Political Decadence in Imperial Germany

EKKEHARD-TEJA P. W. WILKE is director of the Institute for the Study of Nineteenth-Century Europe in Riverside, Illinois. He was born in Pritzwalk, Germany, and lived in various cities and towns in Germany before coming to the United States in 1953.

POLITICAL DECADENCE IN IMPERIAL GERMANY

Personnel-Political Aspects of the German Government Crisis 1894-97

Ekkehard-Teja P. W. Wilke

59

Illinois Studies in the Social Sciences

UNIVERSITY OF ILLINOIS PRESS

Urbana Chicago London

© 1976 by the Board of Trustees of the University of Illinois
Manufactured in the United States of America

Library of Congress Cataloging in Publication Data

Wilke, Ekkehard-Teja.
 Political decadence in imperial Germany.

 (Illinois studies in the social sciences; 59)
 Bibliography: p.
 Includes index.
 1. Germany — Politics and government — 1888-1918.
 2. Hohenlohe-Schillingsfürst, Chlodwig Karl Viktor,
 Fürst zu, 1819-1901. I. Title. II. Series.
 DD228.5.W48   320.9′43′084   76-3591
 ISBN 0-252-00571-6

TO MY MOTHER AND FATHER
IN GRATITUDE

Preface

In recent years, partly as the result of the vast amount of archival material that has become available, the question of German aims and policy during World War I has received renewed scholarly attention. Interest in these issues was renewed primarily by Fritz Fischer's book, *Der Griff nach der Weltmacht*, in 1961. Since then, particular attention has been paid to the interrelationship between various economic groups and the policies of the state. Furthermore, specific attention has been focused on the formulation and conduct of foreign policy as it was influenced by domestic political constellations.

This course of events appears to be an important breakthrough in German historical scholarship. Before the publication of Fischer's book, only a few German historians had emphasized the importance of economic factors in regard to foreign policy. In the 1920s and 1930s historians like Kehr, Hallgarten, and Arthur Rosenberg had taken this approach, but for all practical purposes they were ignored. On the whole, German historians continued to assume that the state, although influenced to a degree by various domestic groups and constellations, stood above parties and party policies. They defended the idea of the primacy of foreign policy in general and the foreign policy of Germany in particular. After 1945 historians who held that the state was merely a tool in the hands of economic interest groups, and who were severely critical of the Germany of 1914, received greater political attention and encouragement. While the one group tended to underemphasize, the other seemed to overemphasize the importance of economic influences. Only recently has the latter position gained greater acceptance and given rise to a more balanced and more accurate analysis.

Books like Fischer's *Griff nach der Weltmacht* and his more recent *Krieg der Illusionen* (1969) have stimulated serious and scholarly debate with participation from all sides. With the extensive use of unpublished material it has now been possible to sketch in detail German domestic and foreign policy, as Norman Rich's *Holstein* (1965), J. C. G. Röhl's *Germany without Bismarck* (1967), and other studies illustrate. Furthermore, it was quite natural that the renewed debate over the old "war guilt" question--now phrased as "war aims"--took into account the specific composition of the German Empire, especially since many historians have become attracted to the concept of "modernization." Although not entirely new, it is "new" with regard to the degree of emphasis and the available data.

During the latter part of 1967 Röhl's book, *Germany without Bismarck: The Crisis of Government in the Second Reich 1890-1900*, was published in England and soon thereafter in the United States and in Germany.[1] Making extensive use of unpublished material,[2] Röhl (limiting his study to the problem of distribution of power within the government) in essence argues that after the dismissal of Bismarck in 1890 there followed a period of struggle for power out of which the Kaiser in 1897 emerged as the victor, the "decisive figure" who determined imperial policy. The book has received many laudatory reviews.[3] Obviously, much work went into it, and in many ways the study is quite informative and stimulating. On the other hand, Röhl's conclusion is neither fully convincing nor universally accepted. In fact, one well-known historian, Geoffrey Barraclough, goes so far as to state: "I shall be surprised if many historians endorse this [Röhl's] view."[4] My own conclusion is that it was *not primarily* the Kaiser but members of the bureaucracy who in effect carried off the victory in mid-1897, although I do not ignore the political importance of Wilhelm II.

While in 1890 with Bismarck's dismissal the recognizable focus of power was lost, the dismissal of Caprivi in 1894 signified the disintegration of political power into the hands of various contending factions. The many personnel changes in mid-1897 might have provided a basis for re-establishing a more or less stable political system. Eventually, however, the change in 1897 turned out to be a process of mere pseudomodernization.

To some extent my study of the German government crisis of 1894-97 may be regarded as the exposition of one aspect of the complex process of political modernization (or, phrased differently, a period of "critical adjustment"). Nevertheless, we fully realize that although accepting October 1894 as a convenient (and justifiable) beginning and June 1897 as the end of the narration, the "crisis" of the German government neither actually began in 1894 with the dismissal of Chancellor Caprivi (or for that matter in 1890 with the dismissal of Bismarck) nor ended in 1897 with the replacement of several ministers (or even in 1900 with the appointment of Bülow as chancellor).

We are confronted with a complex picture of struggles within the government and at the same time among the various political parties and pressure groups. A similar situation of competition for control existed within the government between factions of the bureaucracy, the court, and the monarchy. To complete the complexity of the situation, we are furthermore faced with the struggles between the government and the nongovernmental political groups. My study is limited to a detailed analysis of the struggles within the government in order to show where and how political power within the government was concentrated and how it shifted, or "behaved," at this level during a period of critical adjustment. In a situation where neither the chancellor nor the monarch provided sustained political leadership, the bureaucracy found itself in a dangerous and crucial position. The investigation ends in mid-1897 when the first recognizable phase of the process of adjustment was ended, and the process of consolidation was begun under the period of Bülow's secretaryship. This process under Bülow needs a separate investigation. My study is to serve as a contribution toward a more comprehensive analysis, and a more complete picture, of the history of the Second Reich.

The particular approach and limitation of this investigation--
that is, the emphasis on crises in governmental personnel and the
emphasis on Berlin--need no specific justification. Yet it seems
that this approach--especially toward the years 1894-97--is not as
exclusive and limited, or even untenable, as has been implied most
recently in Stegmann's work.[5] The time under consideration was a
period in which traditional structures had been seriously weakened
and new ones (as well as modifications of former ones) were in the
process of formation and developing toward political participation.[6]
The new emphasis on social history, social structures, on the socioeconomic basis of political parties and on interest-group structures
has of course been extremely fruitful. At the same time it may be
necessary to guard against the temptation to replace one extreme
approach with another--whether it appears in the form of substi-
tuting the formula of "primacy of foreign policy" with that of
"primacy of domestic policy" or in the form of placing too little
emphasis on personalities as a means to compensate for having tra-
ditionally underemphasized structural, socioeconomic factors.

I would like to express my thanks to the following archives and
libraries for having given me permission to use archival material:
the Institute for Social History in Amsterdam; the Deutsche Zentralarchiv in Potsdam and Merseburg; the Bundesarchiv in Koblenz; the
Staatsarchiv in Hamburg; the Sächsische Landesarchiv in Dresden;
the Bayerische Geheime Staatsarchiv in Munich; the Württembergische
Hauptstaatsarchiv in Stuttgart; the Badische General Landesarchiv
in Karlsruhe; the Geheime Staatsarchiv in Berlin; the Politische
Archiv des Auswärtigen Amts in Bonn; the Pfälzische Landesbibliothek
in Speyer; and the National Archives in Washington, D.C.
I would furthermore like to thank the late Prince Franz Josef
Hohenlohe-Schillingsfürst for permission to use the Hohenlohe papers
in the Schillingsfürst Archive in Schillingsfürst (now moved to the
Bundesarchiv in Koblenz); Freifrau von Seyfried for permission to
use the Marschall Diary in her possession in Oberkirch; and Dr.
Zinsmeyer, director of the Badisches General Landesarchiv, who
secured permission for me to use the Grossherzogliche Familienarchiv
in Karlsruhe.
Special acknowledgment goes to Professor J. Alden Nichols of
the University of Illinois, who, having previously directed the
dissertation which is partly incorporated in this study, read the
entire manuscript and made many valuable suggestions and comments.
Professor Nickolas Nelson and editor Mrs. Bonnie Depp of the University of Illinois Press were so kind as to suggest many stylistic
changes. Valuable comments were also given by a number of other
scholars.
Indiana University substantially supported my research in the
form of various research grants; special thanks go to the efficient
staff in the Indiana University library system.
Finally, I would like to thank my wife, Carol, for her active
support at all stages of this project.
The translations when not otherwise indicated are my own. The
study was completed in early 1971.

NOTES

1.   It was published in London: Batsford, 1967; Berkeley and Los Angeles: University of California Press, 1967; Tübingen: Rainer Wunderlich Verlag, 1969.

2.   Such as the Prussian Ministry of State minutes, the Eulenburg Papers, the Badenese ambassadorial reports (apparently only the copies in the Karlsruhe Ministry, not the files of the Berlin embassy), the Bosse Papers, the Marschall Diary (apparently not including, however, the year 1897), and several others. Röhl does not use the reports of the Bavarian, Saxon, and Württemberg embassies in Berlin.

3.   See, for instance the reviews by T. S. Hamerow, *American Historical Review*, 73 (June, 1968), 1554; B. S. Viault, *Annals of the American Political Science Academy*, 337, 171-172; A. Ramm, *English Historical Review*, 84, no. 330 (Jan., 1969), 130-132; M. Balfour, *Historical Journal*, 12, no. 1 (1969), 187-190; as well as reviews in *Economist*, 226 (Jan. 13, 1968), 51; *Choice*, 5 (Mar., 1968), 115; and the *Times Literary Supplement*, Mar. 21, 1968, p. 291.

4.   Barraclough review in *New York Review of Books*, 10 (Mar. 14, 1968), 35. See also the reviews by W. T. Angress in *Journal of Modern History*, 41, no. 2, 253ff., and that by E. Fehrenbach in *Historische Zeitschrift*, 212, no. 1 (Feb., 1971), 185-188.

5.   Dirk Stegmann, *Die Erben Bismarcks. Parteien und Verbände in der Spätphase des Wilhelminischen Deutschlands. Sammlungspolitik 1897-1918* (Köln, 1970), p. 14f.

6.   For example, see the general comments of Fritz Fischer, *Krieg der Illusionen. Die deutsche Politik von 1911 bis 1914* (Düsseldorf, 1969), Chs. 1-4, esp. pp. 43ff.

Contents

Principal Characters

Berlepsch, Hans Hermann von (1843-1926)—Serving in the Prussian government since 1862; Prussian Minister of Trade, 1890-June, 1896.

Bismarck, Herbert Graf (Fürst) von (1849-1904)—Oldest son of Otto von Bismarck; serving in the Foreign Office since 1873; Foreign Secretary, 1886-90; Prussian minister, 1888-90.

Bismarck, Otto Graf (Fürst) von (1815-98)—Active in politics since 1847; Prussian representative to the Bundestag of the Germanic Confederation, 1851-59; Prussian ambassador to Russia and France, 1860-62; Prussian Minister-president, 1862-72 and again 1873-90; Chancellor of the North Germanic Confederation, 1867-70; and Imperial Chancellor, 1871-90; remained active in politics until his death in 1898.

Boetticher, Karl Heinrich von (1833-1907)—Active in the Prussian government since 1862; Secretary of the Interior and Prussian minister, 1880-97; also vice-president of the Prussian Ministry of State, 1888-97; president of the province of Saxony, 1898-1906.

Bosse, Robert (1832-1901)—In the Prussian government since 1868; Prussian Minister of Ecclesiastical Affairs, 1892-99.

Brefeld, Ludwig (1837-1907)—After a variety of bureaucratic posts in the Prussian government, he became Prussian Minister of Trade, June, 1896-1901.

Bronsart von Schellendorf, Walter (1833-1914)—Younger brother of the former Prussian Minister for War, Paul Bronsart von Schellendorf; in the military as Prussian officer since 1852; on the General Staff since 1862; Minister of War, October, 1893-August, 1896.

Bülow, Bernhard (Fürst) von (1849-1929)—In Prussian diplomatic service since 1874, holding posts in Athens, Paris, St. Petersburg, Bucharest; ambassador to Italy, 1893-97; German Foreign Secretary, 1897-1900; Imperial Chancellor and Prussian Minister-president, October, 1900-July, 1909.

Information is based primarily upon data given in E. R. Huber, *Deutsche Verfassungsgeschichte seit 1789* (Stuttgart, 1957—), vols. III and IV.

Caprivi, Leo (Graf) von (1831-99)—Active in the Prussian military as officer since 1849; Chief of the Admiralty, 1883-88; Imperial Chancellor, 1890-October, 1894; Prussian Minister-president, 1890-92.

Eulenburg, Botho Graf zu (1831-1912)— After a variety of posts in the Prussian government, he became Prussian Minister of Interior, 1878-81; president of Hessen-Nassau, 1881-92; Prussian Minister-president and Minister of Interior, 1892-October, 1894.

Eulenburg und Hertefeld, Philipp Graf (Fürst) zu (1847-1921)— In diplomatic service since 1877, serving in Munich, Oldenburg, Stuttgart, and again in Munich, 1881, 1894; ambassador in Vienna, 1894-1903; perhaps the most influential personal friend and advisor of Wilhelm II from 1893 to 1897.

Friedrich I, Grand Duke of Baden (1826-1907)—Grand Duke since 1856.

Gossler, Heinrich von (1841-1927)—Serving in the Prussian army since 1860; Prussian Minister of War, August, 1896-1903.

Hammerstein-Loxten, Ernst Freiherr von (1827-1914)—In Hanoverian, later in Prussian, government; Prussian Minister of Agriculture, November, 1894-1901.

Hohenlohe-Schillingsfürst, Chlodwig Fürst zu (1819-1901)—Member of the Bavarian parliament since 1846; Bavarian Minister-president, 1866-70; member of the Free-Conservative Party in the German Reichstag, 1871-77; ambassador in Paris, 1874-85; viceroy (*Statthalter*) of Alsace-Lorraine, 1885-94; Imperial Chancellor and Prussian Minister-president, October, 1894-October, 1900.

Hollmann, Friedrich (von) (1842-1913)—Serving in the Prussian navy since 1857; Secretary of State for the Navy, 1890-97.

Holstein, Friedrich von (1837-1909)—In Prussian diplomatic service since 1860; in the Berlin Foreign Office since 1876; privy councillor (*Vortragender Rat*), 1880-1906; since 1890 perhaps the most important advisor on German foreign policy.

Kiderlen-Wächter, Alfred von (1852-1912)—In the foreign service since 1879; since 1888 privy councillor (*Vortragender Rat*) in the Foreign Office; Prussian representative in Hamburg, 1894; representative in Copenhagen, 1895-1900; representative in Bucharest, 1900-08; Undersecretary of State, 1908-10; Foreign Secretary, 1910-12.

Köller, Ernst Matthias von (1841-1928)—After a variety of bureaucratic posts, police president in Frankfurt, 1887-88; Undersecretary of State for Alsace-Lorraine, 1889-94; Prussian Minister of Interior, October, 1894-December, 1895; president of Schleswig-Holstein, 1897-1901; Secretary of State for Alsace-Lorraine, 1901-08.

Marschall von Bieberstein, Adolf Freiherr (1842-1912)—In the parliament of Baden since 1875; conservative member (*Deutschkonservativ*) in the German Reichstag, 1878-81; Baden's representative in Berlin, 1883-90; Foreign Secretary, April, 1890-

October, 1897; Prussian minister, 1894-97; ambassador in Constantinople, 1897-1912; ambassador in London, 1912.

Miquel, Johannes von (1828-1901)—Having participated in the revolution of 1848 as a radical democrat, he later practiced law and was then mayor of Osnabrück in 1865-69; director of the Discontogesellschafft, 1870-76; lord mayor of Osnabrück, 1876-80, and of Frankfurt, 1880-90; Prussian Finance Minister until 1901.

Posadowsky-Wehner, Arthur Graf von (1845-1932)—In the Prussian government since 1873; Imperial Finance Secretary, 1893-97; Secretary of Interior, 1897-1907.

von der Recke von dem Horst, Eberhard Freiherr (1847-1911)—After holding a variety of bureaucratic posts, he became Prussian Minister of Interior, December, 1895-1899.

Tirpitz, Alfred (von) (1849-1930)—In the Prussian navy since 1865; Chief of Staff of the High Command of the Navy, 1892-95; chief of the East Asia Cruiser Squadron, 1896-97; Secretary of State for the Navy, June, 1897-March, 1916; since 1898 also a Prussian minister.

Waldersee, Alfred Graf von (1832-1904)—In the Prussian military as officer since 1860; on the General Staff since 1866; chief of the General Staff, 1888-91; commanding general of an army corps, 1891-98.

Wilhelm II (1859-1941)—German Emperor and King of Prussia, 1888-1918.

PART I

CHAPTER 1

The Political Foundations
of the Hohenlohe Government

> Such is the fate of great men: with their inner-
> most and deepest thoughts they try to influence
> the course of world events; but in so doing they
> inevitably become involved in the manifold strug-
> gles that surround them. In achieving a remark-
> able effect, they thereby became superfluous.
>
> Hans Delbrück in the
> *Preussische Jahrbücher*, 1890

1

It is by now a commonplace to assert that the Germany of Bismarck and Wilhelm II was undergoing a highly accelerated pace of
socioeconomic transformation, while at the same time the formal
political structure remained basically unchanged. In fact, the
traditional elements (the landed aristocracy and the monarchy)
were reinforced in maintaining their quasimonopoly of political
power. Although it is not the intention of the present study to
narrate or even sketch the economic development of the period under
discussion, the following figures should serve as indicators of the
momentous changes occurring in Germany and which formed the stage,
so to speak, upon which the personnel-political actions took place.

The population in Germany jumped from 40.9 million in 1870 to
49.5 million in 1890 and to 65 million in 1910, while the average
life span during those same years increased from 37 to 50 years.
This population increase was absorbed by the cities so that, whereas
in 1871 a total of 63.9 per cent of the population lived in commu-
nities of 2,000 or less, by 1910 this figure had decreased to 39.9
per cent. This change is also reflected in occupational statistics:
42.5 per cent were still engaged in agriculture and related occupa-
tions in 1882 (as compared with 35.5 per cent in industry), while
by 1907 these figures had changed to 28.6 per cent and 42.8 per
cent respectively. Dramatic changes are also seen in the statistics
for German industrial output: the mining of coal increased from
29.4 million to 191.5 million tons, and the mining of lignite from
8.5 to 87.5 million tons, between 1871 and 1913; production of pig
iron for 1880, 1890, 1900, and 1910 was 2.7, 4.6, 8.5, and 14.7
million (metric) tons; production of steel for the same years was
1.5, 3.1, 7.3, and 13.1 million tons. Pig-iron production in the
United Kingdom between 1880 and 1910 rose from 7.1 to 10.1 million
tons, and that of steel from 3.7 to 7.6 million tons. The tremendous leap of German coal and steel production was equally noticeable
in other industrial-commercial areas as well, such as shipbuilding,

electrical and chemical industries, foreign trade, banking, etc.
Finally, the total real income of Germany amounted to 14.6 billion
marks in the years 1871-75, to 34 billion by 1896-1900, and 48
billion by 1911-13. The average individual income increased from
352 marks to 603 and then to 728 marks respectively.[1]

No doubt the "Industrial Revolution" had hit the German areas
some time before 1870, and it has recently been forcefully demonstrated that these economic changes were the fundamental underlying
cause for German unification. The process of industrialization
with its massive effect upon all facets and strata of society was
greatly stimulated after 1870 by the German political unification,
and consequent uniformization and centralization; by the territorial
annexation of Alsace-Lorraine; and by the French war indemnity pay-
ments. It is, therefore, not a contradiction to say that "during
the period from 1870 to 1914 Germany was transformed from a predominantly agrarian to a predominantly industrial state . . . to a
nation in which technological skill, financial and industrial organization, and material progress became the outstanding features of
public life . . .," since "it is not until 1870-1900 that we have a
veritable torrent of industrial development."[2]

To be sure, Bismarck eventually forced the aristocracy to share
power with the industrialists and forced the monarchy to accept a
strong chancellorship; however, these modifications proved to be
inadequate in the long run. The mounting tension as a result of the
increasing disparity between the body politic and its government was
basically not resolved and became the major issue in Germany after
Bismarck's dismissal. In other words, post-Bismarckian Germany was
forced into facing the problem of modernization.

It is assumed that a government which reflects to the greatest
degree the structure and "atmosphere" of its society is politically
stable. However, there often exists an imbalance (especially during periods of rapid change) which crystallizes politically around
two poles—change and persistence. With increasing imbalance the
tension mounts to a point of confrontation, and the long-term result
of this confrontation often is a compromise and the re-establishment
of a workable political balance. The challenging forces which advocated change are then incorporated into the existing political
structure and thus, by having received a share of power, have "mod-
ernized" the government. This process of political modernization
does of course vary greatly in form, content, and intensity. We
use the term "modernization" to mean the form of adaptation or
response of the government to a changing socioeconomic environment
which had found direct political expression, thereby reducing the
political tension. In Germany the political system had to be modified to enable the government to legislate and carry out the demands
and wishes of its constituency without alienating any politically
important segment. This process was complicated by the preceding
"charismatic regime."[3]

2

In March, 1890, the aged Prince Bismarck, Chancellor of his
German Empire for twenty years, handed in his resignation. The
resignation was hastily accepted by young Wilhelm II, German Emperor
for less than two years and Bismarck's junior by more than forty

years. Wilhelm boasted that he would lead his people into a glori-
ous future, and Hans Delbrück, editor of the liberal *Preussische
Jahrbücher*, expressed the widespread optimism over Bismarck's resignation when he wrote: ". . . deeply moved, but without any political
crisis . . . held together by its new, yet already strong, stable
institutions, the German nation takes leave of the great Bismarck
era in order to begin a new age."[4]

However, Delbrück's statement was not shared by all of his contemporaries. Indeed, it is even possible to detect a feeling of
uncertainty behind the Kaiser's apparent optimism. This feeling of
uncertainty was revealed most pessimistically by Bismarck's son
Herbert, who exclaimed, "That means the dissolution of the Empire
. . .," and who characterized the German state as being ". . . an
intricate structure, which could not endure a trial of strength such
as the dismissal of the creator of the Empire."[5] Bismarck had, in
fact, become an institution, the setting aside of which would vitally
affect the German state.

This is hardly surprising. In the constitution of the Second
Reich, drawn up by Bismarck himself in 1871, the chancellorship was
the crucial office (aside from the monarchy).[6] In fact, the constitution was designed by Bismarck specifically to fit his own relationship with the monarch Wilhelm I. Under this constitution, and
with Bismarck and Wilhelm I, the government usually operated smoothly.
Problems such as federalism versus centralization, Prussia, ministerial responsibility, democratic rights, etc., were not allowed to
arise under Bismarck's "iron hand." Only in 1890 did they become
serious, and ultimately they contributed to the collapse of the
Second Reich after the war and defeat in 1917-18. It is important
to be aware of exactly what the constitution of 1871 was, because
it was in turn "inherited" by Hohenlohe and Wilhelm II, and one
wonders whether the final collapse in 1917-18 could have perhaps
been averted by a different approach on their part.

Basically the 1871 constitution made Prussia the new Germany,
and all entering states were incorporated under the rule of the
Prussian army and bureaucracy. Thus, although having the appearance of constitutionalism, it was in actuality nothing of the sort.
The new constitution was quite specific on matters dealing with
customs and trade but said nothing about individual rights and
freedoms.

The constitution organized the new Reich into a federal state
(*Bundesstaat*) composed of independent states which did not lose
their basic identities. Besides Prussia, there were the kindgoms
of Bavaria, Saxony, and Württemberg; six grand duchies; five duchies;
seven principalities; three free cities; and Alsace-Lorraine. Although sovereignty was in the Reich government, the Reich did not
have an administrative organization (except for the military, foreign affairs, customs, and post and telegraph). The important
matters regarding police, judiciary, fiscal matters, and education
were handled by each of the separate states, and Prussia as the
largest was, of course, the most overwhelmingly in control.

This peculiar position of Prussia in regard to the organization
of the German Reich is the key to the unique characteristics of the
new government. The king of Prussia was the head of the German
Reich (the term *Deutscher Kaiser* emphasized German nationalism over

state rule and avoided giving the impression of having elevated the
king of Prussia over the other kings). The Kaiser was the official
representative of the Reich; he was responsible for international
and foreign affairs, control of the military, and the appointment
and dismissal of ambassadors, and all of the imperial officials,
including the Chancellor. As king of Prussia the Kaiser had additional power--he, or his minister, presided over the federal council
(*Bundesrat*) and naturally controlled the decisive Prussian votes in
that house, chiefly pursuing the Prussian interests, not those of
the Reich.

The legislature of the Reich government was composed of two
parts--the Bundesrat, representing the individual states, and the
Reichstag, representing the people. But here it is important to
note again that the Bundesrat was often the arm of the Kaiser and
at the same time represented the power of Prussia, especially since
the states were represented according to their size and might. Each
state designated its own members to the Bundesrat who voted en bloc
as each state government decided. (Prussia had a total of 17 votes,
Bavaria 6, Saxony 4, Württemberg 4, and so on.) The Imperial Chancellor presided over the Bundesrat, and all laws had to go through
this house. Thus it was Prussia, and consequently the Kaiser, which
controlled the government and had veto power over any changes in the
constitution. Again, the new government was merely a facade of constitutionalism.

The Reichstag, which was supposed to be the voice of the people,
was in actuality almost impotent. It was elected by universal manhood suffrage (all citizens over 25), but did not have very much
power to do any real legislation. Its only "weapon" was to refuse
the budget, but this weapon had proven to be ineffective and illusory in the Prussian constitutional conflicts during the 1860s and
had consequently lost much of its threat. Even the ministers were
responsible not to the Reichstag but to the Kaiser. Thus the real
power of the government lay in the hands of the Prussian government
and the Bundesrat.

Another unique aspect of this constitutionalism was that the
Reich Chancellor--the only minister of the Reich and the one who
appointed the heads of departments of state--was also Minister-
president of Prussia, who was in turn responsible to the Kaiser!
As president of the Bundesrat, the Chancellor had to countersign
all measures approved by the Kaiser, and at the same time his own
position as Minister-president depended solely on appointment by
the Kaiser.

It becomes quite clear that the success of the whole German
constitutional structure rested with the personal union of the
offices of Imperial Chancellor and Prussian Minister-president, the
personal qualifications of the holder of these two offices, the
nature or character of the Kaiser, and finally the relationship between the two.

In contrast to the civilian ministers who had to function
through the Minister-president, the military had direct access to
the monarch, who was the supreme commander of the armed forces.
This relationship removed the military from any direct civilian
checks or controls and made it correspondingly difficult to maintain any uniform Prussian or German policy. Even Bismarck often

complained about the interference of the military in his policy.

And finally, outside the formal constitutional framework there developed a personal staff of the Kaiser--a Civil Cabinet, a Military Cabinet, and eventually a Naval Cabinet--whose duties included carrying on the routine business of government, fulfilling staff functions, and advising the monarch on various affairs. The influence of these cabinets again varied with the personalities who held those positions.

Keeping in mind this German constitutionalism as set up by Bismarck in 1871, as well as the personalities of Bismarck and Emperor Wilhelm I, it is understandable that Bismarck had indeed been the main force that held the German government together--he had all but dictated foreign affairs and had certainly been the dominant factor in shaping German domestic policies. In his overpowering position Bismarck had been able to restrain the influential reactionary (and essentially still feudal) aristocracy, as well as guide the monarchy. Bismarck's strong leadership had successfully balanced the various interest groups within Germany, especially the feudal, agrarian interests of the Junker class and those representing the "modern world"--the industrialists. Furthermore, he had been able to check temporarily the Socialist element by sheer force with the anti-Socialist laws. However, the task of adapting the old order to a rapidly changing world by way of restraining the extreme factions and uniting the moderates had become increasingly difficult, even for a Bismarck. Underlying this was the fact that Bismarck's power was directly linked to his ability to "control" the Kaiser. Under Wilhelm I, who usually supported Bismarck's ideas, this was no problem. The erratic and immature Wilhelm II was more difficult to deal with. Thus by 1890 the Iron Chancellor was seriously considering the possibility of a coup d'état in order to re-structure the Reich.[7] However, by March of that year, with a determined Kaiser opposing him, he had actually lost control of the situation, which cost him the chancellorship.

Bismarck had failed in his task of creating a stable social basis for his political structure, and he left behind him an almost "hopeless situation."[8] It is perhaps no irrelevancy to wonder whether Bismarck would have been able to accomplish such a task had he remained Chancellor for the next eight years until his death in 1898. This, of course, cannot be readily answered. Certain it is, however, that although the situation was increasingly difficult, Bismarck would have continued to provide responsible leadership on the part of the government in foreign *and* domestic policies--a leadership which Germany indeed lacked under Wilhelm II.

As it was, Germany lost the "institution" of Bismarck. Whereas before 1890 the government had been politically identified with Bismarck, after that date it lacked such an identification and, by implication, such an appearance of unity. Germany now had to face three very serious problems, any one of which alone would have been enough to tax all the political ingenuity and strength of the Iron Chancellor. The first problem was the failure of Wilhelm II to provide responsible leadership for the government; second, there was the increasing opposition to the New Course; and finally, there was the breakdown of government unity into various interest groups and cliques. These structural and functional weaknesses provided the framework of the "crisis."

3

In the most recent study of the German government crisis of
1890-1900, J. C. G. Röhl has pointed out that ". . . the German
Government was faced in 1890 with two distinct but related problems.
First, there was the problem of the distribution of power within the
Executive itself. . . . The second problem concerned the relationship between the Executive and the Legislature, and, on a wider
plane, between the State and Society."[9] In other words, the problem was the distribution of power and authority. During Bismarck's
administration there was little doubt, until the very late 1880s,
where the power, authority, and responsibility lay.[10] However, this
situation changed radically in 1890.

For less than two years--from June, 1888, until March, 1890--
did Bismarck remain Chancellor under Wilhelm II. The causes and
events leading up to the break between Bismarck and the Kaiser have
been described frequently and in great detail. Perhaps the underlying cause was the clash of the two personalities. On the one hand
was the old Chancellor (born in 1815), experienced, successful,
autocratic, and accustomed to forcing his will upon all of Europe;
on the other hand was the young Kaiser (born in 1859), lacking maturity and experience, easily influenced but as equally autocratic,
and eager to exercise personally his prerogatives as king and emper-
or. Among the more direct causes for Bismarck's dismissal we may
list such diverse factors as dissatisfied and intriguing subordinates, especially in the Foreign Office and among the military, who
influenced Wilhelm II against the Chancellor; the anti-Bismarckian
maneuvers of the Grand Duke of Baden; and the conflict between
Kaiser and Chancellor concerning the workers, the Social-Democratic
party, and social legislation in general. All of these culminated
in the events of Wilhelm's decrees of February, 1890; the Reichstag
elections of the same month; Bismarck's alleged coup d'état plans
of early March; and the conflict over the Cabinet Order of September, 1852, which forbade direct discourse of the ministers with
the Kaiser without prior consultation with the Minister-president.
All these varied events and factors led to Bismarck's dismissal in
1890.

The Cabinet Order of 1852, although only one of the various
facets of the crisis of Bismarck's dismissal in 1890, highlights
the central problem of authority and responsibility, masterfully
exposed by Bismarck himself. Bismarck used the Cabinet Order (which
for good reason he had invoked early in 1890 and which he had sub-
sequently been ordered by Wilhelm II to revoke) as framework and
theme in his letter of resignation of March 18, 1890. His exposé
was not merely a letter of resignation but a superbly constructed
lecture on constitutional monarchy designed for the young Kaiser.
Bismarck pointed out that before 1848, at the time of absolute
monarchy, there had been no necessity for a "President of the Ministry of State" who would ensure uniformity in the policies of the
government as well as assume responsibility for the results of
those policies. With the year 1848 and the introduction of the
constitutional practice, absolute monarchy had come to an end:

Presidents of the Ministry of State were appointed for
the policies of the state [*Gesamtpolitik*]. It was their
duty to retain the unity and consistency within the Ministry, and the relations of the Ministry to the Monarch
without which a ministerial responsibility, such as the
essence of constitutionalism demands, cannot be carried
out.[11]

In response to this new situation the Order of September, 1852, was
drafted and accepted:

Since then, this order has been decisive in regulating
the relationship of the Minister-President and the State
Ministry, and it alone gave the Minister-President the
authority which enabled him to take over responsibility
for the policies of the cabinet, a responsibility demanded
by the Landtag as well as public opinion. If each individual minister must receive instructions from the monarch
without previous understandings with his colleagues, it
becomes impossible in the cabinet to sustain uniform policies, for which each member can be responsible.[12]

Obviously a revocation of this order would end the legally established constitutional institutions and would mean going back to
absolutism without ministerial responsibility.[13] In a realistic
anticipation of coming events Bismarck continued:

In the case of each of my successors this requirement
[of authority conveyed by the Order of 1852] will become
even stronger than in my case since he will not immediately possess the authority which, until now, has been vested
in me by the fact of a long Presidency and the confidence
of the two late Emperors.[14]

In 1890, after Bismarck's dismissal, Wilhelm II had boastfully
exclaimed that "the position of the commanding officer on the ship
of state has fallen to me. The course remains the same. Full
steam ahead."[15] However, it did not take any keen powers of perception to recognize that the "old" course was, in reality, a "New
Course"--and all too soon it became quite apparent that the one
consistency in this New Course lay in the progressive political
anarchy developing within the top strata of the German government.

Under Bismarck the offices of the German Imperial Chancellor
and the Prussian Minister-president had been (with one brief inter-
ruption) united in the single person of Bismarck. The combination
of these two offices had given him the ideal framework for necessary political maneuverability. Assuming the role of the German
Imperial Chancellor and being responsive to the "liberal" German
Reichstag (elected on the basis of universal male suffrage),
Bismarck could then oppose the more conservative and reactionary
Prussian Landtag (elected on the basis of the three-class voting
system). On the other hand, using his position as Prussian Minister-
president backed by the Landtag, he could cajole the Reichstag into
submission. It was this system of playing off these two opposing
power blocs that usually assured Bismarck his supremacy over both.
Bismarck's position was further strengthened by the fact that a

number of his direct subordinates held positions in both the imperial and the Prussian governments. In the long run, however, this
system undermined political stability and fostered the growth of
excessive political opportunism, as well as gambling too much on
the ability and character of individuals. The system was designed
by Bismarck specifically for himself--and while winning brilliant
tactical victories, even Bismarck became a victim of his own creation in 1890. Contrary to Delbrück's contention, the structure of
the Second Reich was not strong enough to stand without the support
of its creator. This became obvious when Bismarck was replaced in
1890 by Leo von Caprivi, a capable military organizer and an honest,
straightforward man, but one who was in no sense a successful poli-
tician. In March, 1892, the system collapsed when Caprivi resigned
as Prussian Minister-president but retained his position as Imperial Chancellor. The former office was given to Botho Eulenburg,
who had been at one time head of the Ministry of Interior and by
1892 had become one of the leading figures in the conservative ranks.
This structural change left only the monarchy with the ability to
provide *constitutionally* responsible unity and leadership. It was
unfortunate for Germany that this leadership would be determined to
a large degree by the personality of the monarch.

As a result of these changes it was almost impossible for the
New Course government to coordinate its policies and carry through
a successful legislative program. In addition to the administrative
difficulties of having now to coordinate the two offices, the government was now divided severely on account of the different political lines adhered to by the heads of the two parliamentary bodies.
The Prussian Minister-president now became as influential, as powerful, and to a large degree as independent a political force as the
German Imperial Chancellor himself (the more liberal Caprivi),
since Prussia was the overwhelmingly dominant state in the Empire.
The Prussian conservatives could now effectively oppose the liberal
Chancellor by means of the conservative Minister-president. Increasingly, Caprivi had to rely on the votes of the basically clerical
and particularistic (state's rights) Center Party, on the Radicals
(*Freisinnige*), and even on the votes of the Social Democrats for the
support of his legislative program. The German government had become a "house divided against itself." Keeping this precarious
situation in mind, it is surprising that Caprivi remained in office
as long as he did. His dismissal came in October, 1894.[16]

Caprivi's dismissal was a political defeat for the supporters
of the New Course, and thus a victory for the conservatives. However, it remained only a partial victory. At the same time that
Caprivi was forced to hand in his resignation, Botho Eulenburg also
had to take his leave. The conservatives proved to be too weak to
replace the Chancellor with a candidate of their own choosing or to
be able to effect a general conservative reformation of their government. From this point on, German politics plunged into a period
not of a series of crises but one of perpetual crisis[17]--various
political factions, cliques, and persons put in their bids for power,
or at least tried to stop any dangerous competitors from gaining
control.

Here it might be appropriate to give a brief description of the
major political parties. Without question, the backbone of the

Conservative Party was the landed aristocracy, particularly prevalent in the east Prussian areas. After a series of shifts, re-formations, and new formations within the conservatives, there existed in the 1890s three major conservative groups. First, the Conservative Party had pronounced agrarian interests (as expressed most vehemently by the formation of the Agrarian League in 1893) and was decidedly for strong measures against the Socialists and for defending Prussian particularism. Second, although in many respects similar to the Conservative Party, the Free Conservatives emphasized ". . . a national policy along Bismarckian lines . . . an economic policy based upon the interdependence of the Agrarian and industrial interests . . .," and ". . . a good colonial policy."[18] The last party, formally within the Conservative Party until 1896, was the Christian social movement under the leadership of Adolf Stöcker. It combined orthodox (Lutheran) theology, royalism, nationalism, and Christian socialism against the Social Democrats, liberalism, and the Jews.

The National Liberal Party basically represented the broad middle class. Founded in 1867, it emphasized national unity and constitutionally guaranteed freedoms for the citizens. The National Liberals stressed the coordination of a strong constitutional monarchy with a strong, national, representative body. Although the largest party in the Reichstag from 1871 to 1878, they lost their strong position when Bismarck ended his anticlerical free-trade policy, came to an agreement with the Catholic church, and introduced protective tariffs and state monopolies. Many of the party members seceded and eventually formed the Progressive Party. From the 1880s on, what remained of the National Liberal Party usually followed the conservatives, with considerable backing from large industrial and financial interests. The National Liberal Party stood for a strong centralized Reich and for *"Bildung und Besitz"*--education and property--with strong emphasis on typical middle-class economic interests.

The Progressives, or Radicals, sought for Germany to "become a full-fledged parliamentary state." Laissez-faire in economics and politics, antimilitarist, antiprotectionist, opposed to socialism and "statism," they drew their main support from urban areas, elements of the middle class, small merchants, lower officials, and a number of intellectuals.[19]

In 1875 the radical-democratic Lassallean workers and the Marxist-Socialist workers adopted a common program at the Congress of Gotha and became the Social Democratic Party of Germany. Although adopting Marxism as its official dogma in 1875 and again in 1891, the Social Democrats always retained "a strange mixture of democratic and Marxian ideology."[20] The anti-Socialist laws in force from 1878 to 1890, which outlawed the organizational and propaganda activities of the party but not their representation in the Reichstag, did not stop the steady growth of Social Democratic voters. In fact, in 1890 it had become the largest party, and continued to hold that position throughout the existence of the Second Reich. It is necessary to mention, however, that only by 1912 was its numerical size reflected by the number of its representatives in the Reichstag. Having officially adopted the Marxist ideology, their political program was defined. However, for all practical purposes the German

Social Democrats in their political actions showed no signs of being
a revolutionary party; to the contrary, they wanted to establish a
parliamentary democracy within the legal framework of the existing
governmental structure.

4

The second problem facing the New Course was that of resisting
the increasing opposition from the Social Democratic and the Conservative forces, as well as from the monarchy. Not only had the government lost Bismarck, but it had to endure his ever-increasing
criticism. In addition, there were a number of other groups in
opposition to the government who began to use the name of Bismarck
to further their own interests. Thus Bismarck became an effective
rallying point for various conservative and rightist radical groups
who felt their political interests were being betrayed by the new
trend in the foreign and domestic policy of the Kaiser and the new
Chancellor Caprivi. Opposition to the New Course came not only from
the right (the Bismarck Fronde[21] and the Agrarian League) but also
from the extreme left (the Social Democrats), especially with their
renewed political legalization after the anti-Socialist laws had
lapsed by default in the latter part of 1890. Last, but not least,
opposition came from such groups as the anti-Semites and the Pan
German League. The attempt to pursue a middle-of-the-road course
hardly satisfied anybody and only increased political frustrations
and decreased support for the government. Functionally the government became neutralized, and this neutralization spelled defeat in
the form of legislative failure, most apparent in the anti-Socialist
bills and in the military penal code reform. Both of these explosive issues were carried over into the Hohenlohe Ministry.

The question of the anti-Socialist legislation had received a
renewed emphasis. It must be remembered that when Bismarck had re-
oriented the emphasis of his domestic policy in 1878, he had successfully carried an anti-Socialist law through the Reichstag. In
1887 the Reichstag had agreed to extend that law for three more years
without accepting the proposed intensification of its provisions,
and had also expressed the idea that parts of the law should be revised.[22] In 1889-90 the question of the anti-Socialist law had
again come to the forefront. Before the still-existing law could
lapse on September 30, 1890, it was generally agreed that a new anti-
Socialist law should be ready. The point to be emphasized is the
fact that Bismarck and Wilhelm were, as far as the proposed anti-
Socialist bill of 1890 was concerned, in fundamental agreement, even
to the point of using force against the Social Democrats if necessary.[23] However, by February, 1890, the main differences of opinion between Bismarck and the young Kaiser rested not on specific
issues but on personalities. They had become involved in a struggle for personal power, and Bismarck lost, as evidenced by his dismissal from office. As a direct result of this struggle between
Wilhelm and Bismarck, Wilhelm and his ministers were forced to
inaugurate the "New Course" in opposition to Bismarck. Bismarck
had continued his struggle by ruthlessly attacking and counterat-
tacking the policies, foreign and domestic, of his successor
(especially after Caprivi's so-called Uriah letter).[24]

Thus it appears that to a considerable extent political issues

were sacrificed to personal rivalry, and by October 1, 1890, the
anti-Socialist law had lapsed without being replaced. However, the
agitation for action, even for the use of force if necessary, against
the Social Democrats, never completely subsided. "Each time, as it
were," Naumann quite correctly wrote in his penetrating and percep-
tive book, *Demokratie und Kaisertum,*

> . . . when the economic harmony of interests amongst
> the parties of order appears shaky, then the common struggle
> against the Revolution must rescue the unity. For this
> reason the anti-Socialist law and the Kartell were parallel
> phenomena. Since the end of the anti-Socialist law, a new
> attempt is made every two or three years to save the German
> world from threatening destruction.[25]

This was certainly the case since the parties of law and order found
themselves in political opposition--a considerable segment of the
National Liberals in the liberal Reich camp of Caprivi and the agrarian, particularist, Prussian, anti-Caprivi camp. The violent incidents of 1893, and especially the assassination of French President
Sadi Carnot in the summer of 1894, again brought clamor for determined action. The liberal and conservative press (especially the
Bismarckian paper, the *Hamburger Nachrichten*) and the imperial entourage were particularly vehement. Fearing the Socialists and
Bismarck, Wilhelm had ordered the government in July, 1894, to prepare a new anti-Socialist law. However, by then the Caprivi Ministry
had become irreparably deadlocked. The government lacked unity,
leadership, and the united support of the liberal parties.

A second major difficulty in Caprivi's legislative program arose
out of the fact that since 1890 the Kartell party alignment of 1887
had fallen apart and a regrouping of parties had evolved. The basic
result of Caprivi's legislative program (in particular the trade
treaties, which reduced the tariff on wheat and consequently the
profit of the east Elbian landowners, and the reduction of military
service from nominally three to two years) was that the government
lost the confidence of the right wing of the National Liberal Party,
as well as that of the conservative parties. After 1892 Caprivi
had to rely heavily on the left wing of the National Liberals, the
Radicals, the Social Democrats, and, perhaps most important, on the
Center Party. Since the conservatives were the dominant group in
Prussia, this situation also intensified the difficult federal problem of Prussia versus the Reich, constitutionally expressed in the
separation of the office of Imperial Chancellor and Prussian
Minister-president. The main order of the day was struggle for
political control over Caprivi by a variety of interest groups and
bureaucratic factions. The fact that most of the dissatisfied elements within Germany, in addition to the majority of the conservatives, were continuing to play off the image of Bismarck against
the Caprivi Ministry and even joining forces with Bismarck himself,
added greatly to the already precarious position of Caprivi.

The Kaiser had been forced into the New Course during his struggles with Bismarck in 1889-90; he had not chosen it out of his own
conviction.[26] Easily persuaded and sensitive to any form of criticism, Wilhelm soon after 1890 began to abandon the New Course and
the Caprivi Ministry as much as he dared. Having subordinated

political issues to questions of personalities (Wilhelm versus
Bismarck), he found himself caught between Bismarck and the conservatives on the one hand and the liberalizing New Course on the
other. Consistently siding with the conservatives might give the
impression of submitting to Bismarck and thus acknowledging defeat.
On the other hand, siding with the New Course might not only bring
about a decline of royal power but would be violating his personal
convictions and would be in opposition to the powerful Prussian
aristocracy. Wilhelm shunned a clear-cut decision between these
two equally undesirable alternatives. He drifted along, being
influenced first by one faction, then by another, and consequently
failed to provide the necessary leadership for a unified government.[27]

This was the situation when, in July, 1894, the Kaiser responded
to the cries for action (especially from the National Liberals)
against the "forces of revolution" and ordered Caprivi to draft a
new anti-Socialist law. Wilhelm had reached exactly the position
that Bismarck had reached in 1890--stringent antirevolutionary
legislation was needed, and in case the Reichstag rejected it,
there would be a dissolution of that parliamentary body and a
possible coup d'état.

Caprivi himself was not against a new antirevolutionary bill in
principle, but he found it impossible to accept the extreme measures
which the conservatives advocated and which the Kaiser seemed to
accept. In the ensuing struggle which arose partly out of this
issue, Caprivi was dismissed in October, 1894, not without pulling
the conservative Prussian Minister-president Botho Eulenburg with
him and creating an embittered political atmosphere. Such was the
legacy of the antirevolutionary bill which Hohenlohe inherited from
the previous ministry when he replaced Caprivi as Chancellor and
Botho Eulenburg as Minister-president, again "reuniting" the two
offices.

The question of the reform of the military penal code regulation was to cause a more direct threat to the Hohenlohe Ministry,
although it entered less conspicuously into the arena of political
struggle than the antirevolutionary bill. The penal code reform
question soon became primarily a question of power,[28] as had the
antirevolutionary bill.

The military penal code regulation still in force in 1895 had
been enacted in Prussia in 1845 and was based on secret and written
procedure. Only the states of Württemberg and Bavaria had reformed
codes. At various times since 1870 the Reichstag had requested a
reform, and upon these requests a commission had been formed in
1881, which had advocated a number of reforms along the lines that
most European nations had already adopted. The most important
recommendation had been for public oral procedure (replacing the
secret written procedure) with the exception of cases which might
endanger the public peace, morals, or military security. However,
these reform proposals were not accepted. In 1890 the subject was
once again postponed with the argument that there existed no military necessity for such a reform and also that in accepting the
principle of public procedure in dispensing military justice, the
position of the army and the security of the state would be endangered. When Bronsart von Schellendorf became Minister of War in

1893, he had found a reform proposal drafted by the War Department that excluded public procedure. Bronsart, who had promised a meaningful reform of the penal code, ignored this draft and even went so far as to give vague promises to the Reichstag in March, 1894, for an effective reform of the code.

Early in Hohenlohe's chancellorship the Reichstag made a formal move to request public and oral procedure in the dispensing of military justice. Hohenlohe (who had successfully reformed the military penal code of Bavaria when he was Minister-president of that state) and Bronsart agreed to reform the code in such a way that it would correspond to a truly modern conception of law.[29] This inevitably brought them into conflict with the Kaiser, the great majority of the army, and the conservatives. Thus the struggle over the reform of the military penal code as well as the struggle over the antirevolutionary legislation fitted well into the pattern of the struggle that characterized the New Course.

5

The third and last major problem facing the New Course was the disintegration of the government into various groups and cliques. One of the major groups constituted the backbone of the New Course. These men were: Adolf Marschall von Bieberstein, Heinrich von Boetticher, Friedrich von Holstein, Philipp zu Eulenburg-Hertefeld, and Alfred von Kiderlen-Wächter.

Adolf Marschall von Bieberstein, Foreign Secretary under Caprivi, continued in that capacity under Hohenlohe. He now gained additional prestige by being included in the Prussian government as Minister without Portfolio. Heinrich von Boetticher remained Secretary of the Interior as well as Prussian vice-president of the Ministry of State. These two had become indispensable to the Caprivi regime and remained so for Hohenlohe. Moreover, it was these two persons who, in the public image, had become (aside from Caprivi) the principal symbols of the New Course and consequently were defended by its supporters and attacked by its opponents.

Marschall von Bieberstein, or Marschall, as he is usually referred to, had been a successful lawyer, a notable conservative parliamentarian in the Badenese Diet and in the Reichstag, as well as having been Baden's representative to the Federal Council (*Bundesrat*). Having been on fairly amiable footing with the Bismarcks in the middle 1880s, Marschall had slowly and cautiously begun to switch sides during the late 1880s and had increasingly aligned himself with the anti-Bismarck group that had formed during the later part of the 1880s. Marschall had become acquainted with Friedrich von Holstein, a First Councillor in the Foreign Office who had also during this time assumed a more cautious attitude toward the Iron Chancellor. During the Caprivi era Marschall was instrumental in enacting the trade treaties--the reduction of the tariff on grain--between Germany and various nations and had so gained the undying hatred of the conservatives. As Foreign Secretary he had to face strong criticism from Bismarck, who is credited with applying the phrase "Secretary of State foreign to Affairs" to him, as well as having to endure criticism from the Bismarck Fronde and nonaligned opportunistic malcontents.[30]

Heinrich von Boetticher had by 1890 a long and successful

bureaucratic career. During the last ten years of Bismarck's chancellorship he had been, as Secretary of the Interior and as Prussian minister (since 1888 vice-president of the Ministry of State) instrumental in planning and carrying out Bismarck's social legislation. In Boetticher, Bismarck possessed a helper who was devoted and gifted, who was well versed in routine, and who loved to work--he was Bismarck's right-hand man.[31] During the crisis of 1890 Boetticher had tried hard to mediate between Bismarck and his monarch, but when no compromise seemed possible, he had taken the side of the Kaiser. The fallen Bismarck, however, considered the steps of Boetticher as a clear case of treachery, a "stab in the back," and at least partly for that reason, Boetticher received special attention in the Bismarckians' attacks upon the New Course. Because of his invaluable administrative know-how and the concentrated Bismarckian attacks upon him, Boetticher became one of the most important ministerial symbols of the New Course.[32]

The greater part of the power behind the New Course, however, rested with a "camarilla" composed of three men: Friedrich von Holstein, Philipp zu Eulenburg-Hertefeld, and Alfred von Kiderlen-Wächter.[33] Friedrich von Holstein[34] had a long record of service in the Foreign Office. Among his many posts had been that of an attaché to the Prussian ambassador in St. Petersburg (Bismarck) in the early 1860s (a position Holstein had gained upon the apparent request of Ambassador Bismarck himself). He had then served under Hohenlohe and Count von Arnim in Paris. During the 1870s the relationship of Holstein with Bismarck and his family had been on the whole quite cordial; it was Bismarck who was mainly responsible for Holstein's success and position. It was no wonder that, enjoying such a high degree of confidence from the Iron Chancellor, Holstein was looked upon as a Bismarck man before and after 1878, when he was brought to the Foreign Office at the nerve center in Berlin. At that time he undoubtedly was just that.

The first of a series of differences between Holstein and Bismarck seems to have arisen in 1884 over Bismarck's colonial policy. These differences were greatly increased during the mid-1880s as a result of the struggle for power between Bismarck and the anti-Bismarckians, who placed high hopes on the eventual succession of the Crown Prince and future Emperor Friedrich III. Holstein's actions became even more complicated and complex from 1887 on, chiefly as a result of Bismarck's apparently contradictory policy in regard to the Austro-Hungarian and Russian monarchies. Holstein, like Bismarck, had grasped the importance and the danger of the Russian Empire. Lacking Bismarck's overall perspective, Holstein categorically opposed the Russians, thereby trying to rectify the mistakes which he thought he had detected in the policy of Bismarck. He did this by secretly taking steps which contradicted those of the official policy; he began to cooperate actively with Bismarck's enemies, such as Waldersee, the ambitious future chief of the General Staff.[35]

After the accession of Wilhelm II in 1888, Holstein continued his role of actively countering Bismarck's policies, as well as mediating between Bismarck and the crown in the hope of "saving Bismarck from himself." On the one hand, Holstein recognized the importance of Bismarck even after 1888 as a necessary factor for stability, but at the same time he evaluated Bismarck's policy--that of apparent cooperation with Russia against the interests of Austria and his apparent intent to break the Kartell and shift toward the ultramontane party[36]--as disastrous. Bismarck, Holstein thought, was getting old, and it was necessary to slowly "ease him out." In contrast to the situation in mid-1888 (when Wilhelm I, for all practical purposes, let Bismarck make the decisions), Holstein was now confronted with the difficult situation of having to choose between Bismarck on the one hand and the young Kaiser Wilhelm II on the other. Being momentarily impressed with Wilhelm II in 1889, as well as in accord with Wilhelm's apparently strong opposition toward Russia, Holstein chose (after having in vain tried to mediate between crown and Chancellor) the side of the former--the side also of the Grand Duke of Baden and his protégé, Marschall von Bieberstein, as well as of Count Philipp zu Eulenburg-Hertefeld. Henceforth, Holstein was perhaps the staunchest opponent of any form of compromise with the Bismarcks. During the crisis, then, in the words of the most recent biographer of Holstein ". . . Holstein, in working against many of the Chancellor's policies since 1888, was doing so because he believed those policies would lead to a speedy break with the Kaiser and because he thought it essential to postpone that break until Bismarck could be dismissed without endangering the security of the Reich."[37] However, once the break had become inevitable, Holstein decisively sided with the "new order" and became one of its main supporters.

Since 1890, as first councillor in the Political Department of the Foreign Office, it was Holstein who, little known outside intimate government circles, became the main power in determining the course of German foreign policy, especially since both the new Chancellor Caprivi and the new Foreign Secretary Marschall had had little or no experience in that field. Aside from foreign policy, Holstein also began to exert (especially in conjunction with Kiderlen-Wächter and Philip Eulenburg) a significant amount of influence in domestic affairs in order to modify the rash political actions of the monarch and to save the New Course from falling into the hands of the conservatives and the Bismarckians.

Alfred von Kiderlen-Wächter, or Kiderlen, had in many ways a rather similar political background to Holstein's. He had entered the Foreign Office in 1879, serving at various times in Berlin and in foreign posts. By 1888 Kiderlen had been accepted as a confidant of Bismarck (as had been Holstein, with whom Kiderlen now became well acquainted) and, along with Herbert Bismarck (then Foreign Secretary), was selected by the elder Bismarck to accompany the young Wilhelm II in order to keep an eye on him. Again, as in the case of Holstein, the events of 1890 radically altered the previous relationship between the fallen Chancellor and Kiderlen. Since 1888 (and continuing after 1890), Kiderlen had become the representative of the Foreign Office on the trips of the monarch, whom he regularly accompanied. It was in this capacity that Kiderlen became of prime importance to the new government in general and to Holstein in particular. Without relinquishing the duty of liaison official between the Foreign Office and the Kaiser, Kiderlen became ambassador to Denmark in 1895--a post which he occupied until 1899.[38]

The third, and last, member of the "camarilla" was Philipp zu
Eulenburg-Hertefeld, or "Phili" as he was often referred to by his
closest associates. The cousin of Botho, Phili was also Wilhelm
II's most trusted friend (a friendship that began in 1886), whose
advice the monarch sought whenever confronted with difficulty. It
was the fact of this friendship and his ability to retain it, rather
than the kinship to Botho, or to August Eulenburg (the Court Chamberlain), or even his official position as Prussian representative
in Bavaria and since 1894 ambassador to the Austro-Hungarian Empire,
to which Philipp Eulenburg could attribute his extraordinary political importance. It was he, and to a lesser degree Kiderlen, who
provided that necessary link between government and monarchy which
was not provided for in the constitution.[39]
The dangers that this "semi-official camarilla" was faced with
were ". . . one, that it might lose the confidence of either Kaiser
or chancellor; two, that its operations might become known to the
public; three, that the three collaborators (Kiderlen, Holstein, and
Eulenburg) might become too ambitious and fall out among themselves.
By the summer of 1894 the system was threatened by all three."[40]
By 1896 it might be said that the cooperation within this camarilla
had ceased altogether. In particular, Holstein and Eulenburg had
adopted different courses of action as a result of their differences of personality and, closely related to this, of political
philosophy. Especially after December, 1894, they cooperated only
insofar as each one sought to further his own interests. This was
notably so in the case of Eulenburg. Eulenburg was definitely in
the more advantageous position since it was he who commanded the
ear of the Kaiser, while Holstein still had to rely on Eulenburg
as mediator. It was the military penal code regulation reform that
brought about the complete break between Holstein and Eulenburg,
and, with the victory of Eulenburg over Holstein in 1897, the New
Course came to an end. The struggle between Eulenburg and Holstein
thus assumed critical importance for the Hohenlohe era.
Holstein had been aware for a considerable time before 1896 of
the danger that a "personal regime" of the Kaiser might create for
the German Empire. Already during the Caprivi era, Holstein's aim
had been to limit the personal influence of the Kaiser on political
issues.[41] This he had done at first by trying to control Wilhelm
through personal advisors, notably the Chancellor and Eulenburg.[42]
It became apparent that this method was inadequate, when Hohenlohe,
the successor to Caprivi, did not fulfill Holstein's hopes of being
reasonably assertive with the Kaiser, and when he recognized that
Eulenburg could no longer be relied upon for such a task; Holstein
(as Eulenburg observed) hoped to "push the Kaiser against the wall."
By means of such a radical confrontation, Holstein hoped that the
monarch would thereafter leave the policy-making to his ministers.[43]
In effect, it would reduce the position of the Kaiser to that of a
real constitutional monarch. Holstein would also thus get rid of
the most serious source of interference with his own conduct of
policy.
It was over this issue in regard to the Kaiser that Holstein
differed most with his friend Eulenburg. This is reflected with
increasing intensity in their letters,[44] even though from time to
time there was a superficial reconciliation that did not, however,

extend to their respective political convictions. Eulenburg as early
as January, 1894, thought that Holstein would be only too glad to get
rid of him if he could be less dependent upon Eulenburg as indispensable mediator to the Kaiser. In addition, Phili on his account would
have been glad to drop Holstein had he not considered him irreplaceable in foreign affairs and (at least in late 1894), in the words of
Bülow, "the strongest dam which stems the (high tide) waters of the
Fronde."[45] As it was, both maintained their respective positions,
using each other for their own ends and pulling on the same string
only when their interests coincided.[46]

In contrast to Holstein, Eulenburg defended the divine right of
the Kaiser as king of Prussia. Eulenburg was also aware of the
dangers resulting from the personality of Wilhelm. However, using
the phrase "politics is an art to achieve the possible" as a means
of argument,[47] he accepted the Kaiser for what he was, and only tried
to moderate the "personal rule" of the monarch when and where he saw
fit.

An added point of difference between Holstein and Eulenburg was
that Holstein was terrified of any conciliatory move by Wilhelm and
the government toward the Bismarcks lest this re-establish the influence of the Iron Chancellor once again. Eulenburg, on the other
hand, held such a reconciliation necessary (denying, of course, any
real influence on politics by Bismarck) in order to end the devastating effects of Bismarck's attacks, as well as cutting the ground
from under the feet of the Bismarck Fronde. In other words,
Eulenburg wanted to manipulate Bismarck by a reconciliation which
would place Bismarck in the ranks of the government supporters, but
without granting him any real political influence. Thereby, Eulenburg hoped to stabilize the existence of any government that was,
or might be in the future, in control.[48]

6

As is rather obvious, all three of these problems confronting
the New Course government--the lack of responsible leadership, the
increasing opposition to the government, and the disintegrating
ministerial unity--were closely interlinked with each other. One
may perhaps describe "the problem," as well as the New Course in
general, as an attempt at modernization, and as an attempt to return
to "normalcy" after Bismarck. However, by the summer of 1894 the
New Course had run well aground in failing to provide accepted
authoritative and responsible leadership: it had not been able to
replace the Bismarckian institution; it had failed to come up with
a workable legislative program and thereby failed to build a broad
basis of support (the Kartell of Bismarck); and it had failed to
achieve ministerial unity.

The style of politics during the ensuing years fulfilled the
expectations which could be deduced from the failure of the New
Course. It has been said that the history of France opened with a
revolution and ended with an affaire. Similarly, the theater had
replaced politics as the center of public attention in Vienna during the decades before World War I--in fact, Viennese politics had
become theatrical themselves. In the German areas the days of the
Wars of Liberation and the Stein-Hardenberg reforms at the beginning of the century had given way to an artificial display and

emphasis upon power, to contorted and dangerous maneuvers designed
to evade essential political reforms.

It is characteristic of European politics of the latter years
of the nineteenth century to sidestep crucial domestic-political
reforms. Politics disintegrated into tactics of diversion; they
became a mere manipulation of forces and actions designed to maintain the status quo. Imperialism and "affairs" were the characteristic forms of political maneuvering. The specific German brand of
this type of politics expressed itself in its lack of tact, judgment, and proportion; in its general restlessness and infatuation
with visible display of power and force; and in its *Unausgeglichen-
heit*.

It is not original to describe German politics during the time
under consideration as "operettic" or to see it as part of the comprehensive style of the Wilhelminian era—a bombastic facade constructed with an incredible lack of taste and content.

Serious reform was shunned. Trivial issues were often placed
into the center of the political stage and treated as if they were
the essential issues of the day. Feeling little or no responsibility to the body politic as a whole (and having had little experience and no time to learn), parties and individuals were only too
prone to compromise principles for temporary political advantages.
This political immaturity frequently expressed itself in overdepen-
dence on character and the influence of individual persons. Without overshadowing personalities such as Bismarck or Windthorst, the
leader of the Center Party, politics became an interaction of
trivial issues. Common enough became the cases of individuals who
both served and blackmailed their employers at the same time, or
politicians and bureaucrats who wrote notes to themselves, to their
contemporaries, and to posterity, and used questionable shortcuts
and at times strenuous roundabout ways to achieve their objectives.
In broader perspective and seen from a distance, these political
intrigues often display a comical quality.

One is frequently reminded of a court jester surrounded by
other unimportant characters acting out a second-rate tragi-comedy.
The major character is kept off-stage with the exception of a few
lines, and yet the whole cast of players gets its orientation from
him. The cartoon appearing in the satirical weekly *Kladderadatsch*,[49]
depicting Bismarck as the sun in the background around which everything else revolved, was as true during the Caprivi era as it was
during the Hohenlohe era.

The October crisis of 1894; the Marschall crisis of February,
1895; the Köller crisis of December, 1895; the chancellor crisis of
May, 1896; the Bronsart crisis of August, 1896; the crisis over the
Bismarck revelations in October of the same year; the Leckert-
Lützow-Tausch scandal dragging on from October, 1896, to June, 1897;
the Hollmann and Boetticher crises in April and May, 1897; and then
the finale in June–July, 1897—along with numerous minor incidents,
libel suits, and affairs—all conform to the pattern, the style of
politics described above. They are symptomatic and an expression
of political decadence—when politics disintegrates into mere role-
playing and mere theatrical performance.

The New Course had become bankrupt, and the "Newest Course,"
with barely more assets than its immediate predecessor, was

inaugurated in October, 1894, with the chancellorship of the aged
Chlodwig zu Hohenlohe-Schillingsfürst.

NOTES

1. The figures are taken from Hajo Holborn, *A History of Modern
Germany 1840-1945* (New York, 1969), pp. 367-387; J. H. Clapham,
Economic Development of France and Germany 1815-1914, 4th ed. (Cam-
bridge, 1936), p. 285.

2. Koppel S. Pinson, *Modern Germany, Its History and Civiliza-
tion*, 2nd ed. (New York, 1966), pp. 219-220. In general, see also
H. Böhme, *Deutschlands Weg zur Grossmacht, 1848-1881* (Köln, 1966);
H. U. Wehler, *Bismarck und der Imperialismus* (Köln, 1969).

3. See Fred W. Riggs, "Bureaucrats and Political Development:
A Paradoxical View," in Joseph La Palombara, ed., *Bureaucracy and
Political Development* (*Studies in Political Development*, vol. II)
(Princeton, N. J., 1967), p. 162.

4. Hans Delbrück, "Der Kanzlerwechsel," *Preussische Jahrbücher*,
65 (Apr., 1890), 466. See also J. Alden Nichols, *Germany after
Bismarck: The Caprivi Era 1890-1894* (Cambridge, Mass., 1958), p.
39. See further Annelise Thimme, *Hans Delbrück als Kritiker der
Wilhelminischen Epoche* (Düsseldorf, 1955), pp. 16f. and 102f.

5. Johannes Ziekursch, *Politische Geschichte des Neuen
Deutschen Kaiserreiches*, 3 vols. (Frankfurt am Main, 1925-30), III,
3; Ziekursch quotes from Hugo von Reischach, *Unter Drei Kaisern*
(Berlin, 1925), pp. 167-168.

6. The following outline of the constitution is basically
paraphrased from Pinson, *Modern Germany*, pp. 156-163. For a more
detailed discussion and up-to-date bibliography, consult Huber,
Verfassungsgeschichte, vol. III. See also K. Epstein, *Mathias
Erzberger and the Dilemma of German Democracy* (Princeton, 1959
[Howard Fertig, 1971]), pp. 21ff. On the whole question, see also
Huber, *Deutsche Verfassungsgeschichte*, IV, 240ff.; Nichols, *Germany
after Bismarck*, pp. 3ff.; J. C. G. Röhl, *Germany without Bismarck*
(London, 1967), pp. 20ff.

7. For this aspect, see especially Egmont Zechlin, *Staatsstreichpläne Bismarcks und Wilhelms II. 1890-1894* (Stuttgart, 1929),
pp. 3-84; Werner Pöls, "Sozialistenfrage und Revolutionsfurcht in
ihrem Zusammenhang mit den angeblichen Staatsstreichplänen Bismarcks,"
Historische Studien, vol. 377 (Lübeck, 1960); J. C. G. Röhl,
"Staatsstreichplan oder Staatsstreichbereitschaft? Bismarcks Politik
in der Entlassungskrise," *Historische Zeitschrift*, vol. 203 (1966).

8. Rudolf Stadelmann, "Der Neue Kurs in Deutschland," in
Geschichte in Wissenschaft und Unterricht, IV (1953), 547.

9. Röhl, *Germany without Bismarck*, pp. 9-10.

10. See, in general, Huber, *Deutsche Verfassungsgeschichte*,
III, 703ff., 767ff., 809ff., 908ff.; IV, 129ff.

11. The letter of resignation and the Order of 1852 may be
found in Georg Freiherr von Eppstein, ed., *Fürst Bismarcks Entlas-*

sung (Berlin, n.d.), pp. 189-194 and p. 181.

12.   *Ibid.*, p. 190; translation taken from Louis L. Snyder, ed., *Documents of German History* (New Brunswick, N. J., 1958), p. 267.

13.   Eppstein, *Fürst Bismarcks Entlassung*, pp. 189-191.

14.   *Ibid.*, p. 191. On the Cabinet Order, see also Wilhelm Schüssler, *Bismarcks Sturz* (Leipzig, 1921), pp. 164ff.; Huber, *Deutsche Verfassungsgeschichte*, IV, 231ff.

15.   Otto Hammann, *Der Missverstandene Bismarck: Zwanzig Jahre Deutscher Weltpolitik* (Berlin, 1921), p. 25.

16.   See especially Hans Goldschmidt, *Das Reich und Preussen im Kampf um die Führung von Bismarck bis 1918* (Berlin, 1931), pp. 96ff; Nichols, *Germany after Bismarck*, pp. 157ff., 308ff.; Robert Geis, "Der Sturz des Reichskanzlers Caprivi," *Historische Studien*, vol. 192 (Berlin, 1930); Stadelmann, "Der Neue Kurs," pp. 538-564; H. O. Meisner, "Der Reichskanzler Caprivi. Eine biographische Skizze," *Zeitschrift für die Gesamte Staatswissenschaft*, 111 (1955), 559-722; Huber, *Deutsche Verfassungsgeschichte*, IV, 256ff.; Röhl, *Germany without Bismarck*, pp. 110ff.; Zechlin, *Staatsstreichpläne Bismarcks und Wilhelms II*, pp. 87ff.

17.   Ziekursch, *Politische Geschichte*, III, 86.

18.   Kardorff, as quoted in Pauline Relyea Anderson, *The Background of Anti-English Feeling in Germany, 1890-1902* (Washington, D. C., 1939, reprinted New York, 1959), p. 62.

19.   Pinson, *Modern Germany*, p. 169.

20.   Anderson, *Background of Anti-English Feeling in Germany*, p. 112.

21.   On the term itself and the composition of the Bismarck Fronde, see especially Nichols, *Germany after Bismarck*, pp. 101ff.; Hammann, *Der Missverstandene Bismarck*, pp. 25f.; J. Bachem, *Erinnerungen eines alten Publizisten und Politikers* (Köln, 1913), p. 152.

22.   Pöls, "Sozialistenfrage," p. 21.

23.   On this, see Pöls, "Sozialistenfrage," pp. 21ff., 83ff.; Zechlin, *Staatsstreichpläne*, pp. 3ff., 34; Röhl, *Germany without Bismarck*, pp. 50ff.

24.   Caprivi's Uriah letter was a telegram sent to the German ambassador to Austria-Hungary which in rather offensive form was to impede an audience of Bismarck with the Austrian Emperor Franz Josef. Bismarck was to come to Vienna in connection with the wedding of his son Herbert. See Otto Gradenwitz, "Akten über Bismarcks Grossdeutsche Rundfahrt vom Jahre 1892," *Sitzungsberichte der Heidelberger Akademie der Wissenschaften*, 12 (1921) 4ff.; Otto Hammann, *Der Neue Kurs* (Berlin, 1921), pp. 22ff.; Nichols, *Germany after Bismarck*, pp. 198ff.

25.   Friedrich Naumann, *Demokratie und Kaisertum. Ein Handbuch für innere Politik* (Berlin-Schöneberg, 1900), p. 137.

26. See K. E. Born, *Staat und Sozialpolitik seit Bismarcks Sturz Ein Beitrag zur Geschichte der innernpolitischen Entwicklung des Deutschen Reiches, 1890-1914 (Historische Forschungen*, vol. I) (Wiesbaden, 1957), pp. 28ff., 30ff.

27. No adequate biography of Wilhelm II exists. Attempts such as P. Liman, *Der Kaiser, Ein Charakterbild Wilhelms II*, 2nd ed. (Leipzig, 1913), Hans Helfritz, *Wilhelm II als König und Kaiser* (Scientia A. G., Aalen, 1954), as well as a score of others, are interesting but not sufficient. Most studies emphasize the "times" rather than Wilhelm II: for example, the sound study of M. Balfour, *The Kaiser and His Times* (London, 1964), or E. Eyck's *Das persönliche Regiment Wilhelms II. Politische Geschichte des Deutschen Kaiserreiches von 1890 bis 1914* (Erlenbach-Zürich, 1948). The problem of the "personal regime" has also been discussed repeatedly; see Huber, *Deutsche Verfassungsgeschichte*, IV, 178ff., 329ff., and bibliographical note, 178-179. See also Fritz Hartung's excellent articles now in *Staatsbildende Kräfte der Neuzeit* (Berlin, 1961), pp. 376-413; R. Martin, *Deutsche Machthaber* (Berlin, 1910), pp. 1-52; Schüssler, *Bismarcks Sturz*, pp. 2-28; and then also the memoirs of Wilhelm II, especially *Ereignisse und Gestalten aus den Jahren 1878-1918* (Leipzig, 1922). See also W. Götz, "Kaiser Wilhelm II und die Geschichtsschreibung," *Historische Zeitschrift*, vol. 179 (1955); Lamar Cecil, "The Creation of Nobles in Prussia 1871-1918," *American Historical Review*, 75 (1970), 757 note, promising a biography of Wilhelm.

28. Bogdan, Graf Hutten-Czapski, *Sechzig Jahre Politik und Gesellschaft*, 2 vols. (Berlin, 1936) I, 280, 289, 291ff.; Ziekursch, *Politische Geschichte*, III, 86.

29. Hutten-Czapski, *Sechzig Jahre*, I, 281.

30. On Marschall in general, see David Burnett King, "Marschall von Bieberstein and the New Course, 1890-1897" (Ph.D. dissertation, Cornell University, 1962); Ernst Schütte, *Freiherr Marschall von Bieberstein, Ein Beitrag zur Charakterisierung seiner Politik* (Berlin, 1936).

31. August Stein, *Es war alles ganz anders. Aus der Werkstätte eines Politischen Journalisten 1891-1914* (Frankfurt am Main, 1922). On Boetticher, see also Eppstein, *Fürst Bismarcks Entlassung*, pp. 9ff.; article in *Neue Deutsche Biographie*, 8 vols. (Berlin, 1953-59).

32. Eyck, *Das persönliche Regiment*, pp. 47-101.

33. Nichols, *Germany after Bismarck*, pp. 319-320; Huber, *Deutsche Verfassungsgeschichte*, IV, 255-256; Fritz Hartung, "Verantwortliche Regierung, Kabinette und Nebenregierungen im konstitutionellen Preussen 1848-1918," *Forschungen zur Brandenburgischen und Preussischen Geschichte*, 44 (1932), 323, 328.

34. On Holstein, see Norman Rich, *Friedrich von Holstein, Politics and Diplomacy in the Era of Bismarck and Wilhelm II*, 2 vols. (Cambridge, 1965); Helmut Krausnick, *Holsteins Geheimpolitik in der Ara Bismarck, 1886-1890* (Hamburg, 1942); *Friedrich von Holstein,*

Die Geheimen Papiere Friedrich von Holsteins, 4 vols. (Göttingen,
1955-63) (this is the German edition, ed. Werner Frauendienst, of
The Holstein Papers, ed. Norman Rich and M. H. Fisher, 4 vols.
[Cambridge, 1955-63]); Helmuth Rogge, *Holstein und Hohenlohe. Neue
Beiträge zu Friedrich von Holsteins Tätigkeit als Mitarbeiter Bismarcks und als Ratgeber Hohenlohes* (Stuttgart, 1957); Rogge, *Friedrich von Holstein: Lebensbekenntnis in Briefen an eine Frau*
(Berlin, 1932); Günter Richter, "Friedrich von Holstein, Ein Mitarbeiter Bismarcks," *Historische Studien*, vol. 397 (Lübeck, 1966).

35. On this generally, see Rich, *Holstein*, I, 174ff.; Krausnick,
Holsteins Geheimpolitik; Richter, "Holstein," pp. 141ff.

36. The Kartell was a government coalition between the National
Liberals and the Free Conservatives and Conservatives, created by
Bismarck in 1887. The "ultramontane party" refers to the extreme
clericals within the Catholic, particularistic Center Party. See
Huber, *Deutsche Verfassungsgeschichte*, IV, 150.

37. Rich, *Holstein*, I, 283.

38. Ernst Jäckh, ed., *Kiderlen-Wächter der Staatsmann und
Mensch*, 2 vols. (Stuttgart, 1925), I, 13f., 84ff.

39. Nichols, *Germany after Bismarck*, pp. 319ff.; Huber, *Deutsche
Verfassungsgeschichte*, IV, 255. On Eulenburg, see also Rich,
Holstein, I, 229ff., 289ff.; Johannes Haller, *Aus dem Leben des
Fursten Philipp zu Eulenburg-Hertefeld* (Berlin, 1924), inadequately
translated by Ethel Colburn Mayne as *Philipp Eulenburg: The Kaiser's
Friend*, 2 vols. (New York, 1930); R. C. Muschler, *Philipp zu Eulen-
burg: Sein Leben und seine Zeit* (Leipzig, 1930); Hartung, "Verant-
wortliche Regierung," pp. 319-320.

40. Nichols, *Germany after Bismarck*, p. 320.

41. Hutten-Czapski, *Sechzig Jahre*, I, 241; Haller, *Eulenburg*,
p. 168; King, "Marschall," p. 208.

42. Hutten-Czapski, *Sechzig Jahre*, I, 221, but see also p. 237.

43. Haller, *Eulenburg*, pp. 178, 212; Hutten-Czapski, *Sechzig
Jahre*, I, 241.

44. See especially Haller, *Eulenburg*, pp. 192-195; Holstein,
Geheime Papiere, III, 545-549; Rich, *Holstein*, II, 484-487, 506-508.

45. Haller, *Eulenburg*, p. 179. Bülow to Eulenburg, 15.X.94,
Eulenburg Papers, 32, Bundesarchiv, Koblenz (hereafter cited as
B.A. Eul., plus the number).

46. Haller, *Eulenburg*, p. 198; Eulenburg to Bülow, 16.III.96,
B.A. Eul. 40; however, compare Rich, *Holstein*, II, 508.

47. Haller, *Eulenburg*, p. 183; Rich, *Holstein*, II, 506.

48. Eulbenburg to Bülow, 25.XII.94, B.A. Eul. 33. Eulenburg
writes: "The system that I support with the Hohenlohe Chancellorship in relation to Bismarck also greatly upsets Holstein. It is
the same old story of either love or hate. A middle position does
not exist for our friend."

49. The cartoon is reproduced in Nichols, *Germany after Bismarck,* following p. 242.

CHAPTER 2

The October Crisis

The Liebenberg days-of-the-chase will mark a
decisive incision in German politics. . . .
With the new turn begins the policy of Wilhelm
II which is completely detached from the past;
and the appointment of Hohenlohe we do not regard
as the termination of the erupted crisis, but only
as a temporary disguising of it.

Die Nation, November 3, 1894

A Catholic Bavarian as Chancellor and Prussian
Minister-President, a Protestant (Rotenhan) in the
Foreign Office, a Badenese as Secretary of State
in the same office, a Württembergian as Viceroy--
that will make for quite a fuss amongst the arch-
Prussians.

Baronin von Spitzemberg,
October 29, 1894

Count Caprivi and Count Eulenburg have gone and
Prince Hohenlohe and von Köller have replaced them.
What has thereby changed?

Reichsbote, November 1, 1894

1

In August, 1894, Philipp Eulenburg wrote a long letter to the
Grand Duke of Baden asking him for advice.[1] The situation in Berlin
was clearly getting out of hand--even for such a shrewd and able
manipulator as Phili Eulenburg. At various other times during the
history of the New Course, Eulenburg had been instrumental in smoothing things over, especially in personnel crises. However, when personnel crises were complicated by concrete political issues, Eulenburg was not as effective. Twice during the New Course he had had
to face such critical situations--in 1892 and now in 1894. In both
cases Eulenburg lost the control which he had presumed that he held,
and found himself calling upon the Grand Duke of Baden for help.
The Grand Duke, a key figure in the Bismarck crisis of 1890, important in 1892, was to set the general guidelines to the solution for
the latest difficulties in Berlin--difficulties which, during the
summer, had become acute over the antirevolutionary bill.[2]

In 1894 in response to Eulenburg's pleas the Grand Duke sent
his minister Arthur von Brauer to the various capitals of the German

states to report on the general state of affairs as well as on
specific sentiments about antirevolutionary legislation. Brauer
started with Berlin. His first report from that capital was written on September 12, 1894, and was followed up by three more before he moved on to Munich.[3] "The immediate political impressions,
which I was able to gain during my short stay (it is only 24 hours),"
Brauer reported,

> are hardly of an encouraging nature. That the existing
> government here completely lacks a unified leadership,--
> in order to recognize this it is not necessary to first
> travel to Berlin. . . . But I nevertheless was very sur-
> prised to observe to what degree the confusion [*Zerfahren-
> heit*] has already progressed. Were one still to speak
> today about dualism within the government, one would be
> guilty of euphemism. It is not a dualism, but at least
> a "Quaddrualism" if one may create such a term. Caprivi,
> Eulenburg, Miquel, Posadowsky oppose each other, each with
> his entourage, as 4 large hostile parties who are complete-
> ly at odds except in the fact that it is "impossible for
> the present state of affairs to continue and that His
> Majesty has to decide Himself." "A government of His
> Majesty" as a unit [*Einheitsgedanke*] is simply no longer
> existent. In every case, consequently, one can only say
> what "the Caprivi faction" or "the Miquel faction" thinks
> or does; what, however, the government has in mind, no man
> knows since no one knows whose opinion will be victorious.[4]

Aside from the specific issue--that is, the antirevolution bill--
Brauer reported that it was also possible to look at the situation
as a struggle between Prussia and the Reich. In other words, it
was a new version of the federal problem--Botho Eulenburg, Miquel,
et al. against Caprivi, Posadowsky, *et al*. "It is less a personnel
question," Miquel told Brauer, "than a question of organization.
The dualism is the main cause of the present situation. First and
foremost, this dualism must be removed; on this there cannot be any
doubt, no matter what position one holds in regard to the personnel
question."[5] An important point to note here is that personalities
were, to an increasing degree, playing a conspicuous part in policy-
making, especially since the monarch held the key position. As
Miquel himself said, "Every objective opposition is being interpreted as a personal one."[6] This was often, if not always, the
case. It was the Kaiser who was in a position to decide the issue;
and, more often than not, his decisions were based not on objective
criteria of policy but, subjectively, on criteria of personality.
Thus there was actually no consistent policy. To make things even
more inconsistent, since the Kaiser was very easily influenced,
each side struggled to gain control over him in order to get his
support and, thus, to gain victory.

"All parties to which I have thus far alluded," Brauer continued in his report,

> are so bent on maintaining their respective positions that
> I believe that His Majesty will now *finally* have to make
> a decision in the personnel question. It is, however,

characteristic that no faction is certain of victory; that
no faction even feigns such confidence in victory. Such
is the situation that nobody knows to which side His
Majesty will lean and some think a *tertius gaudens* could
well become the inheritor of both.[7]

The Kaiser was in an admirable position at this point to play
the role of the absolute monarch, to realize all his apparent ambitions. Thus it is easy to conclude that he actually did realize
his goals--that he intentionally retained the "dualism apparently
only sympathetic to Him,"[8] and liquidated the crisis by smoothing
over the differences between Caprivi and Botho Eulenburg. This was
the course of action that Wilhelm II actually did take at first,
but he then changed his mind and relieved both of their duties. At
first glance the net result was the same, and yet on closer inspec-
tion was quite different. The Kaiser's action had not come on his
own initiative. Not knowing what to do, he once again had turned
to his most trusted friend Phili Eulenburg, who then managed affairs
for him. The clear impression of the whole crisis is that while
Wilhelm was the key figure as a result of his official position, he
had become a pawn in the factional power-play among the Caprivi
faction, the Botho faction, and the Phili faction.

On the basis of the reports sent by Brauer, the Grand Duke was
ready to reply to Phili's request for help. "The most urgent and
most important problem," the Grand Duke pointed out, "is to secure
for the German Reich a methodical, strong government."[9] Without
such a position none of the various problems, including the threat
of the anarchists and the Socialists, could be coped with effectively. Furthermore, as the result of this confrontation of the two
major groups in Berlin (Caprivi and Botho Eulenburg) and also because of the caution displayed by the other German state governments in relation to these two groups (illustrated by their position
in regard to the antirevolution bill), "a new government must be
formed, so that one may proceed systematically. However, this
requires that such a government will slowly become more secure and
that it develops a new basis."[10] In order to do this, it was desirable that a crisis not be triggered over the antirevolutionary bill.
Basically, then, the Grand Duke was calling for a united government
based on broad and popular acceptance and under strong leadership,
unburdened by the past ministry and personalities and free to move
in the direction of *"Sammlungspolitik"* within the framework of
constitutional monarchy. The Grand Duke wrote:

> As much as a serious struggle against anarchism and
> socialism is necessary, one must unfold the banner only
> at the time when one is strong enough . . . to that end
> I count, first and foremost, the uniting of all forces
> for law and order.--Nowadays it does not suffice any more
> to sound the call to unite; one must also have mediating
> forces on hand and these are, first and foremost, the
> ministers as political leaders.[11]

After all these deliberations the Grand Duke suggested that the
offices of Minister-president and Chancellor be reunited in the person of the aged viceroy (*Statthalter*) of Alsace-Lorraine, Prince

Chlodwig zu Hohenlohe-Schillingsfürst. "He has, to be sure, attained a high age," the Grand Duke admitted; however, Hohenlohe was the only person known to him "who stands above parties and who knows the custom in the political leadership, resp. in the diplomatic tradition." Not only did Hohenlohe stand above parties and benefit from a long tradition in the diplomatic service, but "he has broad, clear perception and great firmness of conduct once a decision has been made. He has his own ideas and thus is not dependent upon status seekers. . . ."[12]

The Grand Duke was aware of Hohenlohe's age, but he felt that the advantages outweighed, by far, all objections. This was especially so since he proposed "a strong support of this dual office, or expressed better still a (partial) relief of the holder of these offices," in the form of an office of Vice-Chancellor and Vice-Minister-president to be united in one person. For this post, the Grand Duke suggested Philipp Eulenburg. The possibility of Hohenlohe's backing out, the Grand Duke wrote further, made him decide to look upon the Vice-Chancellor, "so to speak, as a *coadjutor ium jure succedenti.* Then there will develop no interruptions and no ambitions will arise."[13]

These suggestions of the Grand Duke seemed to have considerable merit. It would make the best use of Hohenlohe's international esteem and party aloofness, and at the same time would supply the necessary positive firmness and strength (a quality lacking in Hohenlohe) by means of the vice-chancellorship under Phili. To some extent this position of Eulenburg had already been in existence throughout the New Course, the main novelty here being that it was transforming an unofficial position into one of constitutional legality. Despite the apparent contradiction, then, it seems that from the point of view of the Grand Duke the selection of the personalities of Hohenlohe and Philipp Eulenburg was well considered, especially in view of the relationship of Eulenburg to the Kaiser, and to the Grand Duke, not to mention the expected cooperation ("domination") of Eulenburg and Hohenlohe, and the family ties between Hohenlohe and Wilhelm. The idea was, of course, based upon the questionable assumption that the intimate relations between Eulenburg and the Kaiser would remain as they had been.

In addition, it seems also that the Grand Duke had more in mind than just the immediate crisis when he suggested a vice-chancellorship. One of the serious shortcomings of Bismarck had been his failure to train an adequate successor. Building a vice-chancellorship into the constitutional machinery would not only alleviate this problem but also curb the danger of a disastrous struggle for power in the event of a Chancellor crisis. Creating a vice-chancellorship would regulate and stabilize the succession problem by way of a constitutional amendment to the Bismarck system.

The key to the success of the Grand Duke's plan (given his assumptions), however, rested on the acceptance of Phili Eulenburg. Consequently, the refusal of Phili to accept this constitutional responsibility (assuming that he could have functioned in such position!) may well have been one of the main causes for the failure of the Hohenlohe Ministry.

The Grand Duke had also suggested, in case of Eulenburg's refusal, Bülow for that post.[14] However, Bülow was ready to accept only in mid-1897, and his position as Secretary of State for Foreign

Affairs amounted in actuality to precisely that of the Vice-Chancellor position that the Grand Duke had in mind. The succession
problem (until Bülow came to Berlin) was thrown open to widespread
speculation, intrigue, and power play; and the disruption in the
government, instead of having been eliminated, became worse than
ever. The struggle to gain the support of the Kaiser continued;
however, there now developed a struggle to control the Chancellor
as well--a struggle which only ended with the coming of Bülow to
Berlin in 1897.[15]

2

Having looked at the October crisis from this point of view, it
is now important to concentrate on the key figure of Phili Eulenburg. At almost the same time that Phili wrote to the Grand Duke
asking for advice, he also wrote to the Kaiser that, as a result
of the deadlock between Caprivi and Botho Eulenburg concerning the
antirevolutionary bill, the Kaiser would eventually have to choose
between them.[16] Phili did not tie himself down to either party,
but clearly seems to have tried to influence the Kaiser in Botho's
favor. Thereupon the Kaiser, in the true fashion of his personal
regime, conferred with Botho, assuring him of his confidence and
taking a direct stand against Caprivi, so much so that Botho could
be confident of being the next Chancellor. This became quite evident in the Kaiser's speech of September 6 at Königsberg.[17]

Under the influence of this speech (which was followed up by a
letter from the Kaiser two days later announcing that the king of
Saxony, in particular, and the other German governments as well,
would support a coup d'état policy), Caprivi did write out his
resignation. However, after some thought he decided not to send it
off; rather than resign, he would fight it out to the end, no matter
how hopeless. Yet by October 12 the situation had changed. Phili
Eulenburg, steering the Kaiser into the camp of Botho, had to a
large degree done so on the assumption that the Prussian Finance
Minister Miquel was on the side of Botho. During the Ministry of
State meeting on October 12, Miquel unexpectedly abandoned Botho
and supported Caprivi instead. The chances of Botho becoming
Chancellor with the backing of Miquel and Phili had been considered
strong enough. Now, however, with Miquel's change of sides and
with the Grand Duke's advice to accept what clearly was a compromise Chancellor (in Phili's point of view), as well as with Phili's
increasing doubts as to whether the rest of the German states would
support Botho and a coup d'état policy, Phili now began to use his
influence to bring about a compromise between Botho and Caprivi.
It was at this point that he gladly accepted the advice of the Grand
Duke of Baden (with the significant exception in regard to his own
appointment).

The Kaiser, too, changed his mind accordingly. As a result of
new incidents indicating the Kaiser's confidence in Botho, Caprivi
had written out a second letter of resignation on October 23 and
this time had even mailed it. It was not accepted, whereupon Botho,
coming to Liebenberg (Philipp Eulenburg's estate), demanded his own
resignation. This, too, was refused. Thus, when the Kaiser left
Liebenberg the next day for Berlin to confer with Caprivi, he had
two unaccepted letters of resignation in his hand. But he also had

Phili's suggestion to replace both, if necessary, with the choice of the Grand Duke--that is, Prince Hohenlohe. This choice the Kaiser accepted.[18]

It has been said that it·was as the result of an article appearing in the *Kölnische Zeitung* on October 25 (which rather accurately reported the conversation between Wilhelm and Caprivi some days before and which the Kaiser regarded as a breach of confidence) that Wilhelm impulsively decided to dismiss Caprivi and Botho Eulenburg. It seems clear now that even before the 25th, Philipp Eulenburg and the Kaiser had decided to dismiss them both, and the main question for them was merely whether Hohenlohe would accept.

This was an example of the personal regime of Wilhelm. It is true that none of the responsible institutions and persons seemed to have any significant influence upon the decisions of the Kaiser --however, it seems equally apparent that the Kaiser consistently followed the advice of his trusted friend Philipp, first in supporting Botho, then to effect a compromise and retain both, and, when this compromise failed, to dismiss both and appoint Hohenlohe.

3

What Eulenburg thought was needed in mid-October, 1894, was a compromise Chancellor--a man, Eulenburg had suggested to the Kaiser when he was looking for a new Chancellor to replace Caprivi, "who is neither conservative nor liberal, neither ultramontane nor progressive, neither ritualist nor atheist. . . ."[19] Prince Hohenlohe, the choice of the Grand Duke, seemed to be just the man that Eulenburg was looking for. Hohenlohe was a Bavarian but had defended Prussia's dominant position in Germany already before 1870. He had been Bavarian Minister-president, later had become the German ambassador to France, and for a number of years had held the office of viceroy in the provinces of Alsace and Lorraine. With these qualifications he was much better prepared for the position of Imperial Chancellor than his predecessor. In addition, he was respected enough among the foreign nations not to impair the esteem of the German government. Hohenlohe was Catholic and there was adequate reason to expect a favorable response from the important Center Party; however, he was not orthodox enough to alienate the Protestants. Hohenlohe was conservative enough not to run into violent conservative opposition immediately. He was assumed to be weak enough to give the different political parties, factions, and cliques hope that he might be easily controlled, and he was old enough to give rise to the expectation that he would be replaced within a reasonable amount of time. Hohenlohe's nomination gave the embattled political factions a breathing spell during which they could reorganize their forces and look for a suitable candidate of their own, with the intention of replacing the old Hohenlohe when the time seemed most promising. Hohenlohe was also acceptable to the Kaiser, who thought him more manageable than his predecessor (especially so since Hohenlohe was the Kaiser's uncle), as well as acceptable to Eulenburg (probably, in part, for the same reason).[20]

Another important consideration in Hohenlohe's favor was his relationship to Bismarck. After 1866 Hohenlohe had generally supported Bismarck's policies--so strongly, in fact, that he had been viewed in the south German states as a Prussian. In 1874 Bismarck had replaced his enemy in Paris, the German ambassador to France, Count Arnim, with Hohenlohe. In 1880 Bismarck had called him into the Reichstag as Vice-President, and in 1885 had asked him to accept the office of viceroy of Alsace-Lorraine. In addition, during the time of the *Kulturkampf*, Hohenlohe had generally sided with Bismarck.[21]

Since 1890 Hohenlohe had adopted the officially correct attitude and backed off somewhat from the old Chancellor, but not radically enough to be identified with the new regime.[22] Thus without much difficulty he was able to pick up the threads again in late 1894, following up a letter with a visit to Friedrichsruh, Bismarck's estate.[23] Although Bismarck apparently had some reservations about Hohenlohe as Chancellor, he seems to have appreciated Hohenlohe's "ability in statesmanship," and it was probably with sincerity that he wished Hohenlohe "good success and courage."[24] At the same time, Hohenlohe's close associate Hutten-Czapski[25] had, in order to bring Hohenlohe closer to Bismarck, approached Stumm, the influential industrialist and Bismarckian, as well as Herbert Bismarck.[26] Earlier he had already made the acquaintance of Hugo Jacobi, the editor-in-chief of the *Berliner Neueste Nachrichten*, who was closely connected with the Bismarck circles.[27] Hutten-Czapski now pursued this connection still further.[28] By August, 1895, Hohenlohe even thought that he possessed the means to stop the attacks on Boetticher,[29] attacks almost certainly originating in Friedrichsruh and eagerly picked up by the Bismarck Fronde.

On the other hand, Hohenlohe had never identified himself with either the Bismarck Fronde or with Bismarck. While he was anxious to continue the cordial relations with the old Chancellor, especially again after 1894, he very cautiously and characteristically had inquired whether this attitude would be acceptable to the people who constituted the backbone of the New Course government.[30] Again, ever since he had met Holstein in Paris (attached to his ambassadorial staff), he had kept in contact with him.[31]

Hohenlohe, therefore, stood above the identification with the pro- or anti-Bismarckian factions and could be expected to assume his new office with a relatively clean slate and a minimal amount of initial opposition. He could be expected not to continue the Bismarck-Caprivi antagonism on the one hand, and not to prepare for Bismarck's comeback in any form on the other. Moreover, Hohenlohe could serve as a useful and sorely needed protective shield against the devastating attacks that Bismarck and the Bismarck Fronde had in the past hurled against the government.[32]

Hohenlohe was the personification of what has been described as "compromise liberalism."[33] However, in 1894 the German government was not so much in need of compromise liberalism, as of determined and responsible leadership. Quite logically, since this was lacking, and even more so than in the days of Caprivi, the result was a *bellum omnium contra omnes*.[34] In somewhat different words, "the result was that the diverging tendencies and personalities gained even greater freedom of action than under Caprivi."[35] Various ministers and other persons in the government, such as Hohenlohe, Köller, Miquel, Holstein, Kiderlen, and the Colonial Secretary Paul Kayser, began (if they had not done so already) to associate themselves more closely with the press. The various ministries, especially the Foreign Office (Holstein, Kiderlen, Marschall, and the official press information agent Otto Hammann) already had well established press bureaus.[36] Mutual suspicion became a common phenomenon; the fear of being spied upon by police officials constantly gained ground.[37]

What about Kaiser Wilhelm? After all, he had wanted to become his own Chancellor. However, one must assume that this position would signify not only an increase of power but also an increase in the obligation to provide responsible leadership. It is one aspect of the tragedy of Wilhelm II that he did not know what responsible leadership meant; nor did he have the chance to educate himself, or to be educated, in this respect, either before or after 1888. Doubtless he did have power; however, this is only one of the prerequisites for a successful monarch. Wilhelm lacked stability and consistency, that is, a consistent political program into which this power could be channeled.

Now, more than before, it was important for the various political factions, groups, and cliques to plunge into a series of backstage maneuvers in order to gain control over the Kaiser (as well as over persons who were influential or who held positions of responsibility and power), or for those people who held such power to obtain control. The disunity and chaos in the top strata of the German government would assure the initial success to those who would be able to maintain their influence over key personalities, especially over the monarch.[38]

As to Hohenlohe, it was precisely his weakness--the overcautiousness and reluctance to take a firm stand, as well as his age-- that recommended him for the position to Eulenburg. He was recognized as a compromise Chancellor, as a transition, a preventative move, and a figurehead.[39] Hatzfeldt, the German ambassador to England, wrote: "Under the circumstances I, too . . . consider it (the choice of Hohenlohe) the best possible one that could have been made. Rash actions will hardly have to be feared and other candidates who could have been objectionable (*bedenklich*) have thereby been kept away."[40] Berchem, Undersecretary of State in the Foreign Office until 1890, sized up Hohenlohe's position by observing that Hohenlohe would have to accommodate himself or be crushed (". . . *er wird zwischen Oben und Unten ordre pariren müssen oder zerrieben werden* . . ."),[41] and Brauer spoke of the general attitude in Berlin toward Hohenlohe as "the best solution for now."[42]

4

The Hohenlohe Ministry was far from united.[43] Both Heinrich von Boetticher--vice-president of the Prussian Ministry of State and Secretary of the Interior--and Marschall--retaining the position of Secretary of State for Foreign Affairs but now being included in the Prussian Ministry--were taken over from the Caprivi administration. These two, especially Boetticher,[44] had become indispensable to Caprivi and would remain indispensable to Hohenlohe[45] unless a major change in the nature and direction of the government should occur. These two, and to a degree also Berlepsch, Minister of Trade, symbolized the New Course; with their dismissal the New Course would most certainly come to an end in the eyes of the public.

Holstein continued to hold the position of First Councillor in the Foreign Office, extending his considerable influence over Marschall and to a lesser degree at times even over Hohenlohe. Phili Eulenburg, too, continued in his role as mediator, unofficial advisor, and personal friend of the Kaiser. Johannes von Miquel, the radical of 1848 who had become one of the leading conservatives in the government, remained in his position as Prussian Finance Minister, but his influence and ambition reached far beyond his official position with the hope of even extending it under the weak Hohenlohe.[46] Bronsart von Schellendorf, Minister of War since 1893, had become identified with the New Course, especially after he had taken a stand in favor of the reform of the military penal code regulation. However, the new Prussian Minister of the Interior, Mathias von Köller, appointed against the wish of Hohenlohe, was an ardent conservative who was soon to "curry the favor"[47] (and become the mouthpiece[48]) of the Kaiser, and become the "enfant terrible" of the ministry. It must be remembered that the inclination of certain ministers toward a more liberal direction was in itself no sure indication of their mutual cooperation with other "liberally" inclined ministers.

Hohenlohe clearly recognized the importance of Holstein, Marschall, and Boetticher to his ministry. In most instances too weak to carry out his own political convictions, he began to hold that his chief responsibility as Chancellor would lie in the negative action of delaying so as to moderate the effects of ill-considered actions by the monarch,[49] and thus to prevent them. This policy he carried through with some success, however dangerous the implications in the long run were. These dangerous implications were vividly outlined again and again by Holstein. Hohenlohe's action was, after all, not a cure but only a palliative postponement policy. Holding such a concept of his office, Hohenlohe did not become a mere tool of Holstein, who increasingly believed that direct confrontation would be the only effective solution. In fact, Hohenlohe showed himself at times quite free from his influence. He tried hard not to identify himself with any political group or camarilla, but consciously hoped to mediate between all the factions and maintain a middle-of-the-road policy.[50] Hohenlohe, it must be pointed out in all fairness to him, was in a most difficult position: not only was he uncle to the Kaiser and a devoted monarchist, but at the same time he was dependent upon Holstein, Marschall, Boetticher, and especially upon Eulenburg. Being too weak, too old, and perhaps too gentlemanly to command a dominant position in the government, at the same time conscious of the dangers of the personal rule of Wilhelm II (as well as of the irresponsible handling of political affairs by different groups within the government), and quite aware of the precarious position and condition of his ministry, Hohenlohe worked hard for conciliation no matter what the price in the long run. It is also easy to understand how gossip, rumors, and anonymous press articles and letters, all cleverly placed, timed, and phrased, did achieve some success in their aims and added greatly to the unpredictability and instability of the German political scene during the years in question.

As far as the immediate problems of the government were

concerned, the key to the whole situation remained with the Kaiser and his personality. It is here that Eulenburg had the advantage over all other contestants for power. By applauding rather than criticizing the actions of his Imperial friend, Eulenburg was able to bolster the monarch's self-esteem and strengthen his faith in the correctness of his own actions. To maintain his invaluable position, Eulenburg wisely stayed away from Berlin, only returning (often enough, it is true) at critical moments to the side of the Kaiser.

Philipp Eulenburg had, once again, with the help of the Grand Duke of Baden, been successful in directing the affairs in Berlin to his liking. He had been victorious over the extreme right—the conservatives lined up behind Botho Eulenburg; he had been able to persuade Wilhelm II to adopt his (Phili's) position; he had been able to get the support of the Grand Duke of Baden without, however, accepting the substantive changes of the latter's recommendations— that is, the forcible grooming of Eulenburg for the official position that corresponded to his unofficial influence; and he had kept the "liberals," the former supporters of Caprivi, especially Holstein and Marschall, in line. Yet Eulenburg had not only retained but even strengthened his independent position among the various factions and groupings by being accepted as indispensable to them. He was the only one who clearly held the ear of the Kaiser and could use this influence on him better, and more lastingly, than anyone else. Since it was necessary to get the Kaiser's support for their programs in order to be victorious, each group consequently was faced with the crucial figure of Eulenburg.

In regard to the new Chancellor, Eulenburg held a similar, if not as strong, position as he held with the various factions. It had been quite clear where Caprivi had stood, and clear also that it was hardly possible to bring effective influence to bear upon that honest and stubborn general. The possibilities with Hohenlohe seemed more promising; and, in a similar way as there developed a struggle to "capture the Kaiser," so there also developed a struggle to gain control over the Chancellor. Just as in the case of the Kaiser, Hohenlohe was faced with the former Caprivi group, especially Holstein, Marschall, and Kiderlen; the conservatives, the former supporters of Botho Eulenburg; and, forming a "group" to himself, Eulenburg, behind whom stood Bülow and at times also the Grand Duke of Baden. In between these groups wavered the Kaiser, threatening to change unpredictably from one day to the next, but usually under the strong influence of Eulenburg and under the impression of being his own master.

5

The reaction to Hohenlohe's appointment corresponded to the political situation. In general Hohenlohe was well received.[51] The approval of reuniting the positions of Imperial Chancellor and Prussian Minister-president was unanimous, if for various reasons. However, it was, after all, only a compromise—only a temporary solution for many. Behind the thin veneer of routine noncommittal statements accompanying Hohenlohe's appointment, there are revealed the fears and hopes for the future according to the positions and ambitions of the various commentators. The Free Conservative

Deutsches Wochenblatt might serve as a good example. "The most imperative prerequisite for a strong government that Germany needs perhaps more than ever before," wrote the *Deutsches Wochenblatt*, "is undoubtedly its complete inner unity."[52] Under Caprivi the position of Germany among the powers had suffered heavily; on the domestic scene Caprivi's policy of the trade treaties had led to a "split among the national parties and to an estrangement between the government and the Conservatives with regard to the agrarians . . .," forcing the conservatives into opposition against their own will. The newspaper continued: "It seems to us that it was not the question of how the government should stand with regard to the Social Democrats, but the question of how the breach between the government and the loyal conservatives and the agrarians was to be overcome, which brought about the fall of Count Caprivi."

Then the *Deutsches Wochenblatt* looked at the "systematic agitation called for by semi-official sources" against the Prussian Ministry, especially against Count Eulenburg and Miquel. True, Eulenburg had not been appointed Chancellor—he himself would not have accepted it since that might arouse suspicion about his personal ambitions—and consequently had to be dismissed to bring about, again, the necessary unification of the posts of Chancellor and Minister-president.

Considering Hohenlohe, the *Deutsches Wochenblatt* wrote:

> Prince Hohenlohe has reached an age in which the assumed burden is hard to bear under any circumstances. Received with great sympathies, he guarantees that due to his background and his Bismarckian training he will lead policy in that spirit which alone is able to maintain itself in Germany; in the spirit of uniting all national and law and order elements [*staatserhaltende Elemente*]; in the spirit of conciliation which, whenever necessary, will be coupled with force and determination. Especially in this direction does the personality of the new Minister of Interior von Köller give full guarantee. Is it a coincidence that the Mayor of Frankfurt (Miquel) is being followed into the Ministry by the Police President of Frankfurt? If the harmonious cooperation between both men, which had been the case in Frankfurt, will continue in the Ministry, then this can only be to the benefit of the unified character of the government.

> Whether or not, however, this uniformity can be achieved without further changes in the highest positions remains to be seen. In the case of the new course it is not a question of a person, but a system, and whether or not this will be changed will shape the future—but if it is to be changed, then further alterations in the leading positions will be inevitable.

> It is an advantage of the German constitutional system . . . that such alterations may be accomplished not all at once, but slowly and gradually.

> May the changes, whatever they may be, serve the interest of the nation. Large parts of the population who

have discontentedly stood aside now again look upon the
future developments with hope. The road is free, may the
right man seize the rudder and take a course which leads
the ship of state safely through the dangers which only
frighten the inept sailors.[53]

The *Deutsches Wochenblatt* hoped for an end of dilettantism in foreign policy, an end to the "wretched and dangerous diametrical
opposition of Prussia and Reich." Translated into terms of political goals, this meant for foreign policy "a proud, independent
attitude of the Reich government in all national issues . . . ,
concern for the further expansion of German national character
. . . , increasing the cruiser fleet . . . ," and for domestic
policy, "to hold down the Poles and other enemies of the Reich.
. . ."[54] All this the new government under Hohenlohe was to accomplish, supported by Marschall (who again would behave more in line
with the party he originally had belonged to, the Conservatives)
and the rest of the Prussian ministers, as well as a number of
"uprighteous German men" as advisors.

After expressing praise and confidence, the *Deutsches Wochenblatt* continued with words of advice and warning, and stated its
demands: help agriculture; take energetic steps against the Social
Democracy; regain the support of former Kartell parties, but don't
alienate completely the former Caprivi supporters; and be careful
in dealing with the Center Party. However, the newspaper had to
admit that the Crown Speech had been quite disappointing, and one
week later it already felt it necessary to point out that the good
will of the government would not be enough, that only "deeds,
through measures," could bring about change—the change that would
allow the forces of law and order to predominate in the government.[55]

The comments of the press of the former Kartell parties were
vary similar in content to those presented in the *Deutsches Wochenblatt*. In this connection it is interesting to note that the *Norddeutsche Allgemeine Zeitung* hoped for a reunification of all conservative parties in support of the new government, and the *Kölnische
Zeitung* for a re-establishment of the Kartell with the inclusion,
however, of the "moderate elements" of the Center Party and the
Radicals.[56] In addition, it appeared that one issue upon which such
cooperation might be based was an antirevolutionary program. Even
the *Germania* carefully expressed conditional approval for such a
course.[57]

On the other hand, although in a minority, there prevailed among
some groups a skeptical attitude toward the new ministry. This was
to be expected, of course, from the Social Democratic circles.
However, even Theodor Barth, a leader of the Radicals who had been
one of the staunchest supporters of the Caprivi regime, spoke with
unusual severity: "The fall of Caprivi is the victory of the Prussian Squirarchy. . . . It is in the least interest of the liberal
bourgeoisie to gloss over this situation. . . ." He promised that
the Radicals, having upheld for many years the liberal principles
against Bismarck, would "not sit idly in face of the approaching
reaction."[58]

The conservative *Reichsbote* pointed to Hohenlohe's Bismarckian
training. Then it struck a decidedly particularistic note and

pointed out Hohenlohe's south German origin and his Catholic religion. The *Reichsbote* professed its faith in the Kaiser, that he would never appoint a Chancellor who was not friendly toward Prussia:

> . . . but whether such a man as Hohenlohe is truly living in the spirit of the tradition of the Prussian state (such as is necessary for an individual at the head of the government of this state for the preservation of the continuity of its development) is still open to question . . . we hope that the domestic development of Prussia will not be pushed into un-Prussian directions as a result of the appointment of a Bavarian and Catholic as Minister-President, and consequently injuring the state in its inner stability and strength.[59]

This would be disastrous not only for Prussia but also for the Reich.

In a sense, the choice of Hohenlohe was hoped to provide a way of avoiding a dilemma. To a degree this move was successful; however, it resolved no issues. Nowhere did this become more painfully apparent than during the first Reichstag session of the Hohenlohe Ministry.

NOTES

1. Eulenburg to Grand Duke, as becomes evident in the reply of Grand Duke to Eulenburg, 25.IX.94, G.L.A. Karlsruhe, Grossherzogliches Familien Archiv, 13, Bd. 51 N 14 (the Familien Archiv is hereafter cited as Gr. Fam. Archiv, plus the number).

2. For the role of the Grand Duke of Baden in the 1889-90 Bismarck crisis, see now especially the Marschall Diary for late 1889 and early 1890s; the Marschall reports to the Grand Duke, 1889-90, in Gr. Fam. Archiv.

3. Brauer to Grand Duke, 12.IX.94, 13.IX.94, 14.IX.94, Gr. Fam. Archiv, N 329.

4. Brauer to Grand Duke, 12.IX.94, Gr. Fam. Archiv, N 329.

5. Brauer to Grand Duke, 14.IX.94, Gr. Fam. Archiv, N 329.

6. *Ibid.*

7. Brauer to Grand Duke, 12.IX.94, Gr. Fam. Archiv, N 329.

8. Brauer to Grand Duke, 15.IX.94, Gr. Fam. Archiv, N 329.

9. Grand Duke to Eulenburg, 25.IX.94, Gr. Fam. Archiv, 51 N 14.

10. *Ibid.*

11. *Ibid.*

12. *Ibid.*

13. *Ibid.*

14. See Röhl, *Germany without Bismarck*, p. 120.

15. On the October crisis in general, see Nichols, *Germany after Bismarck*, pp. 340ff.; Röhl, *Germany without Bismarck*, pp. 113ff.; Rich, *Holstein*, I, 416ff.; Gustav Roloff, ed., *Schulthess' Europäischer Geschichtskalender* (München, 1860-1938), 1894, pp. 166ff.

(hereafter cited as *Schulthess*); Karl Wippermann, ed., *Deutscher Geschichtskalender* (Leipzig, 1885-1934), 1894 (II), pp. 3, 9, 79f., 135ff. (hereafter cited as *Wippermann*). See also the reports of Lerchenfeld and Hohenthal in Zechlin, *Staatsstreichpläne*, pp. 207ff.; and their unpublished report in the G. S. A. München, Ges. Berlin 1065, and Sächsische H. S. Archiv, Dresden, Ges. Berlin, No. 249, respectively. It is interesting to note that Hohenthal in his reports emphasized the role of the Eulenburgs, as does Caprivi. See Nichols, *Germany after Bismarck*, pp. 357-358; Theodor Barth, "Umsturz," in *Die Nation*, Nov. 3, 1894; Zechlin, *Staatsstreichpläne*, pp. 87ff.

16. Eulenburg to Wilhelm, 30.VIII.94, Röhl, *Germany without Bismarck*, pp. 113-114.

17. Röhl, *Germany without Bismarck*, pp. 113-114. For the speech itself, see also *Schulthess*, 1894, pp. 139ff.

18. For the above, see Röhl, *Germany without Bismarck*, pp. 114ff., 118ff.; Nichols, *Germany after Bismarck*, pp. 353ff.; see also *Deutsches Wochenblatt* (1894), p. 518.

19. Haller, *Eulenburg*, p. 154; translation taken from Mayne, *Philipp Eulenburg*, I, 262.

20. See Fritz Hartung, "Graf von Hutten-Czapski," in *Historische Zeitschrift*, vol. 153, p. 552; Hutten-Czapski, *Sechzig Jahre*, I, 240; Adolf Wermuth, *Ein Beamtenleben: Erinnerungen* (Berlin, 1922), p. 202; Friedrich von Bernhardi, *Denkwürdigkeiten aus meinem Leben* (Berlin, 1927), p. 177; Stadelmann, "Der Neue Kurs," p. 562.

21. Alexander von Hohenlohe, *Aus meinem Leben* (Frankfurt am Main, 1925), p. 284. See also Paul Liman, *Fürst Bismarck nach seiner Entlassung, Neue vermehrte Volksausgabe* (Berlin, 1904), pp. 147-149; Hans Joachim Zeuner, "Hohenlohe und Holstein: Die Politischen Beziehungen des Fürsten Chlodwig zu Hohenlohe-Schillingsfürst zum Geheimen Rat Fritz von Holstein" (Dissertation, Würzberg, 1955), p. 2.

22. Hutten-Czapski, *Sechzig Jahre*, I, 260.

23. *Ibid.*, pp. 260-261. Ludwig Raschdau, *In Weimar als Preussischer Gesandter; Ein Buch der Erinnerungen an Deutsche Fürstenhöfe 1894-1897* (Berlin, 1939), p. 8.

24. Raschdau, *In Weimar*, pp. 32, 46, but also p. 45; Hutten-Czapski, *Sechzig Jahre*, I, 260; Alexander Hohenlohe, *Aus meinem Leben*, p. 276; Fürst Chlodwig zu Hohenlohe-Schillingsfürst, *Denkwürdigkeiten des Fürsten Chlodwig zu Hohenlohe-Schillingsfürst*, ed. Friedrich Curtius, 2 vols. (Stuttgart, 1907), II, 587.

25. Hans Herzfeld, *Johannes von Miquel; Sein Anteil am Ausbau des Deutschen Reiches bis zur Jahrhundertwende*, 2 vols. (Detmold, 1938), II, 513.

26. Hutten-Czapski, *Sechzig Jahre*, I, 261.

27. *Ibid.*, p. 225. See also Klaus Meyer, *Theodor Schiemann als politischer Publizist* (Frankfurt am Main, 1956), p. 39.

28. Hutten-Czapski, *Sechzig Jahre*, I, 261; Raschdau, *In Weimar*, p. 7.

29. Hutten-Czapski, *Sechzig Jahre*, I, 271.

30. Eduard von Wertheimer, "Neues zur Geschichte der letzten Jahre Bismarcks (1890-1898)," in *Historische Zeitschrift*, 133 (1926), 248-249.

31. Rogge, *Holstein und Hohenlohe*, pp. 15ff.; Zeuner, *Hohenlohe und Holstein*, pp. 3ff.

32. For Hohenlohe in general, see also King, "Marschall," pp. 166ff.; Ziekursch, *Politische Geschichte*, III, 77ff.; H. O. Meisner, "Der Kanzler Hohenlohe und die Mächte seiner Zeit," *Preussische Jahrbücher*, 229 (1932), 35ff.; Jäckh, *Kiderlen-Wächter*, I, 162-164; K. A. v. Müller, "Der Dritte Deutsche Reichskanzler, Bemerkungen zu den 'Denkwürdigkeiten der Reichskanzlerzeit' des Fürsten Chlodwig zu Hohenlohe-Schillingsfürst," *Sitzungsberichte der Bayerischen Akademie der Wissenschaften* (Philosophisch-Historische Abtheilung), 4 (1932), 1-60. See also the good characterization in Herzfeld, *Miquel*, II, 435-436 and Ernst Deuerlein, *Deutsche Kanzler von Bismarck bis Hitler* (List Verlag, 1968), pp. 85ff.

33. Herzfeld, *Miquel*, II, 435.

34. Raschdau, *In Weimar*, pp. 9, 46; Wermuth, *Beamtenleben*, p. 199: ". . . ein hin und her taumeln der Macht." Also see *Ibid.*, p. 212; Bernhardi, *Denkwürdigkeiten aus meinem Leben*, p. 178; Alfred Graf von Waldersee, *Denkwürdigkeiten des General-Feldmarschalls Alfred Grafen von Waldersee*, ed. Heinrich Otto Meisner, 3 vols. (Stuttgart, 1923), II, 329-331, 335-336.

35. Herzfeld, *Miquel*, II, 436.

36. Herzfeld, *Miquel*, II, 438; Raschdau, *In Weimar*, p. 9. See also Otto Groth, *Die Zeitung*, 4 vols. (Mannheim, 1928-30), II, 217ff.

37. So in the case of Waldersee; see Raschdau, *In Weimar*, p. 143. For von Schönborn, the adjutant of Hohenlohe, see Raschdau, *In Weimar*, p. 143. For Miquel, see Herzfeld, *Miquel*, II, 510, and Waldersee, *Denkwürdigkeiten*, II, 350. For Hohenlohe, see Alexander Hohenlohe, *Aus meinem Leben*, p. 305. For Herbert Bismarck, see Hans v. Tresckow, *Von Fürsten und anderen Sterblichen* (Berlin, 1922), p. 57. For Bismarck, see Raschdau, *In Weimar*, p. 49. See also Liman, *Bismarck*, p. 179.

38. See *Hohenlohe*, III, 163-164, 170. Also see Herzfeld, *Miquel*, II, 436; Maximilian Harden, "Notizbuch," *Zukunft*, 2 (1895), 430.

39. See 30.X.94, 9.XI.94, 14.XII.94, Waldersee, *Denkwürdigkeiten*, II, 330, 331, 333; Raschdau, *Unter Bismarck und Caprivi* (Berlin, 1939), p. 365; also the interesting article by Barth, "Umsturz," *Die Nation*, Nov. 3, 1894.

40. Hatzfeld to Holstein, 12.XI.94, *Holsteins Papiere*, III, 430.

41. Berchem to Schiemann (historian and journalist for the *Kreuzzeitung*, as well as friend of the *Berliner Neueste Nachrichten* editor Jacobi), 17.XI.94, Schiemann Papers, No. 40, Geheimes Staatsarchiv, Berlin.

42. Brauer to Grand Duke of Baden, 6.XII.94, Gr. Fam. Archiv, N 329; see also comments of General Löe in Bülow to Eulenburg, 13.V.95, B.A. Eul. 36; also Bülow to Lindenau, 17.XI.94, Bülow Papers, No. 99, Bundesarchiv, Koblenz (hereafter cited as B.A. Bülow, plus the number).

43. Eyck, *Das persönliche Regiment*, pp. 47, 101.

44. On the change of the composition of the ministry, see also Röhl, *Germany without Bismarck*, pp. 122ff.; Herzfeld, *Miquel*, II, 437ff.

45. G. Kotowski, W. Pöls, and Gerhard Ritter, eds., *Das Wilhelminische Deutschland; Stimmen der Zeitgenossen*, Fischer Bücherei (Frankfurt am Main, 1965), p. 34; Herzfeld, *Miquel*, II, 510.

46. On Miquel in general, see Herzfeld, *Miquel*. For Miquel in the Hohenlohe era, see *ibid.*, II, 435–518. On Miquel's reaction to Caprivi's fall and his hopes for greater political initiative, see *ibid.*, pp. 437, 447.

47. Rich, *Holstein*, II, 494. See also Raschdau, *In Weimar*, p. 9.

48. Herzfeld, *Miquel*, II, 438, 458, 459; Varnbühler to Mittnacht, 5.XII.95, Württembergisches Hauptstaatsarchiv, Ges. Berlin E 73 Fasz. 61 (hereafter cited as Württ. H.S.A.).

49. For the many examples see, for instance, *Hohenlohe*, III, 151, 182. See also Hartung, "Verantwortliche Regierung," pp. 329–330.

50. Hutten-Czapski, *Sechzig Jahre*, I, 230, 241, 253.

51. See Brauer to Grand Duke, 29.X.94, Gr. Fam. Archiv, N 329; Jagemann to Brauer, 29.X.94, G.L.A. Karlsruhe, 49–2027; a somewhat more cautious report is the Saxon report of Hohenthal to Metzsch, 29.X.94, Sächsische H.S.A., Ges. Berlin, Nr. 249. See also *Wippermann*, 1894 (II), pp. 145ff.; *Schulthess*, 1894, p. 171.

52. *Deutsches Wochenblatt*, 7 (1894), 517.

53. *Ibid.*, p. 519.

54. *Ibid.* p. 601.

55. *Ibid.*

56. *Wippermann*, 1894 (II), pp. 142, 144, 145, 151.

57. *Ibid.*, pp. 149–150.

58. *Ibid.*, pp. 148–149.

59. *Reichsbote*, Nov. 1, 1894.

PART II

CHAPTER 3

The Legislative Session
of 1894-95

Concerning the present ministerial personnel, we
expect at some time in the future increasing confusion in politics, unrestrained acting, and even
greater unrestrained intriguing, of the various
political forces against each other, recurrent
crises and restless tossing about of the ship of
state.

Die Nation, November 3, 1894

The German parliament, whose session has now come
to a close after ninety-nine days of meetings, may
confidently risk the comparison with the *illiterate*
Parliament of 1404. . . .

Harden, in *Die Zukunft*,
June 1, 1895

In the press the government accuses the Reichstag
of weakness and aimlessness; and the Reichstag
accuses the government of the same. The sad fact
is that both are correct.

Waldersee, June 2, 1895

My policy is this: to try to get along with the
Reichstag.

Hohenlohe, February, 1895

1

Even before Hohenlohe took office, he began to feel the pressures upon him. As a characteristic introduction, Hohenlohe, on
October 26, 1894, had received a telegram in Strassburg from the
Kaiser summoning him and Köller to Berlin without any explanation
other than that it "concerned important interests of the Empire."[1]
Hohenlohe had no idea of what was going on but, being very suspicious of the whole thing, asked his son Alexander to meet him in
Berlin in order to be accompanied by a "trusted advisor."[2] It was
only on the way to Berlin that Hohenlohe came to know, from the
latest newspaper, what had happened, and thus the purpose of the
royal summons.
Before Hohenlohe had arrived in Berlin, various people there
were getting ready for him. Holstein wrote two memos on October
26--one was designed to reach Hohenlohe in Strassburg before his

departure to Berlin; the other was to greet him upon his arrival in the capital. In these memos Holstein gave Hohenlohe various bits of advice (besides appealing to his patriotism and urging him to accept the chancellorship). First, Hohenlohe was "not to accept any binding agreements" before having conferred with him (Holstein). Second, Hohenlohe should retain Marschall—if Marschall were to go, then he would also leave. Third, he was to get Marschall into the Prussian Ministry of State as a counterweight to Miquel—a move which Botho Eulenburg had always successfully resisted. Finally, Hohenlohe was to use his bargaining position of accepting the chancellorship as a means of getting all his personnel demands accepted.[3]

The Grand Duke, Holstein, Kaiser Wilhelm, and Kaiserin Victoria all urged Hohenlohe to accept. So did Phili Eulenburg, who promised (if not quite honestly) to come to Hohenlohe's assistance in Berlin if necessary. Under these circumstances Hohenlohe, probably glad to cap his long and venerable political career with the most distinguished position the German Empire had to offer (and brushing aside the serious misgivings of his wife, who foresaw how thankless a task it was to be), accepted the post of Imperial Chancellor and Minister-president of Prussia and reported to his monarch in his new official role on October 29, 1894. By that time, too, Holstein had conferred with him personally and certainly reinforced the opinions expressed in his memos—this time, however, he suggested that Hohenlohe get rid of Boetticher.[4] By then Hohenlohe had also been exposed to other problems—problems that he had certainly been aware of previously, but now was bound to see in a different perspective: the views of the Kaiser, the intrigues of Miquel and Botho Eulenburg, a very unfavorable portrait of Caprivi, and the retention of Boetticher and Marschall by default, and the like.[5] To be sure, Botho and Caprivi had lost their formal positions. However, while Caprivi (an exceptional case) removed himself completely from politics after October, Botho Eulenburg remained the leader of the conservatives who were in control of the Prussian Landtag.

In a relatively short time Hohenlohe heard the rest as well: warnings against the Kaiser, against the Bismarcks, and against Holstein. He was now also aware of the agrarian pressure groups, the position of the Center Party, and the "federal problem." Thus the varied interest groups and cliques that presented themselves to Hohenlohe could be grouped as follows: first, Holstein and Marschall (to which came Kiderlen); second, Botho Eulenburg as leader of the conservatives (including to an extent Miquel, emphasizing the conservatives and Prussian position); third, the Bismarcks and the Bismarck Fronde (the latter often overlapping with the conservative group); and fourth, Phili Eulenburg and the Kaiser (as well as Bülow and at times the Grand Duke of Baden). Beyond these main cliques there were also the various parties and interest groups which could be broadly grouped into the Social Democrats, the Radicals and the left wing of the National Liberals, the moderate conservatives, the right wing of the National Liberals, and the extreme conservatives. In addition to the above, there were two more problems which to a certain extent overlapped—the religious question (included in the problem of the Catholic Center

Party) and the federal problem (Prussia versus the Reich).

Against the background of this intricately complex and inter-
connected web of personalities, interests, and issues, Hohenlohe
looked upon himself as Chancellor in the following manner: he
would have to iron out differences by moderation and compromise,
stand above personalities and parties by not identifying with any
particular one, and follow a course of moderate conservatism. In
addition, he would try to "cultivate and maintain the cordial
federal relationship with the German governments . . ." and "unite
the elements of law and order upholding the state in order to
bring about stabilization, and if necessary, reconciliation, and
in order to strengthen the unity of the German tribes. . . ."[6]
It was also necessary for him to bring about conciliation with the
conservative agrarians—without becoming a conservative agrarian
himself. He desired to conciliate the Reich with Prussia—without
becoming a particularist. And he wished to defend the interests
of the crown—without contributing toward a personal regime of
Wilhelm and encouraging absolute monarchy. All this Hohenlohe
intended to accomplish not by playing an active role but by being
passive—compromising, postponing, delaying, and mediating by
"calm consideration, patient listening, and waiting."[7]

On December 5 the first meeting of the third session of the
ninth Reichstag convened.[8] As usual the Kaiser opened with a Crown
Speech (*Thronrede*) which in its basic noncommittal attitude appropriately fitted the circumstances, as well as the expectations, of
the Hohenlohe Ministry.[9] In his address the Kaiser emphasized
especially the economic and sociopolitical problems to be solved
with the aid of the Reichstag: "True to the tradition of the fore-
fathers, my High Allies and I consider it the most noble task of
the state to protect the weaker class of the society and to assist
them to a higher economic and moral development. The duty to
pursue this goal with all our might becomes ever more compelling
the more difficult and the more serious the struggle for existence
has developed itself for individual groups of the nation."[10] Since
the state had to maintain the "totality of interests" (*Gesamtin-
teresse*) and "equalizing justice" (*ausgleichende Gerechtigkeit*)
among interests, "the allied governments will continue in their
endeavor to maintain and further the feeling of contentment and
unity amongst the people by easing the economic and social contrasts."[11]

Presumably in order to carry out this goal, the Kaiser then
enumerated the various bills and proposals that might reach the
Reichstag during the session: first on the list was the antirevolutionary legislation which "would strengthen the existing
stability of the State [*Staatsordnung*] in order to oppose more
effectively the destructive conduct of those who attempt to disrupt
the State [*Staatsgewalt*] in the carrying out of its obligations."[12]

Then followed plans to amend the Reich penal laws in accordance
with accumulated experience; a new stock exchange in order to
"prevent the danger to which the public welfare is exposed by the
misuse of the stock-exchange form of commercial intercourse,"[13]
which was basically a proposal to protect the commercial and trade
elements against "dishonest means" and "dishonest competition";
and finally, financial reform (including a new tax on tobacco) so
as to assure adequate and independent Reich finances.

The two main subjects to be brought up in this new session of the Reichstag were the antirevolutionary legislation and the finance reform proposals. Both had been subject to considerable discussion before Hohenlohe's appointment, and Hohenlohe himself contributed no important new measure to the legislative program, which he had inherited from the previous ministry. Despite the resignation of Caprivi, the Kaiser (as well as the Ministry of State) had accepted Caprivi's anti-Socialist bill, and Hohenlohe could do nothing but follow suit. Although somewhat reluctantly, Hohenlohe intended to conduct *Sammlungspolitik* under the banner of antirevolutionary legislation.[14]

It must be remembered that the antirevolutionary bills that Hohenlohe took over had had their immediate origin in the summer of 1894. At that time the Kaiser (for reasons of personal security) and especially the National Liberals (for the safeguard of law and order, and property) had clamored for such antirevolutionary legislation. Thereupon both Botho Eulenburg, still Prussian Minister-president, and Caprivi, still Imperial Chancellor, had set to work. Both groups—Eulenburg, representing Prussia, and Caprivi, representing the Reich—had worked in secrecy from (and perhaps even against) each other; Caprivi always kept in mind the necessity of acceptability to the Reichstag and to the other German states, as well as possibly the idea of compromising and countering the correctly expected severity of Eulenburg's proposals. Eulenburg, on the other hand, used his proposal as a means to an end. And this end, it was suspected, was two-fold—first, a change of governmental personnel in favor of conservative and agrarian interests, and second, a means to precipitate a conflict with the Reichstag so as to be able to reform the election law.[15]

Up to the middle of October, possibly even up to the Ministry of State meeting on October 19, the two "versions" were kept a strict secret. In that meeting it was Caprivi's proposal which the Ministry generally accepted (with minor changes and after the Kaiser had given his opinion). Even as this proposal stood then, Caprivi would, according to Secretary of State Nieberding, have made some changes anyway before introducing it into the Federal Council—changes which Hohenlohe later proceeded to make.[16]

On the other hand, "the Eulenburg proposal," reported Jagemann, Baden's representative in Berlin, "remains a historically remarkable document. It contains the academic solution . . . showing which governmental means are possible against revolutionary efforts, with omission, to be sure, of the best and oldest . . . namely that of banishment."[17] In Eulenburg's very comprehensive proposal the Social Democrats, the anti-Semites, the agrarian reformers, possibly the clerical liberals, and even those who spoke out in any way for a change of government (individually or collectively) would be subject to punishment.[18]

These, then, were the two proposals concerning the antirevolutionary legislation. However, what was important was the fact that the October crisis had been triggered directly by these antirevolutionary bills (although actually of much longer standing than the summer of 1894), and both Chancellor and Minister-president had been replaced by Hohenlohe.

As mentioned before, Hohenlohe had accepted Caprivi's proposals

with relatively minor changes. He did make it clear that he wanted
to delete from the proposed bill "anything that would give the law
the character of an anti-socialistic law."[19] His reasons were
several—partly because it was still too vague in parts, partly because he saw the futility of opposing the Social Democrats (as such,
actually a desirable thing) by means of anti-Socialistic legislation,
since it would only lead to a conflict with the Reichstag and
actually strengthen the cause of the Social Democrats. This was
exactly what Hohenlohe did not want.[20]

On November 7 the Ministry of State accepted the Caprivi-Hohen-
lohe proposal;[21] on November 29 the Federal Council did the same;[22]
on December 5 the Reichstag received the bill, officially entitled
"Proposal of a bill regarding changes and amendments of the penal
code, the military penal code, and the law concerning the press."
On December 7 Nieberding introduced this bill, which consisted of
a proposed change of nine paragraphs on the penal code and one
paragraph on the press. The main point of the bill was to make it
a crime for anyone to attack "religion, the Monarchy, the family
or private property by way of insulting remarks in a form that
endangers the public peace."[23]

2

The opening of the Reichstag gave some promise for a successful
session. The commencement of the third session on December 5 was
the last meeting in the old Reichstag building; on the 6th it was
held for the first time in the new building. The Kaiser's speech
had been fairly well received by the House, and the representatives
were still in a "state of expectation" about the specific content
of the bills soon to be introduced. They certainly were also
expectantly awaiting the debut of the ministers.[24]

However, this seemingly positive attitude did not last long.
Before the Reichstag had opened, a shadow had already been cast by
an alleged bomb assassination attempt in Magdeburg in early November,
which left the Kaiser open to influences advocating strong action.
Even Hohenlohe stiffened his attitude against the Social Democrats.[25]
This seems indicative, especially in the case of the Kaiser, of the
lack of firm conviction in regard to the antirevolutionary bill.
In addition, on the same day (December 6) that Jagemann was writing
his rather optimistic report on the Reichstag to Brauer, there occurred an incident in that House which also boded ill for the future.
The Reichstag President v. Levetzow, a conservative, opened the
session with the customary cheer for the Kaiser, and some Social
Democrats, including Liebknecht, deliberately remained seated.
Rumors of dissatisfaction and demands for firm action immediately
circulated.[26] Hohenlohe suggested criminal proceedings against
Liebknecht, a proposal which the Reichstag turned down. Then a
commission was created to tighten up the parliamentary procedure,
which in due time was also rejected. Finally, a law was adopted
on February 16, 1895, giving the president the right to exclude
a member from the meeting (*Sitzung*) "in case of gross procedural
violation."[27]

Soon after the Liebknecht embarrassment, in the latter part of
March, the Reichstag rejected a motion to send a telegram to Bismarck

on his eightieth birthday. Levetzow laid down the presidency in indignation (the 2nd vice-president Böcklin followed suit), and both positions came into the hands of Center Party members von Buol and Spahn.[28]

It was already early in the third meeting that the Reichstag was plagued by the lack of a quorum—the president (still Levetzow) and many members of the Reichstag as well were becoming bored with the whole show. For many the whole parliament, maintaining a brittle, outward respectability by artificial means, had become a farce. Moreover, by many (not least the Kaiser) it was treated with outright contempt. However, no matter how ridiculous the Reichstag appeared to a considerable number of its own members, to the Kaiser, or for that matter to the various ministers, it was still an important political factor, even for those who were prepared to stage a coup d'état from above. In the last analysis, neither the Kaiser, nor Hohenlohe, nor the bulk of the ministers and official and unofficial advisors were prepared (if for various reasons) to take that step—no matter how disturbing the few advocates for radical measures were to the policial equilibrium.

3

The antirevolutionary bill[29] had been officially brought into the Reichstag on December 17. But, Singer, a Social Democrat, called attention to the lack of a quorum, and discussion was postponed until January 5, 1895, and then again to January 12. As to be expected, the Social Democrats categorically opposed the bill, as did the Radicals, the National Liberals, and both conservative parties supporting the government—the latter complaining that the bill was not an exceptional law (*Ausnahme gesetz*) and did not go far enough. The position of the Center Party was somewhat ambivalent: they declared their support for the bill, with certain modifications and additions. Then the bill was handed over to a commission. Neither the Reichstag as a whole nor the commission showed great zeal in pursuing the bill. It was meant to be and was accepted as a political rather than a technical bill, and the fervor of those groups who had made the greatest noise for antirevolutionary legislation during the previous summer of 1894 had considerably cooled off. The government was literally stuck with the bill.

Already by early March successful passage of the bill had become doubtful. The decisive Center Party made its influence felt and, by "clericalizing" the proposals, made it unacceptable also to the National Liberals. Even among the members of the Center Party sitting on the commission there was no one capable of enforcing party unity. Some seemed anxious to retain the bulk of the government's proposal; others intended to change the substance of the original bill beyond all recognition. In summing up the pros and cons for success of the bill, Jagemann reported on March 9 that points favorable for success would be:

1) the efforts of such representatives who want to follow His Majesty as much as possible to redeem the Königsberg promise;

2) the inner inclination which does exist for individual
points even amongst the Radicals . . . ;
3) that one does not want to completely concede to the
Social Democrats the drama (which they mockingly will
take advantage of) that the parties of law and order
could not agree on anything;
4) that among the latter, specifically the party which
according to its nature would be most designed for
restraint, has (as a result of its Frankfurt escapade
of last autumn) launched the ship into the sea and,
consequently, must *volens nolens* help somewhat to
bring it into port.[30]

On the other hand, Jagemann summarized the points working against
a successful conclusion as follows:

1) the bungling of the Center and the consequent irritation
(partly sincere, but partly only exaggerated) which
it caused in other circles;
2) the fear of the anti-Semites who are very effective
agitators, and the pressure of the democratic elec-
torate even upon members of the Center, as well as
the press;
3) the combining with the pulpit paragraph [*Kanzelparagraph*] which makes possible the change of position
for the National Liberals.

Jagemann added, "The worst is that it throws a dim light upon the
general political conditions, apart from the bill in question."[31]

Increasingly, public opinion and the press turned against the
antirevolutionary bill, which was losing its former appearance and
apparently putting on clerical garb. The Center was seriously
divided, torn between maintaining its nature as Catholic and particularist, and becoming the government party per se.[32] The conservatives turned away partly because of the Center Party's changes
in the bill, partly because they were being disappointed by the
government in their agrarian demands. The National Liberals sensed
the failure and ardently looked for a face-saving reason to desert
the bill. Even the unity of the government became threatened.
Some ministers still supported the bill. Others, especially Köller,
clearly let it be known that they had lost all interest in the bill
and that, regardless of the outcome, separate legislation would be
introduced in Prussia.[33] They claimed that the National Liberals,
who had been instrumental in the whole affair, had been misled by
Minister Miquel, who had used the issue to oust Caprivi and, having
achieved this, had lost all interest in the issue.[34]

Many began to advise complete withdrawal of the bill, or at
least its death in the commission, and they took action to influence various persons to effect such an outcome. Their motives
could be construed not only politically and objectively but also
personally (subjectively); they were acting not against the bill
as such but against the government, the Center, Hohenlohe, the
Kaiser, etc.[35]

By early March even the Grand Duke of Baden thought it advisable to convey his opinion to Hohenlohe, after having decided that

nothing could come of the bill either in the Reichstag or in the commission. Very diplomatically, the Grand Duke reviewed the change of public opinion as revealed by the press, especially the *National-Zeitung* and the *Münchener Neueste Nachrichten*. He pointed out that almost certainly the bill would not pass, and he concluded with an exposition of the advantages of complete withdrawal by the government. The government would regain the initiative, would still be free to approach the same subject in the future, and would also gain some freedom of action in regard to other bills still pending. Besides, the Social Democrats would not be granted the triumph of a government defeat, would not be able to pose any more as martyrs, and would lose the "aura of glory." To overcome Hohenlohe's personal scruples to such a move (the Grand Duke pointed out that reminders of the school bill and the school-bill crisis of a few years before were not lacking), the Grand Duke closed his letter by pointing out that Hohenlohe had taken over the bill "only as an unavoidable inheritance and [is] not responsible for its content. . . . If you withdraw the bill now," he continued, "then you very considerably ease your difficult task and strengthen the basis for the formation of a party of order since the need of such a party is felt by many." He was confident that the Federal Council as well as the Kaiser (perhaps with his help if Hohenlohe so wished) would gladly agree.[36]

Hohenlohe had not yet reached the point of surrender. In his reply to the Grand Duke six days later he began by expressing the hope that at least part of the bill (in response to a necessity recognized for years) could be successfully brought through—that, after all, no definite decisions had been reached in the commission. More decisive, however, were the other reasons Hohenlohe gave: the decision to postpone the bill for a year should have been made at the time of his appointment in 1894, but now, regrets notwithstanding, it was too late; a complete withdrawal at the present time could be construed as victory of the press over the government. "As much," he continued, "as I do accept the necessity to take into account public opinion, nevertheless in the present case I am not able to dismiss my concern that a retreat at this time will earn the government the reproach of being weak and unsteady in its decision." The government, as well as the other German states, would still vote against unacceptable proposals. Before taking any action, Hohenlohe would await the outcome of the commission.[37] However, both Hohenlohe and the Grand Duke agreed that in the event of governmental rejection, the explanation for such a move should be used to "characterize the weakness of the party-standpoints in this question."[38]

Despite the special effort on the part of Hohenlohe to speed up the work of the commission, that body took its time. Just as in 1894 when the whole bill seemed to have been used for tactical purposes by Miquel and Eulenburg to oust Caprivi and his system, and would be in the fall of 1895 again, so now it was used (especially on the part of the Center and the conservatives) as a political bargaining tool to get clerical and agrarian concessions. The Center Party had, after all, answered the government bill with the proposal to repeal the Jesuit Law of 1872,[39] and followed it up with other measures, which had been struck from the constitution, that were designed to give the Catholic Church more freedom of

action.[40]   The conservatives, led by the agrarians, introduced the
Kanitz bill, which in effect called for state subsidy for agriculture and thus state subsidy for the agrarian aristocracy.[41]   The
Reichstag, however, had bundled the Kanitz proposal off to a commission, and the Kaiser and the government had not shown great
enthusiasm for fulfilling the agrarian wishes which that faction
thought it had detected in the "promise" of the Kaiser to them in
his Königsberg speech of September, 1894.[42]   Besides the left-wing
parties and groups, it seemed that by March only the National
Liberals were genuinely and thoroughly disgusted with the whole
situation—as well they might be.

By the middle of March, the prospects of the antirevolutionary
bill had been reduced almost to nothing when suddenly its fate
seemed to change, the result of a partial change of attitude in the
Center Party. One is almost tempted to say that the Bismarcks had
intervened. The Reichstag had debated the question whether they
should send Bismarck a congratulatory telegram or not; the majority,
including the Center Party, had voted it down. The Kaiser was, at
least publicly, outraged—as was the conservative faction. The
conservative Reichstag president had resigned in indignation, and
the Center took over the presidency. It was now the Center Party
which was burdened with the minor but irritating problems of parliamentary procedure; and, more important, it was quite sensitive
to the widespread outrage against its rejection of the Bismarck
telegram as unpatriotic. The Center did not want to reinforce its
image of a purely negative party. It wanted, so it almost seems,
to take the place of the National Liberals, and (with qualifications, of course) become respectable in its own right. Along with
the acceptance of the antirevolutionary course, it was understandable that now, in such a delicate situation where its reputation
as a responsible party was at stake, it began to make concessions
—concessions that reached the point even of consenting to the
deletion of the *Kanzelparagraph*.[43]   It became even more difficult
to hold the party together; at least it seemed that the bill would
be saved and that the Center would show itself capable of acting
as a responsible government party under the new, not the "liberal"
Caprivi, government. The Center leadership, especially Gröber and
Dr. Lieber, tried very hard to play the part of the government
party per se, as well as to appease the wrath of the conservatives
and of the Kaiser. However, this was not yet to occur.

4

By early May the commission had completed its recommendations.
On May 8 the amended bill was reintroduced into the Reichstag for
a second reading and was torpedoed by the government—it fell on
May 11. A third and last reading was not even necessary. What
had happened?

In the latter part of April Hohenlohe had still been determined
to see the bill through, more hopeful of successful outcome than
before because of the Center's change of attitude (and despite the
growing impact of the Liberal and Radical press).[44]   The Kaiser
considered the idea of ordering the Federal Council to reject the
amended bill, to withdraw the original bill and repeat the

performance of the school bill under Caprivi (urged on, no doubt, by a part of his entourage and some newspapers). But he had decided against this course of action after learning the view-points of the king of Saxony and the prince regent of Bavaria (which, in fact, were similar to Hohenlohe's). Boetticher and Marschall concurred.[45]

Despite the precarious position of the various parties (for example, the Center, the conservatives, the National Liberals, and even some Radicals) which had finally been won over to supporting the revised bill, the Reichstag would very likely have passed the commission bill, with some minor changes. However, there was lack of unity in the government. Both Köller (who gave every indica-tion of being against the bill no matter what the outcome because it was not strong enough) and the Prussian Minister of Justice Schönstaedt frightened the Reichstag with ill-considered[46] speeches (or perhaps well-considered and deliberately aggressive on the part of Köller). These speeches, taken together (the Reichstag had already grown accustomed to Köller's rude and unmannerly ways), were "too much for this sick bill."[47] If that was not enough, the defense of the bill by the rest of the government representatives, although sincere, had either a negative effect (in the case of Nieberding), or was practically nonexistent (in the case of Hohenlohe). Thus the combination of general opposition to the bill, party disunity (especially the Center), increased public pressure, and lack of coordination (perhaps even subversion) on the part of some ministers, convinced Hohenlohe (probably on May 10) to drop the whole bill.[48] The government returned to its original proposal, indicated that it would not accept any changes, and came to an agreement with Levetzow, Kardorff, and Benningsen that the conservatives, Free Conservatives, and National Liberals would vote against the bill. The Center was stuck with the charge that they had killed the bill not only in substance but also formally by not completely backing down from its amendments.[49] Thus was the anti-Socialist bill completely rejected.

The result was dismal indeed for the government and the parties of law and order alike, as well as for the moderate and extreme left. The Center had been used (or rather misused), especially by the National Liberals, to cover up their own embarrassment, incom-petence, and even impotence. Again the Center Party had found it impossible to continue playing its historical role and be a govern-ment party at the same time, despite having a Catholic Chancellor.[50] Its efforts to do so were rewarded with even greater dissension among its own ranks, an outraged press and public opinion, and no improvement in its relationship with the government. The Center Party came out of the fray with a sense of indignation and frustra-tion.

The National Liberals for their part also were highly embar-rassed, having shown lack of strength and conviction. They, too, had a vague feeling that they had been used (by Miquel and the conservatives) but were reluctant to admit and face the reality of their political situation. They were, it almost seems, twenty years behind the times.

The conservatives also had to acknowledge failure, since their own version of the bill had cost Botho Eulenburg the minister-

presidency and since they were not able to use their support for the
new bill as an effective bargaining device for conservative agrarian
interests. It remained for them to look into the future, legislate
for Prussia, and then overwhelm the Reich. The Reich institutions
had obviously shown themselves imcompetent—this held true for the
Reichstag as well as for the Chancellor. However, while the Reich
Chancellor now could not be dominated politically, there was a much
better chance to dominate the Prussian Minister-president, perhaps
even by reversing the decision of October, 1894. Jagemann wrote,
"The conservatives are visibly pleased that nothing has been accomplished . . . [because] in most areas a negative course of Prince
Hohenlohe's parliamentary campaign will shorten his time in office
and in this manner give the agrarians opportunities" (originally
written as: ". . . give the agrarians free course of action.").[51]
Maintaining the conservative political position could not be achieved
on the Reich basis and was rejected; it could be maintained only on
the basis of particularism. Monarchial federalism was accepted by
the conservatives so long as it did not effectively interfere in
their "particularistic" domination of Prussia. In other words, the
conservatives operated politically as though there had been no
changes after 1866. To be sure, a long-standing historical tradition of an independent and powerful Prussia (which still was the
key element in the Second Reich) was on their side. This gave
the conservatives a remarkably simple political program (as often
in cases of reactionary groups) which was *apparently* backed up and
validated by actual political power in proportion to their claims
(that is, the position of Prussia in the Reich), Yet while their
program was simple, clear, and firm, their actual political position was not. It was practically impossible to formulate a political program that conformed to the reactionary ideology, and to
effectively carry it out in the "real" political situation of the
mid-1890s. A pre-1866 conservative mentality pervaded the bulk of
the party at a time when the relative power position had actually
shifted with the events of Bismarck and the Reich.

The gap between rhetoric and action that was so conspicuous in
the conservative ranks was even more pronounced on the other extreme
of the political spectrum—with the Radicals and Social Democrats.
It was not, as they claimed, as a result of their actions that the
bill did not materialize, and little satisfaction could the collapse
of the bill give them. Whatever formal political strength they had
was derived from imperial institutions, especially the Reichstag
election law (based on universal manhood suffrage). As a result
of the apparent Radical victory (which they had "won" not by the
result of their political action but by default), there was the
danger now, more than before, that the place of struggle might not
be the Reich, where the left was in a much more favorable position,
but in the various states, especially Prussia, where the conservatives would possess an overwhelming advantage.

During the whole affair the government had shown its lack of
leadership, indecisiveness, and severe internal disunity. The
resultant emerging public image discredited the Hohenlohe regime
perhaps as much as Caprivi's had been, and those parties that continued to support Hohenlohe did so not out of conviction, but out
of fear of the possible successor of Hohenlohe. The analogies to

the school-bill crisis were very real indeed.

However, the real defeat in the wake of the antirevolutionary bill came to the National Liberals and the Reich government. After all, the Reich government had, at least to an extent, accepted a procedure of parliamentary responsiveness by introducing legislation in response to popular clamor. The obvious lesson was that the government could not depend upon the Reichstag, more specifically, upon the National Liberals. In the government's eyes the Reichstag had proven a decisive failure. The Reich government could not legislate a measure, which was (at least in part) in response to popular clamor, through the Reichstag; both Reichstag and Reich government had failed. Varnbühler aptly pointed out that while the government had given up some of Caprivi's parliamentary support on the left, it had not been able to find an adequate equivalent on the right.[52]

More will be said later about this issue in a slightly different context. It is sufficient to say here that in May, 1895, the question of Reich versus Prussia remained almost identical to that in October, 1894. In both cases it ended in a stalemate. However, in 1894 "Prussia" (the conservatives) had gained a victory of sorts but still had been forced onto the defensive. Now in May, 1895, the way seemed open for them to take the offensive, even to dominate the Reich government by either gaining control over Hohenlohe or replacing him with a candidate of their own choosing, thus reducing the power of the Reich.

5

In summarizing the work of the Reichstag session of 1894-95, the *Europäische Geschichtskalender* states that the "indecisive dispute" (the debates over the antirevolutionary legislation) had absorbed a large part of the parliamentary activity and that "little positive had been accomplished" in other areas.[53]

In fact, the anti-revolutionary question had received the main attention within as well as without the Reichstag, the main reason being partly in the nature of the question: in its obvious relevance for a large number of people and its inclusion of a number of other issues and problems.

The Center Party had successfully used its crucial position to get a revocation of the ban on the Jesuits in Germany. Hompesch, one of the leaders of the Center, introduced this request as early as January 17, and it was accepted by February 20.[54]

The conservatives, as has been seen, had asked for concessions to subsidize agriculture in the form of the Kanitz bill, and much time had been spent debating the plight of agriculture. However, while their requests for generous subsidy were rejected by the State Council (*Staatsrath*) as well as by the Ministry, the Kaiser, and the Reichstag, a number of "small means" to aid agriculture were accepted (such as the tax on liquor and an increase in the premium on sugar). The monetary question, that is, the question of the gold and silver standard (in order to increase the price of wheat), was dilatorily handled by relegating it to a proposal for an international regulation.[55]

Neither the reform of the penal code nor the finance reform

which Miquel had planned had been accomplished by the time the
Reichstag closed. The same was true, despite many debates, of various proposals on social legislation. The only positive result was
that these debates seemed to indicate "an introduction and stimula-
tion for a new series of social legislation."[56]

In contrast, and despite a number of political difficulties as
has been seen, the Reichstag did pass the naval requests. This was
done as a result of the willingness of the Center to cooperate with
the government, and because of the skill of Marschall and the confidence he commanded in the Reichstag, especially among the Center.[57]

Finally, a number of issues were for various reasons simply
postponed for a future Reichstag session. Most notable among these
was the military penal code reform. A proposal had not yet been
worked out that could be handed to the Reichstag. However, Bronsart,
the Minister of War, announced in the Reichstag in early March that
"he would either get a reform proposal passed in the Reichstag or
hand in his resignation in case he could not succeed."[58] This
definite promise of action was to become a major source of difficulty during the next twelve months. Although the reform would
finally be accepted in 1898, it contributed directly to Bronsart's
dismissal in August, 1896, and to the vulnerability and steady
weakening of the Hohenlohe government.

Considering everything, the positive achievements of the Reichstag session had indeed been meager. Hardly anyone had been satisfied, and in fact the image of the Reichstag seemed to have
suffered greatly. Thus the Kaiser and his entourage, and even the
Chancellor, decided to ignore the next session by introducing as
few and as insignificant bills as possible.

Worse, perhaps, was that the session had clearly shown the
weaknesses of the Hohenlohe government. The political deadlock and
stalemate were to continue. With much justification could the
Radical Eugen Richter lament the helplessness and disjointedness of
the government and go so far as to hold up Bismarck as an example.[59]
Lerchenfeld reported that although as a result of the closing of the
Reichstag for the summer, the atmosphere had somewhat calmed down,
the many disquieting rumors continued, owing to the indecisiveness
of the government and the conflicts within the ministry on various
issues (e.g., Köller versus Berlepsch on social reform; Hohenlohe,
Marschall, and Boetticher versus Miquel on agrarian matters).
Lerchenfeld pointed out that the outcome of the session had only
too well proven the inability of the government to accomplish anything in the Reichstag. Hohenlohe, Lerchenfeld wrote, had hoped
to use the antirevolutionary bill to unite the parties of law and
order with the government, but instead, the campaign had weakened
the Reichstag and various parties and it had considerably undermined the authority of the government. Lerchenfeld then pointed
out that the most critical aspect of the whole situation was that
"the position of the government with regard to the conservative
party, without which it is impossible to govern (*regieren*) in
Prussia and with which the Reich in the long run cannot get along,
is as poor today as at the time of Caprivi's resignation." This
situation left the conservatives open to radical agrarian and
anti-Semitic influences to such an extent that no future government would be able to satisfy the conservatives. "A good part of

the guilt for the present situation," Lerchenfeld concluded, "rests
with Prince Bismarck. . . . Whether one likes it or not, he does
possess the greatest authority in the Reich [*Er besitzt einmal die
grösste Autorität im Reich*] . . . ; and, after a short period of
relative restraint, [Bismarck] has now reopened the struggle with
full force."[60]

It was only fitting that the press circulated rumors about a
ministerial crisis and about the imminent resignations of Berlepsch,
Bosse, Boetticher, and Marschall.[61] Hohenlohe had failed to break
the Caprivian political deadlock, and the political forecasts could
not be very favorable. This is true whether one considers the Reichstag performance of the government or whether one reviews the struggle among the various personalities and interest groups during that
same period, as we shall attempt in the following chapters.

NOTES

1. *Hohenlohe*, III, 1.

2. *Ibid.*

3. *Ibid.*, p. 2.

4. *Ibid.*, p. 3.

5. *Ibid.*

6. *Ibid.*, pp. 9–10. Saxon embassy report, 5.XI.94, Sächsische
Hauptstaatsarchiv, Ges. Berlin, No. 249.

7. Günther Blieffert, "Die Innenpolitik des Reichskanzlers
Fürsten Hohenlohe-Schillingsfürst 1894–1900" (Dissertation, Kiel,
1950), p. 18.

8. On the Reichstag session, see also *Wippermann*, 1894 (II),
pp. 163ff., and 1895 (I), pp. 10ff.

9. See Auswärtiges Amt, Abt. A, Acten betreffend Thronreden,
Beurtheilungen derselben sowie der Reichstagsangelegenheiten in der
Presse, Deutschland No. 125, Nr. 2, Bd. 3, especially Dönhoff to
Hohenlohe, 7.XII.94, Politsches Archiv des Ausw. Amts, Bonn.

10. *Schulthess*, 1894, p. 177.

11. *Ibid.*

12. *Ibid.*, pp. 177–178.

13. *Ibid.*, p. 177.

14. Hutten-Czapski, *Sechzig Jahre*, I, 266; Karl Bachem,
Vorgeschichte, Geschichte und Politik der Deutschen Zentrumspartei,
9 vols. (Köln, 1927–32), V, 386; Blieffert, "Innenpolitik," p. 34;
Saxon embassy report, 5.XI.94, Sächs. H.S.A., Ges. Berlin, No. 249.

15. See Jagemann to Brauer, 26.X.94, 31.X.94, G.L.A. Karlsruhe,
Ges. Berlin, 49–2027.

16. Jagemann to Brauer, 31.X.94, G.L.A. Karlsruhe, Ges. Berlin,
49–2027.

17. *Ibid.*

18. *Ibid.*

19. Blieffert, "Innenpolitik," p. 33; Marschall Diary, 31.X.94, 29.X.94; Jagemann to Brauer, 31.X.94, 5.XI.94, G.L.A. Karlsruhe, Ges. Berlin, 49-2027.

20. Blieffert, "Innenpolitik," pp. 33-34.

21. Bosse Diary, 7.XI.94, Bosse Papers, No. 8, Bundesarchiv, Koblenz (hereafter cited as B.A. Bosse, plus the number).

22. Blieffert, "Innenpolitik," p. 34.

23. Eugen Richter, *Politisches ABC Buch*, 8th ed. (Berlin, 1896), p. 420.

24. Jagemann to Brauer, 6.XII.94, G.L.A. Karlsruhe, Ges. Berlin, 49-2027.

25. Marschall Diary, 4.XI.94; Marschall to Eulenburg, 4.XI.94, B.A. Eul. 32.

26. Waldersee, *Denkwürdigkeiten*, II, 333; Jagemann to Brauer, 14.XII.94, 13.XII.94, G.L.A. Karlsruhe, Ges. Berlin, 49-2027; Saxon embassy report, 12.XII.94, Sächs. H.S.A., Ges. Berlin, No. 249.

27. *Schulthess*, 1895, pp. 46f. On this issue see also *Wippermann*, 1894 (II), pp. 179ff.

28. Richter, *ABC Buch*, pp. 363-364. Also see *Wippermann*, 1895 (I), pp. 215ff.; Karl Wippermann, *Fürst Bismarcks 80ster Geburtstag* (München, 1895). Varnbühler reports, 23.III.95, 25.III.95, 28.III.95, Württemb. H.S.A., Ges. Berlin, E 73, Fasz. 61.

29. On the anti-revolutionary bill, see also *Wippermann*, 1894 (II), pp. 63, 145ff., 186f.; *Wippermann*, 1895 (II), pp. 79ff.; Herzfeld, *Miquel*, II, 448f.; Adalbert Wahl, *Deutsche Geschichte 1871-1914*, 4 vols. (Stuttgart, 1929-36), III, 582ff.

30. Jagemann to Brauer, 9.III.95, G.L.A. Karlsruhe, Ges. Berlin, 49-2028.

31. *Ibid.* The *Kanzelparagraph* of 1871 made it illegal for an official of a church to use his position in a way that would endanger the public peace. See Huber, *Verfassungsgeschichte*, IV, 700f.

32. Indicative also is a letter to Lieber, 5.II.95, in which the party is charged with conducting a "policy of opportunism." Lieber Papers, Pfälzische Landesbibliothek, Speyer.

33. Jagemann to Brauer, 9.III.95, G.L.A. Karlsruhe. Ges. Berlin, 49-2028; see also Lerchenfeld to Crailsheim, 8.II.95, G.S.A. München, Ges. Berlin, 1066; Marschall Diary, 5.IV.95.

34. Jagemann to Brauer, 9.III.95, G.L.A. Karlsruhe, Ges. Berlin, 49-2028.

35. *Ibid.*; Hohenlohe to Eulenburg, 21.II.95, B.A. Eul. 34. See also Dönhoff to Hohenlohe, 12.II.95, B.A. Bülow 22; Lerchenfeld to Crailsheim, 8.II.95, G.S.A. München, Ges. Berlin, 1066; *Hohenlohe*, III, 44ff.

36. *Hohenlohe*, III, 46-47.

37. Hohenlohe to Grand Duke, 6.III.95, G.L.A. Karlsruhe, Gr.
Fam. Archiv, N 412; see also Brauer to Jagemann, 6.III.95, G.L.A.
Karlsruhe, Ges. Berlin, 49-2028, and Grand Duke to Nokk, 8.III.95,
G.L.A. Karlsruhe, Gr. Fam. Archiv, Bd. 13, 55 N 18.

38. Hohenlohe to Grand Duke, 11.III.95, G.L.A. Baden, Gr. Fam.
Archiv, N 413.

39. The Jesuit Law of 1872 made it illegal for the Jesuits to
establish and maintain Jesuit establishments in Germany and, in
case of German Jesuits, could limit their freedom of movement. See
Richter, *ABC Buch*, pp. 163-165; Huber, *Verfassungsgeschichte*, IV,
704ff.

40. Bachem, *Zentrumspartei*, V, 387-388.

41. On the Kanitz bill, see Richter, *ABC Buch*, pp. 181-187;
Huber, *Verfassungsgeschichte*, IV, 1079ff.

42. Here see also Herzfeld, *Miquel*, II, 473ff.

43. Lerchenfeld to Crailsheim, 31.III.95, 11.V.95, G.S.A.
München, Ges. Berlin, 1066.

44. This was also true of Marschall. Varnbühler report, 1.V.95,
Württ. H.S.A., Ges. Berlin, E 73, Fasz. 61.

45. Lerchenfeld to Crailsheim, 11.V.95, G.S.A. München, Ges.
Berlin, 1066; Marschall Diary, 18.IV.95, 26.IV.95, 2.V.95.

46. Marschall Diary, 9.V.95.

47. Lerchenfeld to Crailsheim, 11.V.95, G.S.A. München, Ges.
Berlin, 1066; Varnbühler report, 12.V.95, Württ. H.S.A., Ges.
Berlin, E 73, Fasz. 61.

48. Hutten-Czapski, *Sechzig Jahre*, I, 267f.; Lerchenfeld to
Crailsheim, 11.V.95, 15.V.95, G.S.A. München, Ges. Berlin, 1066;
Jagemann to Brauer, 4, 11, 13.V.95, G.L.A. Karlsruhe, Ges. Berlin,
49-2028.

49. Jagemann to Brauer, 11.V.95, G.L.A. Karlsruhe, Ges. Berlin,
49-2028.

50. See Varnbühler report, 12.V.95, Württ. H.S.A., Ges. Berlin,
E 73, Fasz. 61.

51. Jagemann to Brauer, 11.V.95, G.L.A. Karlsruhe, Ges. Berlin,
49-2028.

52. Varnbühler report, 12.V.95, Württ. H.S.A., Ges. Berlin, E 73,
Fasz. 61.

53. *Schulthess* , 1895, p. 323.

54. *Ibid.*, pp. 24, 49; Blieffert, "Innenpolitik," pp. 60ff.

55. *Schulthess*, 1895, p. 323; see also Blieffert, "Innenpolitik,"
pp. 48ff.

56. *Schulthess*, 1895, p. 324; see also Blieffert, "Innenpolitik," pp. 44ff., 53ff. See also *Wippermann*, 1895 (I), pp. 41ff., on finance reform and on social legislation, Herzfeld, *Miquel*, II, 440f.

57. See Blieffert, "Innenpolitik," pp. 57ff.; Hans Hallmann, *Der Weg zum deutschen Schlachtflottenbau* (Stuttgart, 1933), pp. 142ff.; *Schulthess*, 1895, pp. 50ff. The sympathy that Lieber, for instance, had for the navy in 1897 was as true then as already in 1895. See, for instance, Capelle to Lieber, 10.XII.97, and also Navy Secretary Hollmann to Lieber, 20.V.97, Lieber Papers, Pfälzische Landesbibliothek, Speyer.

58. Richter, *ABC Buch*, p. 331.

59. See Saxon embassy report, 15.V.95, which includes the article "Minister im Parlament" of the *Freisinnige Zeitung*, Sächs. H.S.A., Ges. Berlin, No. 250.

60. Lerchenfeld to Crailsheim, 16.VI.95, G.S.A. München, MA III, 2673.

61. Saxon embassy report, 10.VI.95, Sächs. H.S.A., Ges. Berlin, No. 250; also Varnbühler report, 20.V.95, Württ. H.S.A., Ges. Berlin, E 73, Fasz. 61.

CHAPTER 4

Holstein, Eulenburg, and the Newest Course

That His Majesty is driven by his character to
repair the damage done to the Prussian Monarchy
by the . . . much trumpeted combination of the
ruling statesman and the hero-Kaiser is a kind
of force of nature. If we support him, we must
regard the counter-currents not so much as
aroused by any fault of his, *as the expression
of a conflicting principle*. If, however, we feel
opposed on principle to this trait of the Kaiser,
we must resign our office.

> Eulenburg to Holstein,
> December 2, 1894
> (Rich, *Holstein*, II, 487)

We are two loyal royalists, but our goals are not
quite the same. *You* are nearby and see only the
individual peak; I, from a distance, can see the
whole mountain range--and the clouds gathering
behind it. You think of the Kaiser, I think of
the dynasty as well. . . .

> Holstein to Eulenburg,
> January 1, 1895
> (Rich, *Holstein*, II, 489)

1

"Though the separation of offices [that of Reichchancellor and
Prussian Minister-president] had ended, the political conflict which
had made it unworkable continued."[1] This had been amply borne out
by the 1894-95 legislative program. One does get the impression
that there was a lack of sincerity as far as issues were concerned;
often it seemed that the issues in the legislative program were used
merely as a means to an end. Based on previous experience, both
Radicals and Conservatives had found that they could not win on
issues, and therefore had to gain control over personalities. The
antirevolutionary bill had, to an extent, been used to discredit
Caprivi and Hohenlohe (and their supporters), in addition to the
Radicals, the Center Party, and the Reichstag. Although not denying
the inherent merit of Miquel's financial reform, it too clearly
would have given Prussia (Miquel) supremacy in Reich finances.[2]
The military penal code reform very quickly was also to become the
source of a power struggle between the Kaiser (backed by his entourage, the army, and the conservatives) and the Reich (Hohenlohe and

his supporters). Personnel politics, although still reflecting the general political situation, thus became of critical importance, since specific political issues could not be successfully handled if the former could not be effectively controlled. The key figure in this situation was the Kaiser and king of Prussia. To ensure victory over the Kaiser, it was also necessary to gain control over the Chancellor, thereby not only strengthening one's own position but also neutralizing an important figure who otherwise could be used to bring pressure upon the Kaiser.

We have already had occasion to review the composition of the various groups and their interests. As before, Eulenburg retained the extremely important position as indispensable mediator between the "New Course" and the Kaiser. On the other hand, Eulenburg also had to operate within certain given limits. Once Hohenlohe had become Chancellor, Eulenburg was in a sense dependent upon the retention of Hohenlohe, since another change of chancellors would have gravely, perhaps even irreparably, damaged the position of the "moderate" government and cost Eulenburg his political influence. This later happened with Bülow. Moreover, Eulenburg also was dependent upon Holstein, whom he considered indispensable in foreign affairs; and Holstein might resign under a different chancellor. With the political atmosphere growing more polarized and tense, the position of Eulenburg in particular, but other persons within the government as well, became increasingly hazardous and called for an increasingly cautious and complex response. In this and the following chapter we want to analyze the actions and influence of Eulenburg from November, 1894, to mid-1895.

2

On November 1, 1894, Philipp Eulenburg presented his account of the October crisis to Bernard Bülow, his friend in Rome. The account is noteworthy in several respects and deserves close attention. Eulenburg wrote:

> I almost believe that I am the only one in the position to completely lift the veil. As a result of my connections, I get—unfortunately—a deeper insight than most; and the aversion for the awful mess of human passions and endeavors compels me to objectivity. . . .[3]

He went on to say that, more than was generally known, the Kaiser had become tired of Caprivi:

> However, the entourage of the Kaiser did know this, and incited with the persistence of aversion against an individual who, during 4½ years, has not been able to gain *one single friend* at court.[4]

According to Eulenburg, this opposition increased as a result of Caprivi's policies in regard to the three-year military service, to the conservatives, and to the agrarians—policies which "heightened the hatred of the military entourage of the Kaiser up to the point of folly."[5] As a result of his consequent isolation, Caprivi came under the influence of his staff, who fought for their own interests by forcing the Chancellor to maintain his anticonservative position, for which they had been responsible in the first place:

> Thus it came about that officials, who really were
> conservatives, or at any rate moderate conservatives,
> arrived at the extreme left wing, counted upon the co-
> operation of the democratized Center and even spoke
> without alarm about the fact that one may possibly
> count upon the votes of the Social Democrats.[6]

Eulenburg said that this group consisted, among others, of Marschall, Holstein, the journalist Fischer, and "really the whole Foreign Office and it did not matter that these persons, again, stood in vehement, personal opposition."[7]

The idea, Eulenburg continued, to stand behind the Chancellor should be appreciated, since it originated in the "ethical motive" to prove to Europe that the government of the Kaiser was powerful and possible after the resignation of Bismarck, and despite Bismarck. Eulenburg added that he himself had taken this position but after three years (since Bismarck's dismissal) thought the point had been made and then allowed himself "privately to consider at times other combinations as well."[8] Because of Caprivi's turn to the left, the Kaiser's entourage and the Prussian Ministry had had reason for "serious reflection." The struggle began in the press, then the Kaiser turned against the press director in the Foreign Office, and finally in the Königsberg speech he sided with Botho Eulenburg. In doing so, Phili was careful to point out, the Kaiser did not accept the position of the agrarians, but wanted to "help Caprivi" by effecting a compromise and bringing the conservatives back into the camp of the government. But this action of the Kaiser, according to Phili, marked the beginning of the end of the Caprivi regime because no side was ready to back down; each hoped for complete victory. However, Phili continued, the "either-or" solution upon which both parties had based their calculations turned out to be incorrect; instead, in conversations that he had with the Kaiser, the name of Hohenlohe appeared as the only acceptable successor.[9]

From this account of Eulenburg's, then, it is evident that his role had changed somewhat. Beginning as a supporter of the New Course by providing the necessary, but extraconstitutional, link between government and the monarch in order to maintain a function- ing machinery, he now took up a position which Bülow liked to describe as "royalists *sans phrase*"—using his position to keep both extremes in check and slowly changing the composition of the government to fit his own scheme. The strongest force holding the New Course together up to 1894—the fear of Bismarck—had become so weakened that Eulenburg and, consequently, the monarch discarded it.

What Eulenburg was essentially doing, and the role which he saw himself occupying in the future, was basically a Bismarckian one. The system of personal relationships such as between Bismarck and Wilhelm I was to be perpetuated. As Bismarck had been, Eulenburg was confronted with containing the right and the left. He hoped to do so successfully by virtue of his influence with the monarch and by maintaining intimate contact in both camps. By appearing indispensable to each, he hoped to skillfully play off one side against the other. At the same time, both Eulenburg and

Wilhelm would retain a well-functioning bureaucratic machinery that they hoped to control; after all, most of the personnel of the state machinery had grown up in the Bismarckian system and, feeling a strong hand above them (which Eulenburg in conjunction with Wilhelm—and Bülow—had in mind to provide), would have accepted without resistance.

This analogy, of course, fails when one compares the personalities. Yet it is necessary to keep in mind that while Bismarck and Wilhelm I *could* work effectively together, Bismarck and Wilhelm II could not—just so, Eulenburg was able to adapt to Wilhelm II but could hardly have worked well with Wilhelm I.

While Eulenburg had freed himself from the fear of Bismarck, this was still his key instrument in defending his position. He used it in a positive as well as a negative way. The threat of Bismarck's return kept Holstein and the Foreign Office in line and in reliance upon Eulenburg. But by promising a Bismarck-Wilhelm reconciliation, Eulenburg gained considerable support from the various conservative groups and at the same time took some of the wind out of their sails and transferred it to his own.

3

The problem of Bismarck had been a crucial one before as well as after 1890. It was the inability to cope effectively with this problem—of squaring the circle, so to speak—that had finally cost Caprivi his position. Bismarck was a major concern of Holstein. Holstein showed himself quite adaptable to new situations and personnel changes, especially when under pressure. Caprivi went, and Holstein remained, even ready to sacrifice Boetticher at that point (October, 1894); eventually the whole ministry slowly changed in a way which could not meet with Holstein's approval: Berlepsch, Bronsart, Hollmann, Boetticher, and finally Marschall himself resigned—and every time, Holstein could rationalize himself into accepting the changes. However, on one question he did not compromise—the Bismarcks, father and son.

It is not surprising, then, that Holstein, during the time of Hohenlohe's appointment, bombarded Eulenburg with communications concerning the question of a projected visit of the new Chancellor to Bismarck.[10] As Holstein saw the situation on October 28, one day before the official announcement of Hohenlohe as Chancellor, the Bismarck Fronde was trying to undermine Hohenlohe's position by persuading him to visit Bismarck immediately. They had already, wrote Holstein, won over Hohenlohe's son Alexander, who carried great weight with his father. Holstein thought such a visit would be disastrous, that Hohenlohe would lose all prestige by appearing as the puppet of Bismarck. This would also decisively change the relationship of the Kaiser to Bismarck—Wilhelm II would be dominated by Bismarck. Holstein advised Phili either to write to Hohenlohe "in the most forceful possible style," or to tell the Kaiser to discourage Hohenlohe from the idea of the visit (this would have to be done, Holstein added, "before H. [Hohenlohe] discusses the subject in his own way." In the meanwhile, he advised Eulenburg not to "lay out your cards" until Hohenlohe's appointment and a settlement of the question of the Bismarck visit. "Otherwise," he warned, "we can still experience in the next few days surprises similar to that [for Hohenlohe] on Friday."[11]   One day later, on October 29, Holstein became still clearer: probably realizing that he could not prevent Bismarck from being completely ignored, Holstein proposed that the Kaiser alone keep the dealings with Bismarck in his own hand.   "Whenever the communication between Hohenlohe and Bismarck does start, then nobody knows how far it goes." He pointed out that under pressure from the press, which might taint himself and Marschall as the "sole obstacles to the re-establishment of cordial relations to Prince Bismarck," he would not hesitate to resign.[12]

Holstein's position was motivated by sincere political concern and fear of losing his position, both based on his assessment of Bismarck's still enormous weight in German political life. However, Eulenburg had found his own solution—he explained cautiously to Holstein that in order not to shock Hohenlohe, he had agreed in principle to such a visit, but at a later date. Bismarck would come through Berlin early in November and Hohenlohe could invite him for breakfast—an invitation that would more than likely be rejected. The next move would have to come from Bismarck, and Hohenlohe and his supporters would have regained command of the situation.[13]   Perhaps Holstein, as often when Bismarck and the Bismarck Fronde were involved, had become too nervous. Nevertheless, Holstein's suspicion had been correct. Hohenlohe *had* written to Bismarck before the death of Bismarck's wife on November 27, and had politely asked for an audience; then, at the news of the death, he had renewed his request. Hohenlohe was refused both times; however, a visit at a later date was suggested. Holstein wanted to make sure that Hohenlohe would be just as effectively barred from Bismarck as his predecessor had been, and thereby—another important consideration—very likely force Eulenburg (and the Kaiser) to remain on his side and re-cement and perpetuate the already shattered camarilla. The idea of Alexander Hohenlohe possibly quieting the Bismarckian opposition by visiting the prince and giving his son Herbert a post as ambassador was unacceptable to Holstein, as well as, for the time being, to Eulenburg. And so the combination of Bismarck's negative replies and the advice of Eulenburg, Holstein, Kiderlen, and finally also the converted Alexander forced Hohenlohe to postpone his visit.[14]

The opportunity of re-establishing communication came when Prince Bismarck's wife died on November 27. This opened up the most convenient basis for communication between Hohenlohe and Bismarck, and led to the visit in mid-January, 1895. For the eyes of the public the connection between the new government and Bismarck was purely formal and noncommittal.[15]   Behind this facade, however, connections with Friedrichsruh were much more than merely "formal," a situation attributable to Eulenburg and Alexander. Holstein must certainly have been aware of these connections and also aware that at the same time his political influence in Berlin was becoming ever more dependent upon Eulenburg. Eulenburg had agreed "in principle" with Holstein, yet this had not strengthened Holstein's position in any effective way. On the contrary, it must have increased his frustration. It seems that the Bismarck visit and the exasperating evasiveness of Eulenburg at least helped to stimulate the notable exchange of letters between Holstein and Eulenburg, clarifying their respective political standpoints.

The question of the Bismarcks was by no means the only disquieting event during late October and November. There was also Hohenlohe's son Alexander, a political figure whose importance in Berlin
had not yet been thoroughly gauged. Various people had warned
Alexander of Holstein, of Fischer, and of Marschall,[16] and he had
shown his independent opinions on the Bismarck question. He had
contact (and who knew to what extent?) with the pro-Bismarckian
journalist and editor of the *Berliner Neueste Nachrichten*, Hugo
Jacobi, who circulated in one of his newspapers the suggestion that
Marschall should replace Boetticher and thus make room for Herbert
Bismarck.[17] And besides, Alexander had independent ideas about his
father's position, as well as his own, in the new political constel-
lation.

Ministerial posts had not yet been decided upon, thus adding to
the insecurity of the time. Also, the project of getting Eulenburg
to Berlin and "pinning him down" came to nothing; Eulenburg politely
bowed out. No doubt the Foreign Office in Berlin, despite the verbal
notes from Eulenburg, was able to recognize the direction in which
he was moving. His intentions became clear in his letter to Wilhelm
on November 3, 1894, in which he reported on the new state of affairs
in the Wilhelmstrasse: "The alignments of the persons came about
very quickly. Holstein is an old admirer of the Prince, who in
turn thinks much of Holstein. Men such as Lindenau, Pourtales,
Kayser, etc. who support Holstein and are especially devoted to him
accepted, as did Holstein, the decision of Your Majesty with much
gratitude and joy."[18] Eulenburg said that Marschall had survived
the crisis by pure chance. But he might be quite useful as a parliamentary Secretary of State as long as he left foreign policy
alone and concentrated only on trade-political questions; now
Hohenlohe, a very competent diplomat, was there to balance the positions of Marschall and Holstein in foreign affairs. The appearance
of Alexander in the Foreign Office, continued Eulenburg, created
some consternation and would do so for some time to come: "I have
tried to convince the [Foreign] Office as to the usefulness of this
son. For, in fact, the Prince would hardly last without his help—
it is indicative of his common sense, to get his explanation from
an old and truly devoted friend of the father [namely himself,
Eulenburg]."[19] Eulenburg went on to say that the general effect of
Hohenlohe's entry was that "*in Prussia* the conservative tone would
again receive greater emphasis," and thereby the balance of Hohenlohe's position would be reinforced. This renewed emphasis on
conservatism found the fullest acclamation, according to Eulenburg,
in those circles that had formerly supported Caprivi only because
they wanted to prove that a successful government after Bismarck's
resignation was possible (and not because they liked Caprivi's
"radicalism").

Summarizing Eulenburg's letter thus far: Eulenburg was rehabil-
itating the Foreign Office—the "men around Caprivi"—and in so
doing, protecting Hohenlohe from negative influence that might
prejudice the Kaiser into taking rash action. Just as Eulenburg
had excused the Kaiser by pointing out that in his actions against
Caprivi he had actually wanted to help him, so now Eulenburg excused
the former attitude of the Caprivi supporters by interpreting their

actions as having been in the best interests of the monarchy.
Then Eulenburg continued:

> In my long discussion with Prince Hohenlohe in Berlin
> I have, in regard to the handling of affairs of the For-
> eign Office, strongly recommended three points, which the
> Prince heartily approved of. I told him that the only
> point that matters is that Your Majesty would get a
> certain degree of confidence to the Foreign Office which,
> after all, is the main mouthpiece of the commands and
> instructions of Your Majesty.
> This would include:
>
> 1) that His Majesty must under any circumstances
>   receive immediate notice of all, even half-way
>   important events. . . . This maxim the Chancellor
>   must make an absolute duty for, among others,
>   Marschall.
>
> 2) that the semi-official press must undergo a *total*
>   change. . . .
>
> 3) the Prince is to enforce unity in the Foreign
>   Office with uncompromising severity. . . .
>
> I hope that I have given adequate expression to the ideas
> of Your Majesty with these maxims, which I repeated to the
> Prince twice in a most forceful way, and which he intends
> to follow to the letter.[20]

Eulenburg closed the letter by adding that he had told Hohenlohe
that it would be absolutely necessary to maintain "sincere harmony
with the military attachés and absolute cooperation with the
navy."[21] This second part has a distinctively different tone from
the first part of the letter. Now Eulenburg assumed the role (with
more truthfulness than many another role) of the Kaiser's advocate
and executioner and was indeed obviously catering to the taste of
the monarch.

4

As important as Eulenburg had been during the four years under
Caprivi, it seems that his full influence developed only after the
stubborn general had left office and Prince Hohenlohe had taken his
place. To a degree Holstein and Eulenburg were really struggling
against the same forces—the court and the military surrounding
of the Kaiser; the extreme left; and the reactionary, agrarian,
extreme right. While Holstein adopted the tactic of stubborn
resistance, however, Eulenburg decided to divide the opposition,
"join" the various factions, and then overcome them individually.
This tactic was not new with Eulenburg, but it was fully applied
during the October crisis of 1894 and henceforth. To be sure,
in early November Eulenburg told Marschall that the Kaiser "will,
as a matter of fact, do everything that the Prince wants him
to."[22] This was not quite correct, although Phili did not have
to fear from determined interference and opposition of the monarch.
This condition in itself was reassuring to Eulenburg, but aside
from its precariousness (owing to the necessity of always keeping

a watchful eye on Wilhelm), the "danger" of the situation was far
from over. Eulenburg had now to perform a two-fold task: one, to
watch over (and "control") the Kaiser; and two, to watch over (and
"control") the Foreign Office, or at least neutralize its opposition
to his own aims and those of the Kaiser. This meant keeping Holstein
in line, as well as Marschall and Bronsart, and dominating Hohenlohe
and his most influential immediate aide, his son Alexander.

As has been indicated above, the specific problem of the
Bismarck visit had on the surface been resolved. However, the problem of Bismarck in general had not been resolved at all. Even over
the proposed visit, Holstein still expressed anxiety—in fact, he
eventually felt it necessary to hand in his resignation on February
1, 1895. At any rate, Holstein (and he wasn't the only one) perceived an increased activity against the Kaiser and against the
Foreign Office and largely attributed it to the Bismarck Fronde.
The apparent momentary independence of Hohenlohe on the question
of Bismarck's visit—that is, Hohenlohe's inquiry to visit Bismarck
made *before* Bismarck's wife had died,[23] and the idea of both Hohenlohes to bring Herbert Bismarck into the Foreign Office—was a real
enough threat, especially to an already highly suspicious person
like Holstein. The court case which Marschall began against the
Westdeutsche Zeitung (a Jacobi paper), during which the whole
Kladderadatsch affair (still very recent and pertinent) was again
revived,[24] confirmed Holstein in his suspicions. The situation may
perhaps be illustrated also by Waldersee, the general and Chancellor-
aspirant who had fallen into royal disfavor some years before and
since had been a staunch opponent of the New Course. Waldersee, in
his Altona exile, noted in his diary, "As to myself, I now do have
the hope to get into a better relationship with the Kaiser again and
at some time in the future intend to take steps."[25]

On November 9 and again on the 11th, Holstein wrote Eulenburg
letters which were similar in content. One letter was triggered by
a Harden article in the *Zukunft* behind which Holstein suspected
Friedrichsruh connections: "The police are, as you know, not at
our disposal. A different police, a different Minister of Justice,
and a different reputation of the Kaiser among the population—
these are the three pre-requisites for such articles to cease."[26]

Two days later, after noting that "Varzin" was working on the
problems of getting rid of Boetticher, of elevating Marschall to
the post of Secretary of the Interior, and of introducing Herbert
Bismarck into foreign affairs, and linking these ambitions with the
renewed attacks in the press, he again pointed out the need for an
"energetic and reliable" police president. Holstein implied
Richthofen's removal along with that of Lucanus, whom he accused,
among other things, of working against Hohenlohe. He lamented,
". . . One tries to prevent the 'New Course' from consolidating itself . . .": "Among the public the sentiment against the Kaiser
is extremely bad. . . . *Things can not continue like this much
longer*. The Bismarcks know this. Let Hohenlohe resign today, and
the Kaiser will no longer find a Chancellor who does not have the
following program: political union with Bismarck at any price e.g.
Canossa for the Kaiser."[27]

Then Holstein continued, "The Kaiser has no idea of all this; he
behaves so unpredictably, so that even I am at times worried for his

mental stability. . . ."[28] As an example Holstein cited Wilhelm's
nasty treatment of Marschall, who was now thinking about resigning
although he was indispensable for handling the Center Party and
was the most important figure in the ministry. Holstein ended:
"A.E. [August Eulenburg], Lucanus, and Richthofen replaced with
better elements, also *you here*, that would be in my eyes, the
beginning of improvement."[29]

Holstein urged Hohenlohe and Eulenburg to make various changes.
But while stressing the Bismarck danger to Eulenburg in the advice
he gave Hohenlohe, Holstein placed greater emphasis on the necessity
of strengthening the position and actions of the Chancellor in
relation to the monarch.[30]

In appearance the October ministerial crisis slowly began to
abate. On November 19 Hammerstein-Loxten accepted the post of
Minister for Agriculture, and four days later Schönstedt became the
new Minister of Justice.[31] Against these positive tokens of a
"return to normalcy," Holstein also saw the increased attacks on
Boetticher and Marschall and the increased aversion of the Kaiser
toward the latter. It was becoming doubtful (and justifiably so,
as time was to show) that even Eulenburg would come to Berlin as
the result of the monarch's reservations and Phili's own arguments.[32]
Berlepsch felt insecure in his position; rumors of the resignations
of Boetticher and Marschall persisted.[33] Holstein had hoped that
his own personnel proposals would greatly increase the chances of
success of the new Hohenlohe regime in the times ahead, difficult
enough already without a Bismarck problem and a Wilhelm II. But
his proposals were rejected. In fact, none of the many other major
personnel changes which Holstein had proposed as highly desirable
to both Eulenburg and Hohenlohe precisely in order to assure a
greater amount of stability and protection from both the monarch
and the Bismarck Fronde had been put into effect.

Dismayed (perhaps somewhat disillusioned) by the Kaiser's conduct during the first few weeks of the Hohenlohe administration,
but more so over Eulenburg (and to a lesser degree probably also
over Hohenlohe), Holstein became more pessimistic. His letter to
Eulenburg on November 27 shows clearly his frustration. He expressed
keen insight into the political ills of Germany; however, he could
suggest only one remedy, which he could not implement without
Eulenburg's support. Holstein wrote: "I can understand that you
don't like the present order of things, at least in Germany. Who
does? Only those who want a Bismarck dictatorship or a republic.
That the regime of Wilhelm II forms a transition to one of these
two governmental systems—this is a possibility I unfortunately
cannot exclude." Then he characterized the relationship of the
Kaiser and Hohenlohe as an "operetta government but not one which a
European people at the end of the nineteenth century will put up
with." He could well understand why Eulenburg did not want to come
to Berlin and that the

> matter can rest there so far as I am concerned: why
> should I always be the one to push. But no one can tell
> what phases we will go through by spring. By that time
> things may have been lost that can never be recovered.
> The capricious arbitrariness of His Majesty is growing

in proportion to the indignation of all classes of the
people against it. What may happen as a result of these
two opposing currents . . . we will have to await philo-
sophically.[34]

When Hohenlohe left, Holstein, would "use this opportunity" in turn
to resign also.

5

Eulenburg's immediate reply was that "incredible performance"
in which he "was able to ignore an entire century of political
development in Germany."[35] Here we have, to be sure, a highly emotional defense of the royal absolutism of Wilhelm II not only in
spirit but also in content, reaching its ultimate in the expressions
the "King of Prussia has the constitutional right to rule *auto-
cratically*" and "if now the Kaiser steps forward as personal ruler,
he has a perfect right to do so." Eulenburg's belief in the
"Providence" of the Kaiser to rule the kingdom himself and in the
"star of Prussia" underscores this emotional approach. "It is a
hard thing to say," Eulenburg continued, "but the creation of the
German Reich, that is, the transfusion of liberal South German
blood into Prussian, *the combination of the ruling statesman and
the slumbering hero-Kaiser*, have been the ruin of the Prussian
monarchy." It was impossible to fuse liberal south German ideas
with autocratic Prussian ideas. This was truly an expression of
conflicting principles. In Eulenburg's view Wilhelm was driven by
his character to resolve this contradiction by way of reasserting
his autocratic, "personal" rule. However, Eulenburg also pointed
out that "the personal rule of a king is now only conceivable with
the Conservatives." It is not clear here if Eulenburg took this
attitude because he accepted the necessity of conservative support
in order to regain the personal rule (the necessary prestige which
Eulenburg was afraid only a successful war would provide) or because
he took into account constitutional changes after 1848. He does
become very clear with regard to Holstein's attitude:

> If we support him, we must regard the countercurrents
> not so much as aroused by any fault of his *as the expres-
> sion of a conflicting principle*. If, however, we feel
> opposed on principle to this trait of the Kaiser, we must
> resign our office. To serve the Kaiser and at the same
> time constantly to consider his activity as personally
> ruling king as minor pin-pricks—this belongs *equally* in
> the realm of *insurmountable* contradictions.[36]

Perhaps Holstein's pessimistic letter of November 27 was intended
more as a radical means to get Eulenburg aroused into action after
everything else had failed, but it was to no avail. He did not,
however, give up trying to get him to act. In his letter to Eulenburg on December 4 not only was he able to substantiate his case
further by "the latest Bismarckiana" (the conversation between
Jacobi and Alexander Hohenlohe), but he made his position even
clearer—he was trying to save the monarchy (for him this would only
be possible in the form of a constitutional monarchy). In order to
do so, there would have to be stability, which meant, among other

things, neutralizing the extreme right as well as the Bismarck
Fronde; both groups were working against stability in order to
create a situation in which they might take power. As a consequence, Holstein was trying to prevent any dilemmas, especially
regarding the relationship of the government to parliament; to
introduce moderate legislation that might be accepted; and to preserve Wilhelm's freedom of action in relation to Bismarck. Although Holstein agreed that a successful war would have a very
good effect, he dismissed this idea as impractical. He continued:

> As to the governing with only the conservatives, I
> had thought that we were in agreement for a long time
> that the *King of Prussia* possibly, but certainly not
> the German Emperor, could govern *exclusively* conserva-
> tive. For this very reason, we both were against an
> antirevolutionary bill for the Reich, but in favor of
> a *strong* one for Prussia. So, since neither is possible
> —war and conservative reaction—one must try to muddle
> along with the existing Reichstag factor.[37]

No doubt neither Holstein nor Eulenburg meant literally what
they wrote to each other. To some extent they each had in mind
a "shock method," which they had applied successfully before.
However, their basic approach toward the political problems was
clear enough. Was Holstein more realistic and objective than
Eulenburg? Eulenburg's letter of December 5 must be carefully
evaluated. It was essentially a spontaneous emotional response
to Holstein's frank critique of the Kaiser. In defending the
Kaiser, Eulenburg quite obviously was carried away and put ideas
on paper which he himself accepted in practice as unrealistic
even if he believed them in theory. "When one," he immediately
wrote, "begins to write in broad sweeps, then one ends up at times,
as a result of logical deductions, with peculiar results. This
also must have been the case," he admitted, "in my last letter."[38]
True enough, severe qualifications might not be taken alone as proof
of a retraction by Eulenburg, since he designed the letter with his
recipient in mind. It was, after all, a reply to Holstein's letter
of November 27[39] and was specifically written in defense of Wilhelm.

As to the rest of Holstein's views, Eulenburg was careful to
point out (the questionable fact) that "we are in agreement as to
the *handling* of matters. . . ."[40] Perhaps a better estimate of
Eulenburg in this connection may be gained not by overemphasizing
the "incredible performance" but by taking into account and giving
at least equal weight to his letter of December 27 to Holstein
and his letter of January 7, 1895, to Bülow. He wrote that Holstein
should not forget that his letter of December 2 was a reply to him,
that he (Eulenburg) regarded the Kaiser as his friend, and that
the letter was a personal defense. Then Eulenburg reassured Holstein
of his objectivity and independence from "everything and everyone,
even the Kaiser." He had not become a "Court-Conservative of the
newest type," and consequently had not "deprived the Hohenlohe system, so to speak, of its equilibrium" (an accusation which Holstein
had made in his letter to Eulenburg on December 24 [41]). He emphasized that he was, and only could be, a "very moderate Conservative." He pointed out that they both recognized the necessity of

moving "closer to the Conservatives without giving them both hands"
and even indicated that this was done so at least partly to prevent
personal action of the monarch!—that actually he and Holstein were
acting on a common basis to oppose the "personal regime." The rest
of the letter continues in the same tone. He expressed disgust over
the "court" (but pointed out that their ideas, such as getting Botho
Eulenburg the chancellorship, were not to be taken seriously); he
agreed to the necessity for stability and consequently Hohenlohe's
retention; and he drew attention to Hohenlohe's willingness to "take
energetic steps against the police."[42] Yet the Eulenburg letter of
December 2 was indicative of the general approach which he was taking
in politics—a basically emotional, if not to say mystical, approach
with which he nevertheless hoped to achieve real political success.

If Eulenburg's letter of December 27 was intended to calm Holstein,
it did not do so. Holstein not only maintained his previous tone but
in his reply on January 1, 1895, made further additions to his case,
specifically against Wilhelm's "frivolous regime," by taking examples
from Wilhelm's interference in foreign affairs.[43] The effects of
these personal actions, Holstein argued, were not considered by
Eulenburg. Moreover, in light of the presented facts Holstein
inquired about the position of the Chancellor, adding again that if
Hohenlohe left, he would follow suit if he had not already resigned
as a result of the Henckel affair.[44]

Perhaps the best document illustrating Eulenburg's opinions at
this time was his letter to Bülow on January 7, 1895: "The interesting letter of Holstein of 1.I makes me think and has the same effect
as the Scirocco. In face of certain facts the courage begins to lag
and I fight against it with arguments, which he himself must recognize as arguments of one who is not convinced himself. Deep down I
have not lost the confidence in His Majesty, . . . but it is more of
a feeling than a conviction. A feeling which suffers under the
Scirocco." For the most part Eulenburg recognized the validity of
Holstein's arguments. He appreciated Holstein's "downright extremely
difficult, embarrassing" position, and he accepted Holstein's fear
of the Bismarcks as valid:

> Germany carries a heavy burden in the daemonic nature
> of Bismarck. Jupiter Amaman! They now worship their
> Jupiter in the form of a bull under whose horns and hooves
> the whole organism aches.
> That is really the crux of their woe. We would much
> easier accustom ourselves to the peculiarity of His
> Majesty if that daemonic force did not rule which darkens
> everything or illuminates the country with flames which
> are not the sun.
> His retention impossible—his leaving impossible! . . . [45]

However, Eulenburg took a totally different approach from Holstein's. Despite the unconditional and open opposition of Holstein
to Bismarck, Holstein did recognize that the Bismarck problem was
not the only one and that the figure of Wilhelm was just as important. Holstein saw that it was necessary to take action (negative
action in one case and positive action in the other) against both.
Eulenburg, on the other hand, was trying hard to excuse the shortcomings of the Kaiser and even to put the blame on Bismarck. At

the same time he did not openly oppose Bismarck, but simply (as he later wrote) would wait until Bismarck died. And in the meantime, he implied, he would muddle through as best he could. He did try to keep Bismarck "in a state of mild dis-contentment" and thereby to neutralize him as much as possible—an approach which was bound to fail, since it was based on a gross misjudgment of Bismarck.

Reflecting on the differences between Eulenburg and Holstein, one might say that Eulenburg ignored the historical development of Germany since 1848 while Holstein did not. In this sense much more of a political realist, Holstein was trying to find a workable solution between the monarchy, the bureaucracy, and the parliament. The goal of checking the absolutist tendencies of Wilhelm II did not automatically mean subordination to bureaucracy, although this would have been the eventual result. It seems that Eulenburg also tried to restrict the Kaiser, but by way of personal relationships. Thus the supreme power would rest in Wilhelm and Bülow and Eulenburg! Holstein's plan to restrict the Kaiser proceeded by way of strengthening the Chancellor in relation to the monarch and, until that had materialized effectively, influencing the monarch through Eulenburg's mediation. For this system to work smoothly, it was of great importance for Eulenburg to perpetuate his influence over the Kaiser. There is no doubt that Holstein in such a situation would be one of the key figures, but he would also have been less able to "control" both Hohenlohe and Eulenburg. The ideas of Holstein were in important ways quite similar to those of the Grand Duke of Baden and, one might add, to those of Bismarck, as his various articles in the *Hamburger Nachrichten* seem to indicate. Certainly Bismarck and the Grand Duke could not be accused of trying to subordinate the Kaiser to the bureaucracy or to inaugurate a full-fledged parliamentary regime. All three were trying, it seems, to save the monarchy from the monarch.

However, aside from the basic similarity—a means to restrict the Kaiser—the dissimilarity of approach was crucial. The Grand Duke, Eulenburg, and Bülow intended to restrict the Kaiser by strengthening and perpetuating the "personal regime," that is, by bringing to bear upon the Kaiser personal influence. Holstein, on the other hand, hoped to restrict the Kaiser by way of a strong chancellorship based upon, and controlled by, the bureaucracy. Finally, the conservatives worked for a strong chancellorship controlled by themselves. Paradoxically, a victory of the conservatives (dominating the Prussian Landtag) over the Kaiser thus meant a victory of Prussian particularism as well as a victory of the Prussian parliament. A victory of the bureaucracy, on the other hand, meant a victory over the particularist forces—a victory of the Reich—but a defeat of the parliamentary idea. The policy of the conservatives had strong Bismarckian overtones, but while Bismarck himself looked for a way to curb the Kaiser without capitulating to either the liberals or the conservatives, the conservatives only thought of defending their particularist interests.

It was obvious that Holstein was bound to fail. Yet while he may have felt this in some of his more pessimistic moments, he came at times remarkably close to success, always basing his actions in the last analysis on the hope—even certainty—that eventually even Eulenburg must see things his way and come over to his side. Holstein

was not usually a bad judge of character. He knew how malleable and
impressionable a character Eulenburg was; what he misjudged in the
case of Eulenburg was the amount of consistent influence he could
exert upon him—Eulenburg was exposed too much to influences contrary to Holstein's political convictions. In fact, by 1895 Holstein's influence with Eulenburg had become negligible. For all
practical purposes Holstein's critique of Wilhelm had made Eulenburg "immune" to Holstein; in this, Eulenburg was supported considerably by a mutual friend—Bülow.

7

Bülow had conveyed to both Holstein and Eulenburg his political
views as far as the situation in late 1894 and the immediate future
was concerned. These views were: "no further changes in key positions"[46] and, as far as the basis of government was concerned, to
govern with the "natural pillars of the Reich," the conservatives
in the north and the National Liberals in the south. Apart from
that, however, Bülow strongly supported Eulenburg against Holstein.
It almost appears that Bülow was afraid of Holstein's power and was
using Eulenburg to neutralize Holstein, but without letting Holstein
become aware of this lest Holstein wreck his ambitious career.

Bülow attributed the motivations of Holstein's pessimistic outbursts (in letters to Eulenburg and to himself—letters which they
both then interchanged to reinforce their confidence in each other)
to purely personal reasons: Holstein was afraid of losing power in
Berlin as a result of personnel changes. On the other hand, wrote
Bülow, Holstein's conception also worked in favor of the Kaiser's
interests, since "apart from the fact that Holstein is (with certain
restrictions and under definite pre-conditions) hardly replaceable
in the Foreign Office," he would do anything to prevent changes in
key positions, and "at the moment, we need first and foremost con-
tinuity." Consequently, the longer Hohenlohe, Marschall, and Holstein were kept in office, the better. However, if Hohenlohe were
to die, then Bülow would personally favor Botho Eulenburg as successor. He continued:

> The only question is whether he (as a result of the
> biased attitude of the hostile press, but in reality in
> the eyes of the North German bourgeoisie, the entire West
> and the entire South) has a too-pronounced reactionary
> appearance. If we do not face an immediate large domestic
> action; [and] as long as His Majesty wants to maintain con-
> tact with the liberal elements and as long as it is
> necessary to take into account especially the attitude
> of the South . . . ,

then, perhaps, Hohenlohe-Langenburg would be a more opportune candidate.[47]

Bülow had expressed similar ideas in his reply to Eulenburg's
letter of December 10, in which Eulenburg included not only his letters to Holstein but Holstein's letter as well. In light of this
evidence, Eulenburg certainly expected words of assurance and com-
fort from Bülow against Holstein's trenchant attacks. Holstein,
replied Bülow, wanted to prevent a closer contact between Bismarck

and the Kaiser, and he wanted to prevent the New Course from turning away from the liberals and toward the conservatives. Consequently, he tried to prevent any possibility of a Reichstag dissolution. In case of a conflict or "policy of confrontation" it would be difficult to hold either Holstein or Marschall, or even Hohenlohe, and in case of a confrontation policy "the full support of His Highness [Bismarck] would hardly be dispensable."

Along with eulogistic praise for Eulenburg and deep understanding and sympathy for his position and action, Bülow added that as the result of the last 30 years Prussia could not put itself into opposition to Germany; that a successful defensive war would have its merits; but that Wilhelm II "must not have major failures . . . after the dismissal of Bismarck and the poisoned and poisoning activity of the 'Fronde' our beloved Kaiser must be successful. . . ." Bülow agreed with Eulenburg to some extent: although he saw the "cliffs" in the nature of the Kaiser, he saw even more his positive qualities, and added that "the often present dissatisfaction . . . directs itself even more against the 'how' than against the 'what' in the actions of the Kaiser." Bülow was optimistic for the future: "In time," he held, "Kaiser and nation will get accustomed to each other. . . ." As Eulenburg had already correctly observed, Bülow added, "the times strive for a new form, in which to fuse Imperium and liberty. With seriousness, caution, prudence, constancy this form eventually will be found. First and foremost constancy! We have gone through only too many changes. . . ."[48]

Especially in regard to Bülow's reflections on the synthesis of *imperium* and *libertas*, one is strongly reminded of the attempts to synthesize intellect and power (*Geist* and *Macht*) and "Liberalism and Nationalism." Just as power and nationalism became dominant, so *imperium* would dominate liberty in Bülow's own time, as expressed in the program of world policy and the building of a fleet. The new form of Bülow was in essence merely an imitation of the old Bismarckian form, and the synthesis eventually turned out to be "Power-Nationalism-Imperium."

While Bülow was jotting down his reflections and generally providing guidelines for his friend Phili to follow, Holstein's second main cause for worry—the Bismarcks—flared up almost immediately after he had been reassured: the matter of Hohenlohe's visit to Friedrichsruh.

8

On December 1, 1894, Alexander had a long talk with the editor of the *Berliner Neueste Nachrichten*, Hugo Jacobi, a friend of Bismarck. Jacobi had been in Varzin, and he conveyed his impressions and the conversation he had had with Bismarck. The main political points that Alexander noted down immediately following this interview (and which he sent to Eulenburg) were that Bismarck's interest in current politics was keener than ever and "not only motivated by the interest for his son, but by the idea that he personally would get the power into his hands either directly or indirectly."[49] Bismarck favored Hohenlohe's becoming Chancellor ("It is a pity that he had not already taken over the position 4 years ago . . ."), and in order for Hohenlohe to maintain himself as Chancellor, he would have to "clean up the Augian Stables," or he would succumb through the same intrigues as did Bismarck himself—that is, Hohenlohe should get rid of Boetticher, Marschall, and Holstein. Furthermore, Alexander reported that in regard to Bismarck's 80th birthday, the suggestion made by Jacobi and Bismarck's doctor Schweninger (for Bismarck to stay in Berlin for that event) was favorably received by the old Chancellor as well as by his son Herbert. Bismarck said that he could use Henckel's apartment; he would not want to live in a royal palais, since there he would be a "prisoner,"[50] Alexander concluded that "at any rate we have to take into account that even in the future we will not yet have to deal with an old man bent by the heavy blows of fate, but with the same old Bismarck as he always was."[51]

In a first step to counter the catastrophe of a Bismarck in Berlin on his 80th birthday, Hohenlohe suggested "that in that case . . . it would be, to be sure, desirable for you [Eulenburg] to strengthen the ministry here by your becoming a member."[52] The effect of this news concerning Bismarck, as may easily be imagined, played a considerable role in the debate between Holstein and Eulenburg, which took place roughly at the same time.[53]

On both "objective" accounts, then, Holstein's fear over a realization of a tough line in domestic politics with a Chancellor like Botho Eulenburg, and the return of Bismarck in some form, were not without considerable foundation. As we have seen, Holstein and Eulenburg agreed in principle on these two issues. However, while Holstein proposed and worked for a more or less "radical" solution (he took his moderate conservatism seriously, based on the reality of the German political experience of the last 50 years), Eulenburg felt compelled and confident to meet the crisis in a more subtle way. The unwelcome and disquieting critical voice of Holstein he tried to reject, with self-justification and Bülow's professed support.[54] Eulenburg also received further support on his stand against Holstein from Alexander, who wrote, "In regard to Holstein's excitement, please don't get alarmed. My father, as well as I, slowly come to know both his excellent qualities and his little weaknesses."[55] No doubt some of the arguments used by Holstein's opponents also made an impression on Eulenburg. In this way, Holstein was more or less isolated,[56] his influence to a considerable degree was neutralized, and Eulenburg was free to make his own preparations to maintain the stability of the government (with the illusion of his personal inclinations and idiosyncrasies), as well as to meet the Bismarck problem on his own terms. As far as this latter problem—the Bismarcks—was concerned, Eulenburg found a solution: he advised that if Bismarck actually would come to Berlin (of which he was not sure; he suspected Jacobi to be the initiator of such a politically astute move of the Bismarck Fronde), then the Kaiser was to give him "Bellevue [castle] or something else. He [Bismarck] then will be in a situation of dependence," and Bismarck then could not very well accept Henckel's apartment. It is interesting to note that not only Holstein but Eulenburg as well, was quite suspicious of Henckel's ambitions. Eulenburg made this clear when he said to Wilhelm, "But to have the chance that Bismarck will clear the way [to the Kaiser?] for him, by staying with him, will induce him to work strongly for this combination [Bismarck staying in Henckel's apartment]." Yet it was Eulenburg's plan to counter Bismarck, not Hohenlohe's to get Eulenburg into the ministry, that was ultimately accepted.[57]

NOTES

1. Röhl, *Germany without Bismarck*, p. 126.

2. See especially Herzfeld, *Miquel*, II, 430ff.

3. Eulenburg to Bülow, 1.XI.94, B.A. Eul. 32.

4. *Ibid.*

5. *Ibid.*

6. *Ibid.*

7. *Ibid.*

8. *Ibid.*

9. *Ibid.*

10. Holstein to Eulenburg, 28.X.94; 29.X.94, B.A. Eul. 32.

11. Holstein to Eulenburg, 28.X.94, B.A. Eul. 32.

12. Holstein to Eulenburg, 29.X.94, B.A. Eul. 32.

13. Eulenburg to Holstein, 29.X.94, B.A. Eul. 32.

14. See *Hohenlohe*, III, 5-6. See also Arthur Brauer, *Im Dienste Bismarcks, Persönliche Erinnerungen* (Berlin, 1936), p. 395; Saxon embassy report, 27.XI.94, Sächs. H.S.A., Ges. Berlin, No. 249.

15. A certain amount of speculation naturally circulated, accompanied by the usual attacks on Boetticher and Marschall. See Saxon embassy report, 23.I.95, Sächs. H.S.A. Ges. Berlin, No. 250; Krüger report, 17.I.95, Staatsarchiv Hamburg, A IV C 6, Bd. II.

16. Holstein to Eulenburg, 30.X.94, B.A. Eul. 32.

17. Saxon embassy report, 10.XI.94, Sächs. H.S.A., Ges. Berlin, No. 249. It was the *Westdeutsche Zeitung* against which Marschall consequently was to bring a libel suit.

18. Eulenburg to Wilhelm, 3.XI.94, B.A. Eul. 32.

19. *Ibid.*

20. *Ibid.*

21. *Ibid.*

22. Marschall Diary, 5.X.94.

23. Jagemann to Brauer, 13.XII.94, G.L.A. Karlsruhe, Ges. Berlin, 49-2027.

24. Marschall Diary, 20.XI.94. On the *Kladderadatsch* affair, see H. Rogge, "Die *Kladderadatsch* Affaire," *Historische Zeitschrift*, 195 (1962), 90-130, and below, p. 108, notes 20 and 21.

25. Waldersee, *Denkwürdigkeiten*, II, 329-330, 30.X.[94].

26. Holstein to Eulenburg, 9.XI.94, B.A. Eul. 32. See also Rich, *Holstein*, II, 485.

27. Holstein to Eulenburg, 11.XI.94, B.A. Eul. 32.

28. Holstein to Eulenburg, 11.XI.94, B.A. Eul. 32.

29. *Ibid.*

30. See *Hohenlohe*, III, 11.

31. See also the Saxon embassy report, 14.XI.94, Sächs, H.S.A., Ges. Berlin, No. 249; Varnbühler to Mittnacht, 19.XI.94, Württ. Hauptstaatsarchiv, E 46-48, No. 1274.

32. *Hohenlohe*, III, 10-13.

33. Saxon embassy report, 6.XI.94, 12.XII.94, Sächs. H.S.A., Ges. Berlin, No. 249.

34. Rich, *Holstein*, II, 486 (Holstein to Eulenburg, 27.XI.94).

35. *Ibid.*, p. 488.

36. *Ibid.*, pp. 487-488.

37. Holstein to Eulenburg, 4.XII.94, B.A. Eul. 33.

38. Eulenburg to Holstein, 5.XII.94, B.A. Eul. 33.

39. Eulenburg to Holstein, 27.XII.94, B.A. Eul. 33.

40. Eulenburg to Holstein, 5.XII.94, B.A. Eul. 33.

41. See Haller, *Eulenburg*, pp. 173-174.

42. Eulenburg to Holstein, 27.XII.94, B.A. Eul. 33.

43. This interference of the monarch in foreign affairs was another reason for Holstein's dissatisfaction; see Röhl, *Germany without Bismarck*, p. 130.

44. Holstein to Eulenburg, 1.I.95, B.A. Eul. 34. For the Henckel reference, see below p. 77. For the Henckel "affair," see Rich, *Holstein*, I, 411-415.

45. Eulenburg to Bülow, 7.I.95, B.A. Eul. 34.

46. Rich, *Holstein*, II, 490.

47. Bülow to Eulenburg, 5.I.95, B.A. Eul. 34.

48. Bülow to Eulenburg, 15.XII.94, B.A. Eul. 33.

49. On Bismarckian articles and Herbert Bismarck, see Alexander to Eulenburg, 14.XII.94, B.A. Eul. 33; 19.XII.94, B.A. Eul. 34.

50. Alexander to Eulenburg, 1.XII.94, 6.XII.94, B.A. Eul. 33.

51. Alexander to Eulenburg, 6.XII.94, B.A. Eul. 33.

52. *Ibid.*

53. See especially Holstein to Eulenburg, 4.XII.94; Alexander to Eulenburg, 6.XII.94, B.A. Eul. 33.

54. See especially Bülow to Eulenburg, 5.I.95, B.A. Eul. 34.

55. Alexander to Eulenburg, 14.XII.94, B.A. Eul. 33.

56. See also Liebenau to Bülow, 8.I.95, B.A. Bülow 99. Liebenau also regarded Bülow as the only possible future Chancellor.

57. See Eulenburg to Wilhelm, 9.XII.94, B.A. Eul. 33, which includes both Alexander-to-Eulenburg letters on Jacobi conversations of 1.XII.94 and 6.XII.94; Eulenburg to Holstein, 10.XII.94, B.A. Eul. 33; Alexander to Eulenburg, 14.XII.94, B.A. Eul. 33, reporting a conversation between Wilhelm and Hohenlohe on this matter.

CHAPTER 5

The Marschall Crisis

His Majesty graciously orders me not to be
annoyed . . .

> Marschall Diary,
> January 1, 1895

It was indeed carnival-time.

> Wilhelm to Eulenburg,
> February 21, 1895

I may be allowed to remind Your Majesty of the
fact that after the Lieber Intermezzo last year,
the resignation of Marschall had been completely
arranged [by me]. Afterwards, Your Majesty had
retained him in the Foreign Office due to opportunistic considerations.

> Eulenburg to Wilhelm,
> January 20, 1896

1

The October crisis and the consequent reshuffling of positions
and personnel had created some anxiety within the bureaucracy. The
stresses and strains resulting in the formal, as well as the real,
political polarization of power after 1892 (that is, the separation
of the Imperial Chancellorship and Prussian Minister-presidency) had
come to a head in 1894 and found, of course, a measure of relief
after October of that year when they were recombined. However, the
basis for political instability had not fundamentally altered, since
October was not a solution but merely a postponement of the problem.
The tension and anxiety were best illustrated in the correspondence
between Holstein and Eulenburg during the last days of 1894. No
matter how serious their differences were, the fact that these differences—that is, their temporary falling out, which seriously
endangered the extraconstitutional link between the bureaucracy and
the monarchy—came to the front and were allowed to develop to such
importance seems to prove that it was not as yet a time of political
crisis. Both Eulenburg and Holstein could still afford to "hiss" at
each other—Hohenlohe's Bismarck visit had been postponed, and the
main debates in the Reichstag still lay ahead (accompanied by the
invariable press commentaries). Therefore, especially when looking
back at September and early October, Brauer was justified in observing that there was "significant change toward improvement." He
continued:

> While I was thoroughly shocked during my presence here
> in September at the terrible anarchy of the whole govern-
> ment machinery, at this *bellum omnium contra omnes within*
> the government, I now was pleasantly surprised how the sole
> fact of a new Chancellor has brought about a complete
> change. The confidence in the leadership and its unity
> has been restored. One has the feeling that, again, a
> *government*—and indeed *one* government—exists. One does
> not, of course, underestimate the difficulty of the situa-
> tion which will now show itself with regard to an unstable
> Reichstag; but, in general, the departure of Count Caprivi
> is felt as a clarification and the appointment of Prince
> Hohenlohe as the best possible solution that was conceiv-
> able for the time being.[1]

Thus the struggles within the bureaucracy, as well as its relationship to the monarchy, were temporarily in suspension; the struggle
with the Reichstag would not begin seriously until January of the
next year.

Yet already by late December things began to change significantly. Conflicts within the bureaucracy resumed their normal level
after the "disruption" of the October crisis. The rift also became
apparent in the various meetings of the Crown Council (*Kronrat*) and
the Ministry of State as they prepared for the new Reichstag session.
In the debate over Miquel's proposed *Komptabilitätsgesetz* on January
4, 1895, Bosse (the Minister for Ecclesiastical Affairs), Bronsart,
Marschall, and the Kaiser, "naturally too rash, as usual" (to use
Marschall's words), took a strong stand against Miquel. Miquel, who
had played an ambiguous role during the October crisis, took the
whole situation as a personal offense and became extremely irritated,
especially with Bosse, to whom he attributed his unexpected defeat.
Although Bosse did not take seriously the thought that Miquel would
resign over this incident, he believed that Miquel would not forget
it.[2] Wilhelm's continuously irresponsible activities affecting
foreign affairs[3] and foreign policy did their share to increase the
general feeling of irritation, especially in the Foreign Office. In
an unsent draft letter, for example, Alexander pointed out: "Two
ways exist in which foreign policy may be conducted in monarchies:
either as in Russia, where the Czar is his own Minister of Foreign
Affairs and where the Minister only carries out the orders; or as it
is here, where the Minister of Foreign Affairs is responsible not
only to His Majesty, but also to the country."[4] Hohenlohe, for his
part, rationalized his actions in the face of such flagrant behavior
by saying that he was "too new in my relationship to the Kaiser" to
make reprimands. "That," Hohenlohe added for his own benefit, "will
be possible later. At the moment it would be too early."[5] Last,
there was the Kaiser's gracious order to the understandably indignant
Marschall not to get upset.[6] Perhaps a more serious conflict was
averted only because of the complacency of both Hohenlohe and Marschall and also perhaps because of their sense of responsibility.

2

As if this was not enough material to cause difficulties in the
near future (especially since in January the Reichstag was now in

session), Wilhelm announced in the Crown Council of January 4 that
the Council of State (*Staatsrath*) should be called together to consider a program to help "suffering agriculture," which the Ministry
of State was then to draft.[7] Apart from the obvious political
ramifications which the announcement of such a program had—since
no one could foretell how closely the monarch might eventually
identify himself with the agrarians—there was also the significance of Wilhelm calling upon the Council of State. The Council of
State was an antiquated structure left over from Prussia's period of
royal absolutism, although it had been reformed during the Stein-
Hardenberg period. In 1854 Bismarck had been appointed to the
council, but it fell into the background and was only resurrected
again in 1884 after a lapse of 30 years. At that time Bismarck
was not specifically designated as a member.[8]

Upon Wilhelm's reference to the Council of State in 1895, there
appeared in Jacobi's paper, the *Berliner Neueste Nachrichten*, an
article expressing its satisfaction that "with the calling of the
Council of State Prince Bismarck has been given the opportunity to
utilize again his capacities in official form for the fatherland":
the article pointed out that Bismarck had belonged to the Council
of State since 1854.[9] The bureaucracy in Berlin immediately went
to work and found that there was as yet no proof of Bismarck's
appointment in 1854. They did find, however, that when the Council
of State was reactivated, it was *de jure a continuatio* of the previous council, and that by express order Minister-president Bismarck
had been appointed its vice-president.[10] The question was: with
the loss of the minister-presidency in 1890, did Bismarck also lose
his vice-presidency of the Council of State? The Bismarckians
answered no, while the anti-Bismarckians responded with a determined yes. The Kaiser decided that "since the matter is, all the
same, doubtful, one would do better to decide it in Bismarck's
favor." Hohenlohe, in the course of his imminent visit (it was
January 12 and Hohenlohe was going to Friedrichsruh on the following day), was to tell Bismarck that he was still considered a member
and would be given, in case of his coming, the vice-presidency
(the Kaiser taking the presidency himself)![11]

Thus the stage was set for at least one aspect of the "Marschall
crisis"—Holstein's threatened resignation, which was most directly
connected with Bismarck. There were, of course, attacks and rumors
in the press, a common occurrence by then, but they never failed to
unnerve Holstein. Unexpectedly, the Kaiser had sent Cuno Moltke to
Friedrichsruh on January 9. This, to Holstein, must have seemed a
repetition of January, 1894, but with a much greater chance for
success, since, among other things, Hohenlohe was not Caprivi and
would be more apt to give in to the pressures (including those of
Alexander and Phili) to re-establish relations with Bismarck. For
Holstein, this was indeed tantamount to Bismarck's return. Then
Hohenlohe himself left for Friedrichsruh on January 13 with the
Kaiser's message for Bismarck to attend the Council of State as
vice-president. These events, together with the Kaiser's proposal
for a program acceptable to the agrarians[12] and his intent to elevate August Eulenburg and Lucanus to Ministers of State, had implications not only for Holstein, but for others as well. Waldersee,
for example, noted that "Hohenlohe's visit to Bismarck upon which

the Kaiser had put much importance, has been to mutual satisfaction.
I believe that soon the peace will be fully restored."[13]   This was
a prediction which came fairly close to reality within the next
three weeks.   Kardorff wrote to his wife as early as January 18
that "in politics it really does look like an impending return to
the old course [the Bismarckian course] in all areas."[14]   This
would mean a removal of Holstein, of Marschall, of Boetticher, and
of Berlepsch—the pillars of the New Course.   At the end of January
and after an intensified press campaign against Boetticher and
Marschall, Herbert Bismarck was promoted to colonel, and Holstein
wrote out his resignation: "As there is no longer any doubt that
my remaining in the Foreign Ministry is among those obstacles that
make the establishment of the closer relations with Prince Bismarck
desired by His Majesty more difficult, I regard it as my duty to
remove the obstacle respresented by my person."[15]

Certainly "the combination of these events" had prompted Holstein
to such a decision and was undoubtedly meant to force Hohenlohe to
take a stronger line against moves to restore Bismarck's influence.[16]
The time lag and the drastic nature of Holstein's response are ex-
plainable.   Until late January he had coped with the situation with
self-confidence and with his usual warnings and suggestions of possible alternatives.[17]   But the promotion of Herbert threw him into
confusion.   For a moment it must have seemed to him that he had lost
control of the situation.   But the reassurance that he surely received from Hohenlohe[18] had the effect not only of bringing Hohenlohe closer to his side but also of removing Hohenlohe somewhat
from Eulenburg's influence.   In this way Holstein could again
influence to a greater degree the possible moves of reconciliation
—in whatever form—that Eulenburg might want to take,[19] since
these conciliatory efforts would require the cooperation of the
Chancellor.

When the second phase of the Marschall crisis opened with a
court festivity on February 6, the first phase had been overcome.
Holstein had decided to remain, had strengthened his position, and
had effectively coped with one aspect of the attack on the government from within its own ranks.

3

On February 7 Holstein wrote to Eulenburg that "the Kaiser rules
with the Cabinets against the organs of the Constitutional government."[20]   This was amply borne out during the next two weeks.   This
time the attack concentrated on Marschall.   It started innocently
enough.   Upon request of the Court Chamberlain Count Egloffstein,
Marschall had invited Dr. Lieber, one of the more important figures
of the crucial Center Party, to the court festivity so that the
Kaiser could perhaps say a few words to him.   However, at the ball
the Kaiser refused Marschall's plea to speak to Lieber and instead
had a long conversation with the ex-Jesuit Hoensbröch—a red flag
to the Center—who had apparently been invited and introduced by
Lucanus.[21]

It is interesting here to note again that during the previous
month an attempt had been made by Hahnke, the chief of the Military
Cabinet, and Lucanus, the chief of the Secret Civil Cabinet, to

elevate August Eulenburg and Lucanus to Ministers of State. This
move had become known only by accident, and Hohenlohe had been able
to prevent it.[22] Had this *coup* come about and been accepted, it
would have solved the problem between the official government (or
the bureaucracy) and the executive, but in an unacceptable manner:
it would have established royal absolutism within the framework of
the constitution. In the situation of 1895 it would have established
the dominance of the "unofficial advisors," especially the cabinets,
over the official government.

Meanwhile in the Landtag the debate raged over an agrarian program, while the Reichstag was occupied with the antirevolutionary
bill. Especially in the Reichstag, the Center Party was crucial to
the success of the government program. Failure of the legislative
program would severly discredit the Reichstag, and could be used as
a lever toward a reformation of that body as well as of the ministry.
It seems that the attack on Marschall and the Center Party could
bring about just such a situation. The appearance of Hoensbröch at
the ball on February 6 proved successful. The Kaiser was dismayed
with the Center Party; he was dismayed with the Foreign Office,
which had not given Hoensbröch a position. The Center was annoyed
at the attention the Kaiser gave to the "traitor" Hoensbröch and at
the neglect of Dr. Lieber.

From Hubertusstock on February 12, the Kaiser suddenly sent
Eulenburg a letter strongly attacking Marschall. According to the
Kaiser, Marschall had forced himself upon him in order to get him to
speak to Dr. Lieber; he had refused because Lieber was a "thorough
scoundrel" and had been invited without his knowledge. The Kaiser
also said that Marschall then went to Prince Heinrich to get him to
talk to Lieber, and Wilhelm added that upon direct questioning the
Court Chamberlain had said that Lieber had been invited "due to
personal urging of Marschall without my permission—shortly before
the festival."[23] The Kaiser's adjutants von Kessel and von Arnim
sent letters with very similar content.[24] Wilhelm clearly expected
Eulenburg, who was credited with having "the personalities of the
Foreign Office under a certain amount of control"[25] (and was thus
equivalent to a "Chief of the Foreign Office Cabinet"), to take
appropriate action.

4

Eulenburg's reactions are plainly documented in his letters to
Wilhelm on February 14 and to Hohenlohe two days later. Eulenburg
began: "Since that first offending behavior against Your Majesty
on the part of Marschall during the visit of Prince Bismarck in
Berlin on January 26, 1894,"[26] Eulenburg had realized the necessity
of Marschall's eventual dismissal. After this almost slanderous
introduction, Eulenburg proceeded to outline a realistic plan of
change. He pointed out that Marschall had been retained in October,
1894, only because of Holstein's advice to Hohenlohe to do so (as a
further accentuation of the "new course" against Bismarck). Marschall's resignation would be considered a victory of the Herbert
Bismarck faction; Holstein would leave, and so would Hohenlohe (that
is, if Radolin were to take Holstein's place). In Eulenburg's view
this would be an unacceptable situation. If the Kaiser were to drop

Holstein, then Hohenlohe would need a person who could replace not
only Holstein but Marschall as well—and this could only be Bülow.
If Bülow came, Eulenburg advised giving Herbert Bismarck a position
and thereby achieve full peace with the Bismarcks, since "Bernhard
is the most valuable official that Your Majesty has; the predestined
Imperial Chancellor who must not be allowed to suffer shipwreck on
account of a feud carried on by the Bismarcks." Eulenburg recapitulated: "With the situation as it is, I can *only* see the possibility
(if a Chancellor crisis is to be avoided and if Marschall must go in
any case) that Your Majesty will also separate Yourself from Holstein
—since the latter will identify himself with Marschall—and to
entrust the office to Bernhard Bülow." He also advised waiting with
these changes until the close of the current Reichstag session,
since ". . . one would, after Marschall's successes, *not understand*
why he should go now, and would see in it a simple victory of the
Bismarcks. Later it would perhaps be possible to invent some kind
of story."[27]

With appropriate changes (considering the nature of the Chancellor) Eulenburg conveyed the Kaiser's grievances against Marschall
to Hohenlohe and suggested the necessary steps for the Chancellor
to take. Significantly enough, Eulenburg again included his own
critique of Marschall, and it appears that this was his true conviction and not just a means to mollify the Kaiser. He pointed out
that ever since January, 1894, "the serious intention to get rid of
M[arschall], had always been maintained," that it was only to
accommodate Hohenlohe's wish that Marschall had been retained in
October. The change would probably come after the current session
of the Reichstag, and Hohenlohe should not identify himself with
Marschall. Eulenburg continued: "When someone is unable to gain
for himself even a mediocre position at court during a period of
five years, well then, the matter is hopeless and I believe it is
better, Your Highness, not to become an advocate when there is nothing to be gained." He suggested Bülow as a replacement, and suggested a position for Herbert.[28]

For an understanding of Eulenburg, it is of considerable interest
to evaluate his critique of Marschall. The atmosphere in which Eulenburg felt most secure and where he was at his best was the world of
the courtier. The direct opposite was the case with Marschall.
Moreover, while it is correct to look at Eulenburg as the "mediator"
between the court and the government, it is also correct to view
Marschall as the "mediator" between the Reichstag and the government. Eulenburg's position rested almost entirely on the world of
the court, while Marschall's was based primarily on a constitutional
government with a strong parliamentary element (he had come, after
all, from the world of southwest German liberalism). Marschall's
position was by no means negligible, as the considerations of
Eulenburg to get rid of him (and also his retention until mid-1897)
do show, but it was in comparison to the court decidedly secondary.
Eulenburg acted basically in the interest of the court, as a courtier
who in his "mediating" role between the court and the government
used the government to neutralize the influence of the Reichstag
and at the same time to gain control over the government—and more
than that, over the Kaiser (only in this respect was he able to join
hands with Holstein). In the words of Waldersee, with a different

approach, but having the same effect: "First and foremost we need an energetic individual who can also handle the Kaiser."[29] No doubt Eulenburg's friendship for Wilhelm was sincere, but it was also a rationalization for his own benefit.

While Eulenburg responded quickly to Wilhelm's letter and prepared for the dismissal of Marschall, he did not neglect also to inquire in the Foreign Office and get their version. In response, Marschall gave his version of the whole affair. He placed the attack on his person in its context by reviewing the position of the Center Party. He pointed out that in all major issues, e.g., the military budget, the naval increase, the antirevolutionary legislation, the Center had supported and was still supporting the government without demanding compensation for itself. He pointed out the absolute necessity for the Center Party to support the government, and the disastrous effect the loss of such cooperation would have.[30] According to Marschall, the apparent effect of Hoensbröch on the Kaiser (as well as the Lieber affair and other influences at work on the Kaiser while he was at Hubertusstock from February 10 to the 13) was a violent anti-Catholic outburst on the part of Wilhelm against the Center and those who in any way seemed to support or cooperate with that party (such as Marschall and Catholic Army officers). As a result of this outburst against the Catholic Army officers, the War Minister Bronsart took offense and had a serious run-in with the monarch.[31] Keeping in mind the increasingly difficult position of the Center leaders in the Reichstag in regard to their constituents (many of whom objected to their leniency toward the government and almost looked upon them as traitors to their party), such Imperial behavior would gravely threaten the balance in the Reichstag and possibly throw the Center back into the ranks of the opposition. One cannot help but feel that this was exactly what was intended by those who brought about the scandal. With regard to himself, Marschall pointed out that Lieber had been invited to the court festivity before he (Marschall) ever suggested, among other possibilities, Lieber's name (it appears that this had been done by August Eulenburg[32]); that he had, during the course of the evening festivity, approached the Kaiser on this subject only once and, when very unexpectedly receiving a negative reply, had never brought up the subject again.[33]

5

To further complicate the situation, there existed several additional elements. The first is the so-called Hollmann crisis. This was the result of a proposal circulated within the Navy by von Knorr, chief admiral of the High Command of the Navy. This proposal pointed out the necessity for a colonial army. However, this army was to be under the jurisdiction of the High Command, not the Navy Secretary. Although the friction between the Naval High Command and Hollmann (the Navy Secretary) arose to some extent out of a lack of demarcation of authority between these two structures, it was usually the High Command which tried to extend its direct and indirect control over naval affairs. It played a similar role in opposing the official Reich government as that of the Military Cabinet in regard to the War Ministry and held a significant

position in the ranks of the advisors around the Kaiser. Hollmann
had countered the High Command's attack by threatening to resign if
the document were not retracted. Hohenlohe supported him, since,
among other reasons, the resignation of Hollmann would have had a
very negative effect upon the proposed naval budget (an attack on
Hollmann as Navy Secretary was at the same time an attack upon
Hohenlohe's own position, and the proposal of Senden, chief of the
Navy Cabinet, encroached not only upon Hollmann's sphere but upon
that of Marschall as well).[34] The friction between Wilhelm's adjutant, Major Schele, and the Undersecretary of State for Colonial
Affairs, Kayser, was not as important, but it added to the general
consternation and was also indicative of the general state of
affairs, specifically the opposition of the unofficial influences
(the court) on the one hand and the official government (secretaries
and ministers) on the other.

A second disturbing element to complicate matters was provided
by a report of the Prussian ambassador to Saxony, Count Dönhoff.
According to Dönhoff's report, the Saxon King Albert had spoken in
favor of a radical solution to the present problems, especially in
dealing with the Reichstag and the Social Democrats. Yet as late
as January of the same year the Saxon king had been decidedly
against any such dangerous measures.[35]

Finally, Botho Eulenburg had indicated to the Center that he
favored the renunciation of the Jesuit Law, a step, Botho pointed
out, that Hohenlohe could not take. It was a step to curry the
favor of the Center (while at the same time the Center was being
strongly denounced to the Kaiser).[36]

As we have seen, Marschall, in his letter to Eulenburg on
February 17, tried to set the story straight as a result of the
attacks against him and in answer to Eulenburg's inquiry. However,
Marschall was not the only one who took time to inform Eulenburg.
Alexander Hohenlohe, Holstein, and Franz Fischer (the Berlin correspondent for the *Kölnische Zeitung* and close to Holstein) all did
the same.[37] Probably with a considerable amount of disgust did
Marschall note in his diary, "Throughout the day, Holstein and I
(and not we alone) write long letters to Philipp. What a state of
affairs; one has to constantly trouble oneself not only with foreign
states, but also with His Majesty and his irresponsible advisors."[38]
Bronsart's outburst that all the irresponsible advisors of the
Kaiser deserved to be hanged[39] expressed the same sentiment if in a
somewhat less refined manner.

Taken altogether, the various incidents fit into a recognizable
pattern which very strongly suggests, as Marschall, Holstein, Alexander Hohenlohe, the Chancellor himself, and even Eulenburg believed,
a more or less concerted effort on the part of the conservative
opposition—the Bismarck Fronde, the agrarians, the entourage of the
Kaiser (that is, the court)—to create a crisis whereby the Hohenlohe
Ministry and its New Course policies would come to an end. From
this point of view it was a follow-up to the October crisis in 1894.

It will be remembered that although Eulenburg inquired from
Holstein what actually happened in Berlin, he had already prepared
for the removal of Marschall. He had presented his plan to the
Kaiser in his letter of February 14 and to Hohenlohe two days later.
Eulenburg hoped to separate Hohenlohe from Marschall so that, as he

expressed it to Wilhelm on February 18,[40] the Kaiser had a free hand
vis à vis Hohenlohe in requesting Marschall's removal. Hohenlohe
basically agreed with Eulenburg: they would retain Marschall until
summer, but "what may happen in the summer, is a different question."[41]
However, this attitude was characteristic of Hohenlohe and did not
necessarily mean that he fully agreed with Marschall's dismissal.
Even Holstein, who had stood in defense of Marschall not so much out
of personal consideration but from a desire to keep one of the more
successful government spokesmen in the Reichstag, in a letter to
Bülow indicated his readiness to adjust to the dismissal of Marschall
and perhaps even of Boetticher. He wrote: "Those who urge His
Majesty to get rid of Marschall soon, only work toward the crash.
The Center would presumably retort to Marschall's dismissal with the
rejection of various bills. Then would come the dissolution with
the agrarian program." The new Reichstag, Holstein continued, would
be dominated by the extreme left and the extreme right, and thereby
the influence of the Kaiser would be paralyzed. Led by Herbert
Bismarck (with his father in the background), the right would not
consider the wishes of the Kaiser. Holstein continued: "Briefly
then, if Marschall is under all circumstances to be removed here and
possibly placed in Boetticher's job, as the Bismarcks demand, even
that might be arranged decently if enough time is allowed. In four
months, that is *at the end of the sessions*, you could be brought in;
in about seven months, Monts could be brought in." "But," he added,
"I fear that emotion is stronger than (objective) consideration."[42]
This was very similar to what Eulenburg had in mind, and even Holstein's assessment of the Herbert Bismarck problem did fit well into
Eulenburg's plans. Eulenburg, as mentioned above, had spoken of a
"Herbert Bismarck party" and intended to bring Herbert into the
Foreign Office under Bülow.

The letters written by Fischer, Holstein, Marschall, and Alexander Hohenlohe did not reach Eulenburg (who had been in Munich) until
his return to Vienna on February 20. With this new information, or
"atmosphere-sketches" (*Stimmungsbilder*) as he preferred to call them,
Eulenburg set to work again. To Hohenlohe he wrote:

> As a matter of fact, the affair Marschall-Lieber does
> appear in a different light.
> But the picture of the situation that I received can-
> not change my opinion that, *in the long run*, Marschall
> is unretainable.
> From the chaos of communication I even have the im-
> pression that the whole resultant unrest has its roots
> in the wish of His Majesty for resignation.[43]

Eulenburg's letter to Wilhelm (in which he included, rather
indiscreetly, it would seem, Alexander's letter) made the same
point—"atmosphere-sketches" from Berlin, from which he gathered
that there was a commotion in government circles in Berlin—and he
added, ". . . I believe that all these people do not recognize the
heart of the whole matter: that Your Majesty wants to separate
Yourself from Marschall and that this intention casts its sha-
dows. . . ."[44] Only then, "so that all will go all right," he
pointed out the dangers of dismissing Marschall immediately.

Thus all the arguments and facts of the situation with which

he had been bombarded—and they were not even all for an unconditional retention of Marschall—did not change Eulenburg's mind and
actions. He alone, so he imagined, had fully understood the real
issue and was carrying out the wish of his Imperial friend (and very
likely at the same time his own inclinations).

However, instead of Imperial praise, which Eulenburg probably
thought he deserved and very likely expected, the Kaiser told him
not to take the story too seriously, that he was laughing over it
already; even the wounded Marschall could stay and be somewhat
consoled. "It was indeed carnival-time," Wilhelm ended the telegram and asked Eulenburg to make use of this message as soon as
possible.[45] Wilhelm followed up this telegram with another message: "My dear Philippus, the content of the current letter has
dumbfounded me with astonishment! Such a *galimatias* of nonsense
as Crown Prince Alexander has dreamed up has seldom been put
on patient paper." Alexander's exposé (of February 17 to Eulenburg)
Wilhelm brushed away as nonsense, a carnival's dream, completely
untrue, a fairy tale. He pointed to specific incidents to prove
that he was not opposed to members of the Center Party and that
Catholic officers had been promoted. The Hollmann crisis, he wrote,
did not exist.[46] Wilhelm stated emphatically that he was happy with
the old Hohenlohe, and that Eulenburg had disturbed his peace with
his reorganization: ". . . let all men, whom you push around as if
they were Halma figures, simply remain in their posts! Thank God
that it is carnival-time, otherwise I would have become quite angry
with you."

This sudden change of the Kaiser must indeed have been a shock
and embarrassment to Eulenburg. He had, to an extent, exposed himself to the "Holstein group" in his readiness to drop Marschall;
even more important to him as a courtier, he had "annoyed" the
Kaiser with these plans. Quite naturally Eulenburg tried to excuse
himself on the grounds of having been misinformed, that he had
acted in accord with an Imperial wish. He promised to be "very
clear to the fairy-tale tellers," and to take into his hands the
"education" of Alexander.

In the wake of Wilhelm's change of mind (owing, as Eulenburg
correctly perceived, mainly to the Kaiser's fear of a big reshuffling in the government and not to any objective re-evaluation of
Marschall), Marschall's dismissal for the time being was pushed
into the background. Eulenburg did not (and neither did Wilhelm)
abandon the idea of getting rid of Marschall. With the separation
of Hohenlohe from Marschall, which Eulenburg thought he had accomplished, he wrote, "Therewith then it is arranged that Your Majesty
is able to separate Yourself from Marschall after some time *without
a crisis*, which I, out of many reasons, consider as correct—when
the time is harmless. For a replacement *without* the large changes,
which Your Majesty seems not to wish, I shall yet find means and
ways."[47]

The last act of the specific Marschall crisis was provided by
Eulenburg posing as a successful mediator: he defended the Foreign
Office against court intrigue and shielded it from rash and ill-
considered Imperial moods. In false modesty and not without reason,
he added that his intervention really had not been "necessary,"
since the Kaiser was anxious to please Hohenlohe.[48] Even his

disagreement with Holstein was smoothed over, although it was a superficial reconciliation.[49] He himself had accepted the necessity of no changes during the current Reichstag session. This opinion was also held by Holstein, Hohenlohe, and particularly by Bülow. (Bülow, kept abreast of events by Holstein and Eulenburg, stood fast by his dictum: build stability and confidence, institute no major changes.)[50] On the same day, February 22, Eulenburg cabled to Bülow: "*Orâge à Berlin passé.*"[51] To be sure, the role in which Eulenburg presented himself to Marschall and to Holstein was not incorrect, but nevertheless remained only a half-truth. He did, after all, stand firm to carry out the Kaiser's wish of gradual reformation of the government, and did not hide that fact, either from the Kaiser, or Bülow, or Holstein and Hohenlohe, even if he did convey his plans with an eye to the respective recipients.

6

By late February the Marschall crisis abated. The dictum of "no change at the present moment" had been re-established and accepted by the principal actors. Hollmann had his way in the struggle with the Naval High Command. Marschall was able to get Reichstag approval for all four cruisers which the Kaiser had demanded, and the Kaiser showed his more gracious side to Marschall, who then dismissed the whole "affair" as a mere court intrigue.[52] Moreover, Hohenlohe, with the help of Eulenburg, reconciled Lieber to an extent by telling him that the only reason the Kaiser did not speak to him at the reception was because the Kaiser did not want to increase his difficult position as leader of the Center Party during the current Navy and antirevolutionary legislation debates.[53] Then Hohenlohe left on February 25 for Vienna, from which he came back a few days later in good spirits. Even Eulenburg seemed to resume his former relationship with Holstein, who accepted the renewal of friendly relations partly because he realized his dependence upon Eulenburg (in regard to the Kaiser, to the court, and to Bismarck), and partly because, at least as far as short-range political configurations were concerned, their aims were similar (i.e., Bismarck's visit to Berlin on his eightieth birthday was coming up in the days ahead). However, he had no illusions about Eulenburg's nature and aims.[54]

The Marschall crisis seemed to dissolve without any lasting negative effects. As a matter of fact, even the prospects of the legislative program briefly appeared in a brighter light. However, despite the salvation of the facade of stability in the ministry and the few encouraging signs in the Reichstag, this appearance was very deceptive.

As has been seen, the outcome of the legislative session, measured by its concrete accomplishments with regard to the government program, was anything but successful. As far as the ministry was concerned, it may almost be said that the crisis destroyed the unity—however fragile—of the Hohenlohe government. It is, of course, valid to ask: what unity? Seen in the perspective of the years 1890 to 1897, it is really difficult to speak of unity at all, for the iron grip of a Bismarck that had trained the ministers to be mere bureaucratic instruments had not yet been replaced. The

ministers still lacked a sense of common responsibility, more often
seeing only their own segments and not the totality, yet acting as
if each segment reduced everything else to insignificance. "The
gentlemen," as Hohenlohe well expressed it, "are from former times
used to obey and do not want any freedom which, so they imagine, will
be used by others for intrigues."[55] The ministers remaining after
the October crisis had not basically changed; the crisis itself had
not settled any basic issues. Perhaps one may describe the February
days as the end of Hohenlohe's ministerial honeymoon and, in this
respect, a full return to the "old course" of the New Course.

Under the pressure of the Marschall crisis, the Hohenlohe Ministry had begun to show serious signs of crumbling. It was no longer
true that, compared to December, 1894, the ministry showed some
signs of unity and direction, as Brauer had reported to Karlsruhe.
Marschall's early laudatory comments on Köller had become increasingly critical. Holstein had again handed in his resignation;
Boetticher was again thinking of resigning; Berlepsch asked to be
dismissed; the struggle between the government (the ministry) and
the advisors (the Cabinet) did not die down after February, but the
struggles between the various ministers among themselves increased
significantly. The air was filled with mutual suspicion. All of
this resulted partly from considerations of political issues under
debate in the Reichstag, Landtag, and their committees; partly from
considerations of political issues not introduced in the legislative bodies but influenced indirectly by the political atmosphere;
and partly as a result of a difference of personalities.

The situation of "Hahnke against Bronsart, of Senden against
Hollmann, and of Lucanus against the entire Ministry of State,"[56]
to put Holstein's words into a slightly modified context—that is,
the struggle of the ministry against the court (not the Kaiser)—
thus continued. Moreover, the added element of disunity among the
ministers Hohenlohe describes quite well in his diary:

> All sorts of rumors and intrigues are again circulating.
> Holstein and Marschall accuse Köller of wanting to play
> the leading role in the Ministry; while Köller complains
> that Marschall . . . causes agitations against him. . . .
> I told this to Marschall who wants to clear this up with
> Köller and also with Miquel. The latter has set Köller
> against Marschall. . . . Some ministers, such as Thielen,
> Berlepsch, and Bosse, complain about my lack of energy in
> the handling of the Ministry of State.[57]

Four months later Hohenlohe himself felt threatened by intrigues of
his own ministers, in particular Bronsart and Miquel.[58]

The Hohenlohe Ministry took its hesitant steps into a rather
uncertain future. The atmosphere of uncertainty was not caused,
but was greatly increased, by the February Marschall crisis. The
ministry more often than not reacted rather than acted, precipitated by activities of the extreme right and the extreme left
("Bebel and Bismarck"[59]) and by the legacies from the previous
administration, especially the military penal code reform.

NOTES

1. Brauer to Grand Duke, 6.XII.94, Gr. Fam. Archiv, N 329, G.L.A. Karlsruhe.

2. Marschall Diary, 4.I.95; Bosse Diary, 4.I.95, B.A. Bosse, No. 8. See also Marschall Diary, 5.I.95; Bosse Diary, 9.I.95, B.A. Bosse, No. 8.

3. See, for instance, *Hohenlohe*, III, 26. The Kaiser also tried to gain domestic support for a large naval program. See Krüger report, 9.I.95, Staatsarchiv, Hamburg, A IV C6, Bd. II.

4. *Hohenlohe*, III, 28, note 1.

5. *Ibid.*, p. 27.

6. Marschall Diary, 1.I.95.

7. *Ibid.*, 4.I.95; Bosse Diary, 4.I.95, B.A. Bosse, No. 8.

8. See Heffter, *Selbstverwaltung*, pp. 557, 665.

9. *Hohenlohe*, III, 28.

10. *Ibid.*

11. *Ibid.*, p. 29.

12. See Rich, *Holstein*, II, 490.

13. Waldersee, *Denkwürdigkeiten*, II, 337, 26.I.95.

14. Siegfried von Kardorff, *Wilhelm von Kardorff—Ein nationaler Parlamentarier im Zeitalter Bismarcks und Wilhelms II., 1828-1907* (Berlin, 1936), p. 303.

15. Holstein to Hohenlohe, 1.II.95, in Rich, *Holstein*, II, 490; *Hohenlohe*, III, 32; *Holsteins Papiere*, III, 441-442.

16. Rich, *Holstein*, II, 490, 491.

17. See Holstein to Bülow, 23.I.95, *Holsteins Papiere*, III, 439; Holstein to Eulenburg, 26.I.95, B.A. Eul. 34.

18. See Rich, *Holstein*, II, 491.

19. See Haller, *Eulenburg*, p. 177.

20. *Ibid.*

21. See Holstein to Bülow, 7.II.95, B.A. Eul. 34.

22. Hohenlohe to Eulenburg, 25.I.95, B.A. Eul. 34.

23. Wilhelm to Eulenburg, 12.II.95, B.A. Eul. 34.

24. Kessel to Eulenburg, 13.II.95; Arnim to Eulenburg, 14.II.95, B.A. Eul. 34.

25. See Arnim to Eulenburg, 14.II.95, B.A. Eul. 34.

26. Eulenburg to Wilhelm, 14.II.95, B.A. Eul. 34.

27. *Ibid.*

28. *Hohenlohe*, III, pp. 39-42.

29. Waldersee, *Denkwürdigkeiten*, II, 336.

30. Marschall to Eulenburg, 17.II.95, B.A. Eul. 34.

31. See Marschall to Eulenburg, 17.II.95, B.A. Eul. 34.

32. See *Hohenlohe*, III, 39.

33. Marschall to Eulenburg, 17.II.95, B.A. Eul. 34.

34. On the Hollmann crisis, see Alexander Hohenlohe to Eulenburg, 17.II.95, in *Hohenlohe*, III, 43; Holstein to Bülow, 15.II.95, in *Holsteins Papiere*, III, 144.

35. Holstein to Bülow, 15.II.95, B.A. Eul. 34; see also Marschall Diary, 14.II.95; Bülow to Holstein, 18.II.95, Holstein Papers, vol. 28 6T 120-3854 typescript.

36. Marschall Diary, 21.II.95; Holstein to Eulenburg, 21.II.95, B.A. Eul. 34.

37. Alexander to Eulenburg, 17.II.95; Holstein to Eulenburg, 17.II.95; Fischer to Eulenburg, 17.II.95, B.A. Eul. 34.

38. Marschall Diary, 17.II.95.

39. Röhl, *Germany without Bismarck*, p. 133.

40. Eulenburg to Wilhelm, 18.II.95, B.A. Eul. 34.

41. *Hohenlohe*, III, 39.

42. Holstein to Bülow, 21.II.95, *Holsteins Papiere*, III, 447; translation taken from *Holstein Papers*, III, 500.

43. Eulenburg to Hohenlohe, 20.II.95, B.A. Eul. 34.

44. Eulenburg to Wilhelm, 20.II.95, B.A. Eul. 34.

45. Wilhelm to Eulenburg, 21.II.95, B.A. Eul. 34.

46. *Ibid.*; Eulenburg memo on letter of Alexander to Eulenburg, 17.II.95, B.A. Eul. 34.

47. Eulenburg to Wilhelm, 22.II.95, B.A. Eul. 34.

48. Eulenburg to Holstein, 23.II.95, *Holsteins Papiere*, III, 450.

49. See Eulenburg to Holstein, 23.II.95, *Holsteins Papiere*, III, 450; see especially the indicative letters of Eulenburg to Holstein, 28.II.95, *ibid.*, and p. 451, and 1.III.95, p. 452; 2.III.95, B.A. Eul. 35; Bülow to Holstein, 10.III.95, *Holsteins Papiere*, III, 455.

50. See especially Bülow to Eulenburg, 23.II.95; Eulenburg to Marschall, 22.II.95; Eulenburg to Holstein, 22.II.95; Holstein to Eulenburg, 24.II.95, B.A. Eul. 34.

51. Eulenburg to Bülow, 22.II.95, B.A. Eul. 34.

52. Marschall Diary, 23.II.95.

53. See Eulenburg to Holstein, 23.II.95, *Holsteins Papiere*, III, 450; Marschall to Eulenburg, 25.II.95, B.A. Eul. 34; Marschall Diary, 24.II.95.

54. See Holstein to Eulenburg, 17.II.95, B.A. Eul. 34.

55. Hohenlohe Journal, 3.III.95, *Hohenlohe*, III, 49.

56. See Holstein to Bülow, 7.II.95, B.A. Bülow 90, in Röhl, *Germany without Bismarck*, p. 136.

57. Hohenlohe Journal, 3.III.95, *Hohenlohe*, III, 49.

58. Hohenlohe Journal, 28.VI.95, *Hohenlohe*, III, p. 83.

59. See Seeler's appropriate title for his book, *Zwischen Bebel und Bismarck* (Berlin, 1965).

CHAPTER 6

The Uneasy Summer

Here [in Berlin] we have commotions as usual. The
old councillor who in former days reported to me in
Schillingsfürst used to end his speech with the words:
"Indeed, life is only a struggle." That is certainly
true here also. There is, first of all, the Kotze
affair, in which the cliques Wedell, Lucanus, and
Hahnke fight against the cliques Schrader, Reischach,
Christian Kraft. . . . There is furthermore the
clique Henckel, Waldersee, Herbert Bismarck, Miquel.
. . . I will have a confrontation soon. The old
Wau Wau [Bismarck] bears a grudge because his son
Herbert does not receive the salary of an ambassador
and works against Boetticher and Marschall.

Hohenlohe to his son Alexander,
May 27, 1895

1

To observers of the German domestic scene between October, 1894,
and July, 1897, the Marschall crisis of February, 1895, may appear
as a more or less recognizable entity. With distance and a somewhat broader perspective, we may be in a better position now to
recognize it as a genuine "crisis" by outlining, analyzing, and
inter-relating the various themes which ran parallel, but at times
converged to form the crisis. We have now the historical privilege
to follow the actions of the various participants as well as to put
them into perspective within time, past and future. We may take a
topical and a chronological approach. The direct participants of
those events had often a better knowledge of details and segments of
events, but only when it directly involved them and called for their
action or reaction. Each participant seemed to realize, partly as
a result of circumstances and partly as a result of his own convictions, his own involvement (or the theme that he was particularly
interested in) in the Marschall crisis.

Holstein, for instance, handed in his resignation not because
of the attack on Marschall but because Bismarck might return. For
Holstein it was not Marschall but the Bismarcks who were the central
issue, and while the Marschall affair had abated by early March, the
Bismarck threat as Holstein saw it remained as strong as ever—perhaps even increased, since Bismarck's eightieth birthday was only
four weeks away.

Marschall saw the February days as a particularly clever
intrigue against his person and the Center Party, but only as one

of the many previous attacks he had had to endure since 1890, and
would yet endure as long as he remained in his present position. He
recognized the general aim of the attacks against him, as well as
perceiving, to an extent, the seriousness of the latest incident.
However, he did not realize how close he had actually come to being
sacrificed to his enemies by his "friends." Enveloped in this somewhat false sense of security, he brushed off the "Marschall crisis"
as just another court intrigue.

Hohenlohe and Eulenburg came perhaps the closest to regarding
the February days as a crisis from our more comprehensive point of
view. However, here again, Hohenlohe appears to have seen and
emphasized the threat to his position as Chancellor. Eulenburg,
who, after all, had come up with the elaborate and clever plan for
Marschall's dismissal, must certainly have thought himself as being
in control of the situation—which, as a matter of fact, was not at
all the case.

The Kaiser, finally, gave every indication of not knowing at all
what really was going on.

2

It is possible to interpret events between March and November
of 1895 as directly leading up to the so-called "Köller crisis."
Aside from the fluctuating course of the Reichstag debates, the
question of Bismarck's birthday in April gave rise to concern. On
March 19 Marschall had found out that the Center, together with the
Radicals and the Social Democrats, intended to vote against a Reichstag congratulatory telegram. Marschall tried to prevent this, but
to no avail.[1] On March 23 the motion by the Reichstag President
v. Levetzow to send the congratulation in the name of the Reichstag
was defeated by 163 to 146 votes.[2] Some members of the Center Party
(as well as, naturally, Marschall) were acutely aware, of course, of
the negative consequences of such a move.[3] It provided a cheap,
easy, and effective means to jump on the bandwagon of criticizing
the government, the Reichstag, the parliamentary system, specific
political groups and factions, the Catholics, and so forth—all under
the self-righteous veil of moral and patriotic indignation. It was
also used to attack the Kaiser and his unparliamentary methods, and
at least to a degree to cover ones own failures and difficulties.[4]

We have already had occasion to observe the effects on the Center
Party of the widespread popular accusation of being unreasonable and
unpatriotic, and the consequently renewed effort on the part of
various Center leaders, particularly Lieber, to prove the opposite
without negating the actions and position of the party. However,
in no way did this resolve any basic issues for the Center Party,
either for the party as such (stemming partly from the fact of its
historical position as well as its heterogeneous nature) or for the
Center as the decisive party in the Reichstag in relation to the
government (the problem: "legislature-executive" and Reich-Prussia).
It may even be argued that the congratulatory telegram incident
increased the tensions and frustration within that party and the
Reichstag.

The government found itself in a similar predicament. The
Kaiser boasted that he was ready to dismiss the Reichstag. With

the telegram he sent to Bismarck (a toned-down version of a stronger draft)[5] he clearly showed himself on the side of Bismarck and the Fronde,[6] disregarding the position of the government,[7] which after all had to work with the Reichstag and which could, especially at that moment, ill afford to alienate the Center.

The ministry (particularly Marschall) was thus caught between the "executive" (the Kaiser) and the situation in the Reichstag. The ministers were hardly in a position to choose between them, but could only try to determine the best way to maneuver without alienating either. This turned out to be somewhat easier than expected, since the Center became more anxious to cooperate with the government and since the Kaiser was persuaded to take a "wait and see" attitude. This change of attitude had come about during a conversation between the Kaiser and his Chancellor the day after the Reichstag affair on March 24. Both realized that the government, including the Kaiser, had lost the initiative. They could only react, and even in this case only within a rather narrow limit. It was clearly a position not of strength but of weakness—the government had lost the power to act. They could not dismiss the Reichstag, since there was no government program upon which a new and "better"—more amenable—Reichstag could be returned. Nor could they accept the leadership of the extremes—that is, either Bismarck or the agrarians with their "Kanitz program" (recently rejected by the Kaiser and more recently by the government).[8] Thus the only solution—aside from frustrated verbal outbursts—was to "wait and see," to hope for a new popular power base from which the ministry and the Kaiser could act. In this case it was the reformation of the Reichstag. "I closed with the suggestion," Hohenlohe noted in his diary:

> . . . to await how public opinion in Germany will express itself. In case a general, thorough indignation against the Reichstag does develop, then one can always use this in order to dissolve it, under pressure, so to speak, of public opinion. His Majesty remarked that if this would not result and the German people remain apathetic, then one must wait. . . . It is a question, then, of waiting and as much as possible furthering such a movement [popular movement of patriotism and nationalism].[9]

What a clear recognition of the situation in which the government as well as the Kaiser found themselves; it was also an acceptance of the real power of the Reichstag and, in a sense, of a government restricted by parliamentary power. Despite this, the Kaiser went to Friedrichsruh on March 26 with a shining military entourage and gave a huge dinner.[10] Moreover, the new presidents of the Reichstag, Buol and Spahn, had been invited and were present![11]

Hohenlohe, the Kaiser, and the ministers were caught between the extreme political factions and Bismarck; the only way left open for them was to find a program or issue with which the majority of the public could identify and under which it again could accept (and the monarchy regain) the lost initiative and leadership. By 1895 this rallying program had not yet been found. Wilhelm's hope of using past victories such as Sedan and "official heroes" such as Wilhelm I (both vulnerable in any case, since what was Sedan and who was Wilhelm I without Bismarck?) with high-pressure salesmanship

simply did not offer enough, if anything, to rally public opinion
to his support. Splendor and pomp and empty phrases did not suffice
any more; substance and visibility of real power had to be provided.
The successful formula to achieve this by means acceptable to the
Kaiser and to a large part of the German population was the program
of building a large navy and of transforming Germany from a major
European power (was that not enough to qualify also as a world
power?) to a visible major world power, complete with far-flung
colonial possessions and a fleet to match. These two latter aspects
were not new in 1895—both issues had run into considerable opposition, especially the "limitless Naval plans." However, in both
cases the main objection had been on the means to achieve these aims,
not on the aims themselves.

A preview of this future unveiled itself in that great spectacle
of the inauguration festivals of the Nord-Ostsee Kanal in early
June, 1895, where both pomp and power were skillfully combined.
This festival did not change the political conditions of 1895 or of
the near future, but it did point the way by which the "state," the
ministry, and the monarch could capture public support and thus
seemingly escape the vise of the extremes.[12] The idea of capturing
the support of the vast majority of the people by a display of pomp
and power as a substitute for Reichstag politics may even have been
used as a rationalization for some parliamentarians (as well as
government members) to work consciously toward discrediting the
Reichstag in the public opinion. This would greatly ease general
acceptance of a "government program." However, it would take a
different set of men to carry out this program, a set of men such
as Bülow and Tirpitz that did come in the latter part of 1897.

However, looking at the immediate legacy of the episodes
described above, one comes to the conclusion that they not only
reinforced the standpoint and opinions of the various parties,
cliques, and persons but also were full of embarrassment, pent-up
hostility, and frustration for most concerned.

3

On March 2 Minister of Ecclesiastical Affairs Bosse recorded
in his diary a conversation he had had with Marschall concerning
the political situation:

> He [Marschall] looks very pessimistically upon the
> affairs within the Ministry of State: no leadership,
> Köller! plans are far beyond bounds and not adequately
> considered; the conflict between Berlepsch and Köller,
> if still on a friendly basis, has been expressed very
> clearly; Eulenburg awaits reactivation, but the Reichstag
> lacks all confidence in him. In brief, the prospects are
> as confused as possible and without any prospect for a
> good and reasonable methodical restoration of a sound
> condition.

Bosse agreed with Marschall's analysis of the situation.[13] Judging
from Hohenlohe's journal entry of March 3, the Chancellor had come
to a similar conclusion.[14]

Yet, at the same time, at least a majority of the ministers

found themselves in essentially the same boat. Owing to the external pressures brought to bear upon them, particularly from the Reichstag, Bismarck, and the Kaiser, most of the ministers tried to retain a united front, or were persuaded to hold off their resignations until the Reichstag session had ended. There was one obvious exception, Minister of the Interior von Köller: in contrast to the accepted ministerial code of conduct, Köller proceeded, if somewhat clumsily, to gain the ear of the Kaiser at the expense of his colleagues. Since ministerial unity was based primarily on the consequences of external pressures and bureaucratic convention rather than on voluntary cooperation and collegiate spirit, this action of Köller put a severe strain on the ministry.

Köller was probably not the only one to follow this line of action. There are indications that Miquel did the same.[15] However, whereas Miquel was successful, clever, a brilliant speaker, and capable in his own field, Köller was none of these. One might be tempted to argue that it was his undiplomatic, somewhat clumsy, and all too obvious approach (in line with his personality) that was most objected to rather than the nature of his procedure, which was frowned upon but nevertheless generally accepted. It was more the form than the content of Köller's action which eventually forced his dismissal in December, 1895. The threat to their own positions as ministers had become too obvious and the attack had been too direct, with the consequence that the ministers rebelled—not so much against the crown as against one of their own colleagues—against Köller.

Köller's conduct during the summer was only one of the disturbing factors. Holstein, at times nervous and overly pessimistic but usually justifiably so, pointed out to Eulenburg various other incidents to show the rising level of activity and effectiveness of the opposition: Bismarck had said that the representative bodies of the individual states should take a more active role in foreign, as well as in financial, policies of the Reich; there was new agitation among the Kaiser's adjutants, especially Plessen and Moltke; there was excessive expense for the canal festivals; and there were the increased efforts of Waldersee to gain influence in Berlin.[16] Eulenburg had to agree with Holstein's critical comments on the *aides de camp* of the Kaiser, but he refused to go along with Holstein's remedy of introducing Bissing as a counterweight to Plessen and Moltke. "The idea [of Bissing]," Eulenburg commented in answer to Holstein's letter, "is *absolutely correct* since he would make an abrupt end of any aide-de-camp policy. Bissing is an absolute royalist and would, in case political questions would be intertwined with military ones, take his cue from the Chancellor." However, Eulenburg's own influence was not severely threatened, and perhaps he even preferred the status quo. Bissing was probably less open to Eulenburg's persuasions than, for instance, Moltke.[17]

In the case of Waldersee, Holstein also had a point, although Waldersee had not been inactive since the dismissal of Caprivi.[18] Waldersee's plan was well known—to take radical action against the Social Democrats and the Reichstag; in short, he advocated a *coup d'état* policy.[19]

The Bismarckian attacks were, of course, all too familiar. Yet the timing and the nature of the attacks seem significant. One must be aware, first of all, of the position of the government in mid-1895:

it had just experienced the Marschall crisis and its effects; it had
to bear the burden of Bismarck's eightieth birthday celebration;
Miquel's proposed finance reform and the antirevolutionary bill had
run aground in the Reichstag and in the Ministry of State; and the
Schrader-Kotze affair regained public attention.[20] In addition there
was the ghost of the *Kladderadatsch* affair, in the form of the Bismarckian Henckel von Donnersmarck.[21] It was precisely at this time that
Bismarck advocated a greater amount of action in fiscal affairs on
the part of the individual states, thereby approving, in a sense,
Miquel's plans for increasing Prussian control of Reich finances.
Waldersee's clamoring for determined action against the "revolutionaries" put him on the side of Köller. In addition, Miquel's
apparent support of Köller[22] and of agrarian interests[23] again
clarified the demarcation of political interests: a strong,
conservative Prussia facing a "liberal" (or, better, moderate
conservative) Reich. During mid- and late 1895 this division showed
itself drastically in conflicts over Berlepsch's social legislation,
over Miquel's finance reform, over Bronsart's military penal code
reform, and again over antirevolutionary legislation.

4

In the face of Köller's attacks against proposals for social
legislation (especially in connection with worker protection), and
in the face of Köller's pressure for strong action against the
Social Democrats and his derogatory treatment of the Reichstag
(apparently condoned by the Kaiser) as well as the "deficient leadership of the Ministry of State on the part of . . . Hohenlohe and in
general the lack of any uniform, resolute policy of the Ministry of
State," Berlepsch began to feel himself out of place and somewhat
impulsively voiced his intention to resign. He felt that he "could
not any longer continue with joy and good conscience [as Minister]."[24]
However, Berlepsch was perhaps too conscientious, perhaps also a bit
too much of a bureaucrat, and at any rate not determined enough to
resign on the basis of a realistic assessment of his situation.
Bosse, for instance, although agreeing with Berlepsch (as did most
ministers) about the sad state of affairs in the government and the
Ministry of State, argued against Berlepsch's immediate resignation,
since Boetticher wanted to take his leave after the inauguration of
the canal and since "it has no sense that today the one and in four
the other minister leaves." Berlepsch and Boetticher agreed that
it was necessary to "bring about a frank discussion in the Ministry
of State."[25] Eulenburg opposed Berlepsch's resignation and pleaded
for a solution of the problem within the ministry (as did probably
also Marschall, and then Hohenlohe).[26] Hohenlohe, on his part,
agreed that "the situation in the Ministry of State could not continue in the way it had up to now," that he too disapproved of
Köller's behavior, that he was willing to bring up the whole subject in the Ministry of State at the end of June, and that he "also
for his person must reserve the right to take the consequences which
the present situation necessitates."[27] With these assurances and
promises, Berlepsch was seemingly persuaded to postpone his decision.
Obviously, tension and dissatisfaction among the ministers were
mounting, but, with the exception of Bronsart's somewhat emotional

outburst in February about using the resignation of the entire
ministry to curb the Kaiser,[28] their dissatisfaction centered
around Köller and Hohenlohe rather than the Kaiser.

Hohenlohe was strengthened in his desire to let the Köller-
Berlepsch affair ride by Eulenburg's reports on the Kaiser's
reaction. Before approaching the Kaiser with the subject of
Berlepsch, Eulenburg had (as noted previously) pleaded for post-
ponement and possible solution within the Ministry of State
itself, and he had also mentioned to Marschall that he looked upon
Köller as a lost cause.[29] While in Prökelwitz with the Kaiser,
Eulenburg nevertheless brought up this topic with the monarch.
He must have realized then, if not already before, that Wilhelm
was taking a strong stand against Berlepsch and, thus, supporting
Köller. Accordingly, Eulenburg advised Hohenlohe that it would be
better not to do anything for the time being. A day later he even
suggested that Hohenlohe should write the Kaiser that "after
further information the indicated contradictions have been eliminated
for the time being, or at any rate have been smoothed over . . .,"
but that he, Hohenlohe, would report immediately if the subject again
became acute. Eulenburg also suggested to Hohenlohe that if the conflict could no longer be pushed into the background, Hohenlohe should
speak to the Kaiser without delay.[30]

Berlepsch, however, did not want to wait too long before asking
the Kaiser (in writing) to be relieved of his post. The Kaiser
thereupon called Hohenlohe and informed him that he had not granted
Berlepsch's request for resignation. The Kaiser explained that he
intended to carry out the program of social legislation according
to the decrees of 1890, and the dismissal of Berlepsch would indicate a change of course which he did not intend. On the other hand,
since the Kaiser had been the creator of the decrees, he also held
the prerogative of slowing down their implementation. Apparently
industrial interest groups had been successful in convincing the
Kaiser to view Berlepsch's legislation as a threat to German industry, since Wilhelm added that one could not put too heavy a strain
on German industry and thereby make her unable to compete effectively
with foreign nations. As far as Berlepsch and Köller were concerned,
the Kaiser said, "If Berlepsch fears that the Köller project of a
coalition law alone would give cause to his resignation from the
ministry, then this would be erroneous. One ought not to make a
coalition law without being certain of its acceptance, and must come
to an agreement with the parties beforehand."[31] Now that Berlepsch
had tried to force a clearcut decision, Hohenlohe had to decide
which would be the lesser of two evils—the effect of a Berlepsch
resignation, or the problems arising out of the few bills that
Berlepsch deemed it necessary to introduce: "If Berlepsch leaves
[Hohenlohe reasoned], then Boetticher must go also, and then I am
face to face with Miquel and Bronsart who intrigue against me, and
with Köller who does nothing."[32] However, Hohenlohe ended his considerations with this thought: "For the time being I cannot do
anything since the Kaiser cannot be reached."

Berlepsch, in the meanwhile, was left without any answer to his
resignation. Only on July 31 did Wilhelm reply to Berlepsch, drawing on the same argument he had earlier given Hohenlohe. The
Kaiser said that he wanted to see Berlepsch carry out the social

legislation "which carries a certain degree of sympathy with all parties of law and order." Furthermore, the Kaiser assured Berlepsch of his full confidence and said that he hoped to see Berlepsch's plans for the support and protection of skilled labor as soon as possible, and he rejected Berlepsch's request for dismissal.[33] Thus Berlepsch decided to remain, not for long to be sure (until June, 1896, and without much effect as Commerce Minister), but long enough to act as a determined minister against Köller until the latter's forced dismissal—and long enough to give some embarrassment to the government as the result of the timing of his resignation.

5

On May 15 Prussian Finance Minister Miquel wrote a proposal[34] to the Ministry of State in which he again expressed his wish to participate in formulating the budget bill for the Reich before it was introduced into the Federal Council (Miquel pointed out that the participation of the Prussian Finance Minister in the formulation of the Reich budget had been the case up to 1880 and had been under consideration again in the years 1880-81 and 1890). Miquel also expressed a wish for the Ministry of State to resolve that the Chancellor would (among other things) notify the Prussian Finance Minister of any additional fiscal requests by the various Reich offices (*Reichressorts*) over and above the legislated sum—in such cases agreement should be reached with Prussia first before the adjustments were made known to the other states. Last, Miquel wanted to give the Prussian representative in the budget debates of the Federal Council "discretionary powers."[35] This proposal was probably submitted to the Ministry of State on May 20 and officially presented on May 21.[36] It was sent to Hohenlohe with a cover letter by Humbert, Undersecretary in the Ministry of State, on May 22.[37]

Immediately upon receipt of this communication, Marschall (at Hohenlohe's wish)[38] drafted a long exposé, and Eulenburg (who was with the Kaiser in Prökelwitz) was to bring this, along with other questions, to the attention of the monarch. Marschall pointed out, first of all, that the Prussian Finance Ministry had indeed participated in the preparation of the Reich budget during the 1870s but it had been necessary then because the institutions and personnel of the Reich had not yet been adequately established. However, he added:

> With consideration to the fact that this interlocking
> of Prussian and Reich authorities was contestable not only
> from the standpoint of the Reich constitution, but also
> from the consideration that it would have been suitable
> to help the particularist tendencies that numerously exist
> in the individual states; it seemed to be a considerable
> step forward in the direction of the strengthening and
> consolidation of the idea of the Reich, when . . . by
> Imperial decree of July 14, 1879 the Reich Finance Office
> was created as the central authority.[39]

Then Marschall pointed out the logical implications which would result from Miquel's suggestions: the Chancellor would in effect become an Undersecretary to the Prussian Finance Minister.

It would strengthen all "particularist and decentralizing elements."[40] Hohenlohe wrote that as soon as the first step had been
taken, namely the subordination of the Reich by Prussia in fiscal
affairs, "then the second [step] will soon follow and with this
triumph of Prussia over the Reich's idea all doors will be opened
to all particularist endeavors."[41] Marschall, writing for Hohenlohe,
casually added (not without purpose, since it might be shown to the
Kaiser) that he did not know how serious Miquel really was, either
in his proposal or in his pursuance of it. But the decisive factor
was that this proposal (along with its justifications) was consistent with a tendency "which, in line with my total past, [I] must
resist with a categorical *principius obsta'*."[42] Hohenlohe himself
added to Marschall's exposé in a separate note: "I consider the
action of Miquel a pretentious one, which I will categorically
oppose—if he backs down, all right; if not, it will come to a
break."[43] Thus, while Marschall's notation that Hohenlohe was weak
and helpless[44] was probably quite accurate, when it came to his
personal reputation (as was the case here and again somewhat later
in regard to the military penal code reform), the Chancellor could
be quite obstinate and determined to defend his position. Holstein,
who wrote to Eulenburg on the same day about the same subject,
presented the same viewpoint as did Hohenlohe in practically the
same phraseology. Holstein correctly assessed Eulenburg's fear of
another Chancellor crisis, as Hohenlohe explicitly stated and as
Marschall somewhat more cautiously indicated, and he added, "I
understand that the Chancellor thinks about quitting the field to
Miquel as he told me today."[45]

In Eulenburg's eyes, the credibility of Holstein's letters was
not very high. However, Eulenburg also realized Holstein's advantage in his proximity to Hohenlohe, and it was Hohenlohe whom he was
worried about. Faced with the united front of Holstein, Marschall,
and Hohenlohe, Eulenburg had little choice but to join them. The
form and extent, however, would be determined by the amount of
influence Miquel had been able to bring to bear upon the Kaiser.
Miquel had indeed been active. At several occasions he had pointed
out to the Kaiser the necessity of a greater amount of influence
(*Einwirkung*) of the Prussian Finance Ministry in Reich financial
affairs in order to safeguard the interests of Prussia. This,
obviously, was a very attractive argument. Prussia could not make
financial sacrifices to the Reich. Was this not almost identical
to the position that Prussian conservatives stubbornly upheld—
that Prussia could not be sacrificed for the Reich? On the contrary, Miquel argued, the Reich basically owed its existence to
Prussia and was thus heavily in its debt. The implication was that
the Reich should repay Prussia by supporting the agrarians in the
form of protective tariffs on grain. The Kaiser had never shown
himself to be an extreme agrarian, and he had rejected the Antrag
Kanitz, in fact, as being too unreasonable. Yet he did show himself quite receptive to the appeal of maintaining the interests of
Prussia in the face of the Reich. Although rejecting, it appears,
any limitation of authority of the Imperial Chancellor and the
Secretary of the Treasury in favor of the Prussian Finance Ministry,
the Kaiser tended to take the side of Miquel.

Eulenburg responded appropriately to the situation. He gave

Hohenlohe's "Marschall exposé," as well as Miquel's proposals, to the
Kaiser, but he supported the inclinations of the Kaiser! Eulenburg
could well afford to do this, since Wilhelm himself did not approve
of the extent of Miquel's suggestions. By agreeing with the Kaiser
and at the same time by acquainting the Kaiser with Hohenlohe's objections on this issue, Eulenburg was able to strengthen the Kaiser's
resistance to Miquel. Thus Eulenburg successfully avoided having to
take a stand against Miquel, which might well have affronted the
Kaiser; yet at the same time he prevented Miquel's excessive encroachment on the Reich. It would even be possible for Eulenburg,
if necessary, to tell Miquel that he had supported the idea of
Prussian participation in Reich fiscal matters.

To Hohenlohe, Eulenburg replied that he had presented to the
Kaiser Hohenlohe's views and essentially implied to Hohenlohe that
the Kaiser had agreed with the Chancellor. On the other hand,
Eulenburg pointed out to Hohenlohe (and to Holstein and Marschall),
the Kaiser was not about to sacrifice Prussian financial interests
to the Reich, and consequently Miquel's views would always be of
great importance. However, "the form in which the minister wants to
have his wishes put into practice seemed . . . to go much too far
and at any rate (in this form) was not desired by His Majesty."
Eulenburg continued: "The hearing of the Finance Minister before
the drawing up of the Reich budget by Your Highness has really
always been the actual practice, in the same way that an exchange
of opinions on all Reich finance questions . . . will have
occurred." The inclusion of this assumption was at the same time
a hint to Hohenlohe (and perhaps meant primarily for Holstein and
Marschall); this becomes quite clear when Eulenburg added that "the
Kaiser will, on the whole, accept the viewpoints of the minister."
He immediately emphasized again, "As I said, His Majesty at any
rate rejected categorically the pretention of the minister as far
as it concerned itself with the limitation of the powers of the
Chancellor."[46] Eulenburg's letter thus provided reassurance for
Hohenlohe and, at the same time, rejected the form (but not actually
the content) of Miquel's intended influence, as well as warned
Holstein and Marschall (and Hohenlohe) not to try to change the
ambivalent status quo to Miquel's disadvantage.

Contrary to Hohenlohe's expectations,[47] Miquel backed down and
a serious direct confrontation was avoided. At least on a formal
level Miquel became more reserved than before in regard to his
influence in Reich finances, although he did not give up hope of
implementing his reforms at a future date or of expressing his
views.[48]

6

In the same letter to Hohenlohe in which Eulenburg made it clear
that Wilhelm was on the side of Köller and antagonistic toward
Berlepsch, and that Wilhelm (although rejecting the extreme interpretation of Miquel's financial reform plans) basically sided with
Miquel, Eulenburg also held Hohenlohe responsible for a homogeneous
ministry. He wrote:

The Kaiser . . . declared that he most emphatically
forbids any quarrel, any dispute and any dissension within

the ministry. Your Highness has to provide for this homo-
geneity; the determining of the government maxims is the
affair only of His Highness and Himself [the Kaiser].—He
would "throw out" whoever, by chance, pretends to have
his own ideas . . . the individual ministers must solely
follow the fixed directives.[49]

Obviously, in conveying these words Eulenburg did not see fit to
modify and scale down the Kaiser's temperamental expression. This
advice, reinforced by Wilhelm's talk with Hohenlohe soon thereafter,[50] was sound but inadequate as a basis of conduct; in effect,
it applied only to ministers who, regardless of Hohenlohe's own
opinions and preferences, did not concur in the opinions of the
monarch. Thus Eulenburg warned Hohenlohe not to be too hard on
Miquel. When Hohenlohe finally was forced to take action against
Köller, a grave crisis was the result. On the surface, the Kaiser's
advice was no doubt sincere; it appeared to express his personal
rule. However, was this actually the case? In reality, it was
Eulenburg who directed the show for the Kaiser. Thus Eulenburg's
advice to Hohenlohe was, to a large extent, insincere, especially
when he said that Hohenlohe was in control of the situation and
could do with Miquel and Köller as he liked.[51] Actually Hohenlohe
could only follow Eulenburg's suggestions unless he was trying to
provoke a crisis. Was this the position the Kaiser had taken?
Eulenburg instructed him again:

> The Chancellor—in truly touching admiration and love
> for Your Majesty—wants to avoid at any cost everything
> which might give the impression that he creates inconven-
> iences for Your Majesty. . . . Nothing will harm Your
> Majesty more than if various tendencies were to make them-
> selves felt within the ministry, especially at this moment
> when one wants to *weaken* the Reichstag. The spectre of a
> not completely unified government makes the Reichstag
> appear as the stable element. If the stable element is
> the absolute unity of the ministry under Your Majesty and
> Prince Hohenlohe, then the Reichstag loses.

However, he was quick to add, "The impression that I have gained
does, to be sure, indicate that—not now, but perhaps in the fall
—changes will come in order to maintain this unity. I am sorry,
but I fear that I am not mistaken."[52] This was still not enough.
Soon after Wilhelm had been given his instruction, Eulenburg
revealed his true duplicity when he informed Hohenlohe, "Here I
may be permitted to repeat once again that now His Majesty has
been completely won over for the idea of a homogeneous ministry.
The question will be to strengthen Him more and more in this
idea so that He, in case of a possible crisis, will maintain the
right road in the face of the difficult situations and personal
wishes."[53]
    It, therefore, appears very strongly that while on the one
hand Eulenburg cautiously brought pressure to bear upon the Kaiser
(with the stand of Hohenlohe and Marschall against Miquel) to
moderate his support for Köller and Miquel, he at the same time
used the Kaiser's concessions to influence Hohenlohe! The apparent

long-range goal of Eulenburg was to curtail the power of the Reichstag (perhaps by legislating a change of structure and form of that parliament through itself) as well as that of the Landtag. Yet in contrast to Hohenlohe (who was fed up with the Reichstag but too cautious and afraid to take any action) and the extreme conservatives (who advocated quick and radical action), Eulenburg was politically astute enough to realize that such a goal could not be accomplished overnight, and that certain prerequisites had to be met to assure lasting success. One of the main prerequisites was a stable and unified (uniform?) ministry. It meant retention of certain persons as well as replacement of others. Both these tasks were difficult to achieve and required great skill, since the appearance of stability of the ministry and chancellorship had to be maintained. If this were not done, the situation would get out of hand and open the doors for radical action.[54] The facade of ministerial unity had been preserved to some degree during the first five months of 1895. However, Eulenburg recognized that contradictions within the ministry would be quite likely to come to a head in the fall. He thus prepared for the eventual (and even desirable) changes. Issues had not been settled, only postponed (as in the cases of Berlepsch, Miquel, and Bronsart). Besides, the issue of anti-revolutionary legislation most certainly would come up again in the fall. Eulenburg assumed that time would be on his side: the first half of 1895 had been overcome and the summer months were usually a time of inactivity compared to the rest of the year. In September political activity would again mount. Moreover, having been successful in postponement, Eulenburg would tackle the various problems one by one as they came up.

In comparison to Miquel's challenge, the difficulties arising out of the military penal code reform were much less threatening to the political situation of mid-1895. However, it was clear that the subject could develop into an extremely dangerous one. It would involve Wilhelm as the Supreme Commander of the Armed Forces—a role that was more cherished by the Kaiser than any other and in which he would be more sensitive and stubborn to defend what he considered his prerogatives and his alone (especially when supported by Hahnke, Eulenburg, and his own entourage).

NOTES

1. Marschall Diary, 19.III.95.

2. See Wippermann, *Fürst Bismarck's 80ster Geburtstag*, pp. 68ff. See also Krüger reports, 14.III.95, 19.III.95, Staatsarchiv, Hamburg, A IV C6, Bd. II.

3. See Marschall Diary, 23.II.95.

4. Cf. Marschall's notation: "It is as I had anticipated, the Center looks upon the Imperial telegram as a kind of relief. Naturally, one talks only about that [telegram] now, and not anymore about the [Bismarck telegram] vote of the Reichstag." Marschall Diary, 24.III.95.

5. Marschall Diary, 23.III.95.

6. *Hohenlohe*, III, 53-54.

7. Cf. Marschall Diary, 25.III.95, where he notes that the Ministry of State had on that date unanimously disapproved of dissolution.

8. See *Hohenlohe*, III, 54, note 1, and 56.

9. *Ibid.*, p. 54.

10. Waldersee, *Denkwürdigkeiten*, II, 342.

11. Marschall Diary, 1.IV.95.

12. On the festivals, see *Wippermann*, 1895 (I), pp. 271ff.; *Wippermann*, 1895 (II), pp. 30ff., 180; Hutten-Czapski, *Sechzig Jahre*, I, 268f. Also see G.S.A. München, MA 77272 (Kaiser Wilhelm Kanal Eröffnung 1895); Ernst Engelberg, *Deutschland 1871-1897* (Berlin, 1965), pp. 371f.

13. Bosse Diary, 2.III.95, B.A. Bosse, No. 8; see also Marschall Diary, 3.III.95.

14. *Hohenlohe*, III, 49, 3.III.95.

15. See Marschall Diary, 24.II.95; also, for the role he played during the October crisis, see above, pp. 27, 30.

16. Holstein to Eulenburg, 7.IV.95, B.A. Eul. 35.

17. Eulenburg memo, ca. 8.VI.95, B.A. Eul. 35; see also Eulenburg to Holstein, 16.IV.95, B.A. Eul. 35.

18. For the continuous animosity against the government and Waldersee's renewed activity in 1895, see Waldersee, *Denkwürdigkeiten*, II, 342, 2.IV.95; 345, 9.IV.95; 346, 21.IV.95.

19. See especially Wolfgang Fornaschon, *Die Politischen Anschauungen des Grafen Alfred von Waldersee und seine Stellungnahme zur deutschen Politik, Historische Studien*, 273 (Berlin, 1935), 18ff.

20. See Holstein to Eulenburg, 4.III.95; Eulenburg to Holstein, 16.IV.95, B.A. Eul. 35; Marschall Diary entries for 9, 11, 13, and 14.IV.95; *Hohenlohe*, III, 72. The Schrader-Kotze affair was one of a number of underground clique feuds. In June, 1894, the Master of Ceremonies, Kotze, had been arrested for having written scandalous anonymous letters to prominent figures at court. He was acquitted in April, 1896, but rumors, intrigues, and insinuations persisted. In April, 1896, Kotze fatally wounded Schrader in a duel. See H. Rogge, "Affairen in Kaiserreich," *Die Politische Meinung*, 8 (1963), 65-66.

21. See Holstein to Eulenburg, 7.IV.95, B.A. Eul. 35; H. Jacobi to Eulenburg, 26.IV.95, B.A. Eul. 36. On the *Kladderadatsch* affair, see also H. Rogge's article, "Die Kladderadatsch Affaire," *Historische Zeitschrift*, 195 (1962), 90-130. Some modification, however, might be in order, especially in reference to Holstein-Henckel. In reponse to Cuno Moltke's praise of Raschdau during a conversation which Eulenburg had had with him in Prökelwitz, Eulenburg later filled Moltke in on the *Kladderadatsch* affair in a long exposé: Raschdau and someone else (Bothmer) had furnished the material for

the *Kladderadatsch* attacks. Eulenburg had then written Raschdau
that "as servants of one king, better come to an understanding,"
and followed this up with a personal visit to Raschdau in Berlin.
The result was that the attacks against him (but not against Kiderlen or Holstein!) stopped immediately. Then by way of Axel
Varnbühler, Eulenburg had suggested to Henckel that in order to
"escape the odium, which he had heaped upon himself, . . . he
should not spare money to find the guilty one since this alone
could clear him." However, Jacobi, to whom Henckel had entrusted
this affair, only wrote to Eulenburg that the two guilty ones had
been present at the last dinner of the Kaiser, but that he could
not mention names. Eulenburg continues: "But why did Jacobi
mention no names? Because these two men frequented Henckel's and
were known to him as the originators. The naming of their names
from Henckel's side would give rise for statements that would
compromise Henckel . . . that, however, the Foreign Office (Caprivi
and Marschall) did not start an investigation on the basis of
Jacobi's letter was due in large measure to the fact that the
campaign of the *Kladderadatsch* was not unpleasant to them!!!

"After my suggestion, to discover the guilty ones with Henckel's
money, . . . had failed, and after I knew the names of the guilty
and also knew their frequenting Henckel, there can be no doubt about
Henckel's complicity, at least as accessory.

"Holstein, who has still other reasons against him, knew therefore quite well what he did when he challenged Henckel.

". . . I would be in a position to say many other things still,
but that would lead too far."

In the rest of the letter Eulenburg drew the connection between
the editor of the *Kladderadatsch*, the Raschdau clique, Reuss,
Rantzau, and Harden with Bismarck. See Eulenburg to Cuno Moltke,
15.VI.95, B.A. Eul. 36. See also Hohenlohe to Alexander, 27.V.95:
"Then there is also the clique Henckel, Waldersee, Herbert Bismarck,
Miquel, which intrigues against me . . .," *Hohenlohe*, III, 72; and
in a letter of 28.V.95: "Reischach told me yesterday that one still
works against me [in] Henckel's house . . . ," *ibid.*, p. 73.

22. See Marschall Diary, 3.III.95, 15.IV.95; Holstein to Eulenburg, 16.IV.95, B.A. Eul. 35.

23. See Marschall Diary, 29.IV.95; Krüger report, 10.V.95,
Staatsarchiv, Hamburg, A IV C6, Bd. II.

24. Bosse Diary, 16.V.95, 18.V.95, B.A. Bosse, No. 8; Berlepsch
to Hohenlohe, 15.V.95, *Hohenlohe*, III, 65 (on 17.V.95 and 18.V.95
Berlepsch spoke to Hohenlohe in person); Marschall Diary, 17.V.95.
In general, see also Herzfeld, *Miquel*, II, 449ff.; H.H. Berlepsch,
Socialpolitische Erfahrungen und Erinnerungen (München, 1925),
pp. 42ff.

25. Bosse Diary, 16.V.95, B.A. Bosse, No. 8.

26. Marschall Diary, 17.V.95; Hohenlohe to Eulenburg, 18.V.95,
B.A. Eul. 36.

27. Bosse Diary, 18.V.95, B.A. Bosse, No. 8.

28. See Röhl, *Germany without Bismarck*, p. 136.

29. Marschall Diary, 17.V.95.

30. Eulenburg to Hohenlohe, 23.V.95, 24.V.95, *Hohenlohe*, III, 70, 71-72.

31. Hohenlohe Journal, 8.VI.95, *Hohenlohe*, III, 75.

32. Hohenlohe Journal, 28.VI.95, *Hohenlohe*, III, 82-83.

33. Wilhelm to Berlepsch, 31.VII.95, *Hohenlohe*, III, 86-87.

34. On Miquel and finance reform, see Herzfeld, *Miquel*, II, 438ff.

35. *Hohenlohe*, III, 67-68.

36. Marschall Diary, 20.V.95, 21.V.95.

37. *Hohenlohe*, III, 67-68.

38. Marschall Diary, 22.V.95.

39. *Hohenlohe*, III, 69.

40. *Ibid.*, p. 69.

41. *Ibid.*, pp. 69, 70.

42. *Ibid.*, p. 70.

43. Hohenlohe to Eulenburg, 22.V.95, B.A. Eul. 36.

44. Marschall Diary, 17.V.95.

45. Holstein to Eulenburg, 22.V.95, B.A. Eul. 36.

46. Eulenburg to Hohenlohe, 23.V.95, *Hohenlohe*, III, 70-71.

47. *Ibid.*, pp. 72-73; see also *ibid.*, p. 71, note 1.

48. See Herzfeld, *Miquel*, II, 447. See here Waldersee, *Denkwürdigkeiten*, II, 349, 350; *Hohenlohe*, III, 83.

49. *Hohenlohe*, III, 71; also in B.A. Eul. 36.

50. Holstein to Eulenburg, 25.V.95, B.A. Eul. 36.

51. Marschall Diary, 25.V.95. Holstein, who "misrepresented" Eulenburg, was rebuked for suggesting radical action. See Holstein to Eulenburg, 25.V.95, B.A. Eul. 36; Marschall Diary, 31.V.95; Eulenburg to Hohenlohe, 3.VI.95, B.A. Eul. 36.

52. Eulenburg to Wilhelm, 30.V.95, B.A. Eul. 36.

53. Eulenburg to Hohenlohe, 3.VI.95, B.A. Eul. 36.

54. Bülow wrote that he personally disliked Caprivi and Marschall as much as did Eulenburg, but that he did not want to force the main representative of the New Course into opposition while at the same time helping the conservatives to a victory. Only by holding Marschall (or replacing him with Radolin) would Holstein be kept in office—and to lose Holstein would mean to "open up the strongest floodgate which stems itself against the (high-tide) waters of the Fronde." It would also mean a fiasco in Europe of the policy of the Kaiser since 1890. Changes, Bülow thus advised, should be "from time to time." In this way Eulenburg could also most easily "objectively,

as well as in all personnel matters, bring your own (so great) position into harmony with the future constellations." Bülow to Eulenburg, 15.X.94, B.A. Eul. 32.

CHAPTER 7

Associations Law and Military Penal Code Reform

Telegram of His Majesty to Minister v. Köller about
. . . articles in the Social Democratic press against
Wilhelm I. One is to give a sharp reply and in the
winter a strong coalitions law is to be presented.
So, the previous anti-revolutionary wave starts anew.

Marschall Diary, August 25, 1895

A dark spot on the horizon of our domestic policy,
which could change into a black storm cloud if not
handled with caution and foresight, is the question
of the military judicial reform.

Bülow, memo after conversation
with Eulenburg, August, 1895

1

The celebration of the twenty-fifth anniversary of the German
victories in 1870 had been held with unusual nationalistic and
Wilhelminian pomp and verbosity. One of the high points had been
the laying of the foundation stone for a national monument to
Wilhelm I on August 18. As could be expected, the Social Democrats
showed less reverence for the occasion than Wilhelm felt appropriate
(especially since he hoped to use the occasion as a rallying point
for the nation to support the government—the "program" to assure
a government majority in the current, as well as future, Reichstag).
They staged mass protest demonstrations. In response to the irrev-
erent Social Democrats, Wilhelm demanded a new anti-Socialist law.
The demonstrations were a very clever move indeed on the part of
the Socialists, Wilhelm wrote to Hohenlohe, since they knew that
"in the commemorative celebration of our Great Period it is precisely the person of the old gentleman in which everything once
again unites, to the great annoyance of the revolutionaries."[1] He
also pointed out the impossibility of taking any action in the
Reich, that at any rate the present Reichstag was to get only the
budget, but that something had to be done in Prussia. Furthermore,
Wilhelm suggested as a remedy a short, severe association law outlawing all Social Democratic associations and meetings. A "severe,
sudden attack in the press of the government," the Kaiser held,
"would be accepted with great enthusiasm, would be a good preparation for a successful session in the [Prussian] Lower House." It
would also bring Bismarck into the camp of the government, since he
had already started a successful press campaign against the
Socialists on his own. For that reason alone the government had

to participate, lest it give Bismarck the chance to defend the honor
of Wilhelm I and use the current enthusiasm for himself. Thus:

> With the cue for the sacred memory of the person of
> Wilhelm the Great, we unite the people now in this summer
> in support of us just as with a magic word. And once we
> have gotten them together, then they will not fall apart
> for awhile; they then are "in the fire." Thus: [with the]
> rallying cry "for the observation of the memory of the Great
> Emperor," briskly to work, and let's get at the Social Demo-
> crats by [a campaign of] writings and thundering speeches. The
> Germans we have for us, and last not least [in English in
> original] also the "Old one" [Bismarck]. He will partici-
> pate for the fun of it; which also may be useful to us.
> When the aroused Germans then will be presented with the
> coalition law in the fall, we will get it passed with flying
> colors. We Prussians [will] appear great, and the Reich
> must be ashamed of itself. Lucanus is in complete agree-
> ment with this view and he is to speak with Köller about
> it.[2]

Köller was instructed accordingly,[3] and the press campaign commenced
with an extremely aggressive article in the *Norddeutsche Allgemeine
Zeitung*, and was continued on orders of the Kaiser and of Hohenlohe.[4]
Every line of this "program" of Wilhelm's glaringly revealed his
lack of political maturity and his ignorance of political reality.
Had the experiences of the fall of 1894 been so completely forgotten?
Who took the deification of Wilhelm I seriously, especially when
his minister had been Bismarck? How could a political program be
replaced by a "magic formula" as pretentious and ridiculous as
"Wilhelm the Great?" How could one gain and maintain a majority
with such a slogan? What a gross misjudgment of Bismarck this was!
Finally, what nonsense it was that the "Reich" was being put to
shame by Prussia, and in such a form! It is not surprising that
Holstein saw in this whole business the same means, which had been
successfully used to get rid of Caprivi, to eliminate Hohenlohe and
Berlepsch, and to strengthen Köller and the entourage of the Kaiser.[5]
Hohenlohe did not oppose the Imperial absurdities directly and
firmly, partly because it was not his nature to do so (unless personally engaged), and partly out of the hope that the Kaiser himself
would in due time adopt a more realistic attitude. In fact, Hohenlohe, in writing to the Kaiser, concurred in the hope that general
aversion toward the Socialist excesses would induce the Prussian
Landtag to adopt a strong association law. He also followed the
Kaiser's order to confer with party leaders, pinning them down and
preventing their turnabout when it came to accepting the bill. He
obeyed the monarch in ordering a vigorous press campaign, albeit in
a somewhat more diplomatic form. The only advice that Hohenlohe
felt it appropriate to offer was not to disclose publicly the intention of the government too soon, lest it divide the various parties
on specific points and consequently endanger the success of the
legislation.[6]
Although Hohenlohe did not admit it to the Kaiser personally,
he was becoming increasingly worried. He did not fear an antirevolutionary bill as such but, rather, the extremes to which it

could be carried and the effects it might have on his position and
his ministry. In Hohenlohe's assessment "something" should be done
to take the wind out of the anti-Socialist urgings of the Bismarck
Fronde and of Bismarck himself. He wrote to Eulenburg, "Perhaps
Bismarck really believes in the success of his advice; but perhaps
he only incited in order to let the government, which does not
follow his advice, appear as a weak one." The more Hohenlohe
analyzed the situation, the more embarrassing his prognosis. In
order to take effective steps against the Social Democrats, it would
be necessary to obtain a different Reichstag. However, the elector-
ate would not trust a conservative government. Only if the elector-
ate were to fear the Social Democrats more than it did a possible
conservative coup d'état would the composition of the Reichstag
change and vote for the effective measures. The current proposals
would achieve just the opposite—strengthen the conservative reaction and increase the agitation of the Socialists and of the
Bismarck press. Hohenlohe consequently favored a "steady government, which will not be confused by the agitation articles of the
Bismarck press, which will dispel the . . . fears [of a conservative
reactionary course]. . . ."[7] In other words, Hohenlohe essentially
proposed to do nothing at all. However, this would bring him into
direct conflict with the Kaiser and with Köller. Moreover, he
could trust neither Lucanus nor even Eulenburg—and with good reason,
as he must have realized from the content of Eulenburg's long letter
to him two days later.

2

The Kaiser, according to Eulenburg, gave reason to believe that
he was prepared for a severe action, but showed a good deal of
frivolity on the issue. As far as Köller was concerned, it was
fairly obvious that he also advocated strong action. Aside from
his previous record during the year, he had clearly shown this
preference when, on September 15, he gave Hohenlohe four different
anti-Socialist proposals. He advocated a short, clear, anti-
Socialist law that treated the Social Democrats as revolutionaries
and not as a political party.[8] Thus Eulenburg's reminder that a
major difficulty of a bill would be its representation by Köller[9]
was not really necessary. More informative to Hohenlohe certainly
must have been the position of Lucanus. Lucanus, Eulenburg pointed
out, accepted enthusiastically the introduction into the Reichstag
of a short paragraph which would punish public slander of deceased
German princes, and a short paragraph in the Prussian Landtag
outlawing association (*Versammlungen*) of Social Democrats (as in the
case of Saxony). Eulenburg further implied that he had, to a
degree, changed Lucanus's mind by pointing out that Hohenlohe would
not agree to any extensive action against the Social Democrats,
that in such a situation the Kaiser would have to choose between
this "extensive action" and Hohenlohe, and that the Kaiser would
very likely favor the latter. "Lucanus," Eulenburg wrote, "was
alarmed over it, at any rate he has understood that every action
can be taken only with Your Highness."[10] He then added that he
thought Lucanus had no intention of advocating action on a larger
scale and, in fact, was anxious to restrict the wishes of the

Kaiser, "in the case that Köller would, perhaps, go farther."[11]

As to himself, Eulenburg gave the appearance of being a moderating and mediating agent, as seen in the above words on Lucanus and Köller. Yet at the same time Eulenburg made it quite clear that the Kaiser absolutely wanted to do something against the Socialists. Wilhelm had restricted himself to a few specific (*einzelne*) points, and proposed to move against the Social Democrats at every available opportunity. If the monarch was reasonable (*sich beschränkt*), "as he obviously was," Eulenburg continued, it was advisable that Wilhelm should not encounter resistance.[12] The step-by-step approach and the "restraint" sounded more like Eulenburg's ideas than the unmodified ideas of the Kaiser himself. Sure enough (significantly perhaps), writing from Rominten (one of the several hunting lodges frequented by Wilhelm and his entourage), Eulenburg had to backtrack. It was not so much the Kaiser but Eulenburg who seemed to have modified his position. Although the Kaiser backed off from his expressed preference for strong and quick action against the Social Democrats at the time they "insulted" the honor of Wilhelm I (and he was furious at those who did not take such action), he insisted on the two following points: the proposed paragraph in the Reichstag punishing insults against deceased German emperors and the paragraph in the Prussian Landtag outlawing Social Democratic associations (a step Saxony had already taken).

Rather than supporting the Kaiser's position, which a few days before Eulenburg had defended as a position of restraint that should not be opposed (but to oppose Köller if necessary), Eulenburg now argued against the intended action in the Landtag. The reasons for Eulenburg's objection are even more interesting than the fact of the opposition itself. Eulenburg argued that, first of all, an acceptance of an "enlarged associations law" by the Landtag was not absolutely certain; second, the outlawing of the Social Democratic associations was not adequate; and finally, the resultant concern from the public would not warrant the value of such a bill. The Kaiser had counter-arguments: first, the conservatives would be happy, especially in the wake of the Hammerstein scandal,[13] to support the government in this proposed direction; second, Köller "has the whole Landtag in his pocket"; third, although such a bill would not stop Socialist agitation, it would provide a way out for all those who had been forced to go along with the Socialist leaders within the framework of the associations; and finally, public unrest could not be great, especially when only one very short paragraph would be introduced. The problem of Köller Eulenburg saved for the future. "Today I have not yet discussed the situation of von Köller," he wrote to Hohenlohe, "since other occasional remarks of His Majesty revealed what illusions His Majesty holds with regard to Köller." As for the rest, Eulenburg told the Kaiser that the Chancellor "at the special wish of His Majesty" would certainly be glad to do something "within the limits of the possible," but not more. At the same time he pointed out to Wilhelm that according to Hohenlohe, it "would, in the last analysis, be better to introduce *no* bill at all." Wilhelm remarked that he would not think "to venture so far out that . . . [he] would come into an embarrassing situation and thereby do Prince Bismarck a favor." Furthermore, he gave Eulenburg the impression that he "felt bound by the word he had given to Köller!"

Finally, Eulenburg added his own opinion: one should take thorough action against the Social Democrats and feel strong enough to bear the consequences, or take no action at all. The Kaiser, out of fear for his family, wanted to take effective action by way of the Reichstag and Landtag; if such legal action were denied, only then would he carry through these measures even without legal consent. However, Eulenburg added to Hohenlohe:

> Only this moment seems not to come for a long time since, for the present, I can note that the conviction to play into Bismarck's hands when starting such a revolution, has been too deeply engrained in Him. I almost believe that a serious consideration of these matters will come only after the death of Prince Bismarck [thus Bismarck continued to be the bulwark against radical action, even to be the protector of the Social Democrats—or at least Bismarck was used as a convenient excuse for shying away from radical action] unless an outrageous act of the anarchists would give the Kaiser the means to accomplish what He wants before that time.[14]

Moreover, what the Kaiser wished was, after all, radical action in the style of Köller!

This long communication of Eulenburg was just as little suited to calm Hohenlohe's apprehension as was the one Eulenburg had sent a few days earlier on September 19, since in essence it had become clear that the Kaiser was basically on the side of Köller, that he was mainly restrained by no other than Bismarck, and that Eulenburg did not support the position of Hohenlohe.

Eulenburg's attitude becomes quite clear when one remembers that on September 9 he stated his complete agreement with Holstein against an anti-Socialist law, since this would only serve the purpose of Bismarck; he also agreed that the Imperial speech on the day commemorating the victory at Sedan had, in effect, achieved the opposite, namely the renewed threat of a coup d'état.[15] To be sure, Wilhelm's speech on September 2 (in which he spoke, among other things, about a "horde of people not worthy to be called German"[16]) reasonably led many to expect a full-fledged anti-Socialist law in the near future.[17] Consequently, Lucanus and Marschall toned down the speech of the monarch,[18] and Wilhelm even went to Schönstedt and told him "he would want only one paragraph in order to protect the esteem of the old Emperor; he [Wilhelm] is not so dumb as to do the Socialists a favor in making an emergency law. . . ."[19] The desire, therefore, to get an anti-Socialist law was still quite strong. The only change from the Kaiser's impulsive steps (a step which Lucanus did not take) was that he hoped to get an anti-Socialist law passed in fact without running the risks involved by calling it such. This was also Eulenburg's position. Perhaps Eulenburg was a realist by accepting the Kaiser's wish to "do something" and, in the process of advising on actual proposals, hoped to defuse the explosive situation. On the other hand, he perhaps did not have enough courage and was in danger of becoming a mere royal servant. It would be more appropriate to look at

Eulenburg as a manipulator of forces. His role was not so much that of a mediator but, rather, that of a juggler. Within his requirement of preserving a certain degree of freedom of action (tactically to change his relative position from one side to another), Eulenburg probed Hohenlohe and the Kaiser as to how far his freedom of movement actually, in this concrete situation, extended. He used some of Hohenlohe's arguments with the monarch, some of the Kaiser's arguments with Hohenlohe; and he played the game with Holstein, Lucanus, and others as well. In a sense, Eulenburg was assessing their strength and potentiality in order to be able to use them as effectively as possible to serve his own interests.

3

As the situation presented itself, Eulenburg had to avoid and oppose the extreme positions. Hohenlohe's own natural course—to handle the situation in a dilatory way—fitted well, despite its different base, into the course Eulenburg had to accept. The idea of an associations and coalitions law was not rejected, but neither were any energetic steps taken to implement it.

Hohenlohe again pointed out to Eulenburg that he wanted no action at all, but if one of the four proposals of Köller had to be taken up "at the present time," it should be only an amendment to the already existing associations law.[20] Holstein emphasized the fact that an anti-Socialist law would not increase the protection of the Kaiser but would have the opposite effect—the "imperial closed season lasts only as long as does the recollection of the pro-working group program of '89"—and he even hinted that some of those who advocated radical action might prefer Prince Heinrich over Wilhelm II.[21]

Perhaps the best summation of the position of the core supporters of the New Course on this issue (but transcending by far the narrow confines of the New Course) came in the form of a long exposé by Marschall. Diplomatically and skillfully lauding Eulenburg's efforts (as he had described them in his letter to Hohenlohe on September 21), Marschall, realizing that Eulenburg was not really supporting him, argued against taking any radical action. "We live," Marschall wrote, "in a time of formation of associations" on every social level, and this development, particularly prevalent in the lower socioeconomic strata, could not lack political implications, could not be dissociated from political activity. Marschall saw the "formulation of associations [as] a simply indispensable weapon for the economically weaker groups against the superior strength of capital." In fact, he continued, ". . . one may say that the possibility of a peaceful solution of the social question based upon the reconciliation of the great contrasts between capital and labor, lies mainly in the fact that the weaker elements will unite on the basis of identical interests and will find in this union the strength which they lack if they remain separate." The social question could not be solved by the superficial approach of Köller, that is, by mere anti-Socialist legislation. Nor could it be solved by a mere "strengthening" of the existing laws, since in all probability the dispensation of the law would be deferential, favoring the conservative associations, while at the same time taking

strong action against the Social Democrats. This state of affairs
would increase, not decrease, the danger of the situation, since it
would stimulate "dabbling in secret societies and embitterment.
And these two things have at all times been the ground upon which
assassination attempts against high-situated persons have arisen."
Instead, Marschall continued, the monarch should make full use of
the sympathies that he had acquired as a result of his program of
1890, which had been the reason (still not forgotten among the
workers) of Bismarck's dismissal. The issue of the associations
law would explode in the Ministry of State: "it will hardly be
possible to avoid a crisis, precisely because this action stands
in contradiction to the events of spring 1890." In the Landtag the
difficulties would also be much greater than Köller seemed to
admit: "It is possible that the bill will be defeated, and a
second fiasco in the field of anti-revolutionary action the present
government is unable to bear." Marschall finally pointed out that
the greater the pressure for radical action from the extreme right
and the extreme left, the greater the need for the government, "to
apply the existing laws with severity and justice against transgres-
sion from whatever side they may come; where an urgent necessity
exists, to revise to be sure the law in specific points . . . but
to avoid (large-scale) projects."[22]

The position of Eulenburg was strengthened by approval from
Bülow. Bülow fully endorsed Eulenburg's idea of either a thorough
anti-Socialist law or nothing at all (except to prevent "disastrous
eventualities" such as assassination attempts or effective revolutionary subversion in the Army). A thorough, large-scale action
could only be, according to Bülow, carried out with the cooperation
of Bismarck, and only when the bourgeoisie felt really threatened
by the Socialist danger, and when the clericals were satisfied with
the idea that the state would not use "more extensive means of power"
for starting a new *Kulturkampf*. Bülow did not fail to repeat: no
change of chancellors, but retention of Hohenlohe and the building
of governmental stability.[23]

It becomes clear that although the phraseology was similar, such
as "no *major* action at this time," there was a significant difference in intention. Holstein and Marschall felt confident enough to
dismiss as a negligible force the individuals favoring extreme action.
On the other hand, what Eulenburg, Bülow, and the Kaiser meant by
amending the existing associations law was much different from what
Marschall and Holstein had in mind. By late September and early
October it appeared that two distinct groups had formed which,
although indirectly trying to influence the Kaiser, directly struggled to gain the adherence of the Chancellor to their respective
groups. On the one side appeared Eulenburg, Bülow, and to an
extent, the Kaiser himself; on the other side were the "Foreign
Office," Holstein, and Marschall.

On October 1 Eulenburg reported to Hohenlohe that Marschall's
exposé did not have much success with the Kaiser. In fact, Wilhelm
seemed to have been bored with the report, even antagonistic (Eulenburg presented it by reading it to the monarch, and Eulenburg knew
that his approach would meet with little success). Marschall,
Wilhelm said, should stick to his own business, that his "south
German conception" did not correspond to the Prussian situation.

"I have," Eulenburg added, "exhausted my means with this last attempt.
The important point will, therefore, be now to choose the smallest
of all evils" and to pray for success.[24] To Marschall, Eulenburg
wrote (after thanking him for the exposé) that the Kaiser had not
changed his mind, and that consequently "something" had to be done
in the Prussian Landtag. This was particularly so since "the
Chancellor has shown his willingness to comply with the all-highest
wishes, 'within the range of possibility.'" From this position the
prince could not back down any more without endangering the whole
Hohenlohe regime, nor could he consequently threaten to resign.
Eulenburg did, however, mention the possibility of Hohenlohe personally speaking to the Kaiser about the dangers connected with this
question[25] (it must be added that Eulenburg knew that Hohenlohe
was not very effective in these personal confrontations with the
Kaiser). This approach in handling Hohenlohe might well have worked,
despite Hohenlohe's agreeing with Marschall,[26] had not the Prussian
Ministry of State decided on October 8 to shelve the question by
handling it in a dilatory way. "With the associations law," noted
Marschall in his diary, "Köller makes a poor show," as with all his
proposals.[27] Two days later Wilmowski spelled out the reasons for
the ministry's reluctant behavior on this matter: a proposal could
be given to the Landtag *only* when it was absolutely certain to be
accepted and passed, and this was not the case. The conservatives
as well as the liberals had reservations; the Center might, as a
result of actions in the Landtag, be forced into opposition and
could endanger the Reichstag legislation (especially the civil
code, the *Bürgerliche Gesetz Buch*). Aside from these "tactical"
reasons, Prussia's unilateral steps against the Social Democrats
would harm the Reich idea (*Schädigung des Reichsgedankens*), and
"the Reich would thereby declare its bankruptcy with regard to the
Social Democracy" (to which Hohenlohe penned the comment: "We too
are the Reich"). It would embitter the working classes, and finally,
it would stimulate secret associations and with them criminal
inclinations.[28]

4

While the question of the associations law was thus "disposed
of" for the time being, another matter—the conversion of Prussian
state papers from 4% to 3½%—was neatly "resolved." The conversion
had been announced at a rather inopportune time (on September 10,
probably deliberately), in the form of an article in the *Post*.
Marschall, who called this step "impudence" on the part of Miquel,[29]
informed Hohenlohe about the conversion and Miquel's attitude.[30]
By October 9 Hohenlohe felt it necessary to publish an article
declaring himself publicly against the conversion. Thereupon,
Miquel demanded a disavowal of the article, or he would resign.
However, neither "alternative" became necessary. The Ministry of
State decided against conversion, and Miquel (for the time being)
accepted this decision.[31] In Marschall's words, the "Ministry of
State decides to decide nothing, and with that Miquel is satisfied
too. Thus, much ado about nothing."[32] Some five weeks later an
article appearing in Miquel's newspaper, the *National Zeitung*,
praised "Minister Miquel as a great credit to the far-sighted" for
having fought and prevented the disastrous conversion.[33]

5

The Reich military code (*Reichsmilitärgesetz*) of May 2, 1874, stipulated that "the special jurisdiction over military personnel limits itself to criminal cases and will be regulated by Reich law." The desirability of reforming the military penal code (especially the Saxon and Prussian codes) had already been voiced by various parties in the North German Confederation. However, no reform proposals were introduced into the Reichstag. In 1881, after some years of debate and stalemate, the government explained that a commission was working on the reform proposal; years later, in 1891, the Minister of War replied to an inquiry on the subject that "the work on the proposal is being promoted with all possible means."[34] Especially after 1890 the annual debate over this question became more and more intense, particularly between the Social Democrats and the conservatives.

In October, 1893, Bronsart succeeded Kalterborn-Stockau as Minister of War, and inherited the pressing question of the military penal code. In practical terms it meant the reformation of the Prussian code of 1845 along the lines of the Bavarian code of 1869. The latter was based on a modern conception of law, including verbal and public procedure, free defense and free assessment of evidence, and so on.[35] While in Prussia the military influence was dominant, in the Bavarian code the civil element was clearly predominant.

There were three main "objective" problems in the question of the reform. First was the degree of adaptation to civil procedure, especially in scope, defense, and procedure (written or oral, public and to what degree, etc.); second, the limitation of power of the head of the armed forces and the judge; and third, the establishment of a supreme military tribunal.

The main "subjective" elements were several. First, there was the absolutist role Wilhelm II assumed as head of the armed forces and consequently his opposition to any kind of compromise that seemed to limit his power in this position. Second, there was the problem of particularism (especially in regard to the supreme military tribunal). Third, there was the fear of the conservatives of corrupting the Army and thus losing the remaining bulwark against the Social Democrats. Finally, there was the introduction of the reformed code of 1869 in Bavaria by Hohenlohe (then Bavarian Minister-president and since 1894 Imperial Chancellor), who was consequently forced to stand behind a reformed code, that is, a code with at least a minimum amount of public and oral procedure.[36] In March, 1895, Bronsart, as has been seen, pledged himself to introduce into the Reichstag a reformed code or, if the obstacles were too great, to resign.[37]

Within the government two opposing groups began to form over the military penal code: in the one camp were Hohenlohe, Bronsart, Alexander, Hutten-Czapski, and Holstein; in the other were the Kaiser, his entourage, especially the Military Cabinet and its chief, Hahnke, and, in the Prussian Ministry of State, Köller and also (much less obvious, but crucial) Philipp Eulenburg. In contrast to the previous ministers, Bronsart was ready to act and make his retention as War Minister conditional upon that issue.[38]

On April 29 Bronsart had introduced his proposal into the Ministry of State, and after prolonged debate that ministry unanimously approved the reform. It pointed out to the Kaiser that retention of the right to confirmation (*Bestätigungsrecht*), while the Reich Military Court had only advisory powers, would be impossible—from the political and military standpoints, as well as out of legal considerations. Furthermore, it would be incompatible with the civil code. The ministry proposed, consequently, the abolition of the right of confirmation and supported limited public procedure.[39]

However, the Kaiser was stubborn. While again going along with a Reich Military Court, he refused to yield on both confirmation and (even limited) public procedure.[40] Bronsart was informed by Lucanus that the Kaiser would like to brush the entire issue under the rug, as had been done so often and so successfully before.[41] Perhaps Wilhelm had even ordered Bronsart to drop the issue, as Eulenburg suggested to Holstein.[42] Yet this seems unlikely without resulting in Bronsart's immediate resignation. More likely is that the Kaiser thought that Bronsart had given in, or Wilhelm had told Eulenburg that Bronsart had done so. The Kaiser's response implied a complete bypassing of the Ministry of State (as had been still possible before, but not after, 1848). Hohenlohe fared no better than Bronsart. He tried to approach Wilhelm on the subject on May 31, in an apparently favorable atmosphere (they were taking an outing to the Pfaueninsel), but the Kaiser cut him short: ". . . in this difficult time," the Kaiser informed Hohenlohe, "a minister could not possibly leave his king . . . the Minister of War had accepted His point of view; they were in agreement, and while on the way from Magdeburg to Berlin they had come to an understanding. The presentation [of the bill] to the Ministry of State was only a formality without importance, and He will never give up the right of confirmation . . . and the King of Saxony was just as little disposed toward giving up his right for confirmation."[43] That was all. It is revealing when Hohenlohe continued his *Aufzeichnung* in the following manner: "I now had to ask the War Minister first" to find out if Wilhelm's version had been correct—which in fact, according to Bronsart, it was not. Instead, Bronsart replied ". . . that all that was not true."[44] Hohenlohe had to question Hohenthal, the Saxon ambassador, to find out the actual opinion of the Saxon king.[45] At any rate, probably under the threat of a resignation from Bronsart, Wilhelm had agreed to have the question of the reform submitted[46] and even, at the time of the festivities at Kiel, mentioned to the Saxon king that he had agreed to its submission with limited public procedure.[47]

Despite such an attitude of the Kaiser, neither Bronsart nor even Hohenlohe was willing nor able to drop the military penal code reform issue. A month later, on June 24, the Ministry of State once again deliberated the issue but found itself unable to modify its previous position. Owing only to Bronsart's and Hohenlohe's intervention, a somewhat modified report was sent to the Kaiser. The monarch would be able to use his right of confirmation only to pardon or mitigate or, in case of acquittal, preclude the reopening of a case. In addition, there would be limited public procedure (the public would be excluded in cases of state security,

military interests, or public morality). At the same time Bronsart
ordered a commission under General v. Spitz to redraft the proposal
of 1890, no doubt to bring it in line with the above modifications
accepted by the Ministry of State.[48]

While Bronsart waited for the draft of the commission report
and took seriously Wilhelm's approval of submitting the question,
Wilhelm assured himself that it was only a meaningless formality,
and that he had prevailed over the Minister of War. In fact, it
seems that the Kaiser alone, with almost incredible naiveté, did not
grasp the potential danger still inherent in the whole governmental
structure. As far as he was concerned, the reform question had
been resolved in his favor; Berlepsch had just received the Kaiser's
written confidence and been retained in office. As far as the
Kaiser was concerned, everything seemed to be going well. But
what he forgot to mention to Bronsart was that (under the influence
of Hahnke and then Bülow and Eulenburg[49]) he had been persuaded to
change his mind.[50]   Eulenburg in the meantime took precautionary
steps to defuse the embarrassing military penal code reform. Not
that he was particularly worried; to the contrary, as late as the
middle of November he still did not fear any immediate serious
crisis.[51] Yet the reform was a particularly sensitive issue and
had to be dealt with, lest it be reopened at an unfavorable time
and serve as a political lever in the hands of Eulenburg's opponents. That it in some form would have to come up relatively soon,
Eulenburg was of course fully aware. Bronsart's commission was not
alone concerned with drafting such a reform; the Reichstag, recon-
vening later in the year, would do so, with the support of Bronsart's
previous public statement. In addition, the Military Cabinet under
Hahnke would not rest in its active struggle against Bronsart
(especially in view of his determination to see the reform materialize).[52]

Eulenburg began to plot for the removal of Bronsart. The form
Eulenburg chose was, it seems, to isolate Bronsart and to strengthen
the position of Lucanus and that of the Kaiser. As early as June
22 (that is, two days before the second debate of the Ministry of
State over the reform) Eulenburg wrote to Holstein that Bronsart
thought it necessary for the Kaiser occasionally to ask Bismarck
for advice. He added that the hate against Lucanus was so great
among "certain groups" precisely because Lucanus consistently
agitated against Bismarck.[53]   Hohenlohe noted in his journal for
June 28 that Miquel and Bronsart were intriguing against him—a
suspicion, as far as Bronsart was concerned, which may well have
been taken from Eulenburg.[54]   It is also interesting to note here
that by late September even Wilhelm himself seemed to believe
that it was Bismarck who stood behind Bronsart and his reform.[55]
At any rate, Eulenburg reported the following words of the Kaiser
to Holstein: "The 'Old one' in Friedrichsruh very likely has
incited him [Bronsart] into the military penal code question—
on the one hand, in order to embarrass me; on the other to
promote Bronsart [as Chancellor]. When somebody engages in
making visits to Friedrichsruh, then one cannot be surprised
about certain effects."[56]

To brand someone as a Bismarckian was the surest way to gain
the formidable support of Holstein. Eulenburg was, as was to be

expected, successful.[57] By late September Holstein used exactly the
same arguments for an inconspicuous dismissal of Bronsart as Eulenburg was to suggest to Hohenlohe and to the Kaiser. Holstein wrote:
"The affair with Bronsart is becoming very critical. I believe it
would be *very much* in the interest of the Kaiser if he would dismiss Bronsart over another question, not the penal code regulation.
Otherwise, Bronsart would leave with a tremendous *aureole*, while
the other ministers who had supported him before they knew the
views of His Majesty would be placed in a very difficult situation."[58] Thus, while Holstein used arguments that he knew would
warrant Eulenburg to take action against Bronsart (and thus get rid
of the "Bismarckian" Minister of War), Holstein played directly into
Eulenburg's hands. These maneuvers for gaining Holstein's support
were reinforced by asking Holstein for advice and appealing to his
sense of duty: "Would it be possible for you," Eulenburg asked him,
"to visit me in Vöslau, then please do. You would not only be showing me alone a favor, but perhaps also the state. . . . I am in
need of your advice. Although I am now better able to carry on than
before, I do not wish to. We belong together—I can never dissociate
myself from this idea, which is a good one and a legitimate one."[59]

A supplementary approach to discredit Bronsart by Eulenburg may
be seen in Eulenburg's letter to Wilhelm of August 4 (after Eulenburg had spoken with Hohenlohe) and in a Bülow memo written some
time after August 4 (after Bülow had met with Eulenburg). In the
letter to Wilhelm, Eulenburg cautiously tried to prepare the Kaiser
for a possible "Köller crisis" over Berlepsch's various proposals
and over Bronsart:

> As to Bronsart, the waves have only apparently calmed
> down—as a result of the oil that Your Majesty has poured
> onto the flood. This question, in fact, seems to me not
> to be an easy one in regard to Your Majesty. Hohenlohe
> had identified himself . . . with Bronsart because he
> reasoned that if Bronsart were to resign with *eclat* before
> all of Germany as representative of the reorganization
> of the military courts, he would then possess the popular
> parole with which he could at some future time appear as
> Chancellor; while Hohenlohe, remaining, would to be sure,
> have burdened himself with an odium in the eyes of the
> whole liberalizing Germany. To what extent Your Majesty
> wants to take action in this question I do not know. If
> Bronsart demands the reform . . . in the next session and
> if Your Majesty refused, it could well happen that because
> of the aforementioned reasons with the resignation of
> Bronsart, Hohenlohe would go *also*. Hardly an objection
> can be found against Hohenlohe's viewpoint. Therefore,
> the matter will rest upon the question whether it would
> be possible still to postpone the whole affair—in case,
> that is, Your Majesty would wish no reorganization for the
> time being, or not at all.[60]

Pleading for secrecy, Eulenburg added that "it did, however, seem
important to me to prepare Your Majesty in time for coming
events."[61]

Bülow's memo, obviously intended to be read by the Kaiser,

repeated almost exactly the statements of Eulenburg; only Bülow
suggested even more clearly to Wilhelm what position he should
assume: "If, therefore, in the question of the military judiciary
Your Majesty does not yet, or not at all, want to sacrifice the old
Prussian tradition to the leveling modern spirit of the times," then
the whole issue would have to be postponed lest Bronsart and Hohenlohe resign. Bülow continued that whenever such a postponement had
been achieved, it would be possible to have Bronsart resign over
some other question without having the benefit of "liberal aureole"
and without the resignation of Hohenlohe. This form would, finally,
end the acute and critical nature of the reform question, since
"either the whole thing would slowly be forgotten; or the new
Minister of War would give Hohenlohe the opportunity to declare his
acceptance of the minister's reasons against the reform of the
military judiciary."[62]

We may be permitted here to transgress chronology for a moment
and point out that as late as July, Wilhelm had been—in principle
—for Bronsart's reform and in 1898 did actually accept the "unacceptable" bill. However, faced with the alternative presented by
Bülow and Eulenburg (and no doubt Hahnke and the military entourage
as well) of either upholding the old Prussian tradition or submitting to the "leveling modern spirit of the times" (*nivellierende
moderne Zeitgeist*), Wilhelm did not have much of a choice. It would
thus not be incorrect to state that the Kaiser had been, by August,
persuaded (against his own previous judgment) to oppose the
government and had consequently become a tool of his own advisors—
the Military Cabinet and Eulenburg-Bülow, increasing their own power
at the expense of the responsible government. Instead of trying to
avert a crisis, Eulenburg and Bülow (despite protestations to the
contrary) worked hard to precipitate a crisis. It is true that
both did not want a Chancellor crisis, since they regarded Hohenlohe
as an indispensable figurehead. They worked toward a crisis, however,
that was not supposed to be a crisis—that is, it was not supposed
to carry with it the usual attributes of uncertainty and instability.
Under the veneer of stability they wanted to defuse the military
penal code question by letting Bronsart resign and letting the
Kaiser have "his way," and also by moving toward the right and thus
stealing Bismarck's thunder and eliminating the conservative opposition.

In mid-August Bronsart again conferred directly with the Kaiser;
he was prepared to resign. Wilhelm, however, was not willing to let
him go.[63] Apparently Wilhelm believed again that the result of his
conversation had been indefinite postponement.[64] This could hardly
have been Bronsart's understanding. Similarly, the Kaiser made
himself believe (after a discussion with Hohenlohe on the way to
Danzig) that the Chancellor had agreed not to bring the issue into
the next Reichstag session—a version which did not correspond with
Hohenlohe's own recollection.[65] In fact, neither Bronsart nor
Hohenlohe had any intention of postponing the reform bill. Bronsart
had by mid-October reintroduced the proposal, which included unconditional court procedure and limited public procedure. He had again
been able to get the backing of the Ministry of State ("unanimous
with one exception," namely Köller[66]). Both Bronsart and Hohenlohe
tried to influence the Kaiser to change his mind again—Bronsart by

having the Saxon king (who was not opposed to the bill) approach the Kaiser[67] and Hohenlohe by using the services of the Grand Duke of Baden.[68]

6

While visiting in Strassburg, Hohenlohe took the opportunity to discuss various political issues with the Grand Duke. In this discussion the question of the military penal code reform certainly was of major concern. Independently of Hohenlohe, Bronsart outlined the situation and asked the Grand Duke for advice. The latter then wrote a long letter to Eulenburg suggesting a compromise, particularly in the limited public procedure clause. The Grand Duke said that the Kaiser must give in to Bronsart because the latter was supported by the entire ministry (with the exception of Köller). In order to avoid the appearance of having been forced to accept, the Kaiser should personally introduce the bill in the Reichstag.[69] In addition, in order to make this proposition more acceptable to the Kaiser—to sweeten the pill—the Grand Duke advised the introduction at the same time of a bill for the improvement of the situation of the noncommissioned officers, as well as a plan to reform the organization of the infantry. Bronsart accepted the advice of the Grand Duke, except for the plan for the infantry— there was not enough time to prepare this latter suggestion for the current Reichstag session.[70]

Eulenburg refused to recognize the situation as a real crisis and took his time with a reply to the Grand Duke. Instead, he bombarded Hohenlohe with letters vividly describing the dismay of the Kaiser, who had talked with the Saxon king. Contrary to Wilhelm's former impressions, the Saxon king had also been in favor of the reform. This apparent change the Kaiser had attributed to Bronsart and, behind Bronsart, the intrigues of Bismarck. Since (according to Eulenburg) the Kaiser imperatively wanted to avoid a *belle sortie* for Bronsart over this issue, the Kaiser rejected Hohenlohe's contention that he would have to resign with Bronsart if the latter were dismissed. He suggested that Hohenlohe's staying in office would assure him an enormous increase of prestige in the eyes of the Army and all "rationally thinking people in Germany." Besides, the Kaiser had all the commanding generals on his side and "that carries more weight than *one* Minister of War, who wants to become Imperial Chancellor." Consequently, Eulenburg ended, the Chancellor should try to postpone this issue by all possible means. In addition, Eulenburg said that the Kaiser would speak to Hohenlohe personally the next day (October 30).[71]

The discussion between Wilhelm and Hohenlohe took an almost predictable course. The Kaiser presented his arguments for the agreed-upon postponement of the question. The renewed introduction was, in his eyes, an intrigue of Bismarck, who, just as last year, intended to create a crisis. Disregarding discrepancies in the Kaiser's exposition, Hohenlohe cautiously presented his own case. The result was that Wilhelm again sent Plessen to Bronsart in order to induce that minister to postpone the reform beyond the next Reichstag session and, at the same time, to remain in the ministry, since the Kaiser could ill afford to lose him for the Army.[72]

On the evening of the next day Wilhelm informed Hohenlohe that

he had spoken with Bronsart, and that Bronsart had accepted postponement while he had accepted the suggestion of getting the
opinions of all the commanding generals on the subject: "The
affair," Wilhelm closed, "is herewith disposed of."[73] Hohenlohe,
released of that burden, gladly accepted this compromise.

Only after these events did Eulenburg find it necessary to
reply to the Grand Duke. Excusing himself with the rationalization that the question had reached such an acute state that he
first wanted to await its solution before writing, Eulenburg then
added that "this has now happened—however in a different way than
Your Royal Highness has wished—and it has also modified the
facts. . . ." Eulenburg then quickly reviewed the whole issue,
portraying Bronsart as the "villain." Finally, however, Eulenburg
pointed out that as a result of his mediation, a way had been found
to postpone the military penal code reform (that is, by asking the
commanding generals for their opinions; Eulenburg expected this to
take about nine months). "During a confrontation with Bronsart,"
Eulenburg continued, "Bronsart had, with tears in his eyes, assured
His Majesty of his loyalty and had declared to stay in office and
submit to the inquest." Bronsart had apparently even made rather
practical proposals for a possible bill to supplement the Army,[74]
but not as a compensation for the military penal code reform.
Eulenburg closed the subject: "I have the impression that everybody wants to accommodate himself. Bronsart, I believe, has on
his part changed his tactics after the ministry had suggested his
resignation because then he certainly would have vanished from the
scene without much ado."[75]

A few days later Eulenburg stated to Bülow that he took events
such as the reform question more calmly.[76] Obviously, Eulenburg
thought himself in command of the situation, and must have thought
that he had successfully "mediated" by defending, and essentially
maintaining, the stand against Bronsart (which had become the stand
of the Kaiser). Consequently, Eulenburg could afford to reject and
oppose the position and advice of practically the entire Ministry
of State, Hohenlohe, Marschall, Bronsart, and even the Grand Duke
of Baden. Eulenburg, having won over the Kaiser to their side with
the help of Hahnke, Plessen, and the court, felt, it seems, secure
and confident of success in their opposition to the official
government.

While Eulenburg was thus congratulating himself, investigations
were under way to discover the author of offensive articles that
had just appeared in the press—investigations that were to trigger
the so-called Köller crisis.

NOTES

1. Wilhelm to Hohenlohe, 23.VIII.95, *Hohenlohe*, III, 92.

2. *Ibid.*, pp. 92-93.

3. Marschall Diary, 25.VIII.95.

4. Marschall Diary, 27.VIII.95; Wilhelm to Hohenlohe, 31.VIII.95,
Hohenlohe, III, 94, note 1; Holstein to Eulenburg, 28.VIII.95, B.A.
Eul. 37.

5. Holstein to Eulenburg, 28.VIII.95, B.A. Eul. 37. This was also the opinion of Hohenthal, who wrote of persons within the conservative and National Liberal parties who wanted to use this means to end the Hohenlohe regime. It was possible, he continued, that Eulenburg and his group might work as they did in October, 1894, to replace the Chancellor, but it was not very likely since they would be hard pressed at the moment to come up with a replacement. See Saxon embassy report, 20.IX.95, Sächs. H.S.A., Ges. Berlin, No. 250, and *ibid.*, Foreign Ministry, No. 1079.

6. Hohenlohe to Wilhelm (Entw), no date, but probably 24–30. VIII.95, *Hohenlohe*, III, 93; Wilhelm to Hohenlohe, 31.VIII.95, *ibid.*, p. 94, notes 1, 2.

7. Hohenlohe to Eulenburg, 19.IX.95, B.A. Eul., printed under *"Aufzeichnung"* in *Hohenlohe*, III, 98–99.

8. *Hohenlohe*, III, 98, note 1.

9. Eulenburg to Hohenlohe, 12.IX.95, *ibid.*, p. 98.

10. *Ibid.*, pp. 97–98.

11. *Ibid.*, p. 98.

12. *Ibid.*

13. In July v. Hammerstein, a leader of the conservatives, member of both Reichstag and Landtag, and editor-in-chief of the *Kreuzzeitung*, had been found embezzling funds of that paper for his personal use. See *Schulthess*, 1895, pp. 164, 205.

14. Eulenburg to Hohenlohe, 21.IX.95, *Hohenlohe*, III, 99–101; also in B.A. Eul. 37.

15. Eulenburg to Holstein, 9.IX.95, B.A. Eul. 37; see also his comment to August Eulenburg: "I will of course try as hard as I can to prevent the Kaiser from *provoking* a crisis." 26.IX.95, B.A. Eul. 37.

16. Ziekursch, *Politische Geschichte*, III, 81.

17. See Marschall Diary, 2.IX.95, 3.IX.95, 5.IX.95.

18. *Ibid.*, 2.IX.95.

19. *Ibid.*, 6.IX.95.

20. Hohenlohe to Eulenburg, 25.IX.95, B.A. Eul. 37.

21. Holstein to Eulenburg, 27.IX.95, B.A. Eul. 37.

22. Marschall, 29.IX.95, B.A. Bülow, No. 104; B.A. Eul. 38. See also Marschall Diary, 29.IX.95, and Marschall to Hohenlohe, 29.IX.95, Hohenlohe Archiv Schillingsfürst, Rep. 100 X A–58.

23. Bülow to Eulenburg, 28.IX.95, B.A. Eul. 38.

24. Eulenburg to Hohenlohe, 1.X.95, *Hohenlohe*, III, 112; B.A. Eul. 38.

25. Eulenburg to Marschall, 2.X.95, B.A. Eul. 38.

26. See Marschall Diary, 6.X.95.

27. *Ibid.*, 8.X.95.

28. Wilmowski to Hohenlohe, 10.X.95, Archiv Schillingsfürst, Rep. 100 XXII A-6.

29. Marschall Diary, 10.IX.95. On this see also Herzfeld, *Miquel*, II, 469f.

30. Marschall Diary, 14.IX.95.

31. See Hohenlohe Journal, ca. 10.X.95, Archiv Schillingsfürst, Rep. 100 XXII A-6; Marschall Diary, 10.X.95, 11.X.95; Holstein to Eulenburg, 11.X.95, B.A. Eul. 38.

32. Marschall Diary, 11.X.95.

33. *Ibid.*, 17.XI.95.

34. For all above, see A. Kröber, "Der Kampf um die Reform des Militärstrafprozesses (1893-1898)" (dissertation, Göttingen, 1938), pp. 4-5 hereafter cited as Kröber, "Reform."

35. *Ibid.*, p. 3.

36. See above, p. 14-15; Kröber, "Reform," p. 25; see also Hutten-Czapski, *Sechzig Jahre*, I, 280ff.

37. Adopted from Kröber, "Reform," p. 18, 23ff.

38. See Marschall Diary, 30.V.95.

39. Hutten-Czapski, *Sechzig Jahre*, I, 282; Röhl, *Germany without Bismarck*, pp. 139-140. See also Herzfeld, *Miquel*, II, 454ff.

40. Hutten-Czapski, *Sechzig Jahre*, I, 283.

41. See Marschall Diary, 30.V.95.

42. Eulenburg to Holstein, 22.VI.95, B.A. Eul. 36.

43. "*Aufzeichnung*," 31.V.95, *Hohenlohe*, III, 74.

44. *Ibid.*

45. *Ibid.*

46. See Lerchenfeld to Crailsheim, 28.VI.95, G.S.A. München, MA 77751.

47. Lerchenfeld to Crailsheim, 25.X.95, G.S.A. München, MA 77751.

48. See Hutten-Czapski, *Sechzig Jahre*, I, 283; Röhl, *Germany without Bismarck*, p. 140.

49. Rudolf Schmidt-Bückeburg, *Das Militärkabinett der preussischen Könige und deutschen Kaiser. Seine geschichtliche Entwicklung und staatsrechtliche Stellung 1787-1918* (Berlin, 1933), pp. 208ff.; Lerchenfeld to Crailsheim, 25.X.95, G.S.A. München, MA 77751; Hutten-Czapski, *Sechzig Jahre*, I, 283.

50. *Ibid.*

51. See Eulenburg to Bülow, 12.XI.95, B.A. Eul. 39.

52. See Schmidt-Bückeburg, *Das Militärkabinett*, p. 208. For the consistent struggle between Bronsart as Minister of War and Hahnke as chief of the Military Cabinet, see *ibid.*, pp. 196ff.

53. Eulenburg to Holstein, 22.VI.95, B.A. Eul. 36.

54. *Hohenlohe*, III, 83.

55. Hutten-Czapski, *Sechzig Jahre*, I, 271.

56. Eulenburg to Holstein, 28.IX.95, B.A. Eul. 38.

57. It must be pointed out, however, that Holstein's suspicion in regard to Bronsart did not begin at this time. In October, 1894, Holstein had written to Eulenburg that Bismarck intended Bronsart to be a coup d'état Chancellor; that Bronsart had a "good Bismarck press"; and that in the case of a total crisis Bronsart would suggest that the Kaiser take Bismarck back. See Holstein to Eulenburg, 15.X.94, B.A. Eul. 32. Then there was Bronsart's visit to Bismarck in 1895 which immediately caused a variety of suspicions.

58. See Holstein to Eulenburg, 23.IX.95, B.A. Eul. 37.

59. Eulenburg to Holstein, 11.VIII.95, *Holsteins Papiere*, III, 485.

60. Eulenburg to Wilhelm, 4.VIII.95, B.A. Eul. 37; see also Röhl, *Germany without Bismarck*, p. 140.

61. Eulenburg to Wilhelm, 4.VIII.95, B.A. Eul. 37.

62. Bülow memo, VIII.95, B.A. Eul. 37.

63. Waldersee, *Denkwürdigkeiten*, II, 360.

64. See *Hohenlohe*, III, 115.

65. See *Ibid.*

66. Ministry of State meeting, 8.X.95, 16.X.95; Röhl, *Germany without Bismarck*, p. 141; Grand Duke to Eulenburg, 26.X.95, B.A. Eul. 38; Marschall Diary, 16.X.95.

67. See *Hohenlohe*, III, 114.

68. Röhl, *Germany without Bismarck*, p. 141.

69. Grand Duke to Eulenburg, 26.X.95, B.A. Eul. 38; Röhl, *Germany without Bismarck*, p. 141.

70. See General v. Blume to Grand Duke, 23.X.95, G.L.A. Karlsruhe, Gr. Fam. Archiv, N 321.

71. See Eulenburg to Hohenlohe, 29.X.95, two items in *Hohenlohe*, III, 114; Archiv Schillingsfürst, Rep. 100 XXII A-6; B.A. Eul. 38.

72. Hohenlohe Journal, 31.X.95, *Hohenlohe*, III, 114-116.

73. Wilhelm to Hohenlohe, 31.X.95, *ibid.*, p. 116.

74. This had been proposed to him by the Grand Duke; see above, p. 125. The supplementation possibly was the increase of the four battalions to full battalions.

75. Eulenburg to Grand Duke, G.L.A. Karlsruhe, Gr. Fam. Archiv, N 377; also B.A. Eul. 38 (but not complete letter. Eulenburg there left out the last part, in which he complained to the Grand Duke that he had been attacked in the *Allgemeine Zeitung*, a paper which he, Eulenburg, had won over "for our interests" and he asked the Grand Duke to help put a stop to it). See also Eulenburg to Marschall, 6.XI.95, B.A. Eul. 38.

76. Eulenburg to Bülow, 12.XI.95, B.A. Eul. 39.

CHAPTER 8

The Köller Crisis

Regardless, it is a fact that Köller, since his
unlucky campaign in the Reichstag on occasion of
the anti-revolutionary bill, was considered as
unfit for his post also amongst his colleagues.

Lerchenfeld to Crailsheim,
December 3, 1895

It now becomes more and more apparent that Köller,
in order to place his achievements into a bright
light, has portrayed his colleagues to the Kaiser
for some time already as not energetic enough; and
also he has strengthened the tendency of the Kaiser
to embarrass the Chancellor and not to bother about
the public opinions. This system, to be sure, has
earned him the Imperial confidence. He finally felt
himself so sure that he hardly debated with his colleagues. It appears that during the crisis he continued to downgrade at least some of his colleagues
in the eyes of the Kaiser, and, as it now becomes
apparent, with complete success. . . . Now the entire
press knows exactly how things have happened and
often makes capital out of it for advocation of the
introduction of the parliamentary regime.

Lerchenfeld to Crailsheim,
December 14, 1895

In the evening talked with Boetticher, who talks
about a reconciliation Bronsart-Köller, but then,
however, realizes that the matter is of more profound nature.

Marschall Diary,
November 26, 1895

1

Events occurring in early November, 1895, sparked a crisis that
could have become the gravest and most important event of the decade
after Bismarck's dismissal. Were we to accept the concept of "turning point" as valid in history, then perhaps we might even speak of
a turning point at which history "failed to turn."

The Köller crisis falls conveniently into three main phases.
The first phase really began on November 18, 1895, with Bronsart's

declaration in the Ministry of State that he could no longer work
with Köller; it ended ten days later with the reconciliation of
both ministers. The second phase started on November 26 and terminated with Wilhelm's acceptance of Köller's dismissal on December
2. The third phase, the complications and "immediate" consequences,
came to an end on December 8 with the appointment of Köller's
successor.

On November 4 and 6 the *Münchener Neueste Nachrichten* printed
articles which with reasonable accuracy recapitulated the events
occurring in the Ministry of State meeting over the military penal
code regulation. These articles pointed out that the ministry had
resolved to submit to the Kaiser a reform bill including restricted
public procedure; furthermore, Köller had been the only minister
to vote against the bill. They also stated that Bronsart was
ready to resign if the Kaiser were to reject the public procedure
clause.[1] Soon after there appeared similar articles in the press,
notably one in the *Hannoversche Courier* which attacked Plessen and
Hahnke by name.

Indiscretions in the press were, of course, nothing new. However, apart from the unfortunate timing of the articles, it appeared
that the information must have been intentionally supplied by a
member of the ministry. It is not surprising, then, that Wilhelm
(partly because Hahnke had been attacked directly) and Bronsart,
as well as Hammann, on behalf of Marschall and Hohenlohe, initiated
investigations.[2] While Wilhelm seemed to hold Bronsart and/or the
Foreign Office group as responsible (Marschall had suspected that
the indiscretion would be used to make the Kaiser suspicious of
precisely this group[3]), Bronsart received information confirming
his suspicions against Köller. The difference in information,
especially since both requests for investigations had been given
to the political police under the sectional head of Eugen von
Tausch, is significant and will be brought up in connection with
Leckert-Lützow-Tausch trial.[4] The central point as far as the
Köller crisis is concerned was that Bronsart felt justified in
accusing Köller directly during the Ministry of State meeting on
November 13 of having been directly connected with the *Münchener
Neueste Nachrichten* articles.[5] Moreover, by the 18th Bronsart
could confront Köller with definite evidence and accuse him of
having disclosed proceedings of the Ministry of State. After
first denying this, Köller had to admit that during the recent
Letzlingen hunting excursion (about November 10), in trying to
defend himself, he had talked not only to the Kaiser but also to
Hahnke and Plessen, and to v. Arnim. This evidence had been given
to Bronsart by Plessen and Hahnke. In addition, before the next
meeting convened, Bronsart had announced his decision to boycott
the Minister of Interior by not attending any meeting at which he
was present. Certainly there was also a considerable degree of
resentment on the part of the ministers, particularly Bronsart,
against Köller.[6] Bronsart found Köller's behavior uncollegiate,
and explained Köller's action as trying to save his ministerial
position and Imperial favor in the event of further serious disagreements between the Ministry of State and the Kaiser over the
military penal code reform. However, Köller, it seems, was not
the main recipient of Bronsart's anger. The main cause of friction,

and perhaps Bronsart's main opponent, was Hahnke and the irresponsible Military Cabinet (irresponsible in the sense that it was not
formally responsible to a Secretary of State or Minister but had
direct access to the Kaiser and thus was able to bypass the
established constitutional structures of government). This attitude was emphasized by the fact that Wilhelm had sent Hahnke to
reprimand Bronsart for the *Münchener Neueste Nachrichten* article.[7]
Bronsart extended this resentment to the unofficial advisor of the
Civil Cabinet, Lucanus, and to the Kaiser himself—a general resentment which he had voiced before.[8] The fact that Köller was not the
source for the article in the *Münchener Neueste Nachrichten* (as was
ascertained), but that it had been based upon a report of the
Bavarian military attaché in Berlin and of the Bavarian Minister-
president, Crailsheim,[9] had become by November 18 irrelevant. In
Letzlingen Köller had committed, in the eyes of the ministry, an
inexcusable indiscretion that to them gravely threatened the whole
ministry.[10] It was at that point, rather than on the 4th or even
on the 16th, that the Köller crisis really began. The question
changed its nature from that of a personal question between Bronsart
and Köller to a constitutional question of the entire Ministry of
State and, despite possible reconciliations between the two, had
reached a state of "profound significance."[11]

The ministers accepted the undeniable fact that Köller had
violated proper procedure in a dangerous way, even if many of them
did not hold a personal grudge against Köller or even if some
(such as Marschall and Hohenlohe) suspected that the whole affair
was for Bronsart (in Bosse's words) a welcome incident to assure
him a good and popular exit from the ministry. Hohenlohe belatedly
reminded Köller that reports such as votes in the Ministry of State
should be, if necessary, communicated to the king only by the
Minister-president.[12] Had not the Kaiser himself encouraged Hohenlohe to keep order in the ministry? Wilhelm had suggested strong
action against the ministers, and Hohenlohe had found this advice
sound. So had the ministers themselves, calling for more determined and stronger leadership on the part of the Minister-president.

True to his promise to Hohenlohe, Bronsart did not attend the
next meeting, because of Köller's presence. Yet on the same evening of November 26 he gave Köller an apology (a step apparently
suggested by Boetticher), which Köller immediately accepted.[13] The
apparently irreconcilable ministers of a few hours previous had,
in some way, settled their differences.[14] Thus by the time the
ministers assembled to discuss the case of Köller-Bronsart, the
case had already ceased to exist, although Bronsart was still
highly irritated.[15] In fact, Bronsart was soon to come forward
in favor of a reconciliation between Köller and the Ministry of
State! However, by then (that is, after the 28th) the members of
the ministry could not accept such a solution, a point of view
which soon found unanimity.

2

On November 26, before the Ministry of State meeting, Bronsart
had told Hohenlohe that Köller had spoken not only to the Kaiser
and Hahnke and Plessen but to other officers as well, and that

consequently he, Bronsart, could no longer attend the ministry
meetings while Köller was present.

It was this ministerial "boycott" that prompted Marschall to
act. He explained that as a result of Bronsart's action, Hohenlohe
as Minister-president was obliged to take action himself and to
hear the opinions of the various ministers: "as the situation
stood, I deemed it necessary that something had to be done since
the condition of a minister on strike could impossibly last even
a few days only."[16]

This Hohenlohe did on the same day. He had conversations with
Hammmerstein and Marschall, as well as (probably somewhat later)
with Berlepsch, Miquel, and Thielen. All these ministers condemned Köller's behavior. However, while Hammerstein made it
clear that this act, although not acceptable, would not constitute
a valid enough reason to tell the Kaiser that they could no longer
work with Köller, Hohenlohe recorded that "in the conversation with
Marschall it was noted that a further cooperation with the Minister
of War and Köller would be unthinkable."[17] Marschall's argument,
seconded by Boetticher, was apparently accepted—namely, that it
was an impossible situation for the ministers to boycott Köller.
Hohenlohe decided to inform the Kaiser that the entire Ministry
of State objected to Köller.[18]

Thus Hohenlohe, appearing as the Minister-president of a united
ministry, carried out this decision on the next day (November 28).
He did not get far. The Kaiser, somewhat indignantly and curtly,
insisted on the retention of Köller as the "right man" whom he
counted upon in difficult times.[19] Besides, the Kaiser pointed
out, according to Hahnke's report, Bronsart and Köller had become
reconciled.[20] Hohenlohe, feeling his ministerial position impaired,
sat down and drafted his letter of resignation[21]—the crisis over
Köller was about to turn into a Chancellor crisis. However,
Hohenlohe did not send in his resignation. Instead, he attended
another meeting with the ministers[22] now that the situation had
again been modified by the Kaiser's seeming determination to retain
Köller as his minister.

Some hours before this conference on November 29, Hohenlohe
spoke with Miquel. Miquel, apparently having favored strong action
before and being generally on Köller's side, now did not deem
Köller's actions (to curry the favor of the Kaiser at the expense
of his colleagues) worth a ministerial crisis: "A ministerial
crisis [he told Hohenlohe] ought not develop because of personnel
questions, but because of objective questions, and then all the
ministers ought to stand together."[23] Instead, a Bronsart crisis
seemed in the making.[24]

That afternoon Hohenlohe met with the other ministers—Boetticher, Berlepsch, Thielen, Bosse, Schönstedt, and Marschall.
Absent were Miquel, Hammerstein, Bronsart, and, naturally, Köller.
The main argument against Köller was that without absolute
necessity, he had been indiscreet to the Kaiser, as well as to
other persons, on affairs of the Ministry of State. This fact
would have repercussions in subsequent meetings, since the ministers
would no longer feel free to openly discuss and present their
points of view, especially on issues involving differences of
opinion between them and the Kaiser. Consequently, the only course

of action open to them would be the resignation of Köller or in
case the Kaiser refused, the resignation of the entire ministry.[25]
While perhaps it was true that the "unanimous opinion is that the
prerequisite of a confidential, successful cooperation does no
longer exist,"[26] this unanimity did not include the implications
of a possible ministerial crisis. It was accepted by Marschall,
Boetticher, Berlepsch, Thielen, and very likely Schönstedt.[27]
Hohenlohe had pointed out that both Hammerstein and Miquel, as well
as Bronsart, did not see the necessity of such a crisis. Bosse,
who accepted the view of these latter ministers, emphasized this
fact. Thus the only concrete achievement of the afternoon was the
decision to reconvene next morning in order to hear Miquel,
Bronsart, and Hammerstein.[28]

Accordingly, the ministers met again on November 30, this time
with the exception only of Köller. It was at this meeting that
the ministers agreed on a course of action, with dissent only by
Bronsart. However, by that time Köller, without previous consultation, had committed another act of political folly. On November
29 the police presidium of Berlin, upon orders of the Minister of
Interior, had dissolved eleven Social Democratic associations, among
them the Social Democratic Party (the *Parteivorstand*), on the basis
of an order dating from 1850—even older than the one Bismarck had
found necessary to invoke five years earlier.[29] In addition to the
grievances brought forward against Köller on the previous day, he
was now also accused of not conforming to the political views of
the rest of the ministry and of lacking political tact (making
decisions without consultation with the ministry and with the consent only of the Kaiser).[30] In short, Köller threatened the constitutional position and function of the Ministry of State. That
function was the responsible dispensation of advice through the
Minister-president and the responsible formulation of government
policy. The steps that the ministers unanimously decided to take
were, consequently, not so much a rebellion against the king, or
even against a minister of the king, but rather a defensive move
against one of their peers who threatened their collective constitutional and individual ministerial positions.

The ministers decided (and Hohenlohe accepted) to inform both
Köller and the Kaiser of their request to have Köller resign or,
in case of refusal, to hand in their own resignations. Hohenlohe,
as Minister-president, consequently met Köller on December 1 and,
after initial opposition (Köller emphasized that he did possess
the confidence of the Kaiser), the Minister of Interior submitted
to the will of the ministry and promised to resign. The *Immediatbericht*, put into final form by Boetticher and Marschall, was sent
to the Kaiser on the evening of that same day.[31]

At Wilhelm's request Köller met with him on the morning of
December 2. There was not much time, as the Kaiser was about to
depart with his entourage to Breslau for military maneuvers.
Köller handed in his resignation and it was accepted by the Kaiser.
Both had had to yield to a course of action to which both had vigor-
ously objected and of which both had disapproved. The Minister of
Interior had had to yield to the combined pressure of his colleagues,
the Kaiser to the advice of Eulenburg and to Hohenlohe as Minister-
president of a united and apparently determined Ministry of State.

Köller used the opportunity of the *Immediatbericht* with the Kaiser to discredit the Ministry of State in a most unbecoming and dangerous way. The Kaiser used Lucanus to convey to Hohenlohe his displeasure over the "*Zwangslage*" (position of constraint) into which he had been placed, that only he could "hire and fire" the ministers, and that he accepted Köller's resignation. Finally, Wilhelm asked to have Köller's dismissal kept a secret until he returned from Breslau so that Köller could still attend the opening of the Reichstag as Minister of Interior.[32] There were, as yet, no demands of any kind for "retribution" from the ministry to atone for the humiliation of the Kaiser.

3

When the Bronsart-Köller affair had reached the stage of possibly precipitating a confrontation between the Ministry of State and the Kaiser, and of possibly turning into a Chancellor crisis, Hohenlohe and Holstein informed Eulenburg in Meran. Eulenburg received the news on November 29. It is interesting that Holstein was already emphasizing the role that Plessen had played as informer of the Köller indiscretions to Marschall (seeing Plessen *et al.* as the instigators of the whole intrigue), and he emphasized the unity of the ministry to a greater degree than was actually the case. Moreover, he also indicated—before the November 30 ministerial conference—that the "probable consequences" of those indiscretions would be met by a united ministry. Holstein thus invoked the image of a united ministry for Eulenburg before, in fact, it had come into existence.[33] What neither Holstein nor Hohenlohe naturally wrote was that Marschall and Holstein had to "strengthen" Hohenlohe in his firm insistence on remaining, thus making the crisis inevitable, or (a fact he probably was aware of) that Marschall had persuaded Boetticher to take not a conciliatory attitude but an attitude that would also invariably lead to either Köller's dismissal or a crisis.[34] Holstein did not neglect to inform Bülow (similar to the communications to Eulenburg), except that he stressed somewhat more an imminent Chancellor crisis (he wrote, ". . . while Hohenlohe reads to me his letter of resignation").[35] Bülow quickly telegraphed Eulenburg that Hohenlohe (which meant also Marschall and Holstein) had to be kept in office, and the crisis could be handled by dismissing *both* Köller and Bronsart.[36] A little later Bülow explained his idea to dismiss both ministers—he said that Bronsart had lost the confidence of the Kaiser and that the resignation of both ministers would prevent an appearance of a backing-down on the part of the Kaiser before the rebellious ministry (*einer Schilderhebung*). Eulenburg's and Bülow's first and foremost mission, Bülow wrote, was always the maintenance of the authority and power of the Kaiser (*Autorität und Machtfülle*). In regard to Hohenlohe, Marschall, and Holstein, Bülow said, "Holstein is indispensable with regard to the (difficult and complicated) situation in foreign affairs; Marschall indispensable in the Parliament. The fall of Hohenlohe would . . . again give rise to a feeling of insecurity which, more than anything else of the Fronde, pours water upon the dirty mills of nihilism and socialism." Then, after caustic remarks about Holstein, after mentioning that his brother

Adolph concurred in the opinions of Hahnke and Plessen on the military penal code reform, and after a eulogy to their friendship, Bülow ended his letter.[37]

The particular nature of the crisis, as well as its severity, must have come somewhat as a surprise to Eulenburg, who apparently was not well informed about events in Berlin until November 29, and who had just recently, as far as he was concerned, successfully postponed the military penal code reform.[38]   At any rate, supplied with information from Berlin and advice from Rome, Eulenburg did what was expected of him: Berlin expected him to advise the Kaiser to dismiss Köller;[39] Bülow expected a solution of the crisis without diminishing the power and "face" of the Kaiser, and without losing Hohenlohe, Holstein, and Marschall.

Eulenburg promptly wrote to the monarch and correctly, if somewhat bluntly for Eulenburg, explained that the Kaiser had the alternative of either keeping Köller but losing Hohenlohe and the ministry, or the reverse. He suggested to his Imperial friend that perhaps he was overrating Köller, that he could always be used if necessary in the future. However, at the moment the Kaiser must dismiss Köller, since he had to retain Hohenlohe (using the same arguments as Bülow had expressed to him—stability, difficult foreign situation, the Bismarcks). Invoking God and death, Eulenburg expressed his hope that Wilhelm would find the correct solution. The same night Eulenburg announced his mediating letter to both Hohenlohe and Holstein. To Holstein he added (being familiar with Holstein's opinions on Bronsart) that he would like to see both ministers dismissed, but could not suggest a way to do this.[40] Wilhelm received Eulenburg's letter on December 1, and this might well have contributed to his speedy consent on December 2 to Köller's request, after the firm refusal four days before. The Kaiser then went to Breslau on December 2, and on the next day Eulenburg arrived there.

4

In Berlin Hohenlohe, who had successfully maintained himself through the second phase of the crisis, was now faced with the problem of suggesting a successor to the vacant post. If he thought that the "Köller crisis" was over, he was mistaken.

While the Kaiser was on his way to Breslau (with the Köller interview fresh in his memory and surrounded by his military entourage) and becoming more and more enraged over the "gross insubordination" of the ministers and consequently of his own Imperial "humiliation," Hohenlohe and the ministers deliberated on a candidate to be suggested by him for the appointment. The first possibility (that, according to Lucanus, the Kaiser had suggested before leaving for Breslau), that of Wilhelm Bismarck, was quickly dismissed. The second name (also suggested by the Kaiser, according to Lucanus), Zedlitz-Trützschler, was taken into serious consideration.[41] How serious Wilhelm actually had been with these nominations was open to question. When Hohenlohe asked him two days later (Wilhelm had returned from Breslau and was getting ready to leave for Hanover), he could not recollect having made these suggestions, and in fact, objected to Zedlitz because of the role he had played in the school

bill crisis some years previously. Wilhelm Bismarck was not seriously discussed at all.[42]   In their meeting on December 2 the
ministers decided to suggest a first choice, Posadowsky; a second
choice, Studt (a candidate whom Miquel had suggested); and, as
third choice, Zedlitz-Trützschler.[43]

On the same day that the Reichstag session opened (and it was
no secret any longer that Köller had resigned from his post),
Eulenburg met Wilhelm in Breslau and hurriedly telegraphed to Berlin
that the Kaiser was extremely upset over the action of the ministry
and that he demanded certain "concessions." The crisis was not yet
over.[44]   That, too, was no secret in Berlin: as soon as Wilhelm
had arrived in Breslau, he had sent a special message, dictated to
Hahnke and addressed to Lucanus, expressing his outrage against
the ministry and demanding its collective resignation.[45]   A second,
longer telegram from Eulenburg filled in some details and suggested
a course of action. The Kaiser had ordered Boetticher to tell the
ministers the impermissibility of forcing Köller to resign (so
Eulenburg telegraphed to Hohenlohe) because Köller had possessed
the confidence of the monarch and, if for no other reason, because
of the impression that this step would have with the Social Democrats.[46]   The Kaiser further stated to Boetticher that, if necessary, he would reprimand Köller in the Ministry of State. Instead,
the Kaiser had said (Eulenburg continued to convey the words of
the Kaiser), the ministry had forced him to dismiss Köller. It
was this act of *"majorisieren"* of the monarch that called for concession to an offended king. The "satisfaction" suggested by the
monarch was the resignation of the whole ministry, whereupon the
Kaiser would accept only the resignation of Köller. While Eulenburg begged Hohenlohe to accept this suggestion, he was also quite
anxious to point out that Wilhelm did not hold Hohenlohe responsible
and that, to the contrary, the Kaiser still had full confidence in
the Chancellor and looked upon Bronsart as the originator of the
entire crisis. Eulenburg closed by asking for a personal conference
between the Chancellor and the monarch to effect a compromise, as
well as hinting that Posadowsky would be an acceptable successor
to Köller.[47]

The Kaiser had actually not been as lenient toward the ministry
and to the Chancellor as Eulenburg indicated to Hohenlohe. He
had envisioned (it is perhaps more correct to say that he had been
led to request) not just the resignation of the ministry but a
public resignation. While Eulenburg defended the first idea, he
pointed out that a public resignation would reveal the true reason
for Köller's dismissal, would completely discredit the entire
ministry in the eyes of the public, would result in a Chancellor
crisis—a development which had to be avoided—and would impair
the stability of the government. Consequently, Eulenburg tried
to get Wilhelm to agree to observe strict secrecy about the cause
of Köller's dismissal. It was necessary to prove that dismissal
did not mean a change of system, and taking action against the
Social Democrats would be visible proof enough.[48]

Immediately upon returning to Berlin early on December 4, the
Kaiser sent Lucanus to inform Hohenlohe of his latest opinions on
the crisis. Rather than having all ministers resign, Wilhelm now
thought it better to let no minister resign—not even Köller.

Köller should be given a few months' vacation, and during this interval the Minister of Justice should take his place. The ministers and Hohenlohe, having partly drafted another letter of resignation justifying the action against Köller,[49] found this new proposal unacceptable. Hohenlohe, accepting the advice of Eulenburg, then met the Kaiser in person. The ministers were ready to accept the first proposal of the Kaiser, that is, a joint resignation of which then only Köller's would be accepted. However, they opposed the idea of the vacation. They had thus decided that Hohenlohe should talk to the Kaiser, and if an interview with Hohenlohe were refused by the monarch, they would hand in their collective resignation.[50] The interview was basically successful—at least Wilhelm apparently accepted Köller's resignation and dropped the idea of a vacation. Both, however, stood by their previous arguments. The Kaiser bitterly complained about the Ministry of State and especially about Boetticher and Marschall; Hohenlohe defended the action against Köller using arguments along the same lines as his letter to Wilhelm on December 1. As far as a suitable replacement for Köller, the Kaiser rejected Studt and Zedlitz and, although not rejecting Posadowsky, wanted him to complete the budget. Consequently, as Hohenlohe noted, "they had to continue to search." For the rest of the evening Wilhelm showed no signs of undue wrath or emotions—"again very content."[51]

In their next regular ministry meeting on December 5 the ministers held on to their choice of Studt, but dropped Zedlitz and Posadowsky, suggesting now in second place Regierungs-president Richthofen in Köln. Among the many others considered was also Regierungs-präsident von der Recke in Düsseldorf. In contrast to the other candidates, the only thing the ministers apparently had against von der Recke was that he was too little known.[52] Hohenlohe was to submit the two names, Studt and Zedlitz, to the Kaiser, who had meanwhile, after his short stop-over in Berlin, gone on to Hannover in company with Lucanus (having exchanged the chief of the Military Cabinet in Breslau with the chief of the Civil Cabinet). Lucanus was suspected by Hohenlohe and others as coveting the vacant post for himself,[53] so much so that Hohenlohe even asked—after considerable thought—Lucanus to become minister.[54] At any rate, while in Hannover the Kaiser again rejected Studt (a decision Hohenlohe personally was in favor of and had possibly indicated in some manner to the Kaiser), but offered the post of minister to the second choice, von Richthofen. Richthofen declined, and only then did the Kaiser ask von der Recke, who accepted.[55]

5

Eulenburg had continually been kept informed by Holstein, Bülow, and Lucanus[56] after the Kaiser's departure from Breslau until the nomination and acceptance of von der Recke. However, Eulenburg seemed reluctant to advise the Kaiser on any one individual candidate. Rather, he applied himself to a more crucial task: the rehabilitation of the Chancellor and the ministry in the eyes of the monarch, thus providing the necessary counterweight to the defamations of Köller and the Military Cabinet. Eulenburg had basically sided with the Kaiser and had condemned the actions of

the ministry.[57]   Yet he had also recognized the necessity of maintaining some balance between the cabinets and the responsible
ministries. This balance was in danger of being impaired as a
result of the Köller crisis. First, there was the danger of the
cabinets discrediting the ministry (and by implication the Chancellor), which would strengthen these bodies to such an extent as to
overwhelm completely the ministry. On the other hand, the success
of the ministry in having gotten Köller's resignation might lead
to an overestimation of their own power and inspire them to actions
smacking of western parliamentary procedure, and might even mean
ministerial control over the Kaiser. By December 6, Eulenburg
clearly regarded the extension of ministerial power as the most
acute danger. While having been successful to an extent, Eulenburg
wrote to Bülow that it was yet very necessary to denounce Köller's
insinuation that the decisions of the ministry were arrived at by
way of a ministerial vote. Then Eulenburg continued, "I observe
. . . that the success of that first ultimatum which brought about
Köller's fall encourages Holstein to make use of this situation.
Here he comes close to the Badenese views of Marschall, to the
south German feelings of Hohenlohe, to the ideas of revenge of
Bronsart, and even to the old Democrat Miquel." In this last
sentence, to be sure, there certainly was some truth.[58]   He had
tried to forestall (if necessary at the expense of the ministry)
Holstein's experiments, which were "dangerous as well as useless"
and which the Köller experience might encourage him to pursue by
emphasizing the unity of Chancellor and Kaiser.[59]   To accomplish
this goal, Eulenburg wrote to both Hohenlohe and Wilhelm. To the
Chancellor he pointed out how imperative it was to avoid any
renewed appearance of coercion of the Kaiser on the part of the
ministry in selecting a successor to Köller. Eulenburg remarked
that he had never seen the Kaiser more excited, or more depressed,
than in Breslau. "Were He to get the impression," Eulenburg
warned, "that the ministry to which He had to submit in the case
of Köller takes advantage of its victory, then either a storm will
occur which changes everything and scares the world, or there occurs
a state of the soul which I fear more: the loss of self-confidence."
The self-confidence of the monarch, Eulenburg explained, was absolutely necessary, since with its loss the Kaiser would completely
fall under the influence of Lucanus or some other person. The position of Lucanus, Eulenburg added, would also be greatly enhanced
if the ministry were to prevent the Kaiser from appointing him as
Köller's successor (if this doubtful possibility were actually to
become likely). It would be, Eulenburg worried, a very dangerous
experiment to present the candidates (Studt and Richthofen) in the
form of ultimata inspired by the fear of a remote Lucanus candi-
dacy. Eulenburg placed the greatest emphasis on direct talks
between Wilhelm and Hohenlohe as the form for ending the crisis:
"Should the ministers not submit to that which Your Highness has
discussed and agreed upon with His Majesty, then another dismissal
of this or that minister would enormously strengthen the position
of Your Highness in the eyes of His Majesty. . . ." This would be
true even in the case of Lucanus as minister, since not all ministers would resign and an acceptance of Lucanus despite opposition
would be a form of "reparation and return service."[60]

It is clear that the consequences of Eulenburg's advice to
Hohenlohe would have been the end of responsible government. A
Hohenlohe isolated and even estranged from his ministers and secretaries would never have been able on any issue to stand firm against
a Kaiser supported by the cabinets and Eulenburg. The Chancellor
would become subordinate to and dominated by the Kaiser and, by
implication, to that person or group who controlled the Kaiser.
At the same time, it would deprive the persons or institutions
opposing this "personal rule" of a legal and formal means of
opposition. Specifically, Holstein, Marschall, Bronsart, and
Berlepsch could no longer use the Chancellor as a tool to support
their own positions in their struggle against the unofficial advisors or, as Eulenburg was to see it, against the Kaiser.

The complementary step of Eulenburg's maneuver with regard to
Hohenlohe was to mollify the Kaiser. As in his letters to Hohenlohe, Eulenburg emphasized to Wilhelm that the "center of all
actions" should be based on agreement between Chancellor and
Kaiser. He pointed out that the Chancellor could not allow himself to be used by other forces. If disagreements could not be
avoided at times, the configuration of the Kaiser and Chancellor
opposed to the ministers was permissible (*denkbar*)—never, however,
Minister-president and all the ministers opposed to the Kaiser!
On the immediate question at hand—the appointment of a Minister
of Interior—Eulenburg placed little importance. Although pointing
out Studt, he made it clear that it did not really matter who would
succeed Köller so long as the Chancellor and the Kaiser were in
agreement.[61] Last, almost in the form of an appendix, Eulenburg
justified his action in the crisis to such diverse personalities
as Lucanus and Holstein.[62] With the official dismissal of Köller
(although he retained his title of minister and received the Order
of the Red Eagle, First Class) and the official appointment of
von der Recke, the crisis was considered solved.[63]

6

With the dismissal of Köller and the nomination of von der
Recke as his replacement on December 8, the crisis could have been
over. However, the ousted minister took the opportunity, now that
he was free from ministerial responsibility, to attack his former
colleagues (in particular Marschall and Boetticher) in the press,
and found a very sympathetic response even with the Kaiser.

The *Saale Zeitung* in particular published a Köller interview
which held Boetticher and Marschall responsible for the crisis.
Notwithstanding Köller's denial of its authenticity (but only after
an official *dementi* of the accusations had been made), Köller did
not clearly deny the truth of the statements as such, nor did the
Saale Zeitung back down from its assertion of authenticity.[64] The
crisis, which had begun as a "Bronsart-Köller" crisis, had then
changed into a ministerial and Chancellor crisis, now took on a
new aspect as another "Marschall" crisis. Even Eulenburg felt it
opportune to add in a eulogistic letter to Hohenlohe that the
Kaiser would definitely retain Miquel and Thielen as ministers
and that a change in the other ministerial positions would not be
considered seriously. "I only mention this to Your Highness,"

Eulenburg wrote, "because very likely the traditional oppositions
between Miquel and others (particularly Marschall and Holstein) will
eventually rise again," even if momentarily the cooperation against
Köller had created a kind of "comradeship-in-arms."[65]

Köller and the press campaign against Marschall and Boetticher
were by no means the only obstacles in overcoming the unusual state
of tension that had existed since the middle of November. The Kaiser
himself was rather uncooperative. At precisely the time when Eulenburg was spending considerable effort in consoling Hohenlohe and
when he was proposing stabilization of affairs on the basis of a
common accord between Chancellor and Kaiser, Wilhelm paid a visit
to Waldersee and then went to Friedrichsruh without prior notifi-
cation of—let alone consultation with—Hohenlohe. This added to
the already ample material for speculation in the press. Hohenlohe
accepted this fact passively,[66] but could only have seen it as a
deliberate affront to him. Marschall and Holstein immediately and
actively protested to Eulenburg, and the latter tried to excuse
the monarch's action as a small act of revenge for the Köller
crisis, and emphasized that the confidence of the Kaiser in Hohenlohe was as strong as ever.[67]

"The poison," Eulenburg wrote to Hohenlohe, "which the insulted
Köller poured into the goblet of the Kaiser, is devilish because
it will have a long-lasting effect."[68]   In this Eulenburg was
absolutely correct, especially when he himself contributed to such
an effect. Eulenburg supported the Kaiser's interpretation of the
events as revealing inexcusable ministerial insubordination, and
agreed that satisfaction must be given by the ministry.[69]   Hohenlohe
was not in a mood to continue his opposition to the Kaiser, a role
that he had taken up only reluctantly and which had been a considerable embarrassment to him. Now that the crisis was over, with the
appointment of von der Recke and with the Kaiser's statement that
although condemning the action of the ministry, he continued to
have confidence in that body,[70] Hohenlohe became even more submis-
sive than was usually the case, in order to regain the confidence
of the Kaiser.[71]

Eulenburg had, to a degree, also intrigued against Hohenlohe
and taken sides with the chief of the Military Cabinet, Hahnke,
and the Kaiser on the question of the military penal code reform
itself.[72] He consoled Wilhelm over the loss of Köller by saying
that Köller's political role had not at all ended and, if need be,
he could always be recalled.[73]   Eulenburg further gave no evidence
that he tried to eliminate the Kaiser's distrust of Marschall and
Boetticher and the devious role that they were alleged to have
played in the action of the ministry. In fact, he noted that "it
is not incorrect, what His Majesty told me."[74]   To Holstein he
wrote on the same subject, "Marschall has to be cleared; that is
a main point and I will do everything I can."[75]   However, this
assertion was true only to a very limited extent. Eulenburg had
received a letter from Wilhelm informing him that his own investigations had proven that Marschall alone was responsible for the
Köller crisis. Wilhelm further revealed that "his source" had
characterized Marschall as a thoroughly south German character
"who had not the faintest idea of the King of Prussia, and who
has neither appreciation, nor interest, whatsoever for him and

his unique position, thank God." In Marschall's eyes, continued
Wilhelm's source, it was the Ministry of State that was to command
and to govern and to whom even the king had to submit. The
Münchener Neueste Nachrichten article had been, according to Wilhelm, traced back with considerable certainty to the press bureau
with which Marschall had connections. During a conversation that
Wilhelm had had with Hohenlohe several weeks previously, he had
told Hohenlohe, to the consternation of the Chancellor and his own
secret pleasure, that Marschall aspired to become Chancellor. Then
he had outlined the following program for Hohenlohe: Marschall and
Boetticher would have to leave in the spring after the budget
debates; Boetticher, to be replaced by Posadowsky, would become
Oberpräsident in Magdeburg; and Marschall, to be replaced by Bülow
(who would also get the vice-presidency of the Ministry of State),
would be given an embassy. Wilhelm continued his letter to
Eulenburg:

> Bernhard, my loyal, devoted friend who stands sky-
> high above the parliamentarized ministers in regard to
> reason and energy, will again for me ride the old stal-
> lions with such a tight rein that they will toe the line
> and that they finally learn what it means to be a Prussian
> minister.
>   After all, the Prussian element must again become
> dominant since this alone indeed holds the Reich together
> and the Prince is too old—he cannot look after both the
> foreign affairs and the Ministry of State—and the present
> Vice President is a cowardly wash rag. Bülow is to become
> my Bismarck and just as he threw the Reich together like
> Grandpapa, externally, so do we both domestically want to
> end the chaos of parliamentarism and party cliche.
>   The old uncle was in agreement with my proposals.[76]

Consequently, Eulenburg had to make sure that Marschall was not
dismissed in the near future. Yet despite Marschall's recapitula-
tion of the Köller affair in two long exposés (December 20 and
December 29, which Eulenburg had requested), Eulenburg only
cautiously indicated to Wilhelm that Marschall in fact might not
have been playing the leading role,[77] and then he and Bülow
planned Marschall's careful removal from office at a time of their
own choosing.

7

On November 24 the Hamburger Nachrichten took the opportunity
to refute an article that had appeared some time earlier (perhaps
significantly in the Berliner Tageblatt, whose editor, Levysohn,
was in touch with the Foreign Office[78]) on the Cabinet Order of
1852. The Hamburger Nachrichten maintained that the Cabinet Order
had not forbidden the various ministers to give direct reports to
the monarch unless consented to by the Minister-president, but had
only given the Minister-president the right to be present. The
reason for the order had been to maintain necessary unity within
the ministry—a condition still extremely desirable in the interest
of Prussia and the Reich, with or without the Cabinet Order.[79]
  This was an exposition by Bismarck in which he defended the

powers of the king and at the same time emphasized the need for
enforced unity of the Ministry of State. It was not the differences
of opinion between Köller and the rest of the ministers so much as
Köller's violation of ministerial etiquette that had caused his
dismissal. Thus it is hardly possible to speak of ministerial
rebellion as such but, rather, preservation of an existing formal
structure that had been threatened by one minister.

In fact, it is difficult to substantiate any rebellious mood
on the part of the ministers before, during, or after the crisis.
To be sure, Bronsart had given vent to his frustration by suggesting the collective resignation of the ministry in order to bring
the Kaiser to his senses.[80] However, he had actually remained in
office, despite trying and even embarrassing situations; nor did
he go so far as to support the ministry in its collective stand
against Köller and in face of the Kaiser. Bosse on his part often
confided to his diary opinions similar to Bronsart's. However,
he was apparently a somewhat weak personality and rather dependent upon opinions of others, notably Miquel. When the
time came to take action, Bosse always found excuses.

The real significance of the Köller crisis lay in the degree
of intensity and the outcome of the struggle between the unofficial
advisors of the crown (to whom Köller had appealed and had in a
sense joined) and the official government. On the one side we
find the Military Cabinet, the Naval Cabinet, the Civil Cabinet,
and Eulenburg; on the other (in order to maintain and defend, not
extend, their power) we find Marschall, Holstein, the ministers,
and finally the Minister-president.

Having gained control, to a degree, over the Kaiser, it was
necessary for the unofficial advisors to also subordinate the
Minister-president. However, with the support of the ministers,
specifically Marschall and Holstein, Hohenlohe was made to stand
his ground and resist the opposing forces and the Kaiser. However,
while forced to resist and thereby formally winning the contest of
strength, Hohenlohe's will to resist collapsed in the process and
gave way to full cooperation with the Kaiser. While he formally
maintained his position as Minister-president and official advisor
to the crown, he actually came close to abdicating his post. The
repercussions of this fact for the ministers were that while they
had achieved their goal of maintaining a status quo, Hohenlohe's
personal capitulation had seriously tipped the balance to their
disadvantage. It also had the effect of forcing Holstein to take
more direct action to safeguard the position of the
bureaucracy.[81]

In broader perspective, the effects of the crisis were not
what they should have been but were, in fact, precisely what they
should not have been—namely, the dismantling of the government,
the Hohenlohe Ministry. This process began visibly in June with
the resignation of Berlepsch, soon followed by the dismissal of
Bronsart in August, and ended in June, 1897, with the total
collapse of the New Course. To a considerable degree the Köller
crisis may be viewed as the ministerial equivalent of the *Daily
Telegraph* affair of 1908.

NOTES

1. See *Holsteins Papiere*, III, 502, note 5; Röhl, *Germany without Bismarck*, p. 142; *Schulthess*, 1895, p. 197.

2. See Lerchenfeld to Crailsheim, 6.XI.95, telegram and letter, G.S.A. München, MA 77751.

3. See *Hohenlohe*, III, 123, note; it is interesting to note that at this very time the Ministry of State had initiated legal action against "Unknowns" for apparent indiscretions to the press in connection with the sugar-premium bill. The Literary Bureau, an office of Köller's Ministry of Interior, was suspected, especially since the indiscretions also appeared in "Köller's" newspaper. See Prussian Ministry of State minutes, 5.XII.95, 19.XII.95 (Deutsches Zentral Archiv, Abt. Merseburg, Rep. 90a BIII2b No. 6) vol. 120, and 16.III.96, 20.III.96, vol. 122.

4. See below, pp. 211ff.

5. Röhl, *Germany without Bismarck*, p. 142; Marschall Diary, 16.XI.95; Ministry of State minutes, 13.XI.95, 18.XI.95, vols. 119, 120, DZA Merseburg.

6. See particularly Lerchenfeld to Crailsheim, 3.XII.95, G.S.A. München, MA 77751: ". . . Köller, since his unlucky campaign in the Reichstag on occasion of the anti-revolutionary bill, was considered as unfit for his post also amongst his colleagues"—the more so since Köller had continuously agitated against various ministers. Lerchenfeld to Crailsheim, 14.XII.95, G.S.A. München, Ges. Berlin, 1066. Hohenthal, on the other hand, no doubt intentionally wrote that Köller seemed to have not too many friends in the ministry. See his report, 4.XII.95, Sächs. H.S.A., Ges. Berlin, 5.XII.95; Württ. H.S.A., Ges. Berlin, E 73, Fasz. 61.

7. See Hutten-Czapski to Holstein, 15.XI.95, Rich, *Holstein*, II, 501-502. On Bronsart and Hahnke, see also Schmidt-Bückeburg, *Militärkabinett*, pp. 196ff.; Röhl, *Germany without Bismarck*, pp. 181-182.

8. See Röhl, *Germany without Bismarck*, p. 136.

9. See *ibid.*, p. 142; see also Marschall to Eulenburg, 29.XII.95, B.A. Eul. 39.

10. See also Köller to Hohenlohe, 20.XI.95, and Bronsart to Hohenlohe, 27.XI.95, Archiv Schillingsfürst, Rep. 100 XXII A-6.

11. Marschall Diary, 26.XI.95.

12. See Bosse Diary, 19.XI.95, B.A. Bosse, No. 8.

13. See Marschall Diary, 26.XI.95.

14. See *ibid.*, 26.XI.95, 27.XI.95; Röhl, *Germany without Bismarck*, p. 142.

15. Marschall Diary, 28.XI.95; however, one suspects it was not with Köller but with the *maison militaire*.

16. Marschall to Eulenburg, 20.XII.95, B.A. Eul. 39.

17. Hohenlohe Journal, 27.XI.95, *Hohenlohe*, II, 125-126.

18. *Ibid.*, p. 126.

19. Marschall Diary, 28.XI.95; *Hohenlohe*, III, 126; Hohenlohe
Aufz., 2.XII.95, Archiv Schillingsfürst, Rep. 100 XXII A-6.

20. Marschall to Eulenburg, 20.XII.95, B.A. Eul. 39.

21. *Hohenlohe*, III, 126-127.

22. Called for by either Boetticher or Hohenlohe. Marschall
Diary, 29.XI.95, reads: ". . . Boetticher, who seems to wish a
talk about Köller question. The Prince is somewhat hesitant
(*schwankend*), but Holstein and I strengthen him." Marschall's
résumé for Eulenburg reads: ". . . Boetticher told me that upon
the wish of the Prince a conference of the ministers . . . is to
take place in the afternoon." Bosse wrote: "Boetticher invited
. . . me. . . ." Bosse Diary, 29.XI.95, B.A. Bosse, No. 8. See
also *Hohenlohe*, III, 127, where Hohenlohe does not directly mention
that he asked for the meeting. It might well be that in his
résumé for Eulenburg Marschall intended to de-emphasize the role
of Boetticher and emphasize that of Hohenlohe as Minister-president.
However, it would not seem incorrect to interpret this act as an
independent step of "the ministers." See also King, "Marschall,"
p. 181.

23. Hohenlohe Journal, 29.XI.95, *Hohenlohe*, III, 127.

24. See Jagemann report, 1.XII.95, G.L.A. Karlsruhe, Ges.
Berlin, 49-2028.

25. Bosse Diary, 29.XI.95, B.A. Bosse, No. 8; see also *Hohenlohe*,
III, 127.

26. Marschall Diary, 29.XI.95.

27. *Ibid.*, 30.XI.95.

28. See *Hohenlohe*, III, 127, and Bosse Diary, 29.XI.95, B.A.
Bosse, No. 8.

29. See *Hohenlohe*, III, 135, note; Engelberg, *Deutschland*,
pp. 372f.

30. See Bosse Diary, 30.XI.95, B.A. Bosse, No. 8. Hohenlohe
emphasized, however, that the crisis had not come about as a result
of this action, as indicated in the press. See Saxon embassy
reports, 3.XII.95, 4.XII.95, 11.XII.95, Sächs. H.S.A., Ges.
Berlin, No. 250.

31. See Bosse Diary, 30.XI.95, 1.XII.95, B.A. Bosse, No. 8;
Marschall Diary, 1.XII.95; Marschall to Eulenburg, 1.XII.95,
B.A. Eul. 39; *Hohenlohe*, III, 128-130, to be supplemented by the
drafts of Hohenlohe to Wilhelm in the Journal in Archiv Schillingsfürst, Rep. 100 XXII A-6. See also Marschall's account to Eulenburg in which he anxiously emphasized the point that the ministers
thought it not permissible to force the Kaiser to choose between
Köller and the ministry, and that consequently Köller was asked
to hand in his resignation before the Kaiser was asked to dismiss
him. Marschall to Eulenburg, 20.XII.95, B.A. Eul. 39.

32. See Marschall Diary, 2.XII.95; Bosse Diary, 2.XII.95, B.A. Bosse, No. 8.

33. See Holstein to Eulenburg, 29.XI.95 (two communications), B.A. Eul. 39.

34. See Marschall Diary, 26.XI.95: "In the evening talked with Boetticher, who talks about a reconciliation Bronsart-Köller, but then however, realizes that the matter is of more profound nature." However, it was the same evening that Boetticher suggested to Köller a reconciliation with Bronsart in the form of a personal apology. This Köller did on the same day. See Marschall Diary, 27.XI.95; King, "Marschall," p. 181.

35. Holstein to Bülow, 29.XI.95, B.A. Eul. 39, see also in Rich, *Holstein*, II, 508-509.

36. Bülow to Eulenburg, 29.XI.95, B.A. Eul. 39.

37. See Bülow to Eulenburg, 29-30.XI.95, B.A. Eul. 39.

38. However, he was perhaps better informed than he implied, since it was Eulenburg who "was taken by fear" and telegraphed to Holstein for information. See Eulenburg to Holstein, 29.XI.95, *Holsteins Papiere*, III, 509.

39. See especially Marschall Diary, 30.XI.95.

40. Eulenburg to Wilhelm, 29.XI.95, and Eulenburg to Hohenlohe, 29.XI.95, B.A. Eul. 39; Eulenburg to Holstein, 29.XI.95, *Holsteins Papiere*, III, 509.

41. See Bosse Diary, 2.XII.95, B.A. Bosse, No. 8.

42. See *ibid.*, 5.XII.95.

43. *Ibid.*, 2.XII.95.

44. Eulenburg to Hohenlohe, 3.XII.95, B.A. Eul. 39; see also *Hohenlohe*, III, 132; Marschall Diary, 3.XII.95.

45. Wilhelm to Lucanus, 2.XII.95, Meisner, "Hohenlohe," p. 46.

46. Probably this order was given after November 29, the day on which Köller had undertaken the police action against the Social Democratic associations in Berlin.

47. Eulenburg to Hohenlohe, 3.XII.95, *Hohenlohe*, III, 132-133; also in B.A. Eul. 39; see also letter of Eulenburg to Hohenlohe of same date, *Hohenlohe*, III, 133-134, in which he made essentially the same suggestions as in the telegram but emphasized the emotions of Wilhelm.

48. See Eulenburg to Wilhelm, 3.XII.95, B.A. Eul. 39; see also the Eulenburg Promemoria, 3.XII.95, B.A. Eul. 39.

49. See Hohenlohe to Wilhelm, 4.XII.95, Archiv Schillingsfürst, Rep. 100 XXII A-6. The draft was not finished. It might be that Hohenlohe drafted the letter after his interview with Wilhelm.

50. Bosse Diary, 4.XII.95, B.A. Bosse, No. 8; see also *Hohenlohe*, III, 134; Marschall Diary, 4.XII.95.

51. See Hohenlohe Journal, 4.XII.95, *Hohenlohe*, III, 134-135; Marschall Diary, 4.XII.95, 5.XII.95; Bosse Diary, 5.XII.95, B.A. Bosse, No. 8; Hohenlohe to Eulenburg, 5.XII.95, B.A. Eul. 39.

52. See Bosse Diary, 5.XII.95, B.A. Bosse, No. 8. It is interesting to note that Lerchenfeld pointed out that von der Recke had already been for some time on the list of candidates for an eventual vacancy of the Köller post and got immediate consideration at the time of Köller's dismissal. Lerchenfeld to Crailsheim, 11.XII.95, G.S.A. München, Ges. Berlin, 1066. Hohenthal even mentioned that Hohenlohe, having had some difficulties with Köller in Alsace-Lorraine before 1894, had hoped to replace Köller (who had become minister upon the insistence of the Kaiser) as early as 1894 with von der Recke, who had been "warmly recommended" to him. See report of 11.XII.95, Sächs. H.S.A., Ges. Berlin, No. 250. Very similar is Varnbühler to Mittnacht, 5.XII.95, Württ. H.S.A., Ges. Berlin, E 73, Fasz. 61.

53. See Marschall Diary, 5.XII.95; Holstein to Eulenburg, two communications, 5.XII.95, B.A. Eul. 39; Hohenlohe Journal, 4.XII.95, *Hohenlohe*, III, 135. Holstein suspected that Lucanus had intrigued against acceptable candidates so as to occupy the post himself.

54. See Hutten-Czapski, *Sechzig Jahre*, I, 285-286; Hohenthal report, 4.XII.95, Sächs. H.S.A., Ges. Berlin, No. 250.

55. Lucanus to Hohenlohe, 7.XII.95, and Hohenlohe to Eulenburg, 8.XII.95, Archiv Schillingsfürst, Rep. 100 XXII A-6; Marschall Diary, 7.XII.95; Hohenthal report, 9.XII.95, Sächs. H.S.A., Ges. Berlin, No. 250. On the crisis in general, see also the Jagemann reports of 3, 4, 5, 9, and 10.XII.95, G.L.A. Karlsruhe, Ges. Berlin, 49-2028.

56. See Holstein to Eulenburg, 5.XII.95 (twice); Lucanus to Eulenburg, 5.XII.95; and Bülow to Eulenburg, 5.XII.95 (twice), all in B.A. Eul. 39.

57. See above, pp. 136-37, and also Eulenburg Promemoria, 3.XII.95, B.A. Eul. 39.

58. Herzfeld, *Miquel*, II, 435, where he speaks of a "deep aversion against Prussia."

59. Eulenburg to Bülow, 6.XII.95, B.A. Eul. 39.

60. Eulenburg to Hohenlohe, 6.XII.95, B.A. Eul. 39.

61. Eulenburg to Wilhelm, 6.XII.95, B.A. Eul. 39.

62. See Eulenburg to Lucanus, 17.XII.95, B.A. Eul. 39; Eulenburg to Holstein, 7.XII.95, *Holsteins Papiere*, III, 510-512.

63. See Eulenburg to Hohenlohe, 8.XII.95, Archiv Schillingsfürst, Rep. 100 XXII A-6; Marschall Diary, 8.XII.95, 9.XII.95; Hohenlohe to Eulenburg, 8.XII.95, B.A. Eul. 39; Bosse Diary, 8.XII.95, B.A. Bosse, No. 8.

64. See Marschall Diary, 10, 11, 13, 15, and 16.XII.95; Hohenlohe Journal, ca. 10.XII.95, Archiv Schillingsfürst, Rep. 100 XXII A-6; Köller to Hohenlohe, 11.XII.95, *ibid.*; Wilmowski to Hohenlohe, 11.XII.95, *ibid.*

65. Eulenburg to Hohenlohe, 13.XII.95, B.A. Eul. 39.

66. Holstein to Eulenburg, ca. 26.XII.95, B.A. Eul. 39.

67. See Marschall to Eulenburg, 18.XII.95, B.A. Eul. 39; Eulenburg to Hohenlohe, 19.XII.95, *Hohenlohe*, III, 143-144; Lerchenfeld to Crailsheim, 24.XII.95, G.S.A. München, Ges. Berlin, 1066; Hohenthal reports, 18.XII.95, 24.XII 95, Sächs. H.S.A., Ges. Berlin, No. 250; Jagemann report, 18.XII.95, G.L.A. Karlsruhe, Ges. Berlin, 49-2028.

68. *Hohenlohe*, III, 142.

69. Haller, *Eulenburg*, p. 161; Rich, *Holstein*, II, 497.

70. See Bosse Diary, 12.XII.95, B.A. Bosse, No. 8.

71. See especially Hohenlohe to Eulenburg, 9.XII.95, and Eulenburg's eulogistic reply, 13.XII.95, B.A. Eul. 39; also see Haller, *Eulenburg*, p. 224; Eulenburg to Holstein, 13.XII.95, *Holsteins Papiere*, III, 512; and Rich, *Holstein*, II, 509.

72. Hutten-Czapski, *Sechzig Jahre*, I, 250, 283.

73. Haller, *Eulenburg*, p. 159.

74. *Ibid.*, p. 161.

75. *Ibid.*, p. 189.

76. Wilhelm to Eulenburg, 25.XII.95, B.A. Eul. 39. See also Rich, *Holstein*, II, 501.

77. Eulenburg to Wilhelm, 2.I.96, B.A. Eul. 40.

78. See below, p. 226.

79. Hofmann, *Fürst Bismarck*, II, 335-337.

80. Röhl, *Germany without Bismarck*, p. 136. Compare also Herzfeld, *Miquel*, II, 455, 460ff.

81. See also the sound assessment of the crisis in Engelberg, *Deutschland 1871-1897*, p. 373.

PART III

CHAPTER 9

From Ministerial Crisis
to Chancellor Crisis

Increasing rift between Hohenlohe and Marschall.
After Hohenlohe's success in Köller crisis and the
Engelbrecht affair Holstein, Marschall and Bronsart
push for a decisive crisis, which is to break the
authority of the Kaiser and make him surrender.

Eulenburg to Bülow, March 3, 1896

The clique Holstein-Marschall-Bronsart cannot
possibly weaken dangerously, or even permanently,
our *Maitre*, as long as His Majesty will only remain
patient and sober-minded. If the Kaiser, however,
makes mistakes, it will harm him much more than
anything which this trio may be able to come up with.

Bülow to Eulenburg, March 20, 1896

1

The wrath that Köller had stirred up in the Kaiser with his insinuations against the ministry (as Eulenburg had written to
Hohenlohe) would have a long-lasting effect. Köller's consequent
press campaign certainly contributed its share, and the various
groups and cliques used the crisis as a welcome means to attack the
positions of Marschall, Boetticher, and the New Course with renewed
hope for success.

As shown previously, Eulenburg, although not taking the side of
Hohenlohe, had felt it necessary to defend the Chancellor and
Marschall to the degree of allowing them to continue in office.
However, Eulenburg was ready to place considerable blame for the
whole crisis on the shoulders of Marschall and Holstein—before, as
well as after, the events of the Köller crisis.

Throughout the Köller crisis Holstein had played perhaps an
important part (more indirectly than directly), but certainly not
a key role. He had become quite suspicious of Bronsart before the
crisis had begun, even going so far as to suggest Bronsart's inconspicuous removal from office; and he continued to distrust him after
the Köller crisis had terminated. On the other hand, Holstein had
supported Marschall, Hohenlohe, and the ministry in their determined
stand. Moreover, he had tried—without much success—to influence
the selection of a successor to Köller.

Nevertheless, Eulenburg saw in Holstein one of the main figures,
perhaps even the backbone, of a crisis designed to increase ministerial power at the expense of the rights and powers of the monarch.
The irreparable rift between the two had taken place as long ago as

January, 1894. Then had come the clarification of their respective
positions in late 1894 and early 1895 in the wake of the October
crisis. The main difference perhaps between that time and November,
1895, lay in the accentuation of these different positions. To a
much greater degree than before, Eulenburg seemed to look upon
Holstein as a personal antagonist of Wilhelm. Eulenburg had had
difficulty in clearly distinguishing between personal, private relationships and public, political duties; as Holstein was to put it,
Eulenburg worked for Imperial whims rather than for the true interests of Kaiser and Reich.[1] With regard to Holstein, this confusion
had reached such proportions by late 1895 that the two spheres had
in fact become practically identical, that is, so personal that
Eulenburg remained irrevocably opposed to and could hardly understand Holstein's position. Holstein's criticism, however, went far
beyond mere personal motives (as has been pointed out before,
Holstein was no doubt heavily influenced by Imperial interference
in "his foreign policy" and by his fear of Bismarck)—in contrast
to Eulenburg, no matter how altruistic Eulenburg's personal motives
may have been.

In Eulenburg's opinion (as conveyed to Bülow on November 12,
1895) a new kind of conflict had developed between Holstein and the
unsuspecting Kaiser. It was the result of the "progressively
developing political understanding" of the monarch, which expressed
itself in his progressively independent interference in foreign
policy. This situation was intolerable to Holstein. Only
if a real reconciliation between the Kaiser and Bismarck were to
come about (and this was very unlikely) would Holstein's opposition
to the monarch break into the open. As things stood at that moment,
however, Holstein would not "abandon his most powerful comrade-in-
arms" against the monarch, namely Bismarck! Unfortunately, in the
present state of affairs "Holstein's genius" was irreplaceable.
Eulenburg was caught between Holstein and the Kaiser. "We can,"
he wrote to Bülow, "not possibly dispense with Holstein's genius in
such a difficult situation as is the present one; and on the other
hand, the quick action of His Majesty may, especially in such a
situation, easily cause incidents. That creates for me downright
unbearable predicaments."[2]

Thus the Köller affair had only strengthened Eulenburg's convictions about Holstein, but the crisis had not changed the necessity
of Holstein's guiding hand in foreign affairs. These differences
could not be solved; the task of Eulenburg had become harder. In
the words of Bülow, Eulenburg could only "mitigate, conciliate,
delay." Bülow agreed with Eulenburg's analysis. With just a
slight change in accentuation of the picture Eulenburg had presented,
Bülow portrayed Holstein, Marschall, and Hohenlohe as a solitary
group drawn together by a similar general conception of affairs
(*Gesamtauffassung*). This equation Bülow followed by suggesting to
Eulenburg that "Holstein, as well as Marschall and Hohenlohe, would,
were they to believe that His Majesty would never and under no
circumstances turn to their various enemies (Schweinitz, Waldersee,
Bismarck, Zedlitz, Miquel, Botho Eulenburg, etc. etc.), only see
the contradictions between themselves and His Majesty; and consequently would find the latter increasingly disagreeable and would
want to constrict him more and more. . . ." Bülow continued that

it might not be a bad idea for that trio to know that they were
expendable, that the Kaiser could "in last analysis pretty much do
as he likes and take just about anyone that he wants."[3] While
Eulenburg could justifiably view Bismarck as the "great ally" of
Holstein, at the same time Eulenburg and Bülow were able to use
Bismarck as a threat to keep Holstein, Marschall, and even Hohenlohe in line.

Hohenlohe's determination to resist the wishes and demands of
the Kaiser had been severely impaired as a result of the Köller
crisis, and it is doubtful that Bülow's estimate of him was a
correct one. On the other hand, Holstein did, in fact, become more
determined to limit the influence of the Kaiser. By late December
he could cite further embarrassing incidents. In October, 1895, for
instance, the Kaiser had reacted violently to the suggestion of the
British ambassador in Berlin, Sir Edward Malet, that Germany's
Transvaal policy might have serious repercussions in England. In
mid-December of the same year Wilhelm, during a conversation with
the British military attaché, Swaine, accused England of an
intentionally ambiguous policy and as much as asked England to
join the Triple Alliance.[4] The Köller crisis had shown that Wilhelm,
when confronted with determined opposition by the Chancellor (or
perhaps even by a minister), would back down. It was the combination of these factors which gave rise to their second memorable
exchange of letters arguing for their personal convictions over
political principles in December and January of 1895-96.

One day after the Kaiser's visit to Bismarck in Friedrichsruh,
Holstein expressed his doubt to Eulenburg that the Hohenlohe regime
would last much longer; "for that reason alone already that for the
first time in the new year we both, you and I, have not pulled on
the same rope." Although, Holstein continued, he considered himself
a royalist, he was not for absolute submission to every idea of the
Kaiser, as was Eulenburg; and, he expressed his hope that Eulenburg
would not have to reproach himself (as he did not reproach Eulenburg
now) when he realized what effects his attitude had.[5]

Changing from the general to the specific, Holstein then tried
to gain Eulenburg's assistance in strengthening Marschall and
Boetticher, who had come under heavy attack inspired and carried on
by the Bismarck Fronde (in which Holstein counted Bronsart).[6] Bronsart and Köller, who had been reconciled with Friedrichsruh, as well
as Plessen, had dropped out of the picture. Yet Marschall and
Boetticher were indispensable to Hohenlohe.[7] These specifics were
further elaborated by Holstein in practically identical telegrams
to both Eulenburg and to Bülow. He warned: "An eruption of a
crisis is not impossible since the Kaiser is irritated on account
of Köller's doings, the ministry is irritated about Köller."
Hohenlohe intended to stand and fall with Boetticher (who already
had offered his resignation, which Hohenlohe had refused) and
Marschall. Under the circumstances the Kaiser would be able to get
a coup-d'état Chancellor (since no one else would accept) who would
do violence to the Reichstag "and, depending upon the necessity,
also to the Kaiser. . . . This I prophesize and therefore I warn."[8]
This was essentially a characterization, if not exclusively so, of
Waldersee.

Eulenburg replied on December 19 in two letters—the one

concerning the specific political situation, the other replying to
Holstein's general remarks. Since both Bülow and Eulenburg regarded
the retention of Hohenlohe as a necessity and were consequently
defending and even strengthening the positions of Boetticher and
Marschall, it was easy for Eulenburg to calm Holstein on these points
without deceiving him. Eulenburg summarized the following points:
the Kaiser would absolutely not make personnel changes in the
ministry after a visit to Friedrichsruh; he would neither give way,
nor even give the appearance of giving way, to Bismarck's pressures.
Consequently, even if the Kaiser would like to, he would not dismiss Marschall or Boetticher at this time. Furthermore, the
Kaiser was so intent on keeping Hohenlohe that if the latter
expressed his need for Marschall, the Kaiser would not dismiss
Marschall even under considerably greater pressure than was being
applied at the moment. Holstein's opinion of Bronsart, Eulenburg
continued, was identical with his own; the Kaiser would "prefer to
get rid of him today rather than tomorrow." Köller's perfidies had
to be stopped, Eulenburg agreed. Yet, he continued, despite Köller's
actions and despite the recent visit to Bismarck, the domestic
situation had not changed. Eulenburg said that the possibility of
Waldersee as Chancellor was out of the question, and Hohenlohe's
position was stronger than ever.[9] It was thus easy for Eulenburg
to reply to Holstein's general considerations, that their positions
really were rather similar. As for the rest, Eulenburg brushed
it aside with seemingly calculated frivolity as a greatly appreciated
document of Holstein's friendship.[10] Holstein, however, was not to
be dissuaded from his persistence and general criticism of the Kaiser
and Eulenburg. He continued as before to bombard Eulenburg with
his disturbing and pessimistic prophecies.

In the wake of the Kaiser's interview with the British Colonel
Swaine, during which Wilhelm had said things which could, according
to the outraged Holstein, create a threat of war, Holstein again
wrote to Eulenburg. He hoped this time that Eulenburg would try to
get Hohenlohe (on his way to Vienna) to take a firmer stand against
the interference of the monarch in foreign affairs, or even try to
counsel the Kaiser directly. The Kaiser, Holstein pointed out,
had no political tact, and "initiative without tact is like a flood
without dikes." The Kaiser and the Reich were rushing toward the
abyss. ". . . It has been about a year, my dear Eulenburg," continued Holstein, "since I wrote you a letter in which I expressed
my fears about what now seems to be coming to pass. Today I warn
you again. See to it that world history does not some day picture
you as the evil spirit [*als den schwarzen Reiter*] who was at the
side of the Imperial traveller when he chose the false path." The
constant refrain was that Eulenburg ought not to close his eyes to
reality and should strengthen Hohenlohe as Chancellor in such a way
as to limit the irresponsible and dangerous acts of Wilhelm,
especially in foreign affairs. If this were not done, catastrophe
would most certainly result.[11]

The logical conclusion of Holstein's suggestions was a governmental system where, in fact, the king would have little or no
power.[12] However, an even greater defect seems to stem from a
different source. Holstein had used his "shock-method approach"
so often that Eulenburg had become quite accustomed to it, and

rather than acting on behalf of Holstein, he had become indifferent
to Holstein's advice and disgusted with the advisor. "Holstein gets
on my nerves," Eulenburg had written to Bülow, seeking reassurance.
At the same time Eulenburg informed his friend in Rome that he was
becoming more and more immune to these kinds of crises.[13] Finally,
the last reason why Holstein's threats had become largely ineffective
was because Holstein's most serious warnings had come precisely at
moments when he felt his own sphere of power specifically threatened
by Bismarck or by the Kaiser. In addition, while making his far-
sighted and astute observations on the interest of the state and
the interest of the monarch, his advice almost always coincided
with his own interest, which was the unquestioned maintenance of
absolute control over foreign affairs—and this latter appeared at
least as important as the former. This had become even more obvious
in his letters of late 1895 than in those of early 1895. Quite
understandably, then, Holstein's arguments lost much of their thrust.
Perhaps this is the main difference between the Holstein of late
1894 and the Holstein of late 1895; he had become considerably more
resigned to Eulenburg as he was. At times one has the impression
that he had given up on Eulenburg altogether and that he only hoped
to get him to act on specific issues at specific times.

The rift between Eulenburg and Holstein is all the more deplorable, since modern observers (and contemporaries too) have substantially agreed with the forebodings and prophecies of Holstein.
Holstein's premonitions have to a large extent been borne out by
later events—and even his "judgment of history" on the persons of
Wilhelm and Eulenburg has generally been verified and accepted.
Eulenburg, perhaps in conjunction with Bülow, was decisively influencing the Kaiser at a most critical time.

Knowing that he would fail with Eulenburg in his judgment of
the Kaiser, Holstein did not fare better in inducing Eulenburg to
help strengthen Hohenlohe's position as Chancellor as a counterweight to the Kaiser. Nor did Holstein's similar letters to Bülow
do any good; at least until he had been securely placed in Berlin,
Bülow ostentatiously took the side of Eulenburg. In conversations
and letters to his friend in Vienna, Bülow agreed with a few of
Holstein's factual criticisms, although they were cautiously inter-
spersed between passages of laudatory comments on Eulenburg and the
Kaiser. Perhaps Bülow realized that eventually he would take the
"place" of Holstein and would then be faced with similar impulsive
and irritating improvisations of Wilhelm.

Hohenlohe had gone to his estate in Podiebrad and intended from
there to visit Eulenburg in Vienna. Holstein had supplied Eulenburg (directly and by way of Bülow) with advice about how he should
influence the Chancellor. Bülow did likewise on December 27.
Although eulogizing Eulenburg and the Kaiser, emphasizing their
traditional Prussian royalism (*altpreussische Royalismus*), and
adding insinuations against Holstein and even vaguely hinting at
Holstein's eventual removal, Bülow accepted most of Holstein's
factual criticisms of the Kaiser's interference in foreign policy
and then gave in fact very similar advice! It is this dichotomy
—Bülow's essentially agreeing with Holstein and yet appearing
"all for Eulenburg"—that gives this letter a peculiar ring of
artificiality.[14]

Eulenburg, naturally prejudiced against Holstein's advice and
yet under the influence of Bülow, somewhat modified his position
and accepted some of Holstein's suggestions when he met with
Hohenlohe. He agreed that Hohenlohe should talk to Wilhelm, while
he would write to the Kaiser some time in the future to point out
the dangers of interference in foreign affairs, and that Hohenlohe
should confer with Wilhelm on political matters at least once a
week. However, Hohenlohe was ill equipped to fulfill the function
of a Chancellor who could do justice to Holstein's demands. He
gave every appearance of having been shocked into submitting to
Eulenburg and the Kaiser. He promised to do everything to calm
Holstein and, holding the opinion that Marschall, Holstein, and
Fischer were consciously working toward a parliamentary monarchy,
must have assured Eulenburg of his staunch opposition to these
men. Hohenlohe had come to know that above all he was expected
to defend Prussian interests.[15]

When Eulenburg replied to Holstein and described the visit of
Hohenlohe, he naturally pointed out the steps he had taken to
meet Holstein's objections, but he also shifted the priorities.
He pointed out to Holstein that he regarded the clearing of Marschall
of the accusation that had been made of even greater importance than
the Swaine conversation, and he had been able to convince the Kaiser
of Marschall's innocence.[16] Yet to Wilhelm he wrote that he had
found the Chancellor in exactly the state that he had hoped, "beside
himself over the course of events, which the [Köller] affair took,
to the disgust of Your Majesty, and he is inspired with the passion-
ate, sincere aspiration to win again the full confidence of Your
Majesty." Hohenlohe had said to him, "As Premier of the Prussian
Ministry of State my predominant duty is to represent *Prussian*
interests, and I shall certainly not forget that standpoint when
considering the rights of the Prussian Crown, but regard it as the
line drawn for my guidance." Eulenburg added, ". . . I reflected
inwardly that at any rate the Köller crisis had done that much good
—inasmuch as it had made his [Hohenlohe's] standpoint clear to
him. Hence I see, in working side-by-side with the Prince, for
the future nothing but *good* for Your Majesty. And this was very
manifest in his official and public reception here. He possesses
such prestige in the European world as will not easily be replaced.
Everyone vied in showing him attention."[17] Finally, Eulenburg had
indicated to Bülow that they would have to discuss his future as
soon as possible.[18] This meant, of course, to plan a course of
action to bring Bülow to Berlin.

2

Before Bülow and Eulenburg could meet in Meran, a series of
events had occurred that further strengthened Holstein in his convictions and hardened his determination to resist.

In fact, the new year began with another most embarrassing
scene between Wilhelm and Bronsart. The Kaiser had not been able
to abstain from strongly re-emphasizing his negative opinion of the
military code reform during the annual New Year's speech to his
generals, which resulted in another attempt by Bronsart to resign.
Only after an Imperial apology was he persuaded to remain, but

from Hohenlohe he did not conceal his alarm about the mental
stability of the Kaiser and his grave concern for the future.[19]

In foreign affairs the sensational Jameson raid in Transvaal on
December 30, 1895, and the notorious Krüger telegram of January 3,
1896, had become the focus of attention. The Krüger telegram,
sent to the Boers congratulating them on successfully defending
their independence against British encroachment, aroused violent
and widespread hostility in England. To be sure, neither Holstein
nor Marschall rejected an anti-British policy; on the contrary,
they were to an extent responsible for it and welcomed the outburst
of German public opinion against Britain. However, they (and
especially Holstein) objected to the personal interference of the
Kaiser, behind whom stood the Navy, Senden, and Admiral Knorr. The
result of Imperial interference in the specific case found expression in a compromise: the Krüger telegram, had it not been
for the actions of Wilhelm and the Navy "would never have been
sent"[20] *in that form*. However, Marschall later not only acknowledged
his authorship of the telegram but "defended its timeliness" by
pointing out that it was an expression of the will of the German
people.[21]

The Krüger telegram was quickly followed by another blunder.
Using the wave of strongly articulated anti-British feeling and
his own consequent momentary popularity as a result of the Transvaal
incident and the Krüger telegram, the Kaiser wanted to arouse even
further the public and the press against England in an attempt to
gain support for a huge increase of the German Navy. Foreign policy
had become subordinated to domestic considerations.[22] In addition,
this specific action indicated the basis upon which German "foreign
policy" would be formulated and carried out, with substantial
popular support, under Bülow and Tirpitz.

The Krüger telegram as such was of no serious consequence for
German domestic politics and soon receded into the background. The
issue of the naval increase was, from this point of view, a more
serious matter. Despite the public's anti-British enthusiasm, the
party leaders had refused, to the consternation of the Kaiser, to
go along with an extraordinary naval increase. The exposition of
the Kaiser on the subject for the benefit of a number of Reichstag
deputies on January 18, although apparently well received by his
listeners, did not change the fact of their unwillingness to cooperate in this matter.[23] Marschall, Hollmann, and Hohenlohe agreed
to no additional naval requests beyond those originally proposed
during the current session; the Reichstag members and the Saxon
king voiced their strong objection to the extraordinary naval
expenditures. But at precisely that time a "coalition of the Navy,
Senden and Knorr, the colonial enthusiasts, especially in the form
of the *Kolonialgesellschaft*, and the Fronde" ardently encouraged
the monarch to believe that a large fleet program was necessary
and possible, and did everything to engage the Kaiser in immediate
action toward achieving this goal. Only with some difficulty was
the Kaiser persuaded to postpone temporarily—until the 1897-98
session—the idea of creating a large fleet.[24] The agitations for
a large fleet never did die down completely, and at various times
(especially while defending the budget) they caused considerable
difficulties, even if the relations between Chancellor and Kaiser

were temporarily at their best.[25] However, the Kaiser's public and
private agitation had aroused considerable suspicion among many
parliamentarians and members of the government—last but not least
Holstein—as to the "limitless Naval plans" (*uferlose Flottenpläne*)
and, rather than stimulating unity, reinforced unwillingness among
the ranks in the Reichstag to cooperate and support the government
program.[26]

Describing the atmosphere in Berlin with specific reference to
naval affairs, Lerchenfeld had commended the ability of Hohenlohe
to cope with the situation. However, while Hohenlohe had increased
his respect in the eyes of the Reichstag (Lerchenfeld pointed out),
he had lost in the eyes of the Kaiser, for not being capable of
fulfilling "all-highest" demands. "Accordingly," Lerchenfeld added,
"the position of the current ministry to the Crown remains a precarious one, and for all undercurrents of every variety remains
open."[27] What these undercurrents were Lerchenfeld had summarized
earlier as the combination of the colonial enthusiasts, the naval
enthusiasts, the Naval Cabinet, and the Fronde, to which he later
added Bismarck. As to the effect, he said:

> Unfortunately, ideas such as dissolution of the Reich-
> stag, dictation of a different election law, are very
> widespread among the irresponsible entourage of the
> Kaiser and influence the judgment of His Majesty in a
> way which makes it more than difficult for the responsible
> advisors of the Monarch. Most crises and differences of
> opinion between the Kaiser and his ministers are to be
> traced back to such undercurrents. These influences have
> repeatedly made His Majesty see his advisors as men who
> lack energy, who hinder him in carrying through plans
> for the interests of Reich and Prussia; plans which are
> consistently sanctioned by the other, the irresponsible
> side.[28]

About the possibility of the monarch subjecting his political
acts and "method of governing" to a serious critique after embarrassing experiences, Lerchenfeld was pessimistic but did not want to
give up all hope.[29] Although temporarily confined, the naval issue
constituted a powerful subcurrent which contributed substantially
to governmental instability and the eventual ministerial collapse
in 1897.[30] It was precisely at this point, with Wilhelm discouraged
about interfering further in foreign policy as a result of negative
experiences in his "personal" politics, that Holstein hoped to
find a means of bringing about a stabilizing restriction of the
Kaiser's actions. He had written to Eulenburg:

> You instinctively incline to an autocratic regime no
> matter whether it be Russian patriarchal or *despotisme
> eclaire* on the French model. I am in favour of a moderate
> use of a practicable system of constitutional cooperative
> government which, with the exception of St. Petersburg
> and Constantinople, is in operation in the rest of the
> European and civilized world. My opinion is, I know,
> unfashionable at the court here. "A strong Government
> which can manage without Reichstag" is Admiral von Senden's

ideal, and not his alone. You too belong, perhaps without
knowing it, to those who believe that every political,
military, and legal question is best decided by the Kaiser.
. . . Since it seems to me that a "Government without a
Reichstag" is at present impossible in Germany, I would
prefer that political relations between this Kaiser and
this Reichstag were not made impossible for this Chancellor
so long as he does not believe he can get a better
Reichstag. That the Chancellor is brought closer to his
end by each individual incident where the Kaiser is put
into the position of having to take a decision *before* the
Chancellor, or of having to decide *without* or *against* him,
surely needs no proof. You are thinking of resigning, a
feeling which I share under the existing circumstances.
You are doing so because you are afraid that something
will be achieved which is not my ideal, and that is a
political Jena for the Kaiser—the very thing from which
we have tried for six long years to save him.[31]

To be successful, however, Holstein had to bolster the strength of
Hohenlohe. While Holstein hoped to use the denial of a large naval
program to strengthen Hohenlohe, the latter tried to prevent it
from developing into a serious strain between himself and the
Kaiser.[32]

It was again the military penal code reform, which functioned
as a catalyst in what essentially was a constitutional struggle,
that would trigger one of the two most severe crises of 1896.

In the case of the Köller affair, the attempt to curb the activity of the Kaiser had in the last analysis failed as a result of
Hohenlohe's changed attitude. However, Holstein still hoped to
succeed by using the issues of the Navy and of the military penal
code reform. In fact, Holstein now became more determined to
actively precipitate a crisis that would force the victory, as had
happened during the Köller crisis. Nobody but Holstein could
perform that feat. Already in January Hohenlohe had had the impression that Holstein and Marschall were trying to "strengthen the
position of the Chancellor against Imperial authority"[33] in connection with the proposed naval increase. Although the naval issue
temporarily lost its intensity, the military penal code reform
remained. Here, too, it was Holstein who brought up the subject
and urged Hohenlohe to accept Bronsart's reforms.[34] This general
attitude—of strengthening the position of the Chancellor against
the authority of the Kaiser—Holstein held throughout the crisis.[35]
Holstein's approach was supported to a degree by Lerchenfeld. On
the eve of the May crisis over the military reform he reported
that under the pressure of a united ministry and a determined
Chancellor, the Kaiser would give way; but that neither the War
Minister nor the Chancellor was determined and strong enough; and
that with Bronsart's possible resignation Hohenlohe would have to
struggle alone against the Military Cabinet.[36] Holstein must have
been aware of the consequences of his proposed advice—a possible
general crisis. He knew that on account of the rejected naval
increases the Kaiser was considering a drastic reform of the government by replacing the more cautious ministers with "men of action"—

that is, those thinking about a policy of coup d'état[37] (*Reichs-streich-kanzlerpolitik*).   In this the Kaiser was supported by
his entourage.[38] Holstein certainly saw the dangers of such a turn
of events and warned against it.[39]   However, he knew Eulenburg was
also strongly opposed to a change in the chancellorship.[40]   Holstein
thus probably hoped to succeed in curbing the Kaiser without seriously endangering the position of Hohenlohe.   To some extent he
was justified in this, considering the recent Köller events.
Hohenlohe noted,

> The intention of H[olstein]'s proposal is to use the
> present situation in order to place His Majesty in a
> constrained position . . .; that is, the military penal
> code reform with the inclusion of public procedure be
> introduced only in the Reichstag. Now, so H[olstein]
> thinks, His Majesty will not resist the pressure of the
> ministry and will yield and in this way my position
> will be strengthened to such an extent that one will
> not dare to simply throw me out as is planned.[41]

Hohenlohe, however, was skeptical of Holstein's analysis of
affairs. He saw things in a different light. Holstein's idea, he
conceded, had some merit, but it also caused him grave apprehensions:

> Already Köller's dismissal and the events that have
> preceded it, has shaken my position in relation to the
> Kaiser. He does not forgive me that he, as he thinks,
> made himself ridiculous before Europe by having been
> forced to dismiss Köller. The proposed campaign for the
> military penal code regulation will significantly
> accentuate this discordance and will create mistrust
> that will deprive me of influence of the Kaiser and of
> his confidence for a long time to come.[42]

Moreover, although he would not comply with the advice of Holstein,[43]
he would not, over this issue (as was often the case), be easily
forced into complete submission by the Kaiser. Thus the situation
stood in April, 1896. Holstein, confident that the Kaiser would not
take the extreme measure of getting rid of the ministry, tried to
bring Hohenlohe into strong opposition against the monarch. At
the same time Eulenburg defended the "personal regime" of the
Kaiser and brought to bear all his considerable skills in order to
defeat Hohenlohe, under the veil of compromise, in the struggle with
the Kaiser. Between these two men the weak Hohenlohe stood surprisingly firm for a few months.
    On January 3, 1896, Bülow had written to Holstein that he had
no intention whatsoever of coming to Berlin to take up the chancellorship. He reaffirmed this position emphatically on the 16th.[44]
Between the time of the two letters, however, Bülow had met Eulenburg in Meran, and Eulenburg had reported to Wilhelm that Bülow
was ready to come to Berlin as Chancellor. However, Eulenburg
stressed that "the transition seems to us not to be easy." He
thought that it would perhaps be best to retain Marschall, and
"it might be better to let Boetticher go first." He added the
idea that the attitude of the Bismarck press must also be considered, "since Your Majesty cannot back down in front of a *demand*."

In other words, Eulenburg's chief concern was "to let the parliamentary struggles pass by before a change occurs....A peaceful separation would be very desirable...." Eulenburg also mentioned that Bülow would have to be brought into office in such a way as not to "become loathsome to the South Germans and instantly arouse all liberals." He concluded his letter by stressing the importance of secrecy in regard to his plans for Bülow, ending with the somewhat ludicrous analogy that it was necessary "not to call forth such a commotion in the Foreign Office as was the case in that chicken coop when . . . the hens discovered an ostrich egg...."[45]

With such plans for the future (representing the attitudes of both Bülow and Eulenburg) it was clear enough that sooner or later Marschall would have to leave. Eulenburg also suspected Marschall, a south German, of being on intimate terms with the Bavarian representative in Berlin, Count Lerchenfeld, who, according to Eulenburg, was attempting to become Bavarian Prime Minister; that would constitute, in Eulenburg's words, a "ministry of revenge."[46] Taking into account the attitude of the Kaiser, Eulenburg thought it best to dispose of Marschall at the first favorable opportunity and replace him with Bülow. Again, it was imperative to make the transition as smooth as possible for Bülow. It was thus necessary to keep Hohenlohe in his post to iron out the recent difficulties between him and the Kaiser as a result of the Köller affair. In a letter of February 27, 1896, Eulenburg pointed out to Wilhelm, as he had done before,[47] that "the Prince himself increases ever more his devotion to Your Majesty," as he had been able to observe during Hohenlohe's recent visit to Vienna. Furthermore, Eulenburg continued to present Hohenlohe in the best possible light: he, better than anyone else at the moment, was best suited to be Chancellor because of the skill with which he handled the Foreign Office—"in the Foreign Office his long experience in handling the ambitious, the nervous, and the intriguers" would greatly benefit Bülow, as Foreign Secretary nominally under Hohenlohe. With these words Eulenburg was referring to Holstein, and this letter conveyed the necessity, rather than the desirability, of keeping Holstein. Eulenburg ended by again advising the Kaiser to give Hohenlohe the Imperial confidence that he deserved.[48] To Holstein Eulenburg described Hohenlohe in Vienna (he had gone there in February, 1896) with the following words: "Quite frankly I was not pleased with the Chancellor's political mood while in Vienna. I draw the conclusion from a mass of details that it would be good if I were sometimes to discuss with H.M. the ultimate consequences of Hohenlohe's resignation."[49] In the light of Holstein's general attitude toward the ministry, the Chancellor, and the Kaiser, this letter of Eulenburg's seemed to be designed as a warning to Holstein (also to Hohenlohe) not to push things too far, since the Chancellor was already in a weakened position in the eyes of the Kaiser.[50] Trying to save Hohenlohe and at the same time trying to conform to the viewpoints of the Kaiser was indeed difficult. It was the press campaign that brought the conflict out into the open and initiated the May crisis.

3

At the end of April, 1896, the renewed crisis over the military
penal code reform became acute as a result of a press campaign in
connection with the resignation of General v. Spitz, who was a
supporter of the reform. In particular, the *Kölnische Zeitung* took
up the issue. Hohenlohe at first suspected that it was Holstein's
doing.[51]   As early as March 2 he had noted in his journal:

> The proposal to use the present situation in order to
> force through the question of the military penal code
> reform with the provision for public procedure as decided
> upon by the Ministry of State, is to be carried out by
> suggesting the matter in the press and the Reichstag.
> Then the Ministry of State is to make the categorical
> request that His Majesty permit the draft to be submitted
> to the Federal Council as is. Now, it is believed, the
> Kaiser will have to give in. If this opportunity were to
> be passed up, it is to be feared that the Kaiser will
> dismiss the ministry in the fall without much ado, and
> will try to push through the military penal code reform
> without the public procedure clause, as well as his Naval
> plans, with a different Reich Chancellor and a different
> ministry.[52]

Moreover, no progress had been made at all on the reform question,
and Bronsart was again voicing his intention to resign some time
in the fall.[53]   Holstein's previous record, the Kaiser's communication that no action in the case of the military penal code reform
be taken until the "end of the year," Hutten-Czapski's report that
neither the Kaiser nor the *maison militaire* wished a Chancellor
crisis at the moment, and the warnings against Bronsart and
Marschall from the Kaiser and against Holstein from Eulenburg—all
these were adequate grounds for suspecting that Holstein was
responsible for the action of the press. A few days later, however,
Hohenlohe changed his mind; he then thought that this press campaign had its "origin only in the commotion created in the journal-
istic circles by the dismissal of General Spitz." Somewhat later
he accepted yet another explanation and placed the blame on
Bronsart.[54]

Without further evidence, it is impossible to state whether or
not the press campaign was directly instigated by Holstein. The
suspicions against Holstein were justified, since (aside from previously mentioned factors) he was on intimate footing with Franz
Fischer, the Berlin correspondent of the *Kölnische Zeitung*.[55]
However, the letters of Holstein to Eulenburg on the subject,[56]
together with the long letter of explanation from Fischer (also to
Eulenburg),[57] do give the impression that in this instance the
press campaign was not a direct act on Holstein's part. All that
may be said definitely is that the articles of the *Kölnische
Zeitung* showed a remarkable similarity to Holstein's expressed
attitude.[58]

As soon as the articles appeared, Eulenburg suspected that
Holstein was behind the press campaign,[59] and he interpreted this
as the beginning of the decisive challenge of the "Holstein faction."

The publication of the articles must certainly be taken as a challenge. The press, well informed, not only discussed a topic full of embarrassment to the Hohenlohe ministry but commenced upon a full and frank discussion of the relations between the ministry and the cabinets,[60] which in turn gravely accentuated the struggle between these two elements. In Lerchenfeld's judgment it was quite possible that as a result of the press campaign the Reichstag would combine the question of the four batallions—a subject to be discussed in the regular budget debate—with the military penal code reform and discuss "the relation of the irresponsible military cabinet to the responsible Reich Chancellor," thus placing the entire Hohenlohe Ministry in a dangerous situation.[61] Eulenburg was not, however, unprepared for such a challenge[62]—he had for some time anticipated and planned for future political changes.

In addition to facing other press campaigns that started in April, 1896, Eulenburg was forced to counteract the influence of the *maison militaire* on the monarch[63] (an influence that usually favored radical action, replacing the existing government), as well as to ward off the actions of Holstein and Marschall. This was reason enough for Eulenburg to induce Holstein to be passive for the time being.

Eulenburg described his situation well when he wrote: "Unfortunately all my endeavors to convince the Emperor that it was inadvisable to permit political reports from the military outsiders failed to take effect." He went on to say that owing to the Emperor's increasing distrust of Marschall and the Foreign Office and his diminishing respect for "the venerable figure of Chancellor Hohenlohe . . . the situation grew more and more uncomfortable." Eulenburg was especially concerned about Holstein, who now "turned against His Majesty with the utmost effrontery...." and "literally took it on himself to fight the Emperor and Friedrichsruh," which was in Eulenburg's mind "a lunatic proceeding!" Eulenburg lamented the situation which he found himself in: "Stuck in Vienna, I could neither protect nor advise the Emperor. Nor could I suggest myself to him as Imperial Chancellor, or even force on a crisis whence I should emerge as Chancellor. My conscience forbade me to do that. But I longed for the moment when Bülow should be summoned to Berlin and make it his cardinal business to remedy the impossible conditions caused by the camarilla...."[64] Allowing for his excessive modesty, this statement presents a fair picture of Eulenburg at that time, especially in connection with Holstein. Eulenburg was aware that Holstein also was afraid of a general crisis. The shadow of the returning Bismarck still loomed large in Holstein's mind,[65] and this eased Eulenburg's task considerably in fighting Holstein's activities without forcing his resignation. Moreover, Bülow, too, tried to calm Holstein for the same reason that Eulenburg tried to calm Bülow.[66]

The Engelbrecht intermezzo did not have far-reaching consequences and was soon overcome.[67] Hohenlohe had suffered in the eyes of the Kaiser, but not too much. Against Marschall, however, the monarch had an "insurmountable antipathy."[68] This presented a special challenge to Eulenburg, since even the Kaiser himself was aware of the fact that while Marschall's esteem before the public and in the Reichstag continuously increased, he became more antagonistic toward Marschall[69] (partly as a result of Marschall's increased popularity). Eulenburg wrote to Bülow on March 13 about Holstein, "Increasing rift between Hohenlohe and Marschall. After Hohenlohe's success in Köller crisis and the Engelbrecht affair, Holstein, Marschall, and Bronsart push for a decisive crisis, which is to break the authority of the Kaiser and make him surrender."[70] Hohenlohe, he continued, did not want a crisis and recognized the danger of Holstein. Yet by using the military penal code reform, the press, and the Parliament, the "three conspirators" might be successful in instigating the crisis. Then:

> He [Hohenlohe] will retain Holstein. It may, to the
> surprise of the clique, happen that the Chancellor remains
> and that Marschall and Bronsart have to go.
> Things develop in the direction that the desire of
> the Kaiser will coincide with that of Hohenlohe; I fear
> that then the hour of decision will have come for you.
> At the moment I pursue the course of preventing the clique
> from taking radical steps to filibuster the military penal
> code reform.[71]

Eulenburg seemed to have won over Hohenlohe for the Kaiser (or so he hoped).[72] However, it was not as easy as that.

Eulenburg had thus far progressed fairly satisfactorily. Yet the structure, as everyone was well aware, rested on very explosive foundations, and any partial success did not obscure the fact that the main conflict still lay ahead. To detach Hohenlohe from the Holstein faction was in itself not a very hard task;[73] the only problem was how to bring him into the camp of the Kaiser. Somehow a way had to be found for the Chancellor to compromise his stand on the military penal code reform, since otherwise he would always be in some way tied to Bronsart—and consequently to Holstein and Marschall as well. This was the problem Eulenburg had to solve, and he succeeded to the extent that Hohenlohe finally accepted Bronsart's resignation without handing in his own.

Eulenburg faced other difficulties as well. One of these was what to do with Holstein and Marschall, and how to do it. As much as he would have liked, he could not simply get rid of them in order not to create an untenable position for the future government and for Bülow. Bülow had stated his views on the subject in a letter of March 20. First, "Hohenlohe should not resign in the face of the over-all European situation." Bülow saw "only two really dangerous obstacles" to this course—the military penal code reform and the "encroachments of the *aides-de-camp*." In regard to the former, Bülow wrote that even though he could "completely understand the position of the Kaiser," it was still impossible for Hohenlohe to give in on this issue, since "it would mean such a *capitus diminutio* for him that he would no longer be of any use to His Majesty." In regard to the encroachment of the aides de camp, Bülow observed that "Hohenlohe will rarely protest loudly . . . but it is the nature of the old man that such occurrences may suddenly cause him to disappear without commotion and go to some hidden spot in order to quietly escape all irritations and quarrels."

A second point that Bülow made in this letter was that he

considered it not yet advisable to dismiss Marschall, "especially
after his undeniable parliamentary success," since "it would create
an immense commotion and be everywhere interpreted as a change of
course." Bülow noted that the time was not yet right for such a
"new and completely different direction in politics." Hohenlohe
was "not the man for fighting in domestic politics," and it would
be necessary for a "reconciliation with Bismarck...."
     Third, there was the problem of Holstein: ". . . the propel-
ling force in the struggle of the Chancellor against His Majesty
is not Marschall, but Holstein. Holstein's attitude has gradually become so embittered that even a new Secretary of State would
not be able to keep him in bounds." However, Bülow added that
"Holstein is indispensable in diplomacy, to say nothing of his
personal connections. . ." and that Marschall would be retained
"for the time being on account of Holstein alone. . . ." Bülow
ended with a warning: "The Clique Holstein-Marschall-Bronsart,
cannot possibly weaken dangerously or even permanently our
Maitre, as long as His Majesty will only remain patient and
sober-minded. If the Kaiser, however, makes mistakes, it will
harm him much more than anything which this trio may be able to
come up with."[74] He added that he had tried to calm Holstein,
especially emphasizing that Eulenburg's letters "expressed the
highest approval and friendship of him, Holstein."
     To Bülow's suggestion Eulenburg gave his wholehearted consent,
and conveyed these views (with certain necessary omissions) to the
Kaiser.[75] Quite naturally, then, Eulenburg was extremely careful
not to sever the connection with Holstein, even though their relationship was a "necessary comedy."[76]

NOTES

1. See Holstein to Eulenburg, 26.XII.95, B.A. Eul. 39.

2. Eulenburg to Bülow, 12.XI.95, B.A. Eul. 39.

3. Bülow to Eulenburg, 25.XIII.95, B.A. Eul. 39. See also Röhl,
Germany without Bismarck, pp. 174-175.

4. For this see Rich, *Holstein*, II, 468-469, 498; Röhl,
Germany without Bismarck, pp. 160f., 498; *Grosse Politik*, XI, 5ff.;
X, 251ff.

5. Holstein to Eulenburg, 17.XII.95, B.A. Eul. 39.

6. See Holstein to Eulenburg, 15.X.94, B.A. Eul. 32. At that
time Holstein had heard that Bismarck proposed Bronsart as future
Chancellor. Holstein noted that Bronsart had a "good Bismarck
press," and he would, as soon as a political impasse was reached,
suggest that the Kaiser recall Bismarck. No doubt Holstein's
attitude toward Bronsart was modified somewhat after 1895, but
the basis of suspicion and mistrust certainly persisted.

7. Holstein to Eulenburg, 17.XII.95, 18.XII.95, B.A. Eul. 39.
See also Rich, *Holstein*, II, 497.

8. Holstein to Bülow, 18.XII.95, *Holsteins Papiere*, III, 513-
514; Holstein to Eulenburg, 18.XII.95, B.A. Eul. 39.

9. Eulenburg to Holstein, 19.XII.95, *Holsteins Papiere*, III, 515.

10. *Ibid.*, p. 514.

11. Holstein to Eulenburg, 21.XII.95, Rich, *Holstein*, II, 498-499, but see also same letter in *Holsteins Papiere*, III, 516-517. See, further, Holstein to Eulenburg, 22.XII.95, B.A. Eul. 39, suggesting regular weekly *Vorträge* of Hohenlohe or Marschall; Holstein to Eulenburg, 26.XII.95, 27.XII.95, B.A. Eul. 39; Rich, *Holstein*, II, 498-500; Röhl, *Germany without Bismarck*, pp. 172-173.

12. Röhl, *Germany without Bismarck*, p. 173.

13. Eulenburg to Bülow, XI.95, B.A. Eul. 39.

14. See Bülow to Eulenburg, 27.XII.95, B.A. Eul. 39.

15. Eulenburg to Bülow, 29.XII.95, B.A. Eul. 39. See also *Hohenlohe*, III, 146.

16. See Eulenburg to Holstein, 30.XII.95, *Holsteins Papiere*, III, 518. See also *ibid.*, p. 519; Röhl, *Germany without Bismarck*, p. 175, note 5.

17. Haller, *Eulenburg*, p. 224; quoted from translation by Mayne, *Eulenburg*, I, 331, 332.

18. Eulenburg to Bülow, 29.XII.95, B.A. Eul. 39.

19. See *Hohenlohe*, III, 151; Hohenlohe to Eulenburg, 2.I.96, B.A. Eul. 40; Marschall Diary, 1.I.96.

20. Röhl, *Germany without Bismarck*, p. 165. On the Krüger telegram, see also King, "Marschall," pp. 185ff.; Rich, *Holstein*, II, 466ff.; Langer, *Diplomacy of Imperialism*, pp. 232ff.; *Wipperman*, 1896 (I), pp. 2ff., 15ff., 69, 72f.; Jerussalimski, *Aussenpolitik*, p. 138ff.; F. Meinecke, *Geschichte des deutsch-englischen Bündnisproblems 1890-1901* (Berlin, 1927), pp. 60ff.

21. H. Miquel (son of the Prussian Finance Minister) memo, "Freiherr Marschall von Bieberstein," written about 1912-13 in H. Miquel's Papers, Archiv des Auswärtigen Amts, Bonn. I used microfilm copy T 295, reel 5, in the National Archives, Washington, D.C. See also Lerchenfeld to Crailsheim, 3, 5, and 7.I.96, G.S.A. München, MA 76011. "The Foreign Office," Lerchenfeld wrote in his report of January 7, "cannot have been surprised about the effect of the Imperial telegram upon England. Immediately upon the rise of the Transvaal question, one had been determined to behave in a most energetic way against England—nevertheless, the Foreign Office deemed it necessary to teach England a lesson." One day later he added that according to Marschall, Hohenlohe had encouraged the Kaiser to send the telegram primarily to demonstrate against the audacity of the British press. Lerchenfeld to Crailsheim, 8.I.96, G.S.A. München, MA 76011. See also E. M. Carroll, *Germany and the Great Powers, 1866-1914* (1938; reprinted, 1966), pp. 363ff.; *Grosse Politik*, XI, 1-65.

22. *Hohenlohe*, III, 152; Rich, *Holstein*, II, 504; King, "Marschall," p. 194; Röhl, *Germany without Bismarck*, pp. 166ff.; *Wippermann*, 1896 (I), pp. 60ff., 91ff.; Lerchenfeld to Crailsheim,

18.I.96, G.S.A. München, MA 77689.

23. Marschall Diary, 16.I.96, 18.I.96; Lerchenfeld to Mayer, 18.I.96, and Lerchenfeld to Crailsheim, 26.I.96, G.S.A. München, MA 77689. On the general topic, see also Carroll, *Germany and the Great Powers*, p. 350; H.-U. Wehler, *Bismarck und der Imperialismus* (Köln, 1969), pp. 498ff.; Stegmann, *Erben Bismarcks*, pp. 109f.; Kehr, "Schlachtflottenbau und Parteipolitik 1894-1901"; O. J. Hale, *Publicity and Diplomacy, with Special Reference to England and Germany, 1890-1914* (New York, 1940; reprinted, 1968), ch. V.

24. Marschall Diary, 22, 25, and 31.I.96; Lerchenfeld to Crailsheim, 26.I.96, 28.I.96, G.S.A. München, MA 77689. See also *Hohenlohe*, III, 153, 156-157, 162, 164, 241; Rich, *Holstein*, II, 504-506. It is interesting to note that in the fall of 1895 Wilhelm had already called for an increase of the Navy, to be conveyed to the Reichstag on January 1, 1896! Hohenlohe had persuaded him to ask various party leaders first. Their replies had been completely negative. Finally, Wilhelm had agreed not to present any "all-highest" wishes. Ministry of State minutes, 29.I.96, vol. 121, D.Z.A. Merseburg. See also Saxon embassy report, 4.II.96, Sächs. H.S.A., Ges. Berlin, No. 251.

25. See, for example, Marschall Diary, 23, 24, and 29.II.96 (aide-de-camp v. Arnim tried to win Hahnke for large fleet plans), 5.III.96; Lerchenfeld to Crailsheim, 5.III.96, G.S.A. München, Ges. Berlin, 1067; Varnbühler report, 18.III.96, Württ. H.S.A., Ges. Berlin, E 73, Fasz. 61; Klügmann report, 20.III.96, Staatsarchiv Hamburg, A IV c 6, Bd. III.

26. On the Navy, see also Holstein to Eulenburg, 13, 14, and 25.I.96, B.A. Eul. 40, and 31.I.96, *Holsteins Papiere*, III, 527; Eulenburg to Holstein, 14.I.96, 31.I.96, B.A. Eul. 40; Bülow to Holstein, 31.I.96, *Holsteins Papiere*, III, 528-529; Eulenburg to Wilhelm, 20.I.96, B.A. Eul. 40; Jagemann reports, 30.I.96, G.L.A. Karlsruhe, Ges. Berlin, 49-2029. Varnbühler reported that he had just talked to Hollmann, who had gotten his Navy budget passed by the Reichstag. Hollmann also told Varnbühler that this fact was more likely to make him look suspicious in the eyes of the Kaiser than strengthen his position, since the approval of the Reichstag on his budget meant also a vote of confidence. See report of 2.IV.96, Württ. H.S.A., Ges. Berlin, E 73, Fasz. 61. In general, see also Hallmann, *Schlachtflottenbau*, pp. 171ff.; Kehr, "Schlachtflottenbau," pp. 34ff., 47ff.; Steinberg, *Deterrent*, pp. 31ff., 72ff., 82ff.; Röhl, *Germany without Bismarck*, pp. 168-170; Hans Hallmann, *Krügerdepesche und Flottenfrage* (Stuttgart, 1927).

27. Lerchenfeld to Crailsheim, 8.II.96, 5.III.96, G.S.A. München, MA 77689.

28. Lerchenfeld to Crailsheim, 28.I.96, G.S.A. München, MA 77689.

29. Lerchenfeld to Crailsheim, 17.II.96, G.S.A. München, MA III 2674.

30. For early 1896, see especially Röhl, *Germany without Bismarck*, pp. 169-171.

31. Rich, *Holstein*, II, 506, as taken from *Holstein Papers*, III, 590, 592-594.

32. See Rich, *Holstein*, II, 508; Röhl, *Germany without Bismarck*, p. 168.

33. *Hohenlohe*, III, 161; Rich, *Holstein*, II, 508.

34. *Hohenlohe*, III, 164.

35. *Ibid.*, p. 235; Rich, *Holstein*, II, 484, 519, 543.

36. See Lerchenfeld to Crailsheim, 1.V.96, G.S.A. München, MA 77751.

37. See Rich, *Holstein*, II, 508; *Hohenlohe*, III, 161.

38. *Hohenlohe*, III, 164.

39. *Holsteins Papiere*, III, 528, 532-533.

40. *Ibid.*, pp. 532-533.

41. *Hohenlohe*, III, 181.

42. *Ibid.*

43. *Ibid.*, pp. 164, 170.

44. *Holsteins Papiere*, III, 522, 525.

45. Eulenburg to Wilhelm, 20.I.96, B.A. Eul. 40. I have left out the written comments and changes added to the typescript document. The nature of the handwritten corrections indicates that Eulenburg directly prepared Marschall's dismissal, and that he did not plead for Marschall's retention in 1895.

46. Eulenburg to Holstein, 31.I.96, B.A. Eul. 40 (this part of the letter had been left out in *Holsteins Papiere*, III, 527); *Hohenlohe*, III, 167-169.

47. Haller, *Eulenburg*, p. 190.

48. Eulenburg to Wilhelm, 27.II.96, B.A. Eul. 40. However, compare Rich, *Holstein*, II, 508.

49. *Holstein Papers*, III, 594-595.

50. See also *Holsteins Papiere*, III, 532-533. For events leading up to the "May crisis," see especially the treatment by Röhl, *Germany without Bismarck*, pp. 178-182.

51. *Hohenlohe*, III, 217. In general, see also Röhl, *Germany without Bismarck*, pp. 182-189.

52. *Hohenlohe*, III, 186.

53. Lerchenfeld to Crailsheim, 6.III.96, G.S.A. München, MA 77751.

54. See *Hohenlohe*, III, 181, 189, 199, 209, 216-217, 218, 220. Jagemann reported home that the Military Cabinet was behind the Spitz affair, and that Bronsart tried to force Hohenlohe to a decision on the military penal code reform: 22.IV.96, 23.IV.96, G.L.A. Karlsruhe, Ges. Berlin, 49-2029.

55. Hammann, *Der Neue Kurs*, p. 61. See also Alexander Hohenlohe, *Aus meinem Leben*, pp. 310-311.

56. Holstein to Eulenburg, 1.V.96 (twice), B.A. Eul. 41; also B.A. Eul. 42, pp. 344-346.

57. Fischer to Eulenburg, 1.V.96, B.A. Eul. 41.

58. See Rich, *Holstein*, II, 510. Jagemann reported that the articles had been written by Fischer, although the latter denied this, and indicated that the author was highly competent in military affairs. See Jagemann reports, 28.IV.96, 1.V.96, G.L.A. Karlsruhe, Ges. Berlin, 49-2029. According to the protocol of the Ministry of State, Boetticher mentions Hönig; in his own notes for that meeting he emphasizes Hönig but also mentions Hahn and Fischer. See Ministry of State minutes, 3.X.96, Bd. 123, D.Z.A. Merseburg; Boetticher memo, V.96, B.A. Boetticher, No. 32.

59. Eulenburg to Wilhelm, 29.IV.96, B.A. Eul. 42. The explanatory note mentioning Holstein directly was probably written later. The content of the letter to Wilhelm does not mention, but hints at, Holstein. Not naming him directly was probably done for the Kaiser, who would be suspicious of the Foreign Office and especially of Marschall, rather than Holstein. Eulenburg tried to protect Holstein, lest he become alienated by the Kaiser and oppose the future Bülow government. See Eulenburg to Bülow, 29.IV.96, B.A. Eul. 41.

60. See Lerchenfeld to Crailsheim, 6.III.96, 29.IV.96, G.S.A. München, MA 77751.

61. Lerchenfeld to Crailsheim, 29.IV.96, G.S.A. München, MA 77751. See also Jagemann, who spoke of a "Bronsart Crisis" that could develop into a general crisis; 28.IV.96, 30.IV.96. By 5.V.96, however, he felt the crisis was probably over, G.L.A. Karlsruhe, Ges. Berlin, 49-2029.

62. Eulenburg to Bülow, 29.IV.96, B.A. Eul. 41.

63. See Haller, *Eulenburg*, pp. 246-247; *Hohenlohe*, III, 193ff.

64. Haller, *Eulenburg*, pp. 246-247; written in 1902, and quoted from translation by Mayne, *Eulenburg*, II, 47-48.

65. Eulenburg, "Aufzeichnung" to his collection of papers and observations entitled "Vier Tage in Prökelwitz" (written and arranged in 1902), B.A. Eul. 42. See also Haller, *Eulenburg*, p. 200, note 1.

66. Bülow to Eulenburg, 10.III.96, B.A. Eul. 40.

67. Eulenburg to Bülow, 13.III.96, B.A. Eul. 40.

68. *Ibid*. See also Hutten-Czapski, *Sechzig Jahre*, I, 239.

69. Eulenburg to Bülow, 13.III.96, B.A. Eul. 40.

70. *Ibid*.

71. *Ibid*.

72. Haller, *Eulenburg*, p. 198; *Hohenlohe*, III, 225, 228.

73. *Hohenlohe*, III, 201-203; Haller, *Eulenburg*, p. 197; Hohenlohe to Eulenburg, 24.III.96, B.A. Eul. 40.

74. Bülow to Eulenburg, 20.III.96, B.A. Eul. 40.

75. Haller, *Eulenburg*, p. 201.

76. Eulenburg, "Aufzeichnung," to "Vier Tage in Prökelwitz,"
B.A. Eul. 42.

CHAPTER 10

The May Chancellor Crisis

I am not Chancellory clerk, but Imperial Chancellor,
and must know what I have to say.

> Hohenlohe to Eulenburg,
> May 19, 1896

But what can one do if the Kaiser no longer *wants*
to ride this horse [Hohenlohe.] It is tired and
will not take any more ditches. There is no point
in my singing its praises. I know how gladly it
carries its master, how well the old animal has
ridden in the past, how exactly it understands every
signal during exercises, how well known it is and
how soft and good the sound of its name.

> Eulenburg to Bülow,
> June 8, 1896
> (Röhl translation)

In a word, the Prince risks far less both for his
historical as for his official reputation if he
declares "here I stand, I can do no other, I have
made as many concessions as I could" than if he
risks descending still further down the slippery
road of appeasement.

> Holstein to Lindenau,
> July 27, 1896
> (*Holsteins Papers*,
> translation)

. . . with the disappearance of the crisis Hohenlohe
will be able to spend the rest of his life in office.

> Eulenburg to Wilhelm,
> August 14, 1896
> (Röhl translation)

1

In the last days of April the expected crisis erupted. A telegram from the Kaiser informed Eulenburg: "Prince Hohenlohe is in
poor health and exhausted. Marschall and Bronsart continue in their
unbelievable behavior in a most insolent way, worse than ever before.
Now hell is broken loose, a stroke of lightning will be necessary."[1]
Eulenburg was in Vienna, away from the Kaiser, and therefore

unable to take immediate and direct action. The only step Eulenburg
could take at the moment was to telegraph the Kaiser not to take any
actions since, "in view of such a cunning maneuver executed by the
Holstein group in Berlin, extreme caution is necessary."[2] The telegram was also included in the letter he was just writing to Bülow:

> Forgive me, that I interfere so much in your destiny,
> but I do this, after a most thorough consideration and
> in firm conviction, for your benefit and for the best of
> all of us.
> Despite all the confusion I hope for a postponement
> of the crisis. But I do not believe in the permanence
> of postponement. I beseech you to conceal always and
> from everybody my mentioning Botho Eulenburg. You know
> of course why—and you also know why I mentioned him.
> Unfortunately I do not believe that His Majesty will
> accept him. But I do know how he will act if he is
> confronted with the alternative. It's not for me that
> I mention him (since naturally I would be heavily attacked
> if he came) but for you and the Kaiser.[3]

In this critical situation Eulenburg, afraid that he could not save
Hohenlohe after all, became suspicious of Miquel's going over to
the Bronsart group,[4] and he took the extraordinary step of nominating
Botho Eulenburg as successor. With Botho as the Chancellor, there
no doubt would result a wave of animosity against the whole
"Eulenburg clique," very likely making Phili's advisory role an
impossible one. However, Phili had enough confidence in his ability
to control Botho until Bülow could safely take over affairs.

While Eulenburg advocated such a course of action, Holstein and
Marschall informed him about the crisis and pointed out the danger
to the entire Ministry of State.[5] At the same time Bülow wrote,
"I am always, and for every position, at the disposal of His
Majesty. Only, the nomination of Botho Eulenburg will probably
bring about the rupture with Holstein."[6]

Throughout the early part of May Holstein sent advisory letters
on how to avoid a general crisis. Eulenburg even communicated some
of Holstein's advice to the Kaiser, about looking for a compromise
and about the careful handling of Bronsart.[7] However, he was as far
as ever from helping Holstein and did not miss the opportunity to
include a little jab against Holstein for the Kaiser.[8]

Still, something had to be done to calm public opinion if "all
still pending bills such as the 4th batallions, colonial troops,
reorganization, increase of the colonial troops in southwest Africa,
etc."[9] were to be passed by the present Reichstag. He proposed that
Hohenlohe make some kind of public statement in order to set the
Reichstag at ease. In a footnote Eulenburg added, "As soon as an
interpellation in the Reichstag was to be answered by the Chancellor,
it was an Imperial order. It then lay in the hands of Hohenlohe to
formulate the reply in such a way that the Reichstag would be
satisfied. If the Kaiser would have been calmed over the possibly
too extensive formulation of Hohenlohe in regard to the public procedure—(and that was my job)—the crisis would have been ended
and Hohenlohe's project would have failed."[10] In order to keep
Wilhelm informed about what really happened in Berlin, Eulenburg

sent Holstein's letter[11] and advised the monarch to grant an audience to Marschall but otherwise not to take any rash actions.[12] It was indeed timely advice: on April 30 Wilhelm called the military attachés of the German states and as much as told them that the person behind the press campaign was Marschall. He then emphatically repeated his determined stand against the reform, adding that the kings of both Saxony (which was incorrect, as he was for the reform) and Württemberg were on his side. Wilhelm had also decided to discard his promise to Bronsart to await the opinions of the generals on the reform. The Chancellor had no knowledge of this latter decision and still believed that the reform question would remain in abeyance until the generals reported in the fall.[13]

The audience to Marschall was accordingly granted and took place early on May 4; in general, it was successful[14] and quite in line with Eulenburg's advice. At the same time Eulenburg encouraged the Kaiser in the correctness of his views over the penal reform, which they both believed would be detrimental to the Army.[15] For this Eulenburg reaped the praise (and probably added confidence) of his Imperial friend.[16]

However, Hohenlohe's suggested statement for the Reichstag was to be more than just a political statement. Eulenburg elaborated on the subject that he had briefly suggested before.[17] He wrote to Wilhelm that some public statement would be necessary, but it must be handled in such a manner that "His Majesty ends up without a crisis, and without concession."[18] Therefore, it would be necessary to separate the Minister of War (Bronsart) from the rest of the ministry without discrediting the latter in the eyes of the public—a difficult feat. Eulenburg described three possibilities that were open: the first would be to pacify the Reichstag by submitting the question of the penal code reform to 15 Army Corps leaders with the order to express their opinions in the fall of the year. Having their opinions, the Kaiser would then act as he saw fit. Eulenburg pointed out, however, that Bronsart would not go along with his scheme and thus only Hohenlohe was left to make such a statement. A second possibility would be for the Kaiser to order Hohenlohe to submit the reform not as a motion by Prussia but as a *Präsidialvorlage* in the Federal Council.[19] By this maneuver the Prussian government could submit any number of changes. In this situation the Kaiser would not be responsible any more for what his alter ego, the king of Prussia, did. Besides, the Federal Council would only come to debate the reform in the fall, and thus time would be gained and the present crisis overcome. Also, the proposed reform would have to be as the ministry had already formulated it; otherwise Bronsart would take his leave immediately and the whole plan would come to ruin. The third possibility was to win over Bronsart and persuade him to stay on for a while. However, Bronsart wanted to resign anyway, apart from the military penal code reform, which meant of course a crisis.[20] Thus it was clear that Eulenburg was trying to kill the reform bill and at the same time gain the benefits of such a bill by deceiving the Reichstag.[21] To Holstein as well as Marschall, Eulenburg wrote as though the Kaiser had already accepted one of his three proposals, and he therefore implicitly rejected all

the compromise plans of Holstein and Marschall as not acceptable
to the Kaiser.[22] He used the same tactic with Alexander Hohenlohe,
and Eulenburg hoped that his letters to Alexander would prepare
the Chancellor for the coming events.[23]

Having pulled all these strings, Eulenburg continued to elaborate on his plan: once the statement by Hohenlohe, which necessarily
had to include a definite time at which the reform was introduced
for public debate (in order to calm Bronsart and keep him in office),
the first act would be finished, and the second act could then
begin. Eulenburg saw this second act opening with the Kaiser
suddenly calling a conference with the military leaders, including
the Chancellor and perhaps some of the federal princes, in order to
discuss the reform. Eulenburg thought the German public would
certainly not object to such a conference under the presidency of
the monarch, whatever the outcome might be. Of course, this procedure would be a surprise attack on Bronsart, but this was necessary, lest the effect be wasted. As to the public statement, the
Kaiser was always free to approach Hohenlohe and talk to him about
it.[24]

Wilhelm took up this last suggestion and met Hohenlohe on May
8. Apparently, he seemed confident of his success with the Chancellor.[25] In this conversation it was agreed that Hohenlohe should
give a declaration in the Reichstag "that would be suited to calm
public opinion on this issue."[26] With this step the crisis seemed
averted[27] and, although in a sense it perpetuated the latent ministerial crisis, at the same time it postponed the question until
fall.[28] Wilhelm probably informed Eulenburg about the meeting in
the same tone that the Kaiser later used in a letter to Hohenlohe,
conveying the idea that Hohenlohe had submitted to the Kaiser.[29]
Marschall also described the meeting to Phili, but in a different
light: the meeting had been successful because the monarch seemed
disposed toward leniency. However, continued Marschall, the question was not yet settled, and the best solution would be, then as
now, to submit the reform as prepared by the ministry in the
Federal Council. Judging from the Chancellor's subsequent action,
Marschall's version seems to be the more accurate one, even if he
had assumed too much as a result of Wilhelm's apparent leniency
during the May 4 interview and Hohenlohe's Kaiser conversation of
May 8.[30]

Marschall's letter went directly to the Kaiser "for orientation." Eulenburg added some personal comments, noting that his
impression of Marschall's communication was that Hohenlohe and the
Kaiser were to be forced into a situation which would leave room
only for a definite and positive statement in favor of the reform.[31]
This impression of Eulenburg's was further supported by Alexander
Hohenlohe's lengthy reply to him.[32]

Having done as much as he could from a distance—with dubious
success—Eulenburg then prepared to meet the Kaiser in person.
Notwithstanding possible complications arising out of the fact
that his own name had appeared in the press as a possible future
Chancellor (a fact he also attributed to Holstein),[33] he met the
Kaiser in Prökelwitz after having stopped in Berlin for a short
while. While the Kaiser enjoyed himself on his daily hunting
parties, Eulenburg tried to solve the crisis.

While on the way to the hunting estate Prökelwitz, Eulenburg
had prepared a résumé for Bülow of the impression he had gained in
Berlin: Alexander had completely fallen under the domination of
the Marschall-Bronsart group. Alexander had pointed out to him
that the Chancellor must come up with a statement for the Reichstag "that the entire ministry is in favor of granting the public
procedure in the military code regulation." Eulenburg lamented
that all his strong objections and counter-proposals had had no
effect on Alexander. Despite intense animosity even in the Foreign
Office toward the Minister of War, everybody was under the latter's
spell. Eulenburg saw little success for the Kaiser and expected
the explosion of the crisis at any moment.[34] In this letter, at
any rate, Eulenburg gave the impression that he had dropped his
plan of using a "liberal" public statement on the subject of the
military penal code reform.

Arriving at Prökelwitz, Eulenburg's first act was to inform
the Kaiser about the "actual" state of affairs in Berlin, whereupon the monarch promptly sat down and (in Eulenburg's presence)
wrote a letter to Hohenlohe warning him not to make any statement
in the Reichstag contrary to that agreed upon.[35] He also advised
Hohenlohe to stand firm against any possible intrigues on the part
of some of his ministers and assert his authority against them.
Eulenburg, announcing the Imperial letter that would arrive soon,
also warned the Chancellor not to allow another instance of ministerial insubordination and added that "the prevention of a crisis
will be entirely up to you, as I deem it my duty to say."[36] Even
the Empress was used again to support her husband.[37] Next, Eulenburg wrote to Lucanus asking him to support the Chancellor and
protect him from ministerial intrigue.[38] Then he waited for the
results.

The Chancellor was in a very difficult spot. He was wedged
between Holstein on the one side, who encouraged him to stand firm,
and the Kaiser and Eulenburg on the other, who advised him in the
same way but on the opposite side of the issue. He had resolved
not to abandon his personal position on the question of the military penal code reform,[39] but he was just as resolved not to
capitulate to Holstein, but to try everything to achieve an acceptable compromise with the Kaiser. When Boetticher brought up the
subject in the Ministry of State meeting of May 11, he had to
admit that he was not yet informed about Hohenlohe's projected
statement to the Reichstag. Boetticher promised to convey the
sentiment of the Ministry of State, namely that Hohenlohe get
the written permission of the Kaiser to introduce a reform in the
next session.[40] Hohenlohe (who had gone to Schillingsfürst for a
short rest) had originally intended to make his statement to the
Reichstag without getting specific permission from Wilhelm, but by
the 14th had decided otherwise and thought it best to "cover his
back" with an Imperial consent. He went further than that: in
case Wilhelm wanted to use the Ministry of State proposal as
Präsidialvorlage in the Federal Council, Hohenlohe would deem this
a sufficient statement to the Reichstag.[41] Back in Berlin and with
the help of Alexander, Marschall, and Wilmowski, Hohenlohe modified
his position again, as seen in the telegram he sent to the Kaiser
on May 17.[42] He thought he had now accommodated both the Foreign

Office and the Kaiser, and so he confidently declared in the Reichstag that a reform proposal for the military penal code was in preparation, that he was quite confident that the bill would be brought
before the Reichstag in the autumn, and that "in conformity with
the special requirements that the military establishments require"
it will be based "on modern concepts of law."[43] This declaration
might have been all right had not Hohenlohe received a telegram
from the Kaiser on the previous day that spelled out in detail what
he was to say. Hohenlohe's version did not vary much from the
Kaiser's telegram, but it had a somewhat more positive tone and was
a little less vague about the date.[44]

2

With Hohenlohe's declaration, the Reichstag was satisfied. The
Center, the National Liberals, and even the left showed sympathy
for the difficult position in which Hohenlohe found himself. Hohenlohe's statement was accepted and embarrassment avoided.[45] The
members of parliament, it seems, wanted to be respectable in the
eyes of "the government" and to some degree exercised consideration
for Hohenlohe as a person.
    The first piece of news to arrive in Prökelwitz from Hohenlohe
after the Kaiser's telegram had been sent was his request to make a
statement that the military penal bill would be based upon "the
present conceptions of law."[46] Eulenburg was not too concerned, but
the Kaiser was furious and suspected that "the gang" had forced
Hohenlohe to write the above communication.[47] Then came the big
disappointment: Hohenlohe's letter stating exactly what he had
said in the Reichstag.[48] The Kaiser once more became extremely
annoyed. It appeared to him that Hohenlohe, whom he thought he had
finally won over completely (Eulenburg had helped to strengthen
this impression), had slipped back into the camp of Holstein,
Marschall, and Bronsart.[49]
    Eulenburg indicated to him that it was at least partly his fault
by sending a letter such as Wilhelm had done and with which he had
not been in complete agreement. Now, Eulenburg pointed out, the
situation that he had so much wanted to avoid had become a reality
—the Kaiser was in a straitjacket. Wilhelm then sat down to
draft another note to Hohenlohe, but Eulenburg intervened and
wrote it for him, and before the Kaiser had a chance to read what
had been written, Phili sent it off to Berlin, following it up
with a more lengthy exposition.[50] In Berlin this letter received
a cold welcome and was countered with a stiff reply.[51] For once
the Chancellor adopted a forceful tone, justifying his action by
the favorable effects he had achieved with his statements[52] and
by pointing out that what he had said had in no way contradicted
the words of the Kaiser. He added, "I am not a Chancellory clerk,
but Imperial Chancellor, and must know what I have to say."[53]
However, this note did end on a conciliatory tone.
    Eulenburg was satisfied, since thereby the crisis had been
postponed.[54] The Kaiser became enraged anew, but that was the
least of Eulenburg's troubles. He wrote to Hohenlohe that the
Kaiser had been indignant about the reply for a moment, but had no
personal animosity.[55] The absence of personal animosity was due to

the fact that the monarch was most enraged by that part of the letter
he had identified as being inspired by Marschall.[56] Hohenlohe's
anger also did not last very long, especially since Eulenburg on his
part had replied in a more amiable tone than before and had also
used Alexander Hohenlohe to influence his father, and Marschall
called for a "truce on both sides."[57] Yet Hohenlohe was made aware
of the fact that Eulenburg was definitely still on the side of the
Kaiser by his refusing to yield on the military penal code reform,
and he was told in so many words to dissociate himself from Bronsart
and Marschall.[58] Hohenlohe was ready to compromise, but he also
realized that Wilhelm and Eulenburg would calmly, if not regret-
fully, agree to dismiss him if he did not change his mind.[59]

Apparently Eulenburg still thought that a "compromise" could be
found, and he was absolutely correct.[60] In preparation for a meeting
at Schloss Wilhelmshohe near Kassel on August 8 between the Kaiser
and Hohenlohe, Eulenburg had proposed to Hohenlohe, when he had
visited him at Alt-Aussee on August 3, that he submit a reform plan
to the Federal Council, which would very likely reject it. On the
basis of this refusal Hohenlohe could then go to the Reichstag and
with good conscience postpone the whole reform.[61] In Wilhelmshohe,
then, after a long debate Hohenlohe agreed, first, that Bronsart
could be dismissed; second, that he (Hohenlohe) had time up to
September or even the first of October to make up his mind concerning the military penal code reform; and third, that he should submit
another plan on the same subject that would do justice to both the
Chancellor and the Kaiser.[62]

Having succeeded in saving Hohenlohe from being taken over by
the Bronsart group and from the wrath of the monarch, and having
postponed the reform question without endangering the good will of
the Reichstag, Eulenburg's task now was to induce Bronsart to stay
in the ministry for a while. In this he was aided by the presence
of General von Hahnke at Prökelwitz; after a "frank" talk with
Eulenburg he agreed to the latter's arguments.[63] A momentary
obstacle to Bronsart's retention proved to be an ill-considered
remark of the Kaiser about the minister, as a result of which Bronsart on May 20 expressed his wish to resign. With the help of
Hohenlohe, Eulenburg here, too, succeeded in changing Bronsart's
mind.[64]

3

By May 20 Eulenburg had been successful in overcoming the first,
and in some ways the most critical, stage of the crisis. He had
succeeded in calming the Reichstag by allowing Hohenlohe to make a
statement concerning the military penal code reform bill that made
such promises as would satisfy the Reichstag for a while, but that
would get Hohenlohe into trouble with Wilhelm. Eulenburg, however,
had managed to retain Hohenlohe and had calmed the Kaiser for the
time being.

Eulenburg was now ready to take the next step, which was to
force Hohenlohe to accept the Kaiser's program in its entirety.
That this would not be an easy task to perform, Eulenburg realized
quite well. However, even if Hohenlohe decided to resign rather
than submit, Eulenburg knew with assurance that he could always come

up with a replacement. He could always call on Bülow if the Kaiser refused to accept such other nominations as Botho Eulenburg. In a long letter dated May 24 to his friend in Rome, which included a large number of documents pertaining to the May crisis, Eulenburg kept Bülow up to date:

I quickly outline for you the facts which so decisively influence your future.

For the reason that a collapse might not be possible to avoid, is perhaps imminent, perhaps comes later—at the latest in the fall, the Kaiser touched upon the question of succession. He told me that he neither wants nor is able to take Botho Eulenburg. Lucanus had told him that Botho had shown little energy as Minister of Interior (especially against the conservatives), that he would be unthinkable in the position of the first post of the Reich under such difficult conditions. For this reason he is determined to take you. He is tired of all the crises, he needs a Chancellor who would remain for 20 years or longer.

I replied that if His Majesty would want this, I deemed especially necessary not to place you at the head at such a difficult moment. The danger of exhaustion would be too great. His Majesty did not listen to my further arguments, it seemed to have been a firm decision. I did not insinuate further.

. I have my grave apprehensions. Even if Hohenlohe resigns for reasons of health, it will in any case be interpreted that he resigned because of the rejection of the public procedure in the military penal code reform by His Majesty, and the successor will have all of liberal Germany against him. In addition, the resignation of Marschall would have a very annoying effect, because the latter has gained an increasingly strong position in the Parliament. Finally, the whole conservative party will not understand the resignation of the dashing Minister of War, who is considered to be the most skillful fighter against subversion.

You would find an almost insurmountable situation. As Secretary of State under Botho Eulenburg, on the other hand, you would be temporarily protected and would prepare your position for the Chancellorship. You both, and Posadowsky as Secretary of State for the Interior, would strongly represent the Prussian viewpoint and would stand for a definite attitude. Botho with his infinite skill could hold himself above the water for a while— just long enough for you to prepare yourself.

At the same time Botho's appearance would mean a total "blowing up" of the Foreign Office, of which act you would then be spared. Perhaps I am cruel in this my viewpoint, but one has to create a clearly defined situation, otherwise the meddling continues—a poor state.

This morning I went to Potsdam in order to speak to

Lucanus. I told him without beating about the bush that
His Majesty had mentioned him to me as the opponent of
the Botho-Bernhard project. I would have to explain to
him the reasons why I am for this project. He became
very thoughtful, but finally agreed with me and said
that "he believes that His Majesty had not yet spoken
the final word" on the matter.

I do not know how much Lucanus sees himself threatened by Botho's appearance; neither do I know to what
extent he will give support to my argumentations. My
assurance that I abhor any kind of family politics and
that I would reap inconveniences by Botho's nomination
did not interest him. At any rate, he has modified the
thought of this "too great power of the Eulenburgs"—
and this idea might very well have played a role when
he so ardently advised His Majesty against considering
Botho.

Botho himself to whom I spoke in Prökelwitz declared
that he would not accept the succession, but conceded to
me that he would have to give in to an urgent request of
his king; but at the same time he could not name any
other successor but himself with you as Secretary of
State. I also found out the Prince Bismarck has called
Botho the only successor to Hohenlohe.[65]

How the whole situation would finally develop Eulenburg did not
know, but he did try as hard as he could to influence the course
in his favor. For example, he tried to spare Bülow in order to
assure the latter's success in the future. Eulenburg added:

What I have done so far in the matter has sprung solely
out of the conviction to have served your interest.—But
I do not give myself the right to try to force happiness
upon a friend against his will. The decision rests with
you.

As far as the time of the change is concerned, it is
not easy to come to a decision, but it must be made with
the following considerations in mind:
His Majesty does not concede public procedure in the
military penal reform.

If Hohenlohe leaves for this reason whenever this
question arises, that is, by next fall, he will leave with
that aura of glory that will harm the Kaiser. But he
then also takes his leave with a "crash" and that he
wants to avoid under any circumstances.

Therefore he has to resign early for reasons of health.
That would be in September.

There is still the question whether it is possible to
twist the matter in such a way that the Minister of War
can be made to leave independently from this matter.
Hohenlohe would remain and the bill for the reform could
be tabled throughout the winter until the end of the
next session.

But this I consider hardly possible, just as much so

as that Marschall would remain longer than the Minister
of War.—That would bring the question of your entry
into the Foreign Office on to the agenda of the day.
And the question is if this could be another form of
leading you into the post of Chancellor?[66]

At any rate, Eulenburg prepared for the worst and arranged to
meet Bülow in Vöslau in early June.[67] Then he drew up a document
in the form of a letter to Bülow, read it to him in Vöslau, and
discussed the contents. Bülow agreed with Eulenburg's view. In
the letter Eulenburg pointed out that any number of little incidents could provoke a Chancellor crisis. So far he had been
successful in carrying out the Kaiser's wishes, but now there were
signs that the Kaiser was beginning to lose interest in this way
of handling affairs. Renewed incidents had again upset the monarch
about Hohenlohe, and he had become tired of the repeated and
strenuous attempts at reconciliation. Then there followed a long
discussion on the character of the Kaiser and the difficulty of
his position during the Caprivi era and later, owing to the pressure of Bismarck. Eulenburg came to the conclusion that however
necessary it had been to carry on with Caprivi and Hohenlohe (that
is, with a government based on the Center Party and the Liberals),
it was not (at the third turn of his reign) necessary that the
government revert to its "natural base"—the conservatives.
Eulenburg was confident that the "individuality of the Kaiser
would find its equilibrium in the political life on a basis of
moderate conservatism"—in contrast to the present situation, in
which the "supremacy of liberal-radical or liberal-Catholic
(Center) ideas" imparted the impression of "irresolution" in
German politics. It was necessary, however, to reform the Conservative Party, which had adopted democratic demagogic ways, and
bring it back to unconditional Imperial support. Eulenburg held
the Bismarck Fronde responsible for the deplorable state of affairs,
since the Fronde had forced the government into the liberal camp.
If a conservative reorientation was not brought about, a new disruption would follow very soon. To achieve stability and a conservative reformation, it was necessary for Prussians to dominate
the future ministry. By presupposing that the ministry was a
Prussian one and also "moderate-conservative," the influence of
the *maison militaire* could also be curbed. Eulenburg continued:

> If in general therefore I come to the conclusion of
> the necessity of a swinging turn toward the right, I
> must at the same time express to you my firm conviction
> that this turn must not be "right about face, march,"
> but "half-right, march."
> Only that must come about which came about with the
> change from Caprivi to Hohenlohe. Nothing more, since
> the King of Prussia most certainly cannot, as German
> Kaiser, govern purely in a Prussian conservative way,
> which would amount to Prussian-particularistic way.
> This point touches the weakest spot of the organism
> of the new German Reich: the necessary concession on
> the part of the old Prussian tradition to the liberalism
> of the German Philistine....

Therefore I think that moderate-conservative in
Prussia and moderate-liberal in the Reich will be the
only possible way that one can take.[68]

This was a remarkable statement of Eulenburg's political ideas.
Here he appears to be more responsible than would be expected from
reading his correspondence with Holstein. However, at the same
time it reveals one of his basic weaknesses, which lay in overrating the personality of the Kaiser, overrating his personal
influence on the monarch, and misunderstanding Bülow's character,
as we, after the event, are in a better position to judge.
Eulenburg also shows poor judgment of political reality in general,
in that politics is more than mere personal and personnel manipulation. Eulenburg did recognize the necessity to adapt the government to a post-Bismarckian situation. It also seems that if the
personalities of Eulenburg and Holstein had not been so different,
both could have found a common program and united their efforts to
stabilize the German government on a responsible and moderate-
conservative basis.

The matter of Berlepsch was finally ended during late May and
June. With no ministerial backing, abandoned by Hohenlohe, under
heavy and constant pressure of the agrarians and the industrialists,
Berlepsch resigned on June 27. Two days before Hohenlohe had again
suggested that Berlepsch wait with his resignation for a more
opportune time, and Berlepsch again had not rejected this idea.[69]
Both sides lacked the conviction to postpone once more the inevitable. Hohenlohe put up a stiff resistance against the choice of
the Kaiser, Bitter; but this was a stand against the Kaiser as much
as against the ministers. Neither Bitter nor Hohenlohe's own
choice, Thielmann, was appointed but, instead, Brefeld, a protégé
of the industrialists. Stumm, the most determined opponent of
Berlepsch, had won. At least on this political issue Hohenlohe
was found to be in the ranks of the conservatives like Stumm,
Miquel, Köller, and Bismarck. The New Course had lost the struggle
over the Chancellor. Considering the symbolic significance of
Berlepsch, as "one of the three B's" of the New Course, appointed
in 1890 as Minister of Trade to redirect the social legislation
of his predecessor (Bismarck), it is surprising and revealing how
little actual popular support the New Course ministers held and
how widespread political indifference had actually become. The
Berlepsch resignation was hardly noticed. This fact serves as a
valuable index of the public political climate when considering
further ministerial changes; less than two months later Bronsart
was dismissed.[70]

4

The "long-range" plans of Eulenburg did not deter him from trying to press Hohenlohe into conformity. On June 26 Eulenburg met
the Chancellor and began to work on him with regard to the military
penal code, but without much success. Hohenlohe refused to yield
on this issue. Eulenburg gained the impression that Hohenlohe
would rather resign than give in. Specifically, Hohenlohe had made
it clear that he would leave if Bronsart resigned over the issue of

the military penal code, and that he would resign if Bronsart were
kept but the Kaiser were to reject the public procedure. This is
quite understandable, even disregarding the military penal code
question, since at the same time Bronsart and Berlepsch had asked
for their resignations, so had Bosse. Kayser threatened with the
same step, and even Boetticher seemed hesitant about continuing
in office.[71]   No wonder Eulenburg thought that the Chancellor had
become somewhat "weary of office," but that he would be ready again
to attempt to find a basis of compromise.[72]   In the following
letter—written on board the *Hohenzollern* in Scandinavian waters—
Eulenburg emphasized that Wilhelm would not change his position
on the reform question, and that he wanted to get rid of Bronsart
as well as Marschall.[73]   He reminded the Chancellor that he had,
in early 1895, consented to Marschall's dismissal "if he could
stay in office until the end of the then current session of Parliament."[74]   Marschall was still in office, but he could not last
much longer. Was Hohenlohe, Eulenburg wanted to know, still true
to his words of 1895? The replacement would be Bernhard von Bülow.
Then he added:

> I admit that your Highness might feel bound by the
> statement given before the Reichstag in May—but I do
> not admit that this goes so far that public procedure
> must be accepted as *conditio sine qua non*. Oral pro-
> cedure, supplied defense, are based on the same princi-
> ple, which are in accordance with modern conceptions of
> law.
> I also no longer look upon the argument of your
> Highness "that you owe it to your past not to make any
> concessions in this question," as seriously as before,
> since your Highness put your name under one of the most
> significant documents of the new Empire, the German
> Civil Code.[75]

Eulenburg, on orders of the Kaiser, added that the monarch might
resort to "forceful means," i.e., to dismiss the Chancellor, if
Hohenlohe would not accept this proposal. Moreover, Eulenburg
made it clear that this would be entirely Hohenlohe's fault.
    To soften the impression of the threat, Eulenburg sat down and
wrote another letter immediately in a more conciliatory tone, but
he did not modify any of the facts.[76]   The Chancellor, on his part,
did not yield, but he still did not give up hope of finding an
agreeable solution. He objected, however, to the dismissal of
Marschall as being very inopportune at the moment.[77]   Hohenlohe
began to get the impression that Eulenburg was not mediating for
his cause at all, but was supporting the Kaiser even to the extent
of forcing the monarch against his will to remain firm on the
military penal code reform issue.[78]   He also began to feel that
the Kaiser wanted to get rid of him.[79]   "Under the present circumstances," he wrote to his son Alexander, "I really begin to be
weary of office."[80]
    At least in one respect Hohenlohe's impressions were correct:
Eulenburg had begun to force the issue in order to get a definite
answer. He was even prepared to accept the fact of Hohenlohe's
resignation.[81]

Eulenburg's difficulties had been accentuated by the news of
Bronsart's intention to resign after all.[82]   Bronsart had asked for
his resignation in mid-June and had been given a vacation until
August instead.[83]   However, in early July while on his annual cruise
in Scandinavian waters, the Kaiser was informed that Bronsart had
written his dismissal request and had sent it off some time before.
However, it could not be found anywhere, and Bronsart was requested
to hand it in again[84]—a perfect scene for a comedy.   At any rate,
all this won time in which to meet this new difficulty.

Hohenlohe's weariness of office usually did not last very long.
Possibly afraid of carrying the responsibility for a grave crisis,
Hohenlohe thought it best to remain in office and again accept
Eulenburg's mediation.   Holstein had mentioned this to Eulenburg
and Bülow, and Bülow for his part confirmed the fact from his own
information and likewise communicated it to Eulenburg.   This
probably eased Eulenburg's mind somewhat, but did not change the
tense situation of the moment.[85]

Bülow, as has been shown, was ready to come to Berlin.   However,
only under the most necessary circumstances would he accept the
position of Chancellor immediately after Hohenlohe.   Helping Eulenburg, he suggested that certain points be considered.   First,
Hohenlohe would in all likelihood try to retain Marschall.   This
was especially true since he feared being dominated by Bülow, as
he thought (with some justification) had probably been the case in
Paris 15 years before when Bülow had been his first Secretary.[86]
Therefore it would be more advisable to give him either Radolin
or Saurma as a Marschall substitute.   The second point that Bülow
asked Eulenburg to consider was the fact that if he were to become
Chancellor immediately, there was the danger that Hohenlohe might
take with him the whole ministry "and in particular Miquel!"   With
such a prospect at hand, it would be wise to limit the changes in
personnel for the time being to Bronsart, Marschall, and, at most,
Boetticher.   Miquel, however, should be induced to stay, since "I
am as yet too little familiar with our domestic situation, not to
have a minister at my side who combines both influence with skill
in this regard; what I am lacking could be best supplemented in
the present situation by the appointment of Miquel."[87]   It was also
necessary not to alienate the Center Party because "it is obvious
that we cannot turn against the revolution in its different forms
. . . at the same time."   It would be in the interest of the Kaiser,
Bülow continued, to save him for a later date, and he also pointed
out that in the event of a Hohenlohe resignation there were a
number of possibilities for the position of Chancellor.   Botho,
as Eulenburg had pointed out, was one such alternative.   Botho
could be given Berchem or Brauer as Secretary of State, in this way
emphasizing the "German" (non-Prussian) element in the Imperial
government.   In this case Marschall could easily wait until a
vacancy in an ambassadorial post occurred.   "Marschall must be
taken care of," Bülow wrote, "preferably in Constantinople—otherwise he will become a second Windthorst in the ranks of the
opposition."   The best way to reduce the Hohenlohe resignation
to its minimal danger would be the combination of Prince Hohenlohe-
Langenburg for Chancellor, with Radolin (and Holstein) as Secretary
of State, Phili Eulenburg as Imperial Viceroy of Alsace-Lorraine,

and Botho Eulenburg as ambassador to Austria; the replacement of Boetticher by Posadowsky would in this case be acceptable for the time being.

However, the main issue was to save the authority and the power (*Machtfülle*) of the monarch in the Army and in Germany—authority and power that he had lost since 1890. This could be achieved in two ways: either by forcing the ministers to conform to the will of the Kaiser, or by dismissing all those who did not conform. In both cases Wilhelm would have proven to the Army, the German nation, and the world that he knew how to enforce his will. The dismissal of Bronsart and Marschall, according to Bülow, would be interpreted as an act of Imperial strength against ministerial insubordination rather than Imperial weakness. "I repeat," Bülow ended his considerations, "His Majesty should not even be forced into believing that he only has a choice between Bronsart-Marschall and a Casse-cou policy."[88]

The idea of making Botho Chancellor was not dropped, however, and even Miquel was considered for that position.[89] More good news from Hohenlohe came when he informed Eulenburg that he was working on another compromise plan. No agreement could be reached if the Kaiser held to the phrase "the public is excluded."[90] This proposition could be worked with; a milder phraseology without changing the content could easily be found. That was necessary because it appeared that Eulenburg had given up the idea of elevating Bülow into the Chancellor's chair at a time when he would have to face the military penal code reform issue. He now had come to the conclusion that the Chancellor for the occasion had to be an expendable coup-d'état Chancellor "who would founder on the issues no matter what he did and who he was."[91] For these reasons Eulenburg began to protect Bülow, as he had done throughout the crisis, against the demands of the Kaiser to give Bülow the Chancellor's post. The Kaiser once again accepted Eulenburg's argument and Bülow was saved, but the situation remained as grave as ever. During the first days of August the crisis reached its climax.

While Wilhelm tried to make sure that Bismarck did not object to his fleet program,[92] Eulenburg brought to bear all his ingenuity to influence Hohenlohe. Before meeting the Chancellor in Alt-Aussee in the beginning of August, Eulenburg stopped in Wilhelmshohe to meet the Kaiser. On the way there he jotted down his political plans:

1) *Hohenlohe remains.* In this case
   a) Bronsart replaced by Hähnisch
   b) Boetticher by Posadowsky
   c) Marschall remains through the next session (?) then replaced by (??) Radolin Brinken

2) *Hohenlohe leaves.*
   Bronsart, Marschall, Boetticher follow, at the latest in end of August or first days of September.

In that case

I. *combination* for the event that His Majesty *does not want a policy of force:*
   Botho Eulenburg Reichs Chancellor

Bernhard Bülow Secretary of State and Vice President
of the Ministry of State.

In this combination the most skillful statesmen stand
together in the spheres of domestic *and* foreign policy; it
signifies a Prussian, moderate course with a tendency
against subversion, not against the constitution and
Reichstag. A wearing out of Botho Eulenburg may be expected in a few years, and Bernhard Bülow slides into
his post—now strengthened in parliamentary experience.

II. combination in the event that His Majesty is not
afraid *of forceful measure* or if he is forced to
adopt such a course.

  a) *Bronsart Reich Chancellor*
  Radolin or Brinken Secretary of State (*with* Holstein)

In this case Bülow would have to be spared, since the
violent struggles, once over, would call for a complete
set of new men.
It is not inconceivable that even Bronsart would hold
his own without a constitutional conflict, but the possibility of this is very slight. A Minister of War *eager for
conflict* raised to the position of Chancellor *generally*
means a declaration of war by the government, the sharp
turn to the so-called reaction which would call forth the
most determined opposition in the whole Reich which might
even lead to a suspension of the Reichstag, at any rate
would tremendously increase the difficulties with Bavarians,
Württembergers, and Saxons.

  b) *Waldersee Reich Chancellor*
  Radolin or Brinken Secretary of State (*without* Holstein)

This would be similar situation as in the one above. But
Waldersee does have, in contrast to Bronsart, a certain
popularity in the Reich. [93]

Eulenburg preferred the Botho-Bülow combination, especially since
Bismarck seemed to prefer Botho, and because this was the ablest
combination and was likely to succeed; the administrative apparatus
in Germany would resist any revolutionary changes. However, because the Hohenlohe resignation in every case would severely endanger any following government, the greatest efforts had to be
made to keep him, "provided it does not conflict with the principles
and the honor of His Majesty."[94]
After having seen the Kaiser and discussed the document with
him, Eulenburg noted at the bottom that his program had the complete
approval of the monarch.[95]
Eulenburg set out to work on Hohenlohe. Hohenlohe was not
unaware of Eulenburg's intentions. Eulenburg's telegram announcing
his coming to Alt-Aussee on August 3 upon request of the Kaiser was
indicative. Hohenlohe himself hoped to meet Eulenburg on August 6
in Berlin, where he could get Alexander's assistance, since, so he
wrote to his son, the conference with Eulenburg would determine the
continuation or termination of his chancellorship.[96] Eulenburg,

however, preferred to confront Hohenlohe alone and isolated from
direct influence of the Berlin clique. Marschall was correct when
he noted that Eulenburg had gone to Alt-Aussee to change Hohenlohe's
mind on the reform and to separate him from his advisors, Bronsart
and Marschall.[97] Eulenburg's first day with Hohenlohe, August 3,
was a complete failure (he reported to the Kaiser). However, he
added, "Will continue efforts tomorrow." Wilhelm supplied additional ammunition by informing his friend that "Bismarck is approaching his end," and that therefore Hohenlohe's resignation at this time
would be "treason." The news about Bismarck impressed Hohenlohe
quite a bit. Eulenburg thought that he began to meet with some
success; however, extreme caution was still necessary in order to
retain the little that had been won, which was, as usual, only
Hohenlohe's agreement to think matters over again and then write
to the Kaiser.[98] At this point Eulenburg cited himself as an
example of one "willing to make sacrifices":

> During a sleepless night, in which I sought after new
> arguments and means, I found one more (and Your Majesty
> may graciously forgive me) a recommendation that made the
> greatest impact. I said that if the Prince would make a
> sacrifice, I also would show my willingness to make sacri-
> fices. He knew quite well how difficult it would be for
> me to leave Vienna, but if His Majesty would at all take
> into consideration for a moment to part from the Haus-
> minister Wedel, and the Prince would want me . . . in
> Berlin, I would without hesitation accept everything. . . .
>   Prince Hohenlohe replied: "Under this circumstance
> of course Berlin takes on a different perspective for
> me."
>   I shall be at the complete disposal of Your Majesty.
> But I beg Your Majesty to take me to Berlin, if thereby
> the Prince will remain in his position, because of his
> disposition this may be necessary in order to make Berlin
> more acceptable to him. . . .[99]

Here Eulenburg seems to have been sincere in his proposal, and he
did not fail to affect the Chancellor greatly. However, at the
same time he was probably quite aware that he could avoid Berlin
if the possibility threatened to become reality.[100]
    Under these circumstances Eulenburg was successful with
Hohenlohe. In his own diary Hohenlohe sounded still rather pessimistic,[101] but to Eulenburg he said, "Well, I still hope to find a
way out. I have to reconsider the way once more. I will write
His Majesty immediately,—that I will look for a way out. Then in
a few days afterwards I will make my suggestions."[102] Things having
developed thus far, Wilhelm decided to talk to Hohenlohe in person.
This was acceptable to Eulenburg, but at the same time he advised
the Kaiser not to give any impression of forcing Hohenlohe into an
immediate decision.[103]

5

    The meeting on August 8 between the Kaiser and the Chancellor
was in general successful. At the very least, it again bought some

time. Wilhelm, as well as August Eulenburg, informed Phili of the course of events: the monarch had acted exactly in the way Eulenburg had advised.[104] Perhaps the Prussian ambassador to Bavaria, Count Monts, had contributed to the success by indicating to Hohenlohe, who met him on the way to Wilhelmshöhe, that many south Germans awaited the resignation of the Chancellor in order to use the accompanying crisis and conflict with the Reichstag to push for a further federalization of the Reich.[105]

An added point that might have influenced Hohenlohe was that while he was at Wilhelmshöhe, the Czar had announced his intention to meet the German Emperor at Breslau, and Hohenlohe wanted to use this opportunity to talk to the Czar about his Russian estates.[106] He tried to keep Bronsart in the ministry, but consented to his dismissal when the Kaiser described Bronsart as the main stumbling block between himself and the Chancellor.[107] Bronsart was dismissed on August 14 and "elevated" to the position of Adjutant General.[108]

Although it was known to government officials as well as to the public that Bronsart's position as War Minister had become shaky, his dismissal in mid-August came as something of a surprise. The reaction of the press was the most heated one since Bismarck's resignation in 1890. The majority of papers regarded Bronsart's fate as the outcome of the struggle between the ministry and the cabinet over competency and power. The Saxon ambassador, Hohenthal, on the other hand, tended to de-emphasize the ministry-cabinet struggle and the differences of opinion between Emperor and ministers on specific questions in this case. He believed that the conflict resulted from the fact that the Kaiser seemed to pay more attention to advice given by persons other than his ministers. The replacement of Bronsart by a man like Gossler, Hohenthal regarded as a form of temporary truce between ministers and the unofficial advisors, and the indications pointed toward the development of a cabinet that would confidently accept a struggle for power with the government.[109] Of course, the "camarilla" was not forgotten. Bronsart and Bismarck, neither one a courtier, had fallen victims to the camarilla, the *Leipziger Neueste Nachrichten* had written, and it continued, ". . . and it is characteristic of a camarilla that it proceeds quietly and cautiously, not noisily and with much commotion; that it aims at the possession of real power, not the superficial appearance of power, that it keeps personnel questions in the forefront, not questions of policy. Having almost achieved the main goal, a period of calmness sets in until one crisis to renewed activity and makes new advances."[110] Rather fittingly the *Stuttgarter Beobachter* could write in an article entitled "A Minister Over-Board": "poor ministers, poor chancellors."[111]

Finally, Bronsart himself explained the event to the Grand Duke of Baden. The Kaiser, he wrote, still held him responsible for the press campaign against the Military Cabinet and accused him of wanting to deliver the rights of the crown into the hands of the parliament and to usurp command over the Army. At any rate, his position was hardly tenable after the Köller crisis. Henceforth, Bronsart ended, he will "retreat into a hidden corner in Mecklenburg and without bitterness and anger, as is proper."[112]

As part of the August compromise Hohenlohe was made to feel that he had even saved Marschall for the time being, although perhaps at the expense of Boetticher. However, he also realized, and indirectly admitted, that the compromise had been quite one-sided—that he in effect had backed down.[113]   On August 25 Hohenlohe announced in the *Reichsanzeiger* that the Kaiser intended to introduce a military penal code reform in the Federal Council that complied with the statements of the Chancellor given in the Reichstag on May 18.[114]   Count von Hutten-Czapski, a member of the Prussian Upper House who was on intimate terms with Hohenlohe, congratulated the Chancellor on his "complete political victory."[115]   Hohenlohe was not that optimistic: he judged Bronsart's dismissal to be very detrimental to the position of the Kaiser in the eyes of the public. "It is very sad, and I am rather pessimistic for the future,"[116] he said at the end of the crisis. After all, no vital issues were really settled, and they would come up again soon enough. The Chancellor knew only too well that the political futures of Marschall and Boetticher were very shaky and could bring down the whole government in another severe crisis.

Although some difficulties still lay ahead—namely the liquidation of the military penal code reform proposal itself—Wilhelm, as well as Eulenburg, had gained the impression that the Chancellor crisis had finally come to an end.[117]

In regard to the bill itself, Wilhelm adopted the plan that Eulenburg had mentioned to him long ago: to introduce the bill in the Federal Council rather than in the Reichstag, with the inclusion of provisions for public procedure, and then to kill the bill by attaching amendments. This plan had the approval of the newly chosen Minister of War, Gossler, who had also advised Wilhelm to adopt such a course.[118]   Hohenlohe pointed out to the ministry that Gossler was in complete agreement with him, the Minister-president, in regard to the military penal code reform.[119]

The Chancellor had been won over, but it had taken all the possible devices of pressure at Eulenburg's disposal to induce him to remain in office: praise, appeal to personal and public conscience, and threats. Under the barrage of threats and promises, Hohenlohe had finally yielded, and he could even retain the comforting illusion that he really had not given in at all. Even his son Alexander, who at various times since May 20 had warned his father against a submission made palatable in the form of an illusive compromise, was not able to reverse the situation.[120]

6

Slowly the last remnants of the crisis began to fade, and by the end of August there was again relative but uneasy calm. However, it is apparent that the crisis just overcome was only one step in the plan of Eulenburg, Bülow, and the Kaiser to reform the whole government. The present calm was only a breathing spell to consolidate the partial victory.

Holstein's general attitude toward Hohenlohe, the ministry, and the Kaiser before, during, and after this crisis in 1896 (as well as that in 1897) remained basically the same: he was trying to curb the influence of the Kaiser by strengthening the position of the Chancellor and the ministry. In every issue, therefore, which brought Hohenlohe into conflict with the monarch, Holstein strongly

supported the Chancellor and advised him to take a firm stand,
particularly in the Köller crisis and the question of the reintroduction of the military penal code reform.[121]

Throughout the crisis Eulenburg usually gave the impression
in his letters to Bülow and especially to the Kaiser that there
existed in the Foreign Office a clique working against the Imperial
authority. To Bülow he described this clique as headed by Bronsart,
Marschall, and Holstein, reinforced by Kiderlen and occasionally
also by Alexander Hohenlohe. Wherever possible, Eulenburg cooperated
with Holstein in averting a Chancellor crisis, and even took Holstein's advice a number of times.[122] That, however, did not change
the fundamental facts that Eulenburg distrusted Holstein, that he
tried to limit Holstein's influence in any domestic matter as well
as on any policies contrary to those of the Kaiser and himself, and
that he cleverly tried to undermine Holstein's position to such an
extent that Holstein would become a compliant tool in the hands of
the projected Bülow ministry. It was therefore necessary to conciliate Holstein and even to give in to some of his demands when
they did not vitally affect the basic political strategy.

Eulenburg's letter of February 27, 1896, to Wilhelm has already
been cited.[123] Again, Eulenburg's successful attempts to warn
Hohenlohe about Holstein are known. To Bülow, Eulenburg characterized Holstein, Bronsart, and Marschall as the "three conspirators"
who were working with all available means—press as well as parliament—toward a general crisis.[124] Bülow agreed that Holstein, not
Marschall, was the "driving force in the struggle of the Imperial
Chancellor against His Majesty."[125] Nevertheless, both continually
assured Holstein of their friendship, tried to calm him by posing
as mediators, and made it a point to show themselves in the best
possible light.[126]

When talking about Holstein to Wilhelm, Eulenburg naturally had
to be careful. Eulenburg had no intention of enhancing Holstein
in the eyes of the monarch, yet Eulenburg could not discredit him
so much as to alienate Wilhelm from Holstein, since he was irreplaceable in the field of foreign affairs, and a complete repudiation
might bring about Holstein's active and formidable opposition to
the future ministry. Therefore, Eulenburg always stressed the
necessity of Holstein for the foreign ministry and magnified the
role that Marschall, as well as Bronsart,[127] had played in their
opposition to the Kaiser.

Holstein's own position toward Bronsart during the crisis is
not always clear. To some extent, of course, there was a common
bond between them. Later, however, Holstein seemed to have
dissociated himself from the Minister of War.[128] Perhaps this may
be partly explained by Bronsart's increasingly precarious position
and by Holstein's fear of being identified too closely with the
sinking minister. The suspicion that Bronsart cooperated with,
and took orders from, the Bismarcks also stimulated Holstein's
aloofness.[129] Eulenburg summarized his impressions at a later date
as follows: Holstein feared that Bronsart had allied with Bismarck
and had begun to work toward the dismissal of Hohenlohe, Marschall,
and himself.[130] During the May crisis, then, Holstein's only consideration for Bronsart had been how to use him to turn the total
ministry against the Kaiser. From the evidence of the Eulenburg-

Bülow letters during the May crisis and thereafter, it is quite
reasonable to infer that this latter statement adequately expressed
the opinion of Eulenburg during the time in question.

One other major point of difference between Eulenburg and
Holstein is that the latter was radically against any reconciliation with Bismarck in whatever form, while the former held just
such a reconciliation to be a basic necessity.[131] This fact
alone goes far to explain the relationship between the two.

From the standpoint of Eulenburg, Holstein's role during the
entire crisis of 1896 (and 1897), although important, seems to have
been only a secondary and a negative one. The main aspect was over
the struggle for Hohenlohe—and Hohenlohe, as has been shown, was
never under the complete dominance of Holstein. The main problem
that Holstein presented was how to reconcile him with the future
Bülow government and dissociate him from Bronsart and later from
Marschall. In this task, as well as in all others, Eulenburg met
with resounding success in mid-1897. To be sure, the fact that
Bülow later dropped Eulenburg while Holstein continued to direct
foreign policy may be cited as an "act of poetic justice"; but that
is part of another story. By mid-1896 Holstein had perhaps accepted
Bülow as future Chancellor, but as he warned Raschdau, who had
written an article in the *Berliner Tageblatt* advocating Bülow as
Chancellor, "he should not anticipate the future."[132]

Immediately after the Wilhelmshöhe interview between the Kaiser
and Hohenlohe in early August, 1896, August Eulenburg informed
Philipp about the outcome: "Dear Phili: Well then, postponement,
patchwork until October!" (when the generals had to hand in their
written opinions of the military penal code reform).[133] That is
exactly what had been accomplished. However, given the personality
of Hohenlohe, Eulenburg had gained more than just a temporary
postponement of a Chancellor crisis. Holstein had written him in
June, 1896, that because of Eulenburg's activity "every trace of
resistance—or almost every trace—" had left Hohenlohe for some
time to come.[134] Besides, the decision of the military commanders
could be foretold without much difficulty.[135] That was not all.
Soon after the Wilhelmshöhe conference Hohenlohe had to submit to
long conversations with Lucanus and Hahnke, and it was made clear
to the Chancellor that not the "public procedure" but the "Central-
Imperial military court under the General directly under the Kaiser"
was the important point.[136] If such a military court were not
granted—a condition *sine qua non* for the Kaiser and the whole
reform project—everything would have to be abandoned. As Hohenlohe
well knew, the main opponent to this central military court was the
state of Bavaria, which had no intention of giving up its own independent military court system provided for by the special rights
reserved to it in 1871. Wilhelm had decided to scrap the military
reform bill altogether and at the same time give the Chancellor a
chance to adopt his position without losing so much face that he
would prefer resignation. The Kaiser thought that the Chancellor
had adopted this new proposal,[137] but this was not the case.[138]
Lucanus, in contrast to the Kaiser, seemed more skeptical: he wanted
to speak to Eulenburg in person about the possible future difficulties that could arise out of the negative replies by the Army
officers expected in October.[139] Eulenburg remained calm. He now

believed that Hohenlohe would resign.[140]   On the other hand, he
took into account the "slowness of old heads."[141]
     More serious for Eulenburg was his talk with Marschall, during
which he "was placed in a rather tight spot." Marschall indicated
to Eulenburg that he had gained the impression that Wilhelm wanted
to get rid of him and, if this was so, he would be quite willing to
resign. No wonder Eulenburg was in a difficult position. The
monarch, as well as Eulenburg, would have wholeheartedly agreed,
but Marschall's request unfortunately came at the wrong moment. The
dismissal of Bronsart had not yet been completely digested, and
Marschall's resignation following so closely would have created a
very obstinate Reichstag and a very nasty press. Besides,
Marschall's parliamentary ability could still be put to good use.
Eulenburg was forced to reassure Marschall that, although the
monarch was not entirely pleased with him, he could not resign now.
Eulenburg wrote to Wilhelm, "On the other hand I feel very well that
enduring the next session will not be an easy task for Your Majesty.
This is especially true because Marschall's willingness to stay is
so weak due to Your Majesty's displayed unfriendly attitude, that
Your Majesty cannot afford to deny him a friendly smile in appreciation of his remaining in office. It is this taking of the first
step that necessitates unfortunately the inescapable second one."[142]
     It seems the Eulenburg did not fear a general crisis at the
moment. However, he did recognize that to come to a satisfactory
"solution à la Eulenburg" of the basic problem—the stabilization
of a government suspended in mid-air—would require tremendous effort
on his part.[143]   His attitude did not even change with Hohenlohe's
telegram to the Kaiser correcting the latter's opinion that he had
abandoned the idea of the military penal code reform.[144]   Eulenburg
warned Hohenlohe not to bring up unpleasant Köller memories. This,
Eulenburg, continued, might result in possible rash decisions on
the part of the Kaiser, which, once taken, could not be averted
any more. At the same time Eulenburg pointed out yet again the
willingness of the Kaiser to compromise and to retain the Chancellor
in office. He wrote:

> I found His Majesty very sure of himself and very
> determined in the pressing question—but at the same
> time in a most favorable disposition toward Your High-
> ness, as long as he does not feel defied. It is my
> impression that the elimination of this nauseating
> question will achieve peace for a long time. That, of
> course, is what we are all longing for—and there is
> absolutely no reason to doubt a fruitful cooperation
> between His Majesty and Your Highness, once this *bete
> noire* has been killed. I am even certain of the fact
> that it will then be a genuine pleasure to obtain a
> position for your son Alexander in accordance with his
> wishes.
>   In my estimation His Majesty will (out of consider-
> ation for Your Highness) concede also to the temporary
> retention of Baron Marschall that Your Highness holds
> desirable for practical reasons—and will possibly con-
> sider Boetticher as victim first. . . .[145]

Thus, as before, Eulenburg shrewdly made use of Hohenlohe's fears as well as his hopes. This method of "sugar plum and whip" had worked previously. It worked now, and it had become a principal weapon in the arsenal of mediation so skillfully used by Eulenburg.

Having pacified Hohenlohe for the moment, Eulenburg turned to the Kaiser and again emphasized the necessity of keeping Hohenlohe.[146] On this occasion he also informed the monarch that Hohenlohe sincerely desired to remain in office, and advised him to stall the nomination of Alexander as a district president, since "the prospect for a relief of the purse of the Princess in this rather cynical Imperial princely . . . family is a strong motive for the remaining in office, a kind of patent-axle on the Imperial wagon."[147]

For the time being the annoying question of the military penal code reform receded into the background. The public as well as the Reichstag had been calmed somewhat by Hohenlohe's notice, published in the *Reichsanzeiger*, and they waited for the fulfillment of that promise. Hohenlohe had been persuaded that the Kaiser harbored no ill feelings against him on account of the military penal code reform issue, nor did he want to get rid of him. This promised a period of calm, a fact which Eulenburg did not forget to point out, together with the necessity of Bronsart's dismissal, to the Grand Duke of Baden, who had criticized the events in general and apparently Eulenburg's role in particular.[148]

In perspective, it appears that the first eight months of 1896 existed under the shadow of the Köller crisis. Whereas Hohenlohe and consequently the majority of the ministers had stood their ground throughout 1895, during 1896 Hohenlohe reluctantly, but nevertheless step by step, retreated—and with him the ministers. They lost hope and, from their point of view, legitimacy of action. Neither Berlepsch's nor Bronsart's dismissal turned into crises. The unofficial influences, it appeared, had won a decisive victory. It indeed seemed as if a "kitchen cabinet" was in the making, including such persons as Senden, Hahnke, Lucanus, Eulenburg, and Miquel. Having almost achieved their goal, so the *Leipziger Neueste Nachrichten* predicted, matters would rest for a while, and then would be taken up again. The period of calm was very short, while renewed embarrassments and attacks proved to be destructive to the already crippled Hohenlohe government.

NOTES

1. Wilhelm to Eulenburg, included in letter of Eulenburg to Bülow, 29.IV.96, B.A. Eul. 41.

2. *Ibid.* For the treatment of the crisis, see also Röhl, *Germany without Bismarck*, pp. 184-194.

3. Eulenburg to Bülow, 29.IV.96, B.A. Eul. 41.

4. Eulenburg to Wilhelm, 29.IV.96, B.A. Eul. 41; Holstein to Eulenburg, 3.V.96, B.A. Eul. 42.

5. Holstein to Eulenburg, 1.V.96, B.A. Eul. 41. Part of the same letter is in B.A. Eul. 42.

6. Bülow to Eulenburg, 2.V.96, B.A. Eul. 41.

7. *Holsteins Papiere*, III, 546.

8. Haller, *Eulenburg*, p. 199; B.A. Eul. 41.

9. *Hohenlohe*, III, 219.

10. Eulenburg to Wilhelm, 29.IV.96, B.A. Eul. 42.

11. Dated 1.V.96, it is the one that another letter of the same day from Eulenburg to Holstein describes as "long explanatory letter." Part of the letter is in B.A. Eul. 41, the rest in B.A. Eul. 42. The Kaiser takes up specific issues discussed in that letter. See Wilhelm to Eulenburg, 4.V.96, B.A. Eul. 41. See also *Holsteins Papiere*, III, 546, no. 545, note 1; Haller, *Eulenburg*, p. 199.

12. Eulenburg to Wilhelm, 3.V.96, B.A. Eul. 41. Parts are printed in Haller, *Eulenburg*, p. 199.

13. Lerchenfeld to Crailsheim, 29.IV.96, 1.V.96, G.S.A. München, MA 77751.

14. Bülow to Eulenburg, 4.V.96, B.A. Eul. 41.

15. Haller, *Eulenburg*, pp. 198, 202.

16. Wilhelm to Eulenburg, 4.V.96, B.A. Eul. 41.

17. Eulenburg to Wilhelm, 29.IV.96, B.A. Eul. 42.

18. Eulenburg to Wilhelm, 5.V.96, B.A. Eul. 41.

19. This plan seems not to have originated with Eulenburg but had been presented to the Kaiser in March, 1896, by Hohenlohe and Bronsart. Wilhelm had accepted it, however, very likely with the reservations and intentions that Eulenburg had then put down in writing. See Hutten-Czapski, *Sechzig Jahre*, I, 288-289. By May 14 Hohenlohe thought of suggesting this idea again but dropped it before May 17.

20. Eulenburg to Wilhelm, 5.V.96, B.A. Eul. 41.

21. See *Hohenlohe*, III, 249; Rich, *Holstein*, II, 512.

22. Eulenburg to Holstein, 5.V.96, and Eulenburg to Marschall, 6.V.96, B.A. Eul. 41.

23. *Hohenlohe*, III, 219-220.

24. See Eulenburg to Wilhelm, 7.V.96, B.A. Eul. 41.

25. See *Hohenlohe*, III, 225.

26. *Ibid.*, pp. 220, 225.

27. *Ibid.*, p. 223.

28. Lerchenfeld to Crailsheim, 9.V.96, G.S.A. München, MA 77751.

29. *Hohenlohe*, III, 223.

30. Marschall to Eulenburg, 9.V.96, B.A. Eul. 41; Marschall Diary,

4, 6, and 9.V.96; Lerchenfeld report, 9.V.96, G.S.A. München, MA 77751.

31. Eulenburg to Wilhelm, 10.V.96, and Eulenburg to Bülow, 13.V.96, B.A. Eul. 41. Parts are printed in Haller, *Eulenburg*, p. 200.

32. *Hohenlohe*, III, 220-223.

33. Holstein to Eulenburg, 1.V.96, B.A. Eul. 42; Rich, *Holstein*, II, 510.

34. Eulenburg to Bülow, 16.V.96, B.A. Eul. 42; Rich, *Holstein*, II, 510. Marschall noted that Eulenburg "still tries to scare us" with the danger of a general crisis—implying that this tactic no longer would work. See Marschall Diary, 14.V.96. But Eulenburg succeeded in leaving the impression with Marschall and Hohenlohe of having accepted their arguments, namely, that in the question of the penal code the Kaiser could only lose. See Marschall Diary, 15.V.96; exposé of view of Alexander in his letter to Eulenburg, ca. 6.V.96, Archiv Schillingsfürst, Rep. 100 XXII A-8.

35. *Hohenlohe*, III, 225-226; Eulenburg memo, "Prökelwitz," 16.V.96, B.A. Eul. 41; Eulenburg "Aufzeichnung," "Vier Tage in Prökelwitz," B.A. Eul. 42.

36. *Hohenlohe*, III, 227; Archiv Schillingsfürst, Rep. 100 XXII A-8.

37. *Hohenlohe*, III, 226-227.

38. Eulenburg to Lucanus, 16.V.96, B.A. Eul. 42.

39. *Hohenlohe*, III, 251.

40. Ministry of State meeting, 11.V.96, D.Z.A. Merseburg, vol. 123.

41. Marschall Diary, 9.V.96; Hohenlohe to [Wilmowski?], *Hohenlohe*, III, 224, and rest in Archiv Schillingsfürst, Rep. 100 XXII A-8.

42. Marschall Diary, 16.V.96; *Hohenlohe*, III, 224-225.

43. *Hohenlohe*, III, 229; Archiv Schillingsfürst, Rep. 100 XXII A-8.

44. *Hohenlohe*, III, 228-229; Hutten-Czapski, *Sechzig Jahre*, I, 290ff.; Marschall Diary, 17.V.96, 18.V.96.

45. Lerchenfeld to Crailsheim, 18.V.96, 19.V.96, G.S.A. München, MA 77751.

46. Eulenburg, "Vier Tage in Prökelwitz," B.A. Eul. 42; *Hohenlohe*, III, 224-225.

47. Eulenburg, "Vier Tage in Prökelwitz," B.A. Eul. 42. In fact Marschall had drafted Hohenlohe's telegram of May 17, and "we" also drafted the Reichstag declaration. See Marschall Diary, 17.V.96, 18.V.96.

48. *Hohenlohe*, III, 228.

49. *Ibid.*, pp. 233, 229.

50. *Ibid.*, pp. 229, 229-230; Eulenburg, "Vier Tage in Prökelwitz," B.A. Eul. 42; telegram in Archiv Schillingsfürst, Rep. 100 XXII A-8.

51. *Hohenlohe*, III, 231.

52. *Ibid.* He had brought through the Reichstag the 4th battalions, he had averted the danger of throwing the question of the 4th battalions together with the question of the military penal code reform, and he had on "the question of public procedure" in the military penal code reform calmed the Reichstag.

53. *Ibid.*

54. Eulenburg, "Vier Tage in Prökelwitz," B.A. Eul. 42.

55. *Hohenlohe*, III, 229-230; Eulenburg, "Vier Tage in Prökelwitz," B.A. Eul. 42; Archiv Schillingsfürst, Rep. 100 XXII A-8.

56. Archiv Schillingsfürst, Rep. 100 XXII A-8, which in this case was not correct; Marschall Diary, 19.V.96.

57. *Hohenlohe*, III, 231-233; Marschall Diary, 20.V.96.

58. *Hohenlohe*, III, 230, 235. See also Lerchenfeld to Crailsheim, 27.V.96, G.S.A. München, MA 77751.

59. *Hohenlohe*, III, 235, 240, 243, 249-250, 251.

60. See also Lerchenfeld report, 27.V.96, G.S.A. München, MA 77751.

61. *Hohenlohe*, III, 249-250, 258.

62. *Ibid.*, p. 252.

63. Eulenburg, "Vier Tage in Prökelwitz," B.A. Eul. 42.

64. See Rich, *Holstein*, II, 512.

65. Eulenburg to Bülow, 24.V.96, B.A. Eul. 41.

66. *Ibid.*

67. Eulenburg to Wilhelm, 8.VI.96, B.A. Eul. 42.

68. Eulenburg to Bülow, 8.VI.96, B.A. Eul. 42. See also excerpts and discussion of this document in Röhl, *Germany without Bismarck*, pp. 191-192.

69. See Marschall Diary, 24.V.96; Hohenlohe to Boetticher, 25.V.96, B.A. Boetticher, No. 68.

70. On the Berlepsch dismissal, see Röhl, *Germany without Bismarck*, p. 148; Born, *Staat und Sozialpolitik*, pp. 127ff.; Engelberg, *Deutschland 1871-1897*, p. 271; Saxon embassy report, 1.VII.96, Sächs. H.S.A., Ges. Berlin, No. 251; Varnbühler report, 8.VII.96, Württ. H.S.A., K 51, F 27, Fasz. 12d; Lerchenfeld reports, 28.VI.96, 5.VII.96, G.S.A. München, Ges. Berlin, 1067; Klügmann reports, 28.VI.96 (on Brefeld), 16.VII.96, Staatsarchiv Hamburg, A IV c 6, Bd. III; Bosse Diary, 16.VI.96, 17.VI.96, B.A. Bosse, No. 8.

71. Bosse Diary, 4.V.96, 16.VI.96, B.A. Bosse, No. 8; Bosse to Boetticher, 13.VII.96. B.A. Boetticher, No. 57; Kayser to Hohenlohe, 16.VI.96, Archiv Schillingsfürst, Rep. 100 XXII A-6. Marschall noted that Hohenlohe was helpless again because Bronsart wanted to leave. See Marschall Diary, 16.VI.96.

72. Eulenburg memo, "Gespräch mit dem Reichskanzler," 26.VI.96, B.A. Eul. 42. See also Rich, *Holstein*, II, 513. However, one day later Hohenlohe had thought matters over again and confided in his journal that "if the War Minister would remain in office," things would not be so bad even if Wilhelm refused to make concessions. Archiv Schillingsfürst, Rep. 100 XXII A-8.

73. Eulenburg to Hohenlohe, 5.VII.96, B.A. Eul. 42. See also *Hohenlohe*, III, 242-243.

74. Eulenburg to Hohenlohe, 5.VII.96, B.A. Eul. 42.

75. *Ibid.*

76. *Ibid.*

77. Hohenlohe to Eulenburg, 16.VII.96, B.A. Eul. 42.

78. *Hohenlohe*, III, 254. See also earlier suspicions, Hutten-Czapski, *Sechzig Jahre*, I, 250.

79. Hohenlohe to Eulenburg, 16.VII.96, B.A. Eul. 42.

80. *Hohenlohe*, III, 243.

81. Eulenburg to Bülow, 7.VIII.96, B.A. Eul. 42.

82. *Ibid.*

83. Marschall Diary, 19.VI.96.

84. Eulenburg, "Unterhaltung mit dem Kaiser in Stalheim," 9.VII.96, B.A. Eul. 42.

85. See Eulenburg to Lucanus, 16.V.96; Holstein to Eulenburg, 10.VII.96; Bülow to Eulenburg, 16.VII.96; Hohenlohe to Eulenburg, 16.VII.96 (twice), all in B.A. Eul. 42.

86. Bülow to Eulenburg, 16.VII.96, B.A. Eul. 42.

87. *Ibid.*

88. *Ibid.*

89. Bülow to Eulenburg, 23.VII.96, B.A. Eul. 42.

90. Eulenburg memo, 21.VII.96, B.A. Eul. 42.

91. *Ibid.*

92. See Wilhelm to Eulenburg, 20.VIII.96, B.A. Eul. 43.

93. Eulenburg, "Notizen zur Besprechung auf der Bahn Kiel-Wilhelmshöhe," 1.VIII.96, B.A. Eul. 43. See also Röhl, *Germany without Bismarck*, pp. 194-199.

94. Eulenburg, "Notizen zur Besprechung auf der Bahn Kiel-Wilhelmshöhe," 1.VIII.96, B.A. Eul. 43.

95. *Ibid.*

96. Hohenlohe to Alexander, 28.VII.96, and Holstein to Alexander, 29.VII.96, Archiv Schillingsfürst, Rep. 100 XXII A-8.

97. Marschall Diary, 7.VIII.96.

98. Eulenburg to Wilhlem, 3, 4, and 5.VIII.96, B.A. Eul. 43.

99. Eulenburg to Wilhelm, 4.VIII.96, B.A. Eul. 43.

100. Eulenburg to Wilhelm, 5.VIII.96, B.A. Eul. 43. The end of the affair: three days after Bronsart's dismissal Eulenburg told Hohenlohe that unfortunately he could not come to Berlin. See Eulenburg to Hohenlohe, 17.VIII.96, Archiv Schillingsfürst, Rep. 100 XXII A-8. Hohenlohe to Eulenburg, 21.VIII.96, B.A. Eul. 43; he would come back to the proposal as soon as he could again stand on solid ground. This was in October. However, Eulenburg: "Unfortunately I must decline." Eulenburg, "Notizen," 16.X.96, and Eulenburg to Bülow, 26.X.96, B.A. Eul. 43.

101. *Hohenlohe*, III, 249-250.

102. Eulenburg to Wilhelm, 5.VIII.96, B.A. Eul. 43.

103. *Ibid.* (written in the same letter but under the date of 6.VIII.96).

104. Wilhelm to Eulenburg, 9.VIII.96, and Kiderlen to Eulenburg, 10.VIII.96, B.A. Eul. 43.

105. Monts to Eulenburg, 7.VIII.96, B.A. Eul. 43.

106. Kiderlen to Eulenburg, 10.VIII.96, B.A. Eul. 43. See also Röhl, *Germany without Bismarck*, pp. 175ff., especially pp. 178-179, 198.

107. *Hohenlohe*, III, 235, 251-258. See also assessment of the conference in Lerchenfeld report, 11.VIII.96, G.S.A. München, MA 77751.

108. This plan seems to have originated with Hahnke in order to make Bronsart "*mundtot.*" See Eulenburg, "Aufzeichnungen für Bernhard Bülow," 23.VII.96, B.A. Eul. 42.

109. Bavarian embassy report, 29.VIII.96, G.S.A. München, MA 77751; Saxon embassy reports of 11, 12, 13, 14, 19, 21, 23, and 24.VIII.96, Sächs. H.S.A., Ges. Berlin, No. 251.

110. *Leipziger Neueste Nachrichten*, 27.VIII.96, "Zur Geschichte der letzten Tage," included in Saxon embassy report, Ges. Berlin, No. 251.

111. *Stuttgarter Beobachter*, 17.VIII.96. For the crisis, see also Marschall Diary, 14, 16, 17, 18, and 20.VIII.96; Brauer to Grand Duke, 20.VIII.96, G.L.A. Karlsruhe, Gr. Fam. Archiv, N 330; Bosse Diary, 29, 30, and 31.VIII.96, B.A. Bosse, No. 8; *Schulthess*, 1896, pp. 101-102; *Wippermann*, 1896 (II), pp. 85ff.

112. Bronsart to Grand Duke, 29.VIII.96, G.L.A. Karlsruhe, Gr. Fam. Archiv, N 334; very similar to Bronsart to Bosse in Bosse Diary, 7.IX.96, B.A. Bosse, No. 8.

113. *Hohenlohe*, III, 254–255; Lerchenfeld to Crailsheim, 11. VIII.96, G.S.A. München, MA 77751; Marschall Diary, 15.VIII.96; Bosse Diary, 29.VIII.96, B.A. Bosse, No. 8.

114. *Hohenlohe*, III, 256. See also Hutten-Czapski, *Sechzig Jahre*, I, 294ff.; Marschall Diary, 23, 24, and 25.VIII.96. Marschall by now had come to regard the May 18 declaration in the Reichstag as stupid.

115. *Hohenlohe*, III, 256. But much less optimistic was Brauer to Grand Duke, 26.VIII.96, G.L.A. Karlsruhe, Gr. Fam. Archiv, No. 330. See also Miquel to Boetticher, 25.VIII.96, B.A. Boetticher, No. 84: the statement in the *Reichsanzeiger*, Miquel said, was no doubt pretty nice, but it had not solved the issue. Hohenlohe would be satisfied with a bare minimum of reform, and this minimum he will get if he saves Miquel's budget.

116. *Hohenlohe*, III, 257.

117. Wilhelm to Eulenburg, 13.VIII.96; Eulenburg to Holstein, 14.VIII.96; Eulenburg to Wilhelm, 14.VIII.96 (twice), all in B.A. Eul. 43.

118. Eulenburg to Wilhelm, 14.VIII.96, B.A. Eul. 43.

119. Hohenlohe to Eulenburg, 29.VIII.96, Archiv Schillingsfürst, Rep. 100 XXII A-8; Ministry of State minutes, 11.IX.96, D.Z.A. Merseburg, vol. 124.

120. See Eulenburg to Wilhelm, 14.VIII.96, B.A. Eul. 43.

121. See Werner Frauendienst, "Demokratisierung des Deutschen Konstitutionalismus in der Zeit Wilhelms II," *Zeitschrift für die gesamte Staatswissenschaft*, 133 (1957), 728.

122. For Holstein during this period, see also Rich, *Holstein*, II, 508–519.

123. *Ibid.*, p. 508.

124. Eulenburg to Bülow, 13.III.96, 16.III.96, B.A. Eul. 40.

125. Bülow to Eulenburg, 20.III.96, B.A. Eul. 40.

126. Bülow to Eulenburg, 17.III.97, B.A. Eul. 49. Especially illuminating are the following lines: "I have taken great care to point out to Holstein (in my letters to him) how invaluable you have been . . . [for the government and for him, Holstein]; but [I also pointed out] that there are no limits to your influence . . . I will continue to write Holstein along these lines of reassurance. We have to further our position with H[olstein] mutually. If he would not be under the impression that I do everything to 'influence' you according to his line of thought; that you are not eagerly trying to support the 'system'; then the general situation would become an untenable one...." See also Bülow to Eulenburg, 16.VII.96, B.A. Eul. 42: "I replied to him [Holstein] only in generalities since I do not know how much you have told him and in order not to impair your line of action." Bülow added that perhaps it would be appropriate to scare Holstein with his "terrible visions" of Radowitz, Waldersee, and Herbert Bismarck. However, see also

Holsteins Papiere, III, 581, note 1.

127. See Eulenburg to Bülow, 13.III.96, B.A. Eul. 40.

128. See especially Holstein to Eulenburg, 1.V.96, B.A. Eul. 42; *Holsteins Papiere*, III, 560.

129. Especially Holstein to Eulenburg, 5.V.96, B.A. Eul. 42; Haller, *Eulenburg*, p. 197; *Holsteins Papiere*, III, 560.

130. See Haller, *Eulenburg*, p. 200; Eulenburg, "Vier Tage in Prökelwitz," B.A. Eul. 42.

131. See above, pp. 17, 19.

132. Raschdau to Schiemann, 30.V.96, Schiemann Papers, No. 107, G.S.A. Berlin, Rep. 92. It is interesting to note that this member of the Fronde advocated Bülow as Chancellor! Eulenburg and Bülow knew how to play their game.

133. August Eulenburg to Philipp Eulenburg, 11.VIII.96, B.A. Eul. 43. See also Kiderlen to Eulenburg, 10.VII.96, B.A. Eul. 43; *Holsteins Papiere*, III, 580-581.

134. Holstein to Eulenburg, 19.VI.96, B.A. Eul. 42.

135. See *Holsteins Papiere*, III, 580-581.

136. This had been assumed to be a logical outcome of the proposed reform but had not, as far as Hohenlohe's memoirs go, been mentioned in the Wilhelmshöhe conference in August. See Hutten-Czapski, *Sechzig Jahre*, I, 291.

137. See Eulenburg to Wilhelm, 14.VIII.96, B.A. Eul. 43.

138. Hohenlohe to Eulenburg, 21.VIII.96, 29.VIII.96, B.A. Eul. 43; *Hohenlohe*, III, 254-255.

139. Lucanus to Eulenburg, 13.VIII.96, B.A. Eul. 43.

140. Eulenburg to Wilhelm, 18.VIII.96, and Eulenburg to Grand Duke, 8.IX.96, B.A. Eul. 43.

141. Eulenburg to Wilhelm, 18.VIII.96, B.A. Eul. 43.

142. Eulenburg to Wilhelm, 16.VIII.96, B.A. Eul. 43.

143. Eulenburg to Kaiser in Victoria, 18.VIII.96, B.A. Eul. 43.

144. Hohenlohe to Eulenburg, 21.VIII.96, 29.VIII.96, B.A. Eul. 43; *Hohenlohe*, III, 254-255.

145. Eulenburg to Hohenlohe, 24.VIII.96, B.A. Eul. 43.

146. Eulenburg to Wilhelm, 30.VIII.96, B.A. Eul. 43.

147. Eulenburg to Wilhelm, 24.VIII.96, B.A. Eul. 43.

148. Grand Duke to Eulenburg, 30.IX.96, B.A. Eul. 43.

CHAPTER 11

The Bismarck Revelations and the Leckert-Lützow-Tausch Trials

In all circles here there prevails great excitement about the publication of Bismarck about the Russo-German neutrality-treaty of 1887. . . . The one, especially the semiofficial, group accuses the Prince of treason; the others say that the publication was done with the purpose in mind to bring about an understanding with Russia.

> Spitzemberg Diary,
> November 4, 1896

I am satisfied with the result [Marschall's reply in the Reichstag to Bismarck's revelations]. A triumph of the government over Prince Bismarck would have been politically disgraceful and would have been achieved only with a poor majority, but neither is it a triumph for Bismarck. The government had to speak, since despite all the undying achievements of Prince Bismarck a government must exist after his resignation also and must have the courage of its convictions.

> Marschall Diary,
> November 16, 1896

I deem it of some interest to point out that as of now in three cases the agents of the Political Police have transmitted information proven to be false. . . . I regard the whole system of the secret agents as a failure, since these men are faced with a task they cannot solve, and consequently their reports simply do not correspond with the truth. . . . If von Tausch insists upon having secret agents, this is his own affair. But if these agents dare publicly to slander me, my subordinates, and the Foreign Office, then I resort to publicity [great commotion in the court-room] and denounce their activity in public.

> Marschall in court during
> the Leckert-Lützow trial,
> December 3-4, 1896

I cannot stand it any longer with Marschall! I do not care if 20 Lützows are prosecuted.

> Wilhelm II

1

The May crisis over the military penal code reform had hardly
been overcome (and the subject itself postponed for the time being),
when new events occurred that erupted into another severe crisis for
the Hohenlohe government. The new confrontation arose in the form
of a concentrated attack on the personalities, as well as the
policies, of the German Foreign Office. It came directly in the
wake of the European tour of the Russian monarch in August, September, and October of 1896.

On August 25 young Czar Nicholas II commenced his European tour,
meeting the German Emperor in Breslau and Görlitz from September 3
to September 7. In early October the Czar was in Paris where he was
enthusiastically received. On the return trip Wilhelm met the Czar
again for a short time in Darmstadt and Wiesbaden, and by the end of
the month Nicholas had safely returned to St. Petersburg.[1]

The visit of the Czar in the West, especially his stay in Paris,
created a lively response in the press and from the European governments; this was particularly so in Germany and France. The Czar's
Paris days had shown once again that France had successfully freed
herself from the diplomatic isolation that Bismarck had imposed upon
her. The new Czar Nicholas had confirmed the previous indications
during the reign of his father of a developing Franco-Russian friendship, demonstrated by visits to Cronstadt in July, 1891, and Toulon
in October, 1893. The French no less than the German and Russian
press went to great lengths to point out again this change in the
European diplomatic situation. As much as it had been a diplomatic
defeat for the Germans, it had been, from all appearances, a victory
for the French.[2]

The immediate impressions of the Breslau-Görlitz days in the
minds of the German statesmen seem to have been encouraging. Eulenburg in Vienna had received "good news" from Berlin.[3] This impression was further strengthened by the generally optimistic letter of
thanks from the Russian ambassador in Berlin, Count Osten-Sacken.[4]
Eulenburg in early October even recorded that the old friendship had
again come alive: "The Czar is very straightforward. His Majesty
had the greatest confidence in him and thinks that the days of Breslau and Görlitz will be very fruitful."[5] They hoped that these
fruits would consist of economic cooperation between Germany and
Russia, and eventually a Europe united against the United States.
This would be, it was hoped, "in a sense the program for the new
future of the European world."[6] The Czar, however, had not returned
to Russia right away, but had gone on to Copenhagen, where he had
planned his visit to France,[7] a fact which he had purposely withheld from the Kaiser in Breslau.[8] While the Czar was in Paris, the
Breslau-Görlitz days were re-examined in a more realistic perspective. The follow-up visits between the Russian and German monarchs
in mid-October had been anything but encouraging. Cuno Moltke,
Eulenburg's close friend, informed Phili that Wilhelm, even before
seeing Nicholas in Darmstadt and Wiesbaden, was already in a
depressed mood, since "the Breslau days did not fulfill everything
they had promised."[9] The naive eagerness with which Wilhelm had
tried to restore his Breslau image at Wiesbaden and Darmstadt made
him look slightly ridiculous and tended to achieve the opposite of

what he had wanted. Eulenburg, as well as Hohenlohe, had to listen
to Wilhelm's moods, depressions, hopes, and disappointments over the
Czar; Wilhelm did not conceal his attitude but expressed it rather
openly in court circles.[10] Wilhelm had tried personal diplomacy
and had failed, but in his naive and clumsy way he had been quite
sincere. He had obviously hoped to impress the young Czar and induce
him to reverse the policy of Alexander III toward France by joining
the Austro-German camp. The seeming insincerity of the Czar immediately after Wilhelm's own flights into delusion—delusion stemming
in no small part from wishful thinking and from his inability to
form a sound, realistic analysis of the political situation—certainly tended to increase his mood of depression and resentment.
Eulenburg's reaction to Wilhelm's failure is quite revealing. "Yet
I am not discontented," he wrote to Bülow. "This matter belongs in
the chapter '*personal* experiences' of the Kaiser, and this we
need."[11] This had been one of Holstein's maxims.[12]

2

Such was the general atmosphere when the newspapers began their
critical analysis of "recent" German foreign policy. The *Hamburger
Nachrichten*, as did most other German newspapers, commented on the
recent developments and pointed out Germany's receding position and
her increasing isolation; Germany was being wedged in between two
hostile neighbors. This must be seen as a "consequence of the
fact . . . that during the first year of his administration Count
Caprivi had given up the well cultivated relations with Russia and
Austria-Hungary of the old course as being 'too complicated.'"[13]
On October 24, 1896, Bismarck published in the *Hamburger Nachrichten*
his famous article (the so-called "Bismarck revelations") in which
he revealed the existence of the Reinsurance Treaty between Germany
and Russia, which had not been renewed by his successor. On several
previous occasions Bismarck had alluded to this treaty, but only
an intimate few had been able to understand the full meaning of
these occasional hints.[14]

While the Bismarck revelations as such created only temporary
concern among the leading European statesmen and had no serious
repercussions in international relations, they created an immense
sensation in German domestic affairs for several weeks.[15] The
German press plunged into a heated debate. Mainly, the conservative and "middle party" press defended the viewpoint and action of
Bismarck, while only the Social Democratic, the Radical, and some
ultramontane papers came to the aid of the government.[16] Bismarck's revelations constituted a "public accusation"[17] against the
New Course in general and the Foreign Office—and Holstein and
Marschall—in particular.

Bismarck's challenge was so direct, and the reaction it found
in Germany was so tremendous, that the German government could not
possibly ignore it as far as the public was concerned. It had in
one form or another to give a public account of the conduct of its
foreign policy during the "post-Bismarckian" period. This was
extremely difficult as well as embarrassing. Holstein was not
incorrect when he reviewed the year of 1896 to Eulenburg in the
following manner:

The year 1896 has been an evil year for His Majesty. It began with the Krüger telegram, and ended with the appointment of Muraviev and Queen Victoria's letter, in which she begged her grandson not to come to the Royal Jubilee, and that because of the State of English public opinion! So left and right, with Russia and England, he had played havoc—. . . . People no longer take the sovereign seriously. That is a great peril. For when the hour of danger comes, when the question arises: "Is the Emperor a man who can be depended upon?"—how will that question be answered, in Germany and outside it?[18]

The Krüger telegram had for the moment alienated Germany from England by encouraging German animosity toward England in order to use the aroused public opinion as a means of encouraging the idea of a huge Navy. Moreover, the crisis over Crete certainly was not handled by the German government in such a way as to bring the two countries closer together.[19] At the same time Russia had moved away from Germany toward France.

Bismarck was well aware of the situation[20] and realized it was absolutely necessary to further good relations with the eastern autocracy. The result of the policies of the New Course was that Germany had become isolated from England as well as and especially from Russia. The greatest of Bismarck's fears, a French-Russian alliance—a fear that had been the basis of most of his diplomatic efforts—had become a reality by 1894, and German policy since that time had failed to improve Germany's foreign political position. Under these circumstances, revealing the existence of the Reinsurance Treaty seems to have been the last desperate act of a deeply troubled statesman using even public pressure to curb political irresponsibility rather than the act of an irresponsible man seeking personal revenge.[21]

3

"Bismarck's publication," Eulenburg noted on October 27, "has hit the Foreign Office like a bombshell."[22] Certainly it did, since it constituted a violent and direct attack upon the Foreign Office at its most vulnerable spot, which was Germany's policy toward Russia since 1890. Holstein interpreted Bismarck's move as being conducted against the Triple Alliance,[23] but at the same time was suspicious that it might be designed as a coup on his part to return to Berlin.[24]

The Kaiser, no less than the Foreign Office, was gravely apprehensive about the Bismarck article, especially as it came almost immediately after his keen disappointment over the Czar and thus added insult to injury. Wilhelm regarded it as a personal attack upon himself and could find no adequate explanation why Bismarck had again so suddenly and violently turned against him. His main fear, however, seemed to stem from the possibility of further Bismarck revelations that would discredit him in front of Germany and Europe.[25] August Eulenburg wrote to his cousin Phili in Vienna, "I long very much to speak with you, especially since you can

imagine that the frame of mind of the All-Highest is at the moment,
due to the Bismarck press publication, inconsolable. And this does,
as it were, noticeably affect the general state of mind."[26]   In line
with his impulsive nature the Kaiser intended to take drastic action
against Herbert Bismarck, whom he (as well as the Foreign Office)
at first held responsible for the publication.[27]   However, the military entourage and Hohenlohe succeeded in calming down the monarch.[28]
It was Hohenlohe, most likely influenced by Marschall,[29] who pointed
out to the monarch that a trial of even Herbert would, regardless of
the evidence, only be looked upon as a trial of the retired Chancellor himself. Moreover, this step would "cloud" not only the image
of Bismarck for the German people but also the "esteem of the
German Empire in a downright destructive and dangerously impairing
way."[30]   The Kaiser then dropped the idea of a court-martial.

The Foreign Office had soon decided that the attack came not
from Herbert but from Bismarck directly. Although unable to explain
the specific reason for such an attack at precisely that moment, the
general nature of the attack was obvious; Marschall particularly
felt obligated to defend himself against the charge of a pro-English
policy. He was quick to point out, among other things, that the
central point of the defense of the Foreign Office and Count
August Eulenburg against the press accusations of the journalists
Leckert and Lützow was the rejection of the insinuation that a pro-
English clique was conducting German policy. He did not fail to
mention the strange role that the Berlin police commissary, Tausch,
who seemingly had direct connections with Friedrichsruh, played in
this intrigue. For Marschall, then, the Bismarck attack and its
consequences had one aim in common: to discredit the Foreign Office
by accusing it of succumbing to British influences.[31]

Eulenburg apparently was not too concerned about either the
foreign or the domestic situation. His first step with regard to
the Kaiser after the Bismarck catastrophe was to calm him about the
"shocking publications of the wicked old man of Friedrichsruh."
After assuring the monarch of his sympathy ("the lively sensitivity
of Your Majesty is in truth like a part of me. We both are born
for suffering"), he went on to explain that even though the revelations would result in increased suspicion on the part of Austria
and Hungary toward Germany, it was not a strong enough attack to
loosen the bonds between these countries. Eulenburg explained
Bismarck's motives as being solely a matter of his personality.
Bismarck, he suggested, had become annoyed that he was being held
responsible for the deterioration of relations between Germany and
Russia, which (Eulenburg assured the Kaiser) in fact was the case.
At the end of the letter Eulenburg dealt with Marschall. On the
one hand, he praised him for his "very dignified and well stated
reply" in the official *Reichsanzeiger*; on the other hand, he took
the liberty of making clever, and deliberate, jokes at his expense.[32]
Eulenburg thus made sure that Marschall would not reap any Imperial favors—however slight this possibility might have been—from
his very able defense of the government and crown against Bismarck
and the Bismarck Fronde. He also made sure that he retained his
freedom of action toward Marschall, which had once before, in 1895,
been impaired by the Kaiser.

In several respects Eulenburg's attitude toward the European

tour of the Czar and the Bismarck revelations was quite similar to that of
his friend Bülow. This attitude was, in part perhaps, a reflection of the
latter's views. Shortly before the *Hamburger Nachrichten* article appeared, Bülow had written that he was not very much concerned about
the latest European developments   If Russia, he speculated, were to
attack Austria and Germany, these two powers would have to fight
France, England, and the Poles as well.[33] Such was the diplomatic
"genius" of Bülow(!); little did it improve during his relatively
long period in the chancellorship, which was to begin a few years
later. In contrast to Bismarck's policies, Bülow's lack of concern
in the face of a disastrous and as it turned out correct analysis of
the situation may be characterized as trivial irresponsibility.

Yet, in contrast to most other officials in the Foreign Office,
Bülow seems to have appreciated rather than lamented the Bismarck
article. To be sure, he also recognized that this action would
increase the difficulties of the German ambassadors, especially
those in Vienna and Rome; however, he said, "For the domestic
situation on this Hamburg attack could lead to a clarification.
The elimination of Marschall after this declaration of war from
Friedrichsruh seems impossible to me at the present time, at least
for the duration of the coming parliamentary campaign."[34] Bülow
analyzed the situation and concluded that Marschall was safe for
the time being. Of course, this meant that it was Marschall who
had to bear the brunt of the fighting through the difficult issues
and discredit himself with all the major parties in the process,
while Bülow could save himself for calmer times.

Eulenburg agreed with his friend Bülow. He followed up his
soothing letter to the Kaiser with a personal visit in early November, and he even convinced him that Bismarck had scored only a
very slight, even a "bad," success, which would keep him from pub-
lishing more incriminating material. However, at the same time
Eulenburg was himself quite afraid of just such a move from Friedrichsruh. Moreover, when the Kaiser exclaimed that now all ties
between Bismarck and himself had been broken, "that there would,
henceforth, be no sign of any kind of connection," Eulenburg noted
(for Bülow), "I remained silent. Time heals many wounds. May God
only protect us from an *accentuation* of the contradictions."[35] It
is quite apparent that even while Eulenburg knew that he had to keep
Marschall in office to assure Bülow's success in Berlin, he also knew
that it was fundamental not to sever all the ties with Friedrichsruh.
Although there seems to be no written evidence of any direct connection between Eulenburg and Friedrichsruh for this time, it seems
very probable that Eulenburg did not risk the chance of accident in
having his way, especially considering that perhaps the most important prerequisite of a successful Bülow career in Berlin would be
the attitude of Bismarck and the Bismarck Fronde toward this new
government. On the other hand, it seems quite certain that Eulenburg left this part almost completely to Bülow, since it was Bülow
who knew Herbert Bismarck well and kept in touch with him.[36]

A few days after meeting Wilhelm, Eulenburg paid a visit to the
expendable Botho to inform him about "pending personnel matters."
He found that Botho was still very much interested in becoming
Reich Chancellor, but on his own terms—that is, with Bülow and
without Marschall—since he wanted the job only if his views could

find clear and full expression. Cousin Phili did not disillusion
Botho: he might have to serve as Chancellor for a short time if
any unexpected events—and there were always good chances for that
("With God and His Majesty anything is possible," Marschall had
said[37])—might force Phili to change his tactical moves and goals
temporarily. He did succeed, however, in persuading Botho that
Marschall was still a necessity for the present regime. Moreover,
while at the beginning of the conversation Phili recognized that
Botho's antagonism toward Marschall was greater than he had suspected, at the end he was able to note confidently that "at any
rate, I had the impression that this transition with Marschall will
be possible for a time."[38]   He summed up in his own mind the possibilities of the present situation:

   1) Hohenlohe and Marschall will possibly be swept
   out of office by questions that become acute in the
   Reichstag, by worse revelations, or some other such
   matter (this I doubt). In this case an appointment of
   B.E., B.B. would result (for the latter the only possible
   way to preserve himself for the future).

   2) Hohenlohe stays and Marschall leaves in the spring,
   then B.B. would replace him. Botho would (if Hohenlohe
   immediately died) not even be considered, and Bernhard
   takes over after Hohenlohe's fall (termination).

   3) Hohenlohe becomes ill. Botho will be nominated
   as substitute and Marschall remains for the time being.
   In this case Bernhard would come after a few months.[39]

For the moment Eulenburg thought the second possibility the
most likely, since Hohenlohe was in the best of health and Marschall
was "like an extremely rotten pear, physically and as far as his
ability to carry out his duty is concerned." Then Eulenburg considered the Holstein problem: "Holstein identifies himself with
the block group system Hohenlohe-Marschall, and does not even consider the thought of a possible separation of these two." He
attributed Holstein's recent cordiality solely to Bülow, and
credited the former with the intent to use Eulenburg to re-establish
his dominant position in affairs of state: "When the sky is blue
again, he will again sit on top and we will hear the familiar tune.
But, as a matter of fact, things may turn out in quite a different
way."[40]   Nevertheless, Eulenburg's attitude toward Holstein did not
keep him from following Holstein's advice whenever it coincided with
his own interests. In fact, Holstein at times still proved to be
quite valuable to Eulenburg.[41]

4

   On November 12 Holstein informed Eulenburg that the Kaiser had
called on Marschall and had bluntly told him that the answer to any
Reichstag inquiry concerning the Bismarck articles should be that
these things were "secrets of state." This indeed had been the line
taken by Marschall in the official reply in the *Reichsanzeiger* on
October 27.[42]   Holstein added that "silence however is impossible."[43]
Thereupon Eulenburg wrote Wilhelm the next day, pointing out that

"total silence would no doubt create a bad impression but one word in excess may do much harm. Thus, one must maneuver with caution between these positions."[44]

Marschall, on his side, pointed out the impossibility and the disastrous consequences of such a response.[45] He correctly surmised that ". . . the 'secret of state' that has been announced in the *Reichsanzeiger* covers up for the content of the treaties—in this sense it must remain so—not however the reasons for the non-renewal, the attacks due to British influence, that the government has severed the ties with Russia, and thereby is the cause of Toulon and Cronstadt, etc. . . ."[46] He held that in the Reichstag there existed three groups: the anti-Bismarck majority, the Bismarck followers, and a moderate group which disapproved of Bismarck's conduct and was willing to support the government on the basis of a reasonable official statement. He included here the Center Party and the National Liberals. Under these circumstances, Marschall concluded that a reasonable and objective statement by the government would be well received by the majority of the Reichstag as well as in Europe, while total silence would only intensify discussion on the subject to such a degree that in the end the government would be forced to face the issue under the "impression of a vain attempt to take up the lost battle again." Hohenlohe was of the same opinion, pointing out that silence would be looked upon as "a fearful retreat in the face of Prince Bismarck and as bankruptcy of the government." Under this pressure Lucanus also in time came around to support Hohenlohe and Marschall. The Kaiser finally gave his consent to Marschall's reply, which was delivered during the session of November 16.[47]

In the Reichstag Marschall defended the government ("an extremely difficult task") with considerable ability.[48] Nonetheless, there was no denying that the government was on the defensive and had been placed in an extremely unpleasant situation. This situation was to last at least through the period during which the ministers responsible for the New Course remained in their leading positions. On the other hand, it gave at the same time a new—if brief—lease on life to the New Course ministry, and particularly to Marschall. An immediate dismissal of Marschall would have amounted to a capitulation before Bismarck. Nevertheless, the whole episode had shown how powerful and influential the Bismarck Fronde, and Bismarck, still were in politics,[49] and it had proven once again the indispensability of Marschall to the Hohenlohe Ministry.

That fact, however, was not reflected in the attitude of the Kaiser or the groups surrounding him. Eulenburg had to intervene in early December and point out to the monarch that after the kind of parliamentary feat Marschall had just performed, he could not simply be dismissed without serious consequences to public morale, to the image of the Kaiser, and to the attitude of the majority of the Reichstag. He cordially congratulated Marschall on his "brilliant" success.[50] However, this did not change his viewpoint or his tactics in regard to the Kaiser and Marschall that he had stated ten days previously: "With spring the swallows may fly. Your Majesty knows my viewpoint in this regard and knows that Marshall's brilliant speech on the Bismarck revelations was a double-edged sword for me. As it is, everything depends upon choosing the *right*

moment—and that is certainly not while the Reichstag is in
session."[51]

5

In early October Eulenburg had written to Holstein, "We will get
through the winter all right. I am not troubling myself to look
further. We will simply have to do our best to remove combustible
materials."[52] However, it was beyond their power to do so. In more
than one respect the visit of the Czar had brought forth an intense
and sensational response. Hardly had the *Hamburger Nachrichten* sensation subsided when a scandal of a different nature arose—this was
the Leckert-Lützow trial, followed by the proceedings against Eugen
von Tausch. These two cases remained on the German political scene
up to the time of Marschall's dismissal in June, 1897.

As in the case of the Bismarck disclosures,[53] the Leckert-Lützow
affair originated during the visit of the Czar. At Breslau the
Czar on one occasion had given a toast in which he said that he held
the same sentiments toward Germany as did Kaiser Wilhelm toward
Russia. The Czar's toast was then incorrectly reported as expressing
sentiments toward Germany similar to those of his father, Alexander
III, who had a reputation of being anti-German. Before this latter
version could be disavowed by the German government, it had been
picked up by several newspapers as well as by the majority of the
French press.

The affair over the toast received very serious attention from
Foreign Secretary Marschall when a Berlin newspaper, the *Welt am
Montag*, published two articles (on September 28 and October 4)
maintaining that the false report of the toast had not been an accident, but had been a deliberate act on the part of a camarilla under
British influence. Such a false report was supposedly to help
create a rift between Germany and Russia and, consequently, to force
the German government to lean more heavily toward Great Britain.
The article clearly implied that Count August Eulenburg, the Court
Chamberlain, was responsible for the act of falsification. An
article in the *Staatsbürgerzeitung* also implied that the charge
against August Eulenburg had come from the Foreign Office, specifically from Marschall. It was this attack on Marschall's office
and person that forced him to take action. On October 7 he asked
the monarch's permission to file suit and clear up the whole matter,
a request which met with the full approval and consent of the
Kaiser.[54] However, it was approved by the Kaiser not so much from
sympathy toward Marschall but because the press had also attacked
Hahnke—and this fact had been the cause of Wilhelm's wrath.[55]
Marschall, then, took his case to court and energetically began to
prepare for it. Marschall was aware—at least to some extent—of
his precarious situation and the animosity of the Kaiser toward
him. He seemingly hoped to consolidate his position as well as
gain the respect of the monarch with a successful trial against
the subterranean press intrigues that had, with varying intensity,
accompanied the New Course throughout its existence.[56]

For a time the Bismarck revelations had commanded the full
attention of the government. Even though Marschall had brilliantly
defended the government, the monarch still wished to get rid of

this successful minister who had proven himself once again an invaluable asset of the Hohenlohe Ministry as well as of the crown.[57] Marschall's action against another paper, the *Deutsche Tages-Zeitung*, was a kind of prelude and indication of events that lay in the near future—the Leckert-Lützow trial. Among the many speculations that were voiced about Bismarck's motives for the Reinsurance Treaty revelations was the suggestion in the *Bank und Handelszeitung* that the Czar had originally intended to visit Bismarck but had changed his mind as a result of the efforts of high German government officials. What induced Marschall to take action against the *Deutsche Tages-Zeitung* was an article stating that it had been Marschall himself who had placed this notice in the press. The result of the court action was disappointing. The *Deutsche Tages-Zeitung* was punished, while the real offender remained undiscovered.[58]

On November 24 the situation again became so acute that Holstein felt it necessary to warn Eulenburg of an imminent crisis: "The barometer indicates an approaching storm. . . ." Up till then the public was not aware of this, since no legitimate reasons for any crisis existed, especially after the recent success of Marschall, whose action had (according to the press) "given the government a stronger position in the country and Parliament than at any time since the spring of 1890."[59]

Nevertheless, the agitation against Marschall was reaching a new climax—the same agitation that had started with the resignation of Köller. Marschall was accused of having successfully intrigued against the "most incompetent of all Ministers of Interior," with the help of the press. Marschall, by accident or, rather, because of the "increasing impudence of his opponents," found a clue to the press intrigues against him and the Foreign Office. This clue clearly pointed to Eugen von Tausch as the source of the insinuations. Tausch at the time was head of the political section of the Berlin Police. Marschall then began to prepare his defense against these elements, openly and in court. Holstein further informed Eulenburg that in all probability Tausch would be "exposed." What added to the importance of the Tausch affair was the fact that Waldersee, among others, had "regularly" worked with Tausch. Naturally these elements were now doing everything in their power to attack the present regime with the hope of forstalling a Tausch trial. Holstein further added that the Kaiser was unfortunately lending a ready ear to all those who were urging him to take radical measures in an attempt to bring down the Hohenlohe-Marschall Ministry.[60]

At the same time, Hohenlohe was warned not to let himself be dragged "into the abyss" by Marschall; the opposition of the Kaiser against the Secretary of State, "caused and agitated by the Bismarck friends at the Berlin court," had reached such a feverish pitch that the monarch would rather see Hohenlohe go than retain Marschall. Hohenlohe did not take this warning at its face value, but he realized that his position, and that of Marschall, was a grave one.[61]

Eulenburg took Holstein's warning seriously enough to use it as a basis for writing to the monarch and pointing out to him the inopportune time for a crisis. At the same time he skillfully used flattery: "It haunts me even in sleep the picture of the bad

Old Man who, face to face with Death, falls into fits of rage which hurt his Emperor and the Fatherland." Then he quickly added that he had been very much reassured by the rational and sensible attitude which Wilhelm had displayed throughout the whole Bismarck affair; he had in fact taken the monarch as his example. After this flattery (we know that the facts were to the contrary) Eulenburg carefully approached the question of the monarch's considering the idea of creating a crisis. He had come to the conclusion, Eulenburg wrote, that "with the state of feverish excitement in the country and the narrow-minded fanaticism of the mass who idolize the Old One like Baal," it was best to abstain from any rash actions for the time being. Consequently, he said, the alarming news that had reached him from Berlin could hardly be true. Then he recited the facts that Holstein had supplied and pointed out that "whoever may advise Your Majesty for a crisis at the moment is either a miserable political dilettant or he is *mala fide*. . . ." He ended by assuring his monarch that next spring, after the end of the current Reichstag, appropriate steps could easily be taken.[62] Eulenburg certainly knew how to handle Kaiser Wilhelm. It was the "brilliant adroitness" that Holstein well knew how to appreciate.[63]

Holstein had ably pointed out to Eulenburg the possible consequences of such radical steps as replacing Hohenlohe and Marschall or of dissolving the Reichstag. Public opinion would shift from the Kaiser to the Socialists and Bismarckians.[64] Bülow was of the same opinion; the alternatives produced by such a policy, he conceded, would be either a full-fledged parliamentary system or a return to a Bismarckian system. In addition, Bülow stated, as he had often before, that "the time has not yet come when the majority of the nation will have come to understand with us that neither with the one, nor with the other, but only in royalism *sans phrase* lies salvation." Although he was aware of the weakness of the present situation, any premature action to do away with the "present system" could easily lead to something worse. Bülow added:

> Situations exist where one has to choose the lesser
> of two evils. If Hohenlohe stays, he can under no cir-
> cumstances dispense with Marschall before the end of the
> parliamentary session (especially after his latest success,
> the impression of Bronsart's resignation, the attacks of
> the press against irresponsible camarilla, and in particu-
> lar the latest attack by Bismarck). . . .
> I realize that great demands are often made on the
> patience of His Majesty, but this patience will person-
> ally and politically pay for itself.[65]

He closed by assuring Eulenburg that he had done everything possible to calm both Holstein and Marschall.

Eulenburg was aware that Holstein needed him to support the Hohenlohe-Marschall regime, and they stubbornly fought for the same end, although for different reasons and often with different methods. They both fought the "men of action" surrounding the Kaiser, especially Waldersee, who was bent on a coup d'état.[66] Thus the combined efforts of Holstein and Eulenburg succeeded again in lengthening the life span of the precarious and tottering Hohenlohe Ministry,

despite the active agitation against it. Since both Eulenburg and
Holstein supported Marschall, he was not dismissed, and the court
case took its due course. The court began its public hearings on
December 2 and ended on December 7 after four days of full session.

Marschall's optimism that he would be able to strengthen his
position in the eyes of the monarch and to clear up the press
intrigues was by no means shared by everyone. August Eulenburg
made sure to explain to his cousin Phili why he had taken legal
action. Had it not been for Hohenlohe and Marschall, who practically begged him not to desert the Foreign Office, he would not
have done so. However, it was not until he had secured the
Kaiser's consent that he agreed to file suit. However, this would
be all. As far as the trial itself was concerned, he said, "I will
be—exactly according to your advice—completely passive and await
what may come out of it." This would probably amount to nothing.
August agreed with Phili that Marschall "deceives himself completely
about the success that the court action is supposed to give him.
The opinions of His Majesty about the personalities there are
harsher than ever."[67]

The usually well informed Bavarian representative in Berlin,
Lerchenfeld, reported to his government that this trial was bound
to have some positive results, such as a more careful attitude of
the press toward journalists, a more discriminating practice of
publication, a more careful selection of police agents, and less
likelihood that another Tausch scandal would be possible within the
next few years. However, he regreted that a minister had to take
such a step as Marschall did: "Marschall has . . . entered the
trial with a clearly recognizable inner satisfaction and has therewith once again given proof of his unusual determination and vigour."
On the other hand, "that his conduct concerning the trial is to
his advantage in All-Highest quarters and that his relationship to
the Kaiser will improve, that I do not yet dare hope at the moment."[68]
Even Hohenlohe was skeptical of such a success, since the police
commissar, Eugen von Tausch, whom Marschall suspected as being the
center of intrigue, "is *persona gratissima* with H.M. H.M. has been
told that Tausch eminently guarantees his personal safety. If
Marschall brings the said Tausch to such a point, where he has to
disappear from the scene, H.M. will concern himself little with his
[Tausch's] proven black-guardism but will lament the loss of the
experienced security agent. And Marschall will fare even worse
than before as the cause of this destruction."[69]

Above all, it was Eulenburg who knew how illusory Marschall's
hopes were. As early as October 26 he was able to inform Bülow
that Marschall was making a big mistake in expecting a "generally
rosy mood" as a result of the prospective trial. "Despite the
Lützow trial, his days are numbered," he commented.[70] The animosity
of the Kaiser was too great to overcome: "I cannot stand it any
longer with Marschall! I do not care if 20 Lützows are prosecuted,"
Wilhelm had exclaimed.[71]

Lucanus, who held that in order to avoid a scandal Marschall
should request appointment to an embassy, probably did his part to
intensify further the antagonism of Wilhelm. Admiral von Senden
and General von Hahnke undoubtedly contributed their share, as well
as did, with more caution, Waldersee.[72] Perhaps Finance Minister

Miquel and even August Eulenburg took part in this maneuver to undermine Marschall's position.[73] Wilhelm's attitude, therefore, was
anything but favorable toward Marschall. In this connection Holstein's description of the situation to Eulenburg on November 24
reflected the state of the Kaiser's mind and the influence of those
surrounding him. Well could Eulenburg comment, "*Poverino
Marschall.*"[74]

6

The trial was not prevented, but the Kaiser and his entourage
had made up their minds and would not let themselves be confused by
whatever facts Marschall might uncover. Hohenlohe's probable justification of the proceedings—namely, that the various attacks
against the Kaiser in the foreign press had been committed by
agents of Tausch and thus had not been stopped; that these agents
(especially Normann-Schumann) had been protected by Police President
v. Richtofen; and that consequently Marschall and the Foreign Office
had no choice but to act in the form of a public trial—made no
impression.[75] Such were the conditions under which Marschall
proceeded to defend his own honor and that of the Foreign Office
for four days in front of the public in the Provincial Court I in
Berlin.

The actors in the Leckert-Lützow trial ranged over a vast
spectrum of social respectability. There was the self-styled
journalist Heinrich Leckert, just 19 years old, who had tried his
hand unsuccessfully in the merchant trade. There was Karl von
Lützow, in his fifties, journalist and police agent with a court
record involved in a variety of scandals,[76] a former Bavarian Army
officer with a dishonorable discharge. There was Dr. Karl Ploetz,
editor of the young *Welt am Montag*, "a man probably inexperienced
in press affairs." There was Dr. Berger, who in his *Staatsbürgerzeitung* had consistently attacked the New Course and the Foreign
Office. There was the Hofrat de Grahl, who had taken down and
transmitted the incorrect message to Berlin and who would, some
months later, be removed from his post for having given another
false telegram—that the Kaiser had congratulated Bismarck on his
eighty-second birthday, which in fact had not been the case.[77] In
addition, there were a host of other journalists, police agents, and
government officials. More important than these was the Berlin
criminal commissar, a Bavarian who was responsible for surveillance
over the press and subversive activities, and was the main security
agent of the Kaiser—Eugen von Tausch. Above all towered the figure
of Marschall, who quite early in the show took over the control of
its direction and held the reins throughout.

The issues were less diverse than the actors. The dominant
theme was the attack on the New Course in general and on the Foreign
Office in particular. It was concerned primarily with intraministerial suspicions and disunity, the Köller crisis, the military
penal code bill, and foreign policy in connection with the visit
of the Czar. The trial could well hold its own as one of the
dramatic scandals of the time, with its piquant details of forged
signatures, press intrigues, unmasked front-men, mysterious higher-
ups, hushed-up secrets of state, libelous accusations, and a

measure of sentimentality.[78]

For four days the court listened to the abundant evidence and testimony from various witnesses. Among the more notable scenes was the dramatic arrest of the witness von Tausch on charges of perjury; it appeared that Tausch had been the coordinator, and at times instigator, of press articles that had led to governmental embarrassment, personal slander of high-ranking officials, and intraministerial suspicions. It was articles such as the ones which led to the Köller crisis and those of the *Welt am Montag* designed to create a crisis, that were here subjected to minute investigation—as well as the role that Tausch had played as the official who was responsible (by means of hired agents) for monitoring the press.

We permit ourselves to digress here and present a more detailed narration of the Leckert-Lützow trial. We recognize that it is valid to argue that the space devoted to the trial is out of proportion to the rest of the story. We decided to include it for the following reasons: the trial gives us a good example of one element of the confused and generally unsavory political atmosphere; certain particulars are interesting in themselves for the specialist of this period; consequently, while not significant enough to be translated in its entirety, extensive excerpts of the transcripts are worth presenting in English.

During the court proceedings on December 2, Leckert explained that he had informed Lützow that according to reliable information the editing of the toast at Breslau was due to British influences. He also told the jury that he had written only one article concerning the toast, which was published, but he had given Lützow two manuscripts upon which the latter had based his second article in the *Welt am Montag*. There was much other material brought to bear against Leckert, and in each case Leckert gave very inadequate replies. Even when confronted with the receipts that he had given to Lützow for two articles described as "Eulenburg I" and "Eulenburg II," the defendant declared that these were for the two manuscripts and not for the two published articles. Furthermore, the hurdle that was never overcome was the mysterious informer. Was there even such a person? It was, of course, very unlikely that Leckert had invented the whole story himself, since it constituted only one in a series of attacks against the New Course.

The results of the Leckert testimony were indeed meager. The trial produced many more questions than it had answered. The field was opened wide to implications, suspicions, and speculations. According to Lützow, the main ideas of the two articles came from him. He supposedly got the material from Leckert, who had visited him about September 20. At the time Leckert told him that he had written "some very nice things" of late, especially one about the falsification of the Breslau toast, discussed in many papers at the time. He had sent it to the *Breslauer Generalanzeiger*. Leckert then told him that "the Czar had not said '*que mon pere*,'" rather that the launching into the press of this version can be attributed to British influence, which had gained influence around the Kaiser in Breslau. A higher court official had used his influence, so that this version would be given to the Wolff Telegraph Bureau representa-

tive for transmission."[79] In this manner the wrong version had come
into the press. Furthermore, Leckert had told him that he had been
received several times by Marschall, and that the Secretary of
State, even after the *dementi* in the *Deutsche Tages-Zeitung*, had
upheld everything concerning the toast (as written in the *Welt am
Montag*), and had still shown great interest in the publication of
the manuscript, "in order that the world may get to know how in
this case again the camarilla-government is at work." At this same
meeting with Lützow, Leckert had named Eulenburg, the Court Chamberlain, as one who (according to his source) had "in a sense dictated"
the false version to de Grahl, reporter to the Wolff Bureau. Lützow
as the more experienced newspaperman had offered his services to
Leckert and had taken matters into his own hands; he then had placed
the articles in the *Welt am Montag*.

The chief prosecutor, *Oberstaatsanwalt* Drescher, explained that
the president of the police, von Windheim, had officially taken
steps to inquire into the authorship of the articles, and had asked
Tausch to conduct this investigation. Tausch, then, had used Lützow
as his agent to find the authors and found, "presumably—to his own
surprise," that Lützow had written them. Lützow's report to Tausch
was read in full in the court. It substantiated Lützow's previous
testimony and proved in fact that Lützow had received his instructions from Tausch as an agent of the police.

The second day was concerned mainly with the hearing of the
winesses. De Grahl of the Wolff Telegraph Bureau, who had telegraphed the disputed version of the toast from Breslau to Berlin,
said that he thought that the phrase *"que mon pere"* was used. At
the time he expressed doubt over what he had heard because of the
implication of such words, and he had verified it with the stenog-
rapher of the Secret Civil Cabinet, who reaffirmed its correctness.
Thereupon de Grahl had tried to speak to Lucanus, but was not able
to do so right away. He had sent out the message without Lucanus's
confirmation so that it would be received early enough in Berlin to
appear in the Monday morning papers. The accusation against Eulenburg and himself he rejected as absolutely untrue. The Office of
the Court Chamberlain had never had anything to do with confirming
the official versions of speeches, toasts, or the like; in fact,
that was the responsibility of the Secret Civil Cabinet. Moreoever,
de Grahl took special care to point out that "every journalist by
profession knows, that he receives his court-reports not from the
Office of the Court Chamberlain, but from the aide-de-camp on duty:
and that the text of such speeches are dispatched solely by the
Secret Civil Cabinet and never the Office of the Court Chamberlain."

It would have been interesting to question de Grahl more thoroughly. Before coming to the Wolff Telegraph Bureau, he had been
a correspondent for a conservative paper. More interesting and
indicative, however, is the fact that six months later de Grahl
committed a similar error when he reported falsely that the Kaiser
had sent a congratulatory telegram on the occasion of Bismarck's
birthday. De Grahl was then dismissed.[80]

The most important witness of the day (besides Tausch) was
Secretary of State Marschall. Marschall explained the background
and present state of the relations between the Foreign Office and
the press and the political section of the police. As he

expressed it, ". . . he had for several years for very specific
reasons no longer consulted the political police in regard to the
identification of the origin of articles."[81]   He had good reason for
such mistrust. Almost as soon as the New Course had begun, it had
come under violent and slanderous attacks from a number of newspapers.
By accident Marschall had stumbled across the name of a journalist
who was most likely the responsible person; this was a certain
Normann-Schumann, who at the time was also an agent of Police Commissar von Tausch. By 1892 the Foreign Office had presented their
case to the Minister of Interior, Botho Eulenburg, and had expressly
named Tausch as Normann-Schumann's protector.[82]   However, Botho
Eulenburg had informed Kiderlen-Wächter a few days later, "Unfortunately nothing can be done, since the President of the Police
considers the agent Schumann as indispensable."[83]
   Marschall disposed of the toast controversy with the following
observation:

> I took part in the gala dinner on September 5th.
> After the toast of His Majesty in German, the Russian
> Czar delivered his in French. I presupposed that the
> stenographer of the Secret Civil Cabinet would not be
> in a position to take down French in shorthand, there-
> fore, I immediately noted down the toast of the Czar
> of Russia, as I heard it, and had the text verified
> by a high Russian official, and then handed it to the
> Chief of the Civil Cabinet.[84]

The different version of the Telegraph Bureau had therefore taken
him completely by surprise, and he had immediately ordered an investigation, which ended with Wolff's explanation of de Grahl's
mistake. Thus the matter stood when Marschall had unexpectedly
seen the *Welt am Montag*'s second article, and when the *Staatsbürgerzeitung* wrote about "semi-official press-management."
   The *dementi* that the Telegraph Bureau published disposed of
Marschall's suspicions against that agency. However, soon after-
ward he received a letter from Dr. Ploetz asking him to verify the
content of the *Welt am Montag* article. Hammann met Ploetz and
showed him that he had been misled. Confronted with this evidence,
Ploetz then revealed the name of Lützow. Marschall continued,
"When I came to know that this agent of the Political Police was
involved, I took the matter seriously right away, and it was this
fact which made me bring the matter before a public court."[85]   The
president of the police, whom Marschall questioned, knew nothing
about the affair except that Criminal Commissar Tausch had reported
to him that the article in question had its origin in the Foreign
Office. Tausch was then confronted, and he admitted that Lützow
was "in the service of the Political Police." Marschall said that
at his meeting with Tausch, he "had tried to put all the blame on
Leckert and tried to exonerate v. Lützow as much as possible."
   Turning to the *Staatsbürgerzeitung*, Marschall pointed out,
"For over a year now there had appeared articles in this paper
indicating that one might find the source, from which stemmed the
instigations of high officials against each other, in the Foreign
Office. The *Staatsbürgerzeitung* had in this case again indicated
that the source of the article could be found in the Foreign Office

and had the purpose to bring Bronsart and Köller up in arms against
each other."[86] He also pointed out the connection between the
Staatsbürgerzeitung and the article in the *Münchener Neueste Nachrichten* of November 4, 1895, on the subject of the military penal
code regulation and its discussion in a closed Ministry of State
meeting: "The *Staatsbürgerzeitung* also indicated that the source
of this article should be sought after in the Foreign Office and
that it was intended to embroil the ministers Bronsart and v.
Köller."[87] Actually, according to Marschall, the case was as follows: after the publication of the *Münchener Neueste Nachrichten*
article, Bronsart had ordered the matter to be investigated. This
investigation showed that the inspiration for this article had come
from the Prussian Ministry of Interior, and suspicion was cast upon
Kukutsch and Homan (then working in the Literary Bureau, a branch of
the Ministry of Interior). This information seemed to Marschall
so incorrect that he himself, after consulting with Hammann, conducted his own investigation. From the Minister of War he had
found out that it was Tausch who named Kukutsch as originator of the
article. Tausch, on his part, had referred to Lützow as his source.

To show a similar case, Marschall cited the article of the
Kölnische Zeitung of April 28, 1896, which had included heavy attacks
on General Hahnke in relation to the military penal code reform. At
that time Tausch incorrectly gave as the source Dr. Huhn, who was
receiving information from the Foreign Office. In connection with
Dr. Huhn, Marschall expounded the relationship of the Foreign
Office to the press. He said:

> The press bureau is a necessary evil, the witness would
> like to get along without it, but cannot conduct foreign
> policy without the press, and the Reichsanzeiger is not
> enough. There are a number of newspapers which support the
> foreign policy of the government. They do this by asking
> the press bureau of the Foreign Office for information about
> a particular situation—and this is an important point—
> inquire about the correctness of statements in foreign
> newspapers. But the Foreign Office has never had the
> intention to influence the point of view of these papers
> that received information from it in any way or otherwise
> to influence these papers.[88]

Marschall also stated that reform of "press mismanagement"—something that certainly did exist—must come from within press circles
themselves and not from the Foreign Office.

The next important witness was Eugen v. Tausch.[89] Tausch
declared that he had known Lützow for about five years and had used
him, in his official capacity, to identify anonymous press articles
and the like that might be of interest to the police, but that he
had not demanded of him tasks contrary to personal honor. Tausch
explained the *Welt am Montag* article in the following manner:

> As soon as I had read the articles, I immediately told
> myself, there will be inquiries. I therefore asked Lützow,
> of whom I knew that he had already written a number of
> articles for the *Welt am Montag*, concerning the author of
> the article in the *Welt am Montag*. Thereupon he named

himself as the author. After my inquiring how he could do that, that this was going a bit far, he added that this article had been inspired by Secretary of State von Marschall, who had given Leckert the necessary information.

I thought it unbelievable that the Foreign Office would use such a young man for the placing of such an article. He told me a number of details which strengthened my disbelief still further. I told the whole matter in the form of a report to the President of the Police von Windheim, who naturally also found it quite improbable, and no further attention was paid to the affair. On the next day President von Windheim said to me that he had asked Marschall, and that everything was a lie. Then I called Lützow, informed him of the outcome, and told him that he had been deceived. Thereupon I asked him to give me the development of the whole matter in the form of a report so that I could give it to the President of the Police and that I would not succumb to the suspicion that somebody had added something. . . . In a letter Lützow had once again definitely stated that the matter is absolutely untrue, and from that I have drawn the firm conviction, and still hold it today— that von Lützow was duped and that he himself believed in the correctness of Leckert's words. I should say that I know von Lützow quite well. When one has so much contact and speaks together for five years [as Lützow and I] one knows one another. [90]

Tausch was quite sure, and made this point at various times during his hearing, that Leckert did in fact have an "instigator": "I hold him for much too inexperienced in politics to come up with such a cleverly placed intrigue. His source, of course, may be sought after in other circles than those that Leckert names. The man who pulls the strings, more likely than not, had had it in mind to trip the Secretary of State von Marschall." [91] The reintroduction, especially by Tausch, of this "instigator" aroused Marschall's suspicions. He intervened and commented, "The assumption of the Commissar that Leckert has somebody who is using him as a mere tool, certainly is a very meaningful one for me; but it would be very interesting to know, on what he bases his idea. Doesn't the Commissar know that individuals whom he had employed for the press investigations have simply made up such attacks against the Foreign Office . . . Normann-Schumann." [92]

To Marschall the trial was a chance to rid the Foreign Office of all the false and scandalous accusations under which it had suffered for years. Within the confines of his personal honor, his concept of responsibility to the state, and his offical position, he wanted to clarify this whole affair as thoroughly as possible. To the personal defense of Tausch with regard to Normann-Schumann, Marschall replied,

The Criminal Commissar defends himself against an accusation that I have not even made against him. I only remind him of Normann-Schumann, who also had been used for press-information, and today it has been proved that this same agent von Normann-Schumann himself wrote almost

all the scandalous articles during 1890 to 1893 against
the Foreign Office; the same articles for which von Tausch
asked him to find the author, and that these had been
made up in every case. After the experiences that Tausch
had with Normann-Schumann, I wish him to state more precisely why he holds, especially in this case, that Leckert
must have had someone behind him, and did not make up these
things himself. For me this is very important, since I
foresee that this "instigator" that has been suspended
in the air by Tausch may become the basis for further
suspicions against the Foreign Office.[93]

On the subject of the *Münchener Neueste Nachrichten* article,
Tausch recalled having been ordered by Bronsart to conduct an
investigation of this article. Tausch said that he had employed
several of his agents, among them Lützow. All of the agents came
up with some ideas as to the source of the article; Lützow named the
Literary Bureau of the Ministry of Interior as the source. Even
though Tausch and the representative of the Department of War,
First Lieutenant Gaede, had been skeptical as to the validity of
Lützow's proof (a receipt signed with the name of Kukutsch, who
worked in the Literary Bureau), both Tausch and Gaede "promised each
other not to talk about it." However, Lützow was later proven wrong
in his assumption, and Tausch dropped the matter as of no concern
to him any more. He had not reported anything to Minister v. Köller,
since this lay beyond his official capacity, but he did report every
day to his immediate superior, President of the Police v. Windheim.
It also became apparent that although Köller had talked to Tausch
personally about the affair, Tausch had not mentioned his suspicion
of Lützow's questionable information. As an explanation of this,
Tausch reasoned that Köller had been informed of all this by President v. Windheim, to whom Tausch gave daily reports.[94]

On Friday, December 4, Lützow made his so-called "confession,"
which resulted in a charge of perjury against Tausch on the next day.
The prelude to Lützow's breakdown, the "quasi" duel between Marschall
and Tausch which had begun the day before, continued. Marschall
turned to the article in the *Kölnische Zeitung* about the military
penal code regulation, which had been attributed incorrectly to von
Huhn, a journalist connected with the Foreign Office:

> As far as I know, the Ministry of Interior had con-
> ducted investigations as to the author of the article.
> The probable author was found to be the correspondent
> von Huhn, and this was reported to the highest authority.
> Then I inquired in the Ministry of Interior from
> where this false accusation against von Huhn had come
> and received the reply: "from von Tausch." And upon
> the further question, where Tausch got this information,
> I was told: from a very reliable agent, the name of
> whom, however, had to be kept secret.[95]

Marschall concluded with a general observation:

> I deem it of some interest to point out that as of
> now in three cases the agents of the Political Police
> have transmitted information proven to be false. First

of all in the case of the *Welt am Montag*, then in the
case of the *Münchener Neueste Nachrichten*, in which
case the Literary Bureau of the Ministry of Interier is
informed that the sensational article comes from von
Huhn, who is supposed to have connections with the
Foreign Office. I do not care what agents the
Political Police uses, but when these agents dare to
slander me or officials of my department, then I must
defend myself.[96]

Somewhat later Lützow finally broke down. It was not he, he insisted, who instigated the "clever feat" but his employer, whom
Lützow now identified as Eugen v. Tausch. Lützow's confession was
placed in the record and then read:

On the 27th I [Lützow] received the information from
Leckert [directed against Eulenburg and Marschall as the
source]. On the same evening I gave the article to the
Welt am Montag. During the next week I was with Tausch
several times and, upon his question, told him that I had
brought the matter and that I had received it from Leckert.

The Police Commissar von Tausch received the news with
the greatest enthusiasm because of Marschall being the
source, namely for the reason, as I know, that Tausch
has always had a great animosity against Marschall. He
told me, I should put this whole matter on paper and in
detail once more, since he had the intention to tell the
while affair to the Ambassador Count Philipp Eulenburg in
order to show him once again how Excellency von Marschall
conspires against the associates of the Kaiser. Von Tausch
"squeezed me dry" about this affair as much as possible,
and I told him every detail, because I was absolutely
certain about the truth of Leckert's information. Tausch
did write to Count Philipp Eulenburg, as he told us, in
Liebenberg and informed him, that he had an important
matter for him. Eulenburg replied—as I have seen—
that he would come to Berlin in the near future and would
then be happy to receive him.

In the meantime Tausch asked me to question Leckert
as much as possible, so as to be well-informed about his
source and to produce another article on the next Monday,
so that the matter would not be forgotten. In the meantime I was to report several times, and that I did. Then
he [Tausch] wanted to see to it that the Kaiser would get
to know the whole thing through Eulenburg, so that we
finally would have Marschall caught. . . .

On Monday, after the second article had appeared,
Tausch called me and told me that hell had broken loose
in the Foreign Office and that the President of the Police
had been called. The latter had had no choice but to give
my name. I was to give him once again a complete account,
in order to take it to Philipp Eulenburg. He would cover
up for me and protect me. I should remain calm. During
the whole next week he called me and told me the Foreign
Office is bent upon pursuing the matter further. On

Saturday he told me that he would have to take me into
custody. I was not to say that I had had any connection
with him. Between us it remained as it had been. He
was terribly scared. On Sunday he told me: "The matter
will be very bad for all of us: the Kukutsch affair will
also be revealed. But remain firm." On the 15th he gave
me 100 Mark, and from then on we hardly saw each other.
At the second arrest Tausch again was very frightened. . . .
    The extent of the animosity of Tausch against
Marschall is revealed by the fact that he commanded me
(on October 29th at the time of my second arrest) to
say during the investigation that Hönig, whom Tausch
at that time already knew to be the author of the
Kölnische Zeitung article "Flügel Adjutanten Politik,"
was being received by Prince A. Hohenlohe. This was to
create the suspicion that the article came from the
Foreign Office nevertheless.[97]

Tausch's immediate reaction was to brand the whole document a
complete lie. He did admit that Lützow had been an agent since 1891
or 1892 and that their relationship was very close, but he wanted
to prove that all other accusations were false. The Lützow document was then read in parts, Tausch defending himself on each
specific issue. However, Tausch's replies to the accusations sounded
less convincing than Lützow's statements. As to the relationship
of the political police and Marschall, Tausch emphasized that it was
not the police (that is, himself) but Marschall who had shown acute
antipathy against the former because he was supposedly carrying on
"camarilla-politics." Marschall in turn made it clear in his reply
that he had no personal animosity against Tausch. Then he gave a
very broad sketch of the experiences of the Foreign Office with
the political police. The record had been completely negative.
Almost as soon as the New Course had begun, slanderous attacks
upon it had appeared in the domestic and the foreign press. By
accident the Foreign Office had come to know that the principal
slanderer, Normann-Schumann, was at the same time an agent under
the direct supervision of v. Tausch. This startling fact was made
known to the political police, but no action whatsoever was taken,
and Normann-Schumann remained in the service of the Prussian
Ministry of Interior. At this point the Foreign Office decided to
break off all relations with the police. Marschall ended:

    As it is I have found a certain similarity between
    Lützow and Normann-Schumann. I regard the whole system
    of the secret agents as a failure, since these men are
    faced with a task they cannot solve, and consequently
    their reports simply do not correspond with the truth.
        And if we look at the agents of von Tausch who were
    involved in the cases concerning this trial, we have
    to say that there is not one report that is not entirely
    wrong.
        If von Tausch insists upon having secret agents, this
    is his own affair. But if these agents dare publicly to
    slander me, my subordinates, and the Foreign Office,
    then I escape into the open [a great commotion in the

courtroom] and denounce their activity in
public.[98]

This commotion in the courtroom spread like wildfire. To be
sure, from the beginning of the trial, opinion was divided about
the expediency of conducting a public trial against what was a
Prussian governmental agency. However, Marschall had now provided
a slogan around which the two opposed opinions could rally—"*Flucht
in die Öffentlichkeit*—and the resultant commotion was an indication
of the German political atmosphere. The underlying issues were
the struggle between Germany and Prussia, the "liberal" New Course
and the "reactionary" conservatives, increasing parliamentary responsibility against the class rule of vested interests. Marschall, as
a south German and as representative of the New Course, as well as
Foreign Secretary of the German government, had to face the Prussian
landed aristocracy and the Prussian bureaucracy. It did seem that
Marschall and the Social Democrats were fighting on the same side.
Although a superficial accusation, the course Marschall chose to
take at least pointed in the direction of greater public responsibility in government affairs.[99]

Most of the remainder of that day's session was taken up by
Tausch's defending himself against Lützow's statements, with which
he was systematically confronted. Coming to Count Philipp Eulenburg,
Tausch remarked that he had gotten to know him during the time of
the *Kladderadatsch* affair of 1894, in which Eulenburg had been
interested. Eulenburg had at that time mentioned to him that whenever Tausch came upon some material of interest, he should inform
him of it. This Tausch had done—for the first time in the two
years—in the case of the *Welt am Montag* articles. Why, he was
asked, did he inform Eulenburg about an article in which supposedly
Marschall heavily attacked one of the Eulenburgs? Tausch's answer
was: "But I did not inform him at all about it. I only told him
that I would when he would come by. In the meantime I would have
enough time to clarify everything completely."[100] Yet he had sent
the article. Also, the short letter with the promise of "interesting material" sounded much less harmless than his somewhat naive
defense. Tausch admitted that he had "squeezed Lützow dry," but
of course for the purpose of the political police. Lützow was also
correct in his account of Eulenburg's letter to Tausch: "For years
von Lützow had visited me. One speaks about politics and all kinds
of things. In this way one becomes acquainted—and over a glass of
beer, when he was in my house, I mentioned this in a most innocent
way; I thought absolutely nothing of it."[101] To most of the other
points made by Lützow, Tausch replied unconvincingly.

Again the story told by Lützow, that Tausch had told him Bronsart
believed v. Köller to be the source of the article in the *Münchener
Neueste Nachrichten*, seemed to have been borne out by Marschall's
observations. Marschall maintained, that

When Bronsart came to me in November of last year and
asked for my support in finding the source of the reports,
I had the impression that Bronsart's suspicion of Köller
stemmed from the report of the Criminal Commissar von
Tausch. . . . I also remembered that at that time Bronsart
had spoken about an anonymous letter that contained the

names of Kukutsch and Homann. That certainly is correct,
and the Minister of War Bronsart was quite firm in this
matter, and I can only explain this by assuming that his
firm attitude was based upon the possession of the
receipt. That is the "proof" that Lützow had gotten for
Gaede . . . . and Tausch.[102]

Moreover, Lützow's statements again seemed to be confirmed when
Marschall pointed out, "It is indeed correct that the matter had
first been discussed only after the prosecution of Leckert and
Lützow had begun."[103] Suspecting Lützow, he had gone to Gaede, and
the latter said, "At that time I ordered Criminal Commissar Tausch
on the behalf of von Bronsart to investigate and find the source.
For this purpose he used Lützow and reported to me that the matter
came from the Literary Bureau."[104] By the end of the day Tausch
had not been able to fulfill his promise to disprove Lützow's
accusations as completely false. In fact, just the opposite seemed
to be true. Lützow's confession seemed constantly to gain plausi-
bility.

The last day brought the sensational—if not unexpected—climax
of the whole drama: the arrest of Tausch. Instead of being able to
clear himself, Tausch was taken into custody on a charge of perjury.
Thus Prussian bureaucratic self-righteousness suddenly suffered a
terrible loss of prestige: a Prussian court had arrested a Prussian
official on charges of "strong suspicion of having committed perjury."
Proof of corruption did not need any public admission of guilt. The
facts were too obvious. Who was bound to profit by these exposures?
Certainly the liberal and left-radical opposition to the government
would. However, the agrarian opposition to the government could
also use it for political benefit, by attacking the new post-
Bismarckian regime and thus throwing the blame for the scandal
onto the weak, liberalizing tendencies of the New Course.

The proceedings of the fourth day centered around Count Philipp
Eulenburg and Dr. Levysohn of the *Berliner Tageblatt*. Tausch left
the room, and Eulenburg testified:

> I made the acquaintance of Commissar von Tausch in
> Abbazzia, where he was in the service of His Majesty and
> I was the representative of the Foreign Office. . . . That
> was in February of 1894. Since then I have met him in
> Stettin at the occasion of the visit of the Austrian
> Emperor and at the royal visit in Venice. The Criminal
> Commissar von Tausch plays such a minor role in my life
> that I am not able to recall when I saw him for the last
> time. The last thing I had from him was a letter that
> I received during the last days of October in Liebenberg.
> The letter contained a newspaper article that was concerned
> with the falsification of the toast of the Czar. In this
> letter, also, Tausch asked if it would be possible to meet
> me, because he had something interesting to tell me, or:
> "he had interesting information to give me concerning
> this article." . . . I cannot remember any details of my
> reply. But already at that time I had no intention of
> receiving Tausch, because interesting reports of a police

commissar are of no interest to me if they are not my
concern. I am not used to concern myself with things that
are none of my business. And therefore the letter of von
Tausch found its way into the waste paper basket. My
relations with Tausch were only superficial and social.
There has been no other correspondence between us. Only
one other time he thanked me for the friendliness I had
shown him. Here, where every word is under oath, I
declare it a slander, a malicious invention if anyone
asserts that I had maintained contact with von Tausch,
especially of such a nature as the article of the *Welt
am Montag*. With such intrigues, such slanders as revealed
in this trial, I had never anything to do, and never in
my life will. In mid-October I talked about the trial
with Excellency von Marschall, with the usual frankness
that exists between us. Other than that I have nothing
else to say.[105]

The "friendliness" mentioned by Eulenburg referred to a nomination for a decoration which Tausch had then received. Eulenburg
admitted that he could have written to Tausch congratulating him.
As to Tausch's contention that Eulenburg asked him to write him if
he came across anything of interest, the Count held, "I do not
believe so, not even in the form of a hint."
Another aspect of the relationship among Tausch, Eulenburg, and
Marschall was revealed when Tausch told the court,

> Weeks ago I already told the Police President von
> Windheim, the *Oberregierungsrat* Friedheim and *Geheime
> Regierungsrat* von Muhl: I am very sorry that Count
> Eulenburg did not come here. If he had come here he
> would have come here in response to a letter I had written
> him; this would have given an opportunity to ask His
> Excellency to play the role of mediator between von
> Marschall on the one hand and the police on the other,
> and to clear things up. . . .[106]

This idea seemed strange and almost improbable. Why did not Tausch
let the president of the police talk to Marschall? Tausch explained
that since the former presidents, von Richthofen and Mauderode had
died, he (Tausch) and not Windheim was the best informed man in
press affairs: "I was the only one who was completely oriented on
the latest occurrences." Moreover, coming back to the article,
Tausch maintained that he had sent it to Eulenburg because he
believed that there was someone behind Leckert. Through further
questioning, Tausch admitted that he mentioned to Windheim Eulenburg's coming to Berlin and that he could see him then, but nothing
about having sent an article to Eulenburg. Having before emphatically
stressed the official nature of his acquaintance with Eulenburg, now
Tausch defended his failure to inform Windheim upon the grounds of
the personal nature of his "gratitude." This lack of willingness
to inform his superior was again revealed a moment later in the case
of the Kukutsch receipt (Lützow's proof). First Tausch said that
Windheim had known about it. However, when it became apparent that
Windheim had learned about the Kukutsch affair only a few days ago,

Tausch replied, "That could be, these are such subordinate matters, I only report the important things."

It was, however, not these incongruities in Tausch's testimony that led to his arrest, but the direct contradiction of his testimony with that of the witness Dr. Levysohn, editor of the *Berliner Tageblatt*. According to Tausch, he had gone to Levysohn to get a certain newspaper issue which he did not have any more, and which Levysohn still might have a copy of. Then Levysohn had begun to talk about Leckert, but Tausch had been very noncommittal. Levysohn, on the other hand, maintained that Tausch had paid him a visit to talk about Leckert, not to ask for any newspaper issue (which would be strange for a government official supposed to monitor the press) but that this was only intended as an introduction:

> During the course of the conversation which then
> followed (the details of which I cannot remember), I myself
> came up with the question: . . . who actually are Leckert
> and Lützow? And Tausch told me that Leckert was a man
> who up to now had only been active in feuilleton and
> theatre news. I asked, for which paper? He said: among
> others for the *Tägliche Rundschau*. I asked: How is it
> possible that such a man concerns himself with politics?
> He answered, Lützow is the one fooled by Leckert. Leckert
> has certain connections. I asked: "connections with whom?"
> "With the Foreign Office. And he himself had had an
> interview for the *Tägliche Rundschau* in the Foreign
> Office."[107]

A little later he added:

> . . . every time that he came to me, which happened
> about every one half year in order to get a new spring
> copy, he has in his conversations talked about the condi-
> tions in government circles in such a way especially after
> the fall of Prince Bismarck and the Caprivi era that I,
> confronted with an official, have always been quite
> suspicious and thought it to be a kind of provocation to
> get me to talk in a similar way.[108]

Marschall, at this point, added that he had called Levysohn shortly after the article had appeared in the *Berliner Tageblatt* (something Tausch had neglected to do). Levysohn had told him exactly what he had said in court, except that he had left out Tausch's remarks about the government, and had not disclosed Tausch's name directly. Marschall had replied that the informant was Tausch, which Levysohn did not deny.[109] At this time Chief Prosecutor Drescher called for the arrest of Tausch for having knowingly committed perjury.

The last witness of the day was the editor of the *Berliner Tageblatt*, Gingold-Stärck, who acknowledged that he had become an agent of Tausch about a year previously. He declared that Tausch had never directly spoken to him about any high-ranking government official, or about Marschall specifically, but

> He considered the Secretary of State an usurper of
> that office which he did not deserve—and which actually

belonged to Herbert von Bismarck. Von Tausch had a
different political tendency than von Marschall. As
most opponents of Marschall, von Tausch is a fanatic
Bismarckian and von Tausch said, Marschall is unfit for
his political position—he is not competent for his job
—this position should actually be filled by Herbert
von Bismarck.

I was repeatedly urged by von Tausch to try to get in
contact with the Foreign Office. In particular he mentioned several times the name of von Holstein, whom I
should contact.[110]

However, Gingold was consistently turned down. This latter information was confirmed by Marschall, and Hammann added that when Gingold
tried to get access to the Foreign Office, Hammann called Tausch
about this journalist and had received a "surprisingly favorable
report, fit even for more important political affairs," which
contrasted to almost everything else that he had heard about Gingold.

The other significant point to be mentioned here concerns von
Huhn's authorship of the *Kölnische Zeitung* article. Tausch had
named Gingold as his source. Gingold had indeed named Huhn, admit-
tedly because he was correspondent of the *Kölnische Zeitung*. And
why did he mention this name in particular, seeing that the *Kölnische
Zeitung* had more than one correspondent? Gingold answered, "I did
this only under the prerequisite established once and for all, that
no acts are to be taken against that gentleman." This answer did not
help to clear that already confused picture. Thus with this anti-
climax the court ended the taking of evidence and, in the afternoon,
asked for summaries and gave the sentences.

8

The Leckert-Lützow trial had, as did previous scandals such as
the *Kladderadatsch* affair and the Kotze scandal, given the public
"glimpses into the quarrels and intrigues of the most exalted
circles."[111] However, it had been only a glimpse, and even the
majority of government officials could not get a definite picture
of what really was going on and who primarily was responsible.
Rumors and accusations varied from holding Marschall and Holstein
responsible[112] to giving Bismarck the credit for the slanderous
activities in the press.[113]

On December 6, 1896, Herbert Bismarck wrote to his brother-
in-law, Count Rantzau, about the trial and about Eulenburg in
particular: "Phili seems to have lied his way out of the trial
already . . . on the whole more lies have been said there, and
more perjuries committed, than ever before!"[114] Herbert apparently
meant specifically the representatives of the Foreign Office,
Hammann and Marschall, as well as Tausch and Eulenburg. He generally
seems to have looked upon the trial as a farce.

There is little doubt that Tausch, contrary to his forced
explanations during the trial, did know and cooperate with the
agent Normann-Schumann. Both police presidents Richthofen (whose
confidant Tausch had been[115]) and Mauderode had been warned about
Normann-Schumann but had held him to be indispensable.[116] Tausch

as early as 1891 had received similar warnings. He had known, for
instance, that the author of the slanderous *Saale Zeitung* articles
had been Normann-Schumann, his agent, and yet had given him the order
to search for the author; then he had reported that the source of
these articles could not be found.[117] In addition, Normann-Schumann
had remained an agent for Tausch until the spring of 1893; his dismissal came as the result not of his press attacks upon the Kaiser
and the Foreign Office but because he had become too exposed in a
trial, at which time he had been shown to have worked for various
opposing factions at the same time![118] Again, Normann-Schumann had
used material that could have been received in all probability only
from Tausch. In fact, the information that Tausch had been so
freely conveying to other journalists was almost identical with the
content of many articles by Normann-Schumann.[119] The intimate
letters between Lützow and Tausch after Normann-Schumann's dismissal[120] seem to prove that Lützow took the place of that agent.

During the trial Tausch at various times indicated the existence
of an instigator. In all probability Tausch was correct in this
assertion; this was no less a person than General von Waldersee.
Waldersee had had a number of contacts with the press and also with
Normann-Schumann, especially during 1891. He had used the latter
to bring his attacks against the Kaiser into the press and had given
him considerable sums of money. Waldersee's name was not mentioned
during the Tausch trial because he had been warned by the police
president of such a possibility; Waldersee had asked the latter's
cooperation to keep his name out of the trial, and took steps to gain
the forgiveness of the Kaiser. Last, it was said that he was able
to keep Normann-Schumann out of the country during the critical
days.[121]

Normann-Schumann's boasting about his intimate connection with
Waldersee was generally not taken seriously, except by the Social
Democrats; however, in the light of the above this connection cannot be denied. Waldersee had direct connections not only with
Normann-Schumann but with Tausch as well.[122] Waldersee even wanted
to bring Tausch into the Foreign Office.[123] It was through these
channels, for instance, that in all likelihood the devastating
attack on Boetticher (in 1891) was brought into the press.[124] It
strongly appears, then, that at least the source of the attack upon
the Kaiser and the Foreign Office, as well as on other select persons
was Waldersee and his agents (Tausch *et al.*). With this group it
is possible to associate also Count Guido Henckel von Donnersmarck
(one of the richest industrialists in Prussia and quite prominent
in the ranks of the Bismarck Fronde), although this connection is
not nearly as clear.[125]

Herbert Bismarck had written that Eulenburg had lied his way out
of the trial. This was most certainly the case. Already during
the Tausch trial in May and June, 1897, Eulenburg had to revise his
earlier testimony considerably: he now admitted that "I do not hold
it at all impossible, that I have asked v. Tausch to write me since
I had close contact with him."[126] Tausch, on his part, admitted
that he had helped Eulenburg during the *Kladderadatsch* affair and
had therefore received Eulenburg's support for a decoration; furthermore, a "policeman of his department had often visited Count Eulenburg and had carried messages back and forth." In this connection

it is perhaps interesting to add that the policeman had made the acquaintance of Eulenburg on board the Kaiser's yacht, the *Hohen-zollern*.[127] Eulenburg was in constant touch not only with Tausch but also with Waldersee directly[128] and very likely with Henckel indirectly.[129] Moreover, the letters of Eulenburg to Tausch, although read by the prosecutor, were not mentioned during the trial.[130]

While it is possible with considerable certainty to hold Waldersee responsible for press intrigues, this is not the case with Eulenburg. In all probability he did not have anything to do with them, but only associated himself with this group so as not to lose touch with what was going on behind the scenes. Waldersee never did achieve his objective. As Maximilian Harden, the brilliant, devastating, and exceedingly well informed journalist, put it: he "had to be satisfied, even in his brightest hours, with the semblance of power."[131] The reality of power at the time lay elsewhere, to a considerable extent in the hands of Eulenburg.

In the hope of exposing the real source behind the press slanders, Marschall had taken the course of a public court action, had chosen a "*Flucht in die Öffentlichkeit*," as he himself had styled it. Although hoping to gain specific advantages—the end of the press intrigues and reaffirmation in the eyes of the Kaiser—Marschall's conduct took on more and more the nature of an "act of desperation,"[132] only to end in psychological resignation and removal from his post in Berlin. His action did not bring success. When the whole affair was over in June, 1897, the little men had been caught—Leckert and Lützow. Waldersee had hardly been mentioned, but Marschall was induced to take a vacation that preceded his resignation. Even Tausch had been acquitted in the public trial. Many details that had surfaced during the preliminary investigations for the disciplinary action against Tausch were not mentioned. Generally, these details substantiated the compromising position of Tausch during the public trials. However, others—his connections with the General Staff and the Navy and his dealings in Russian affairs (possibly even as a spy)—were not publicly displayed.[133] The disciplinary administrative action against him dismissed him from his position, but authorized him for a different post with equal rank and salary.[134]

Every year of the so-called "Newest Course" during the Hohenlohe era had its dismal crisis that stood out above all other stresses and strains. For the year 1894 no doubt this was the October crisis, for 1895 the Köller crisis. In 1896 the climactic stress was provided by the combination of the press intrigues against Marschall and the Bismarck revelations, which, as Marschall correctly interpreted, were two aspects of a common onslaught against the Foreign Office and the Hohenlohe Ministry. This is even more true if the renewed discussions over the military penal code reform—as fruitless, inconclusive, and as frustrating and potentially dangerous as ever—are included, since after early August the issue became prominent again in the wake of the revelations.[135]

In May the Kaiser, under the influence of his entourage and his cabinets, had wanted to dismiss Marschall along with Bronsart, and even Hohenlohe's position seemed insecure. However, later Hohenlohe had insisted on Marschall's retention, and while his own position

seemed to gain security, Bronsart was dismissed. Now the attack
had concentrated squarely on Marschall; because he was, of course,
more expendable than Hohenlohe, he had never lost the basic insecurity of his position.[136] While the concentrated attack upon
Marschall did not immediately produce his dismissal from office,
his position had been shattered beyond repair, and six months
later he had for all practical purposes been dismissed.

NOTES

1. *Schulthess*, 1896, pp. 104–105, 222–224, 270.

2. *Ibid.*, pp. 109–110, 224–225, 268–269. But see also Marschall
Diary, 6, 8, and 10.X.96.

3. Eulenburg to Goluchowski, 8.IX.1896, B.A. Eul. 43. See also
Marschall Diary, 5.IX.96.

4. Letter of Count Osten-Sacken, 18.IX.96, B.A. Eul. 43. See
also the very optimistic report of Guttenberg, 9.IX.96, G.S.A.
München, MA III 2674.

5. Eulenburg, "Notizen," ca. early X.96, B.A. Eul. 43.

6. Eulenburg, "Notizen," 4.X.96, and Goluchowski to Eulenburg,
15.X.96, B.A. Eul. 43; *Die Grosse Politik*, XI, 357ff.; Jerussalimski,
Aussenpolitik, pp. 295ff. See also F. B. Traude, "Untersuchungen
zur Entstehung und Entwicklung des Verständigungsgedankens der
Kontinentalmächte 1897 im Lichte der Presse" (Dissertation, Köln,
1933), p. 7; Fischer, *Krieg der Illusionen*, pp. 69ff.; *Schulthess*,
1896, p. 105. For Hohenlohe's skeptical attitude, see *Hohenlohe*,
III, 260ff.

7. *Hohenlohe*, III, 265.

8. *Ibid.*, II, 528.

9. Cuno Moltke to Eulenburg, 20.X.96, and Eulenburg to Bülow,
26.X.96, B.A. Eul. 43. At least outwardly the Foreign Office (that
is, Marschall) was neither surprised nor worried about the Paris
events. See Guttenberg report, 17.X.96, G.S.A. München, MA III 2674.
See also Marschall Diary, 15.X.96.

10. Waldersee, *Denkwürdigkeiten*, II, 373–374; Baronin von Spitzemberg, *Des Tagebuch der Baronin von Spitzemberg*, ed. Rudolf Vierhaus
(Göttingen, 1960), p. 348. See also *Die Grosse Politik*, XI, 369ff., 372ff.
and 385; Marschall Diary, 17, 19, and 20.X.96; Eulenburg, "Aufzeichnung,
Hochzeit Kalnein-Eulenburg und Besuch der Majestäten," X.96, B.A. Eul.
43; *Hohenlohe*, III, 269; Holstein to Eulenburg, 23.X.96, B.A. Eul.
43.

11. Eulenburg, "Notizen für Bülow, Besuch bei Seiner Majestät am
8.XI.96" (written in early November), B.A. Eul. 44.

12. See Haller, *Eulenburg*, pp. 173, 200.

13. *Schulthess*, 1896, p. 109.

14. See Hammann, *Der Missverstandene Bismarck*, pp. 53ff.; *Der
Neue Kurs*, pp. 28ff.

15. *Schulthess*, 1896, pp. 112–119; *Hohenlohe*, III, 270; Spitzemberg, *Tagebuch*, p. 346; Johannes Pentzler, ed., *Fürst Bismarck nach seiner Entlassung*; *Leben und Politik des Fürsten seit seinem Scheiden aus dem Amte auf Grund aller authentischen Kundgebungen*, 7 vols. (Leipzig, 1897–98), VII, 196ff.; William L. Langer, *The Diplomacy of Imperialism* (New York, 1965), p. 347; Eyck, *Persönliche Regiment*, pp. 163ff.; Verlag der *Frankfurter Zeitung*, ed., *Geschichte der Frankfurter Zeitung* (Frankfurt am Main, 1911), pp. 865f.; Waldersee, *Denkwürdigkeiten*, II, 375f.; "Aus dem Tagebuch von Alexandrine Eulenburg," 1.XI.96, and Eulenburg to Wilhelm, 3.XI.96, B.A. Eul. 43. Rich, *Holstein*, vol. II, does not mention the revelations in his discussion of the 1896–97 crisis. See also *Wippermann*, 1896 (II) pp. 131ff.; Brauer, *Dienste*, pp. 397ff.; Lerchenfeld to Crailsheim, 28.X.96, 3, 8, 17, and 23.XI.96, G.S.A. München, MA 76007.

16. *Schulthess*, 1896, pp. 112ff.

17. Jerussalimski, *Aussenpolitik und Diplomatie*, p. 305.

18. Haller, *Eulenburg*, translation taken from Mayne, *Eulenburg*, I, 367–368, 211. See also Jerussalimski, *Aussenpolitik und Diplomatie*, p. 306.

19. See Rich, *Holstein*, II, 477ff.

20. Hermann Hofmann, *Fürst Bismarck 1890–1898*, 3 vols. (Stuttgart, 1913), vol. II, 342f., 350ff., 364; Eduard von Wertheimer, "Neues zur Geschichte der letzten Jahre Bismarcks (1890–1898)," *Historische Zeitschrift*, 133 (1926), 224.

21. See among others Eyck, *Persönliche Regiment*, p. 163; Liman, *Bismarck*, pp. 175f. but also p. 252; Siegfried von Kardorff, *Bismarck im Kampf um sein Werk* (Berlin, 1943), pp. 176–177; Raschdau, *In Weimar*, p. 94; Herbert Bismarck to Harden, 14.X.96, Harden Papers, B.A. Koblenz.

22. Eulenburg, "Notiz, Frühstück bei Marschall mit Reichskanzler, Rotenhan, Holstein, Pourtales, Lindenau," 27.X.96, B.A. Eul. 43.

23. *Ibid.*

24. Holstein to Eulenburg, 29.X.96, 6.XI.96, B.A. Eul. 43. At the same time Raschdau moved against Holstein; see *Hohenlohe*, III, 274.

25. Eulenburg, "Notizen für Bernhard Bülow, Besuch bein seiner Majestät am 8. Nov. 1896" (written in November 1896), B.A. Eul. 44.

26. August Eulenburg to Phili Eulenburg, 1.XI.96, B.A. Eul. 43. See also Waldersee, *Denkwürdigkeiten*, II, 373.

27. Spitzemberg, *Tagebuch*, p. 374; *Hohenlohe*, III, 270; Lerchenfeld to Crailsheim, 28.X.96, G.S.A. München, MA 76007.

28. Waldersee, *Denkwürdigkeiten*, II, 375; *Hohenlohe*, III, 270f.; August Eulenburg to Phili Eulenburg, 1.XI.96, B.A. Eul. 43.

29. *Hohenlohe*, III, 274–275.

30. *Ibid.*, pp. 270–271.

31. See Lerchenfeld to Crailsheim, 8.XI.96, G.S.A. München, MA 76007; Marschall Diary, 3.XI.96, 4.XI.96; below, p. 210.

32. Eulenburg to Wilhelm, 8.XI.96, B.A. Eul. 43.

33. Bülow to Eulenburg, 20.X.96, B.A. Eul. 43.

34. Bülow to Eulenburg, 6.XI.96, B.A. Eul. 44.

35. Eulenburg, "Notizen für Bernhard Bülow, Besuch bei Seiner Majestät am 8. November 1896," B.A. Eul. 44.

36. Fürst von Bülow, *Denkwürdigkeiten*, 4 vols. (Berlin, 1931), IV, 487–488, 584, 590, 632, 644, 483; but see Haller, *Eulenburg*, p. 209, where Bülow writes to Eulenburg that he had not seen Herbert Bismarck for six years. It also seems quite probable that Bülow did not approach the Bismarcks directly, but used the editor of the *Berliner Neueste Nachrichten* (Jacobi) to reestablish contact. See, for instance, Bülow to Eulenburg, 14.IV.96, B.A. Eul. 41.

37. Spitzemberg, *Tagebuch*, p. 347.

38. Eulenburg, 11.XI.96, B.A. Eul. 44.

39. Eulenburg, "Notizen für Bülow," 11.XI.96, B.A. Eul. 44.

40. Haller, *Eulenburg*, p. 204.

41. See Rich, *Holstein*, II, 520ff.; Haller, *Eulenburg*, pp. 249–250.

42. *Schulthess*, 1896, p. 116; Marschall Diary, 27.X.96, 28.X.96.

43. Holstein to Eulenburg, 12.XI.96, B.A. Eul. 44. See also *Hohenlohe*, III, 274.

44. Eulenburg to Wilhelm, 13.XI.96, B.A. Eul. 44. See also *Hohenlohe*, III, 274.

45. *Hohenlohe*, III, 274–275.

46. *Ibid.*, p. 275.

47. *Ibid.*, pp. 275, 278; Marschall Diary, 12, 13, and 14.XI.96.

48. Marschall to Eulenburg, 24.XI.96, B.A. Eul. 44; Spitzemberg, *Tagebuch*, p. 374; Lerchenfeld to Crailsheim, 17.XI.96, G.S.A. München, MA 76007; Marschall Diary, 25.X.96, 28.X.96, 1, 5, 8, 9, 10, 12, 14, 15, 16, 17, and 18.XI.96.

49. *Hohenlohe*, III, 278; Hohenlohe Journal, 16.XI.96, Archiv Schillingsfürst, Rep. 100 XXII A-9.

50. Eulenburg to Marschall, 5.XI.96, B.A. Eul. 44.

51. Eulenburg to Wilhelm, 26.XI.96, B.A. Eul. 44.

52. *Holsteins Papiere*, III, 583; translation from Rich, *Holstein*, II, 520.

53. However, compare Eulenburg, "Notizen für Bülow," B.A. Eul. 44, in which he writes that Bismarck had planned this move with the editor of the *Neue Freie Presse* already in July, 1896. See also Haller, *Eulenburg*, pp. 206–207.

54. *Schulthess*, 1896, p. 146.

55. See Guttenberg report, 2.IX.96, G.S.A. München, Ges. Berlin, 1067. Wilhelm approved, since the press had also attacked the court and General Hahnke. See also Marschall Diary, 7.X.96; Bosse Diary, 7.X.96, B.A. Bosse.

56. *Hohenlohe*, III, 269. See also Marschall Diary entries for October, November, and early December. Among the newspapers involved were the *Welt am Montag*, *Staatsbürgerzeitung*, *Bank und Handelszeitung*, *Deutsche Tages-Zeitung*, *Berliner Fremdenblatt*, *Berliner Tageblatt*, and *Berliner Neueste Nachrichten*.

57. *Hohenlohe*, III, 279; Eulenburg to Wilhelm, 26.XI.96, B.A. Eul. 44.

58. Liman, *Fürst Bismarck*, pp. 176ff.; Marschall Diary, 8.XI.96.

59. *Holstein Papers*, III, 651–656.

60. *Ibid.* Even Marschall and Holstein regarded the "pro-English clique" insinuations as Bismarckian attacks. See Marschall Diary, 21.XI.96. See also *Holsteins Papiere*, III, 586–587.

61. *Hohenlohe*, III, 279.

62. Eulenburg to Wilhelm, 26.XI.96, B.A. Eul. 44; parts in Haller, *Eulenburg*, p. 204.

63. See *Holsteins Papiere*, III, 588.

64. *Ibid.*, p. 586.

65. Bülow to Eulenburg, 4.XII.96, B.A. Eul. 44.

66. Haller, *Eulenburg*, pp. 203, 208.

67. August Eulenburg to Phili Eulenburg, 15.XI.96, B.A. Eul. 44; Marschall Diary, 13.X.96, 14.X.96.

68. Lerchenfeld to Crailsheim, 4.XII.96, G.S.A. München, MA 2674.

69. *Hohenlohe*, III, 269.

70. Eulenburg to Bülow, 26.X.96, B.A. Eul. 43.

71. Haller, *Eulenburg*, p. 205.

72. Eulenburg to Bülow, 26.X.96, B.A. Eul. 43. See also Rich, *Holstein*, II, 522; Waldersee, *Denkwürdigkeiten*, II, 374–381, 382; Haller, *Eulenburg*, p. 210.

73. Haller, *Eulenburg*, p. 210; Waldersee, *Denkwürdigkeiten*, II, 383.

74. Eulenburg to Bülow, 26.X.96, B.A. Eul. 43.

75. "Promemoria" by Hammann to Hohenlohe, XII.96, Archiv Schillingsfürst, Rep. 100 XXII A-9. On the foreign press attacks and Normann-Schumann and Tausch, see Motteler Papers, Nos. 22, 32, 48, 82, 111, 1586, 1593–94, 1596–97, 1600, 1601, 1603, 1605–06, 1610, 1755, 1757, 2323, Internationales Institut für Sozialgeschichte, Amsterdam; G. Fricke, *Bismarcks Prätorianer. Die Berliner*

politische Polizei in Kampf gegen die deutsche Arbeiterbewegung (1871-1898) (Berlin, 1962), pp. 292f., 296f., and his article "Die Affaire Leckert-Lützow-Tausch und die Regierungskrise von 1897 in Deutschland," *Zeitschrift für Geschichtswissenschaft*, 8 (1960), 1579-1603.

76. For his connection with the Hammerstein scandal, for example, see D. von Oertzen, *Adolf Stoecker-Lebensbild und Zeitgeschichte*, 2 vols. (Berlin, 1910), II, 169f. He worked, it appears, for the industrialist Stumm against the court chaplain, Stöcker, and apparently was also involved in the *Kladderadatsch* affair.

77. De Grahl never did reveal his sources. See Hammann, *Der Neue Kurs*, pp. 77f.; Brauer, *Dienste*, p. 401; *Die Zukunft*, vol. 20, p. 138; Pentzler, ed., *Bismarck nach seiner Entlassung*, VII, 284, 289. But see also the report of Varnbühler maintaining that de Grahl did not in fact have an instigator. Württemberg embassy report, 10.IV.97, Württ. H.H.S. Archiv, Ges. Berlin, E 73, Fasz. 61.

78. On the trial and Leckert-Lützow, see *Die Politische Polizei in Preussen: Bericht über die Verhandlungen in Prozess Leckert-Lützow-Tausch am 2., 3., 4., und 7. Dezember 1896 vor dem Landgericht I zu Berlin; Nach stenographischen Aufnahmen* (Berlin, 1896), published by the expedition *der Buchhandlung Vorwärts*, 95 pages. The record of the trial in the archives of the Foreign Office (now in Bonn) is a copy of the daily verbatim reports of the *Kölnische Zeitung*, Auswärtiges Amt, Abtheilung A, Politisches Archiv d. Auswärt. Amts; Akten: betreffend Prozess gegen die Journalisten Leckert u. v. Lützow und den Kriminal Kommissar v. Tausch wegen Beleidigung von Beamten des Aus. Amts, Deutschland 122, No. 3b, Bd. 1. Also: Staatsarchiv Potsdam, Stenographischer Bericht über den Prozess Leckert-von Lützow u. Gen. [to which is added a printed version of the *Norddeutsche Allgemeine Zeitung* with hand corrections at the end], Acta der Politischen Polizei Berlin, U 128 b (13897). See also the records of the political police, betr. die Untersuchung wider die Journalisten Heinrich Leckert, Carl von Lützow und Genossen wegen Beleidigung und verleumderischer Beleidigung, Lit U No. 128 (13895). Since the Tausch trial in May-June, 1897, and his disciplinary investigation following the trial are intimately connected with Leckert-Lützow, consult also references given for these. A record of the proceedings may be found in a number of newspapers such as the *Kölnische Zeitung*, *Frankfurter Zeitung*, *Vorwärts*, and in Hugo Friedlander, *Interessante Kriminal-Prozesse von kulturhistorischer Bedeutung*, 4 vols. (Berlin, 1911), III, 127ff. See also *Wippermann*, 1896 (II), p. 144.

79. *Politische Polizei*, p. 15.

80. See Pentzler, ed., *Bismarck nach seiner Entlassung*, VII, 284-289; Hammann, *Der Neue Kurs*, pp. 77-78. See also Harden in *Die Zukunft*, vol. 20, p. 138.

81. *Politische Polizei*, p. [27?].

82. Auswärtiges Amt, Abtheilung A, Politisches Archiv d. Auswärt. Amts: Akten: betreffend Journalist Normann-Schumann, Deutschland

122, No. 3a secr., Kiderlen to Hammann, 9.II.1897 (microfilm, ACP, Roll 296, National Archives, Washington, D.C.). On Normann-Schumann, see also Motteler Papers, as cited above, note 75; Staatsarchiv Potsdam, Acta der Politischen Polizei Berlin, betr. Ermittelungen in der Disziplinar Untersuchungssache wider den Kriminal Kommissar von Tausch (Anzeige des Normann-Schumann), Ad. Personalia, Lit T, No. 50 [sic] (E452/1); P. A. Bonn, Journalist Normann-Schumann, Deutschland 122, No. 3a, vols. 1-3 [vol. 1 in National Archives, ACP, Roll 296]; P. A. Bonn, Journalist Richard Grothe, Deutschland 122, No. 3c [parts on National Archives, ACP, Roll 335].

83. Kiderlen to Hammann, 9.I.97, Deutschland 122, No. 3a secr.

84. *Politische Polizei*, p. 27.

85. *Ibid.*, p. 28.

86. *Ibid.*, p. 29.

87. *Ibid.*

88. *Ibid.*, pp. 30-31.

89. On Tausch, see records of the political police, personnel file of Tausch, Personalia, Lit T, No. 50 (8451); the pre-hearings of Tausch for his trial, Personalia, Lit T, No. 50c (8452/2); the disciplinary proceedings, Personalia, Lit T, No. 50a (8452); investigations into Tausch's perjury, Lit U, No. 126, vol. 2 (13893), Staatsarchiv Potsdam. See also references for the Leckert-Lützow trial, Normann-Schumann, and the Tausch trial, note 75, note 78, and note 82 of this chapter.

90. *Politische Polizei*, pp. 34-35.

91. *Ibid.*, p. 35.

92. *Ibid.*

93. *Ibid.*, pp. 35-36.

94. Later it was established that the originator of that article had not been Köller. See August Keim, *Erlebtes und Erstrebtes; Lebenserinnerungen von Generalleutnant Keim* (Hanover, 1925), p. 84. See also Rich, *Holstein*, II, p. 495; Hammann, *Der Neue Kurs*, p. 81.

95. *Politische Polizei*, p. 43.

96. *Ibid.*

97. *Ibid.*, pp. 45-47. See also Marschall Diary, 4.XII.96.

98. *Politische Polizei*, p. 50. In the Ministry of State meeting Marschall had already gained consent (in opposition to v. Recke) to relieve Tausch of his oath of secrecy concerning matters of state. See Marschall Diary, 27.XI.96, 5.XII.96, and so did then the police president. See *Politische Polizei*, p. 44.

99. Cf. public reaction in P.A. Bonn, Deutschland 122, No. 2d, No. 1, No. 3b.

100. *Politische Polizei*, p. 53.

101. *Ibid.*, p. 54.

102. *Ibid.*, p. 59.

103. *Ibid.*

104. *Ibid.*

105. *Ibid.*, p. 66.

106. *Ibid.*, p. 68.

107. *Ibid.*, pp. 73-74.

108. *Ibid.*, p. 75.

109. In this case Levysohn seems to be on the side of the Foreign Office. However, see the interesting comment of Holstein about "intimate connections" between Levysohn and Waldersee dating back before 1870. Holstein had thus thought about Waldersee as being behind the troublesome press articles of April-May, 1896. See *Hohenlohe*, III, 234. But see also Wolfgang Fornaschon, *Die politischen Auschauungen des Grafen Alfred von Waldersee und seine Stellungnahme zur deutschen Politik* (Berlin, 1935), p. 30.

110. *Politische Polizei*, p. 78. This is substantiated by Holstein to Hohenlohe, 28.V.96, Archiv Schillingsfürst, Rep. 100 XXII A-8; see also Marschall Diary, 6.XII.96.

111. Harry F. Young, *Maximilian Harden, Censor Germaniae* (The Hague, 1959), p. 90.

112. See the article by Maximilian Harden, "Der Prozess Marschall," in *Die Zukunft*, vol. 19, pp. 475ff. See also Raschdau, *In Weimar*, pp. 103ff., 111, 141; Herbert Bismarck to Rantzau, 6.XII.96, Bismarck Papers, Friedrichsruh.

113. Princesse Radziwill, *Une Grande Dame d'Avant Guerre; Lettres de la Princesse Radziwill au General De Robilant 1889-1914*, 4 vols. (Bologna, 1933-34), II, 47.

114. Herbert Bismarck to Rantzau, 6.XIII.96, Bismarck Papers, Friedrichsruh.

115. Hans von Tresckow, *Von Fürsten und anderen Sterblichen* (Berlin, 1922), p. 56.

116. Auswärtiges Amt; Abtheilung A, Politisches Archiv d. Auswärt. Amt; Akten; betreffend Journalist Normann-Schumann, Deutschland 122, No. 3a secr; microfilm in National Archives, Washington, D.C., ACP, Roll 296. Letter of Lindenau to [Foreign Office], 22.I.91.

117. Hammann, "Aufzeichnung," 21.III.97, Auswärtiges Amt; Abtheilung A, Politisches Archiv d. Auswärt. Amts; Akten: betreffend Journalist Richard Grothe, Deutschland 122, No. 3c; microfilm in National Archives, Washington, D.C., ACP, Roll 335.

118. Hammann, "Aufzeichnung."

119. *Ibid.*

120. See *Politische Polizei*, p. 48.

121. See Waldersee, *Denkwürdigkeiten*, II, 201, 218, 378ff., 396. See also Fornaschon, *Waldersee*, pp. 49, 51, 57; Harden, *Köpfe*, I, 206, 208f.; Hofmann, *Fürst Bismarck*, I, 196. On 23.XI.96 Marschall noted that "he [Waldersee], too, will not be very pleased with the trial."

122. Harden, *Köpfe*, III, 178.

123. Handwritten note by Alexander on memo of Hohenlohe to Alexander, 18.I.97, Archiv Schillingsfürst, Rep. 100 XXII A-7. In this connection it may also be interesting to note that in September, 1896, there was under discussion between the Foreign Office, the Ministry of Interior, and the political police—that is, Tausch—the subject of fighting revolutionary and anarchistic movements more effectively. See Guttenberg to Mayer, 19.IX.96, G.S.A. München, MA 76544.

124. Fricke, "Affaire Leckert-Lützow-Tausch," p. 1586; Rogge, *Holstein und Hohenlohe*, p. 357; Ernst Feder, ed., *Bismarcks grosses Spiel; Die geheimen Tagebücher Ludwig Bambergers* (Frankfurt am Main, 1932), pp. 462ff., 544. Kiderlen to Hammann, 13.II.97, Auswärtiges Amt; Abtheilung A, Politisches Archiv d. Auswärt. Amt, Akten: betreffend des Journalisten Normann-Schumann; microfilm in National Archives, Washington, D.C., ACP, Roll 269.

125. Hammann, "Aufzeichnung," [].I.97., 21.III.97; Spitzemberg, *Tagebuch*, p. 350.

126. Quoted from Harden, *Köpfe*, III, 176-177. "Quite a decent man," Eulenburg had described Tausch in connection with the Kotze affair in mid-1895. See Eulenburg, "Notiz," 23.IV.95, B.A. Eul. 36.

127. Harden, *Köpfe*, III, 176, 178.

128. See also Haller, *Eulenburg*, pp. 165-166.

129. See Raschdau, *In Weimar*, pp. 22, 62, 172.

130. Staatsarchiv Potsdam, Acta des Königlichen Polizei-Präsidiums zu Berlin, die Disziplinaruntersuchung wider den Kriminal Kommissar von Tausch Ad. Personalia Lit. T, No. 50a (8452). The *Strafakten* against Tausch, which include the Eulenburg letters, could (according to letters of Generalstaatsanwalt, Berlin, of 18.III.68, and the Landgerichtspräsident, Berlin, of 10.VII.68) not be located, either in the Landgericht Berlin, the General-staatsanwaltschaft at the Landgericht Berlin, or in the Landarchiv Berlin. On the Tausch trial, see references on Tausch, note 89; P. A. Bonn, Prozess gegen . . . den Kriminal Kommissar von Tausch wegen Beleidigung von Beamten des A.A., Deutschland 122, No. 3b, vols. 2, 3. See further, as in the case of the Leckert-Lützow trial, newspapers such as the *Vörwarts*, from May 26 to June 6 (for trial days of May 25-June 5).

131. Harden, *Köpfe*, I, 198.

132. Herzfeld, *Miquel*, II, 511.

133. On this, see Fricke, "Regierungskrise," p. 1585; [ ] to Hohenlohe, 13.XII.96, Archiv Schillingsfürst, Rep. 100 XII A-9; Hohenlohe to Lucanus, 28.V.97, Archiv Schillingsfürst, Rep. 100

XXII A, Bd. 11; Hohenlohe memo for conference with Wilhelm, 13.XII. 96, Archiv Schillingsfürst, Rep. 100 XXII A-9; Marschall Diary, 16.XII.96, 17.XII.96; Raschdau to Schiemann, 14.II.97, G.S.A. Berlin, Rep. 92; Schiemann Papers, No. 107; *Hohenlohe*, III, 286, note 2.

134. Sitzung des Kgl. Staatsministeriums, 29.I.98, Auswärtiges Amt, Deutschland 122, No. 3b, Geheim, vol. 3.   P.A. Bonn; and again modified on 13.III.99, Acta Disciplinaruntersuchung Tausch, Lit T, No. 50a (8452), Staatsarchiv Potsdam.

135. See the Guttenberg-Lerchenfeld reports of 9.X.96, 30.X.96, 10, 17, and 22.XI.96, G.S.A. München, MA 77751.

136. See Lerchenfeld's description of the general political situation in Berlin upon his return from several weeks in Munich, Lerchenfeld to Crailsheim, 22.X.96, G.S.A. München, MA 77751.

CHAPTER 12

The Disintegration
of the Hohenlohe Ministry

The most favorable solution [for dismissing
Marschall] would undoubtedly be the resignation
of an old ambassador and the subsequent request of
Marschall to replace him. . . .

Eulenburg to Wilhelm,
January 7, 1897

You will have noticed that we are in a crisis, of
course a personnel crisis, since we don't know any
others. It cannot be denied that Marschall's position has become very insecure and the only question
is over which issue he falls.

Raschdau to Schiemann,
February 14, 1897
(Schiemann Papers, No. 107)

We have to get rid of that South German.

[Miquel], early 1897

1

As far as public opinion was concerned, Marschall had won a
brilliant victory in the Leckert-Lützow trial and had reached the
climax of popularity.[1] However, this very fact made him all the
more detestable, and vulnerable, in the eyes of the "decisive
party in Prussia"[2]—the conservative party—and in the eyes of the
Kaiser and his entourage.[3]

Philipp Eulenburg was caught in the middle of the warring
factions. His role of appearing as the "honest broker," a role he
cherished so much and upon which most of his success was based,
came close to being unmasked, which would have seriously impaired
his freedom of political maneuverability. He wrote to his friend
Bülow his misgivings concerning the trial and its aftermath: "My
opinion about the trial is divided. Marschall could not accomplish
anything by way of disciplinary action against Tausch, who had too
much backing from the people surrounding the Kaiser. Therefore,
he had to take action by way of a trial. But it is certainly without precedent that a Prussian minister publicly destroys a Prussian
institution such as the secret police." Eulenburg went on to
describe to Bülow the difficult position in which he had found himself after the trial when he had driven with "the overly proud public
prosecutor Marschall to Moabit [the court building in Berlin]."

Then Eulenburg "had to congratulate him on his undeniably great
success," while realizing that the Kaiser and his entourage were
outraged at the unprecedented affair. Eulenburg stated that he
had therefore tried to "prepare" the Chancellor, Marschall, and
Holstein "for a recognition by the Kaiser that would not live up
to their expectations." Moreover, he had "urgently advised"
Hohenlohe "not to act too victorious" and to prepare for a possible
move on the part of the Kaiser to dismiss Marschall.[4]

Marschall's hour of triumph was only too short; Eulenburg's
analysis had only been too correct. He had foreseen that, whatever the outcome, the trial would be detrimental to Marschall:
"the enemies of Marschall, if the trial shows *little* success will
triumph; but if he would have a big success, would double their
hatred."[5]

While the Leckert-Lützow trial was still in progress, Wilhelm—
this time enjoying a hunting excursion at Sprigge in the company
of his entourage—informed the Chancellor how deplorable Marschall's
action in the trial had seemed to the assembled party. The uniform
opinion had been that Marschall's acts were in contradiction to the
duties of a Prussian minister. Wilhelm made it quite clear that
this was not his opinion, only the impression of "the gathered guests,
coming from all part of the country." His own evaluation would
come—"as is always the case"—after the end of the affair.[6] However,
he had given enough indication of where he stood. He was infuriated
about "the appearance of a Minister of State whose conduct is that
of a prosecutor only and who downright arranges a circus performance
before the public."[7] Wilhelm was probably quite sincere in his
indignation over the "terrible mud"[8] that the trial had brought into
the open; however, rather than judging the situation on its merits—
even Eulenburg did not deny the necessity of Marschall's step[9]—the
Kaiser instantly placed all the blame on the Secretary of State.
In addition, this prejudiced reaction received constant and powerful support from his entourage. One day after the Leckert-Lützow
trial had ended, Wilhelm had sent a telegram to Hohenlohe strongly
criticizing Marschall's conduct. In order to counteract Wilhelm's
verbal and written expressions of dissatisfaction with Marschall,
Hohenlohe did not show the Kaiser's letter to Marschall, since that
might have induced him to resign on the spot. At the same time
he again explained in detail to the Kaiser why the court action had
been necessary and warned that a negative treatment of the Foreign
Secretary might well create a government crisis. In fact, Marschall
had confronted Hohenlohe with the alternatives of either arranging
a conference with the Kaiser or submitting his resignation.[10]

Eulenburg on his part realized the full extent of Marschall's
failure when he met the Kaiser and his entourage on December 8 in
Magdeburg on the train that was to take them to Potsdam together.
Wilhelm took this occasion to complain bitterly about Marschall.
The Kaiser said that he could no longer continue to govern with
him, nor with Hohenlohe; Prussia would go to ruin under such leader-
ship, "that completely misunderstood what the responsibility of
Prussia and its King was." Eulenburg continued in his report to
Bülow, "This psychological difference was inevitably leading towards
catastrophe, if I did not succeed in making a noticeable impression."
But the Kaiser "saw at once that a crisis with Marschall in this

moment of liberal triumph when he is cheered by millions of glasses
of beer every evening, would do the Sovereign endless harm," and
ended with the following observation: "Well, until spring everything is to remain as it is—not any longer—impossibly any longer.
Even old Hohenlohe shall then go."[11]

Thus, when Eulenburg parted from Wilhelm in Potsdam to see
Holstein, Boetticher, and Marschall, he could be reasonably sure
that he had once again won over the Kaiser to his side for the time
being. However, it seems that for the first time Eulenburg had
clearly realized that Marschall's end was definitely in sight and
that he, Eulenburg, could no longer (as he had done throughout
1896) postpone Marschall's resignation into the indefinite future.
He mentioned to Bülow, "But of this you may be sure—the trial has
knocked the bottom out of things. So prepare yourself gradually,
my poor dear fellow. There is time still, but it won't last many
months. We shall have a chance—if God wills—to discuss the
situation in Venice."[12] Eulenburg probably also realized that,
given the Leckert-Lützow trial and with the future Tausch case in
view, his own position and influence might well be endangered. Up
to then, he had been accepted as the confidant and "honest broker"
by the Kaiser, by Hohenlohe, and to an extent by Holstein, Marschall,
and even Lucanus, General Hahnke, and Botho Eulenburg. However, by
defending Marschall and appearing at the trial, he might have gone
too far, and he was afraid that he might have overplayed his hand.
Eulenburg had the impression that everybody was longing for a
change: "—perhaps even August Eulenburg to a degree—nobody wants
to wait any longer. They think H. M. ripe for them to venture on
any word or deed which may precipitate the catastrophe. In regard
to this I am especially suspicious of Lucanus."[13] He was also
afraid that a person or combination of persons would deliberately
leave him out of the picture, lest he again "mediate" and wreck
their plan for getting rid of Marschall and Boetticher, and eventually Hohenlohe.[14]

Consequently, Eulenburg, aware of Marschall's untenable position, began renewed political intimacies with some of Marschall's
most dangerous enemies in order to keep abreast of events, as well
as to be able to direct them. "No one suspects," he added in the
letter to Bülow, "that I see through it all—and the Office has no
idea how combustible I think the situation. I have one aim in
view—to guard H.M. from making a change which will come easier
when Marschall's laurels are forgotten, or at any rate, withered."[15]
In Berlin, Eulenburg did not need to fear Hohenlohe, since the
Chancellor abhorred a Marschall crisis as much as Eulenburg did at
the moment. Holstein was a different matter; he had informed
Eulenburg that "we stand at the beginning of a Tausch-crisis,"[16]
and Boetticher, with whom Holstein had spoken on the same day, gave
the same indication. Eulenburg noted that, as he had foreseen,
the hostility toward Marschall had increased rather than decreased.
The Kaiser was certainly correct when he remarked, as did the
Bismarckian press, the "the public prosecutor had run away with
the Minister," and that this provided too forceful a lever against
Marschall. However, Eulenburg thought a crisis at the moment was
not inevitable.[17] He completely agreed, as usual, with Bülow's
analysis of the situation: "...an abrupt separation from Marschall

and Hohenlohe . . . would bring His Majesty into an impossible
situation." In fact, a separation at that time, "when . . . public
opinion and the press as well as the majority of the parliament
stand on Marschall's side . . . would only be possible if His
Majesty comes to a full reconciliation with Friedrichsruh."
Eulenburg very aptly summed up the present situation in Germany:
"Those forces in Germany that are not on Marschall's side are on
that of Bismarck. Those who are, like you and I, royalists and
nothing but royalists, are only a few."[18] As often, the key to the
whole situation still lay with the Kaiser, and since Eulenburg was
as yet unsurpassed in the handling of his Imperial friend, it also
lay to a great extent with him.

Apparently Holstein—as before—wanted to use Marschall's great
popularity throughout Germany to strengthen the ministry against
the crown. He therefore had advised Marschall to ask the Kaiser
for an immediate interview; if the latter in any way showed his dis-
content, Marschall was to hand in his resignation. As we have seen,
this was the course Marschall followed. However, Eulenburg endeav-
ored to prevent such a renewed "position of constraint" and, in
conjunction with Hohenlohe, tried to gain time to bring his considerable persuasive skills to bear.[19]

By the time Eulenburg paid him a visit, Marschall had despaired
of the possibility of gaining respect in the eyes of the monarch by
"cleaning out" the government by way of the Leckert-Lützow trial.
He complained to Eulenburg that he had an express order from the
monarch to take action against the press intrigues "unrelentingly
and with all available means." It was necessary to give a report
about the trial to the monarch—the more so since Marschall had
(in the interests of the state) withheld information concerning
the instigators of Tausch.[20] Then he added, "I tell you quite
frankly that if I will be treated ungraciously by His Majesty at
this moment, then my honor does not allow me to remain any longer."
Eulenburg tried to persuade Marschall to drop his dangerous thoughts
of resignation, but apparently with little success. Marschall was
not satisfied with Eulenburg's assurance that the Kaiser had calmed
down considerably. He still insisted upon an interview but accepted
a postponement of it until December 10, and accepted Eulenburg's
mediations in the form of a written communication to Wilhelm. After
his conversation with Marschall, Eulenburg reported the whole interview to the Kaiser, and urgently asked the monarch once more to be
as friendly as possible to Marschall in order to forestall the
latter's resignation: "in the event of the possible eruption of
bitterness, Your Majesty will suffer."[21] It is not very pleasant
to compare the Eulenburg who is talking to Marschall with the Eulenburg who is writing to Wilhelm and supposedly mediating between the
two. Indeed, suggesting Marschall's dismissal in the spring was
perhaps the only way to mollify the Kaiser and retain Marschall for
the time being; but then Eulenburg himself wanted to get rid of the
Foreign Secretary as soon as it seemed safe to do so.

Marschall's audience with the Kaiser took place two days later
on December 10. It was a complete success for Eulenburg. Even
Holstein felt that Wilhelm had almost been won over by Marschall's
arguments.[22] Marschall himself had also been quite satisfied, but
remained skeptical about how long his success would last. The

Kaiser appears in no more favorable light when he told Marschall
that he was sorry to have temporarily wavered in the faith of "one
of his best advisors" and that he, Marschall, had behaved magnifi-
cently.[23] As it was, soon enough did the Kaiser show his true
colors. He sharply rebuked Marschall for a Reichstag speech on
Crete and for having overstepped, and pointed out that only he,
Wilhelm, guided foreign policy.[24] Marschall was, however, wide of
the mark in imagining even a temporary amiability. Holstein's
letter to Eulenburg contained such phraseology that one must assume
it to have been a deliberate act to mollify Eulenburg. For this he
had good reason, since apparently Eulenburg suspected Holstein of
being one force behind the recurrent anti-Eulenburg press campaigns.[25]

Kaiser Wilhelm's report to Eulenburg was clear enough. He had
successfully adopted the appearance of conciliation, but his categorical determination to replace Marschall, as well as Boetticher
(even Hohenlohe was mentioned), remained as strong as ever. Moreover,
he made sure that Eulenburg was kept informed about his real intentions and would not be taken in by false reports reflecting his
tactical moves.[26] However, Eulenburg knew the real state of affairs
anyway. He assured his monarch that he had not changed his attitude
in regard to Marschall; that he, too, had come to realize the
necessity of Marschall's dismissal; and that he would work toward
that end without "wavering." Priding himself that he was "in
politics very tough and consistent," he wrote, "The form of a
separation in the spring must be *very* thoroughly planned. The
most favorable solution would undoubtedly be the resignation of an
old ambassador and the subsequent request of Marschall to replace
him; since an exchange with Bernhard von Bülow bears serious doubts
for the latter, in consideration of the existing atmosphere. And it
is too important for Your Majesty that he may find as smooth a
way as possible."[27]

Marschall did not have a chance. In the face of the animosity
of the Kaiser, the political line followed by Eulenburg, and the
continuous and ever increasing agitation against the Secretary of
State by the entourage (Miquel, Lucanus, and Waldersee),[28] there
was no question as to the outcome of the struggle. In addition,
Philipp Eulenburg had been informed by August Eulenburg that the
connection between the Kaiser and the Foreign Office had been all but
severed, and that whenever "an attempt at contact is made, every
time there is a spark, if not an explosion."[29] Along with this,
numerous smaller incidents gave proof of the state of affairs.[30]

It was quite natural that Holstein, who now realized that a
direct defense of Marschall could hardly have any positive impact,
once again became rather pessimistic.[31] Therefore, he changed his
line of argument, adapting it in such a way as to be most effective
in provoking Eulenburg to action. He began to emphasize the fact
that a dismissal of Marschall before the Tausch trial would have
disastrous consequences, and in a letter of January 12, 1897, he
urged Eulenburg that whenever a concrete situation might appear
(that is, the possibility of a direct move against Marschall), he
should not fail to use all his influence to prevent Marschall's
dismissal.[32]

It was in his reply to Holstein that Eulenburg pointed out
directly that his support for Marschall had its limits. The

animosity of the Kaiser—already of long standing—had only increased:
"For a number of years we find ourselves between the friction-peaks
of two incommensurable dimensions." Eulenburg had done all that was
possible (so he stated in his second letter to Holstein) to smooth
over the differences between the Kaiser and the Secretary of State:
"A contradiction such as does exist between the natures of His
Majesty and of Marschall may, at the most, only be decreased—but an
elimination of such cannot be hoped for." He had even arranged a
meeting between Marschall and the Kaiser (that of December 10) which
had been successful but could be of no permanence. Besides, Eulenburg then asked Holstein if it was for the good in the long run to
let these contradictions continue to exist with such acuteness.
"Does not the whole organism suffer thereby?" However, Eulenburg
continued, the state would be harmed even more by the removal of
Marschall at the present time, and he would do everything in his
power to prevent Marschall's dismissal before the conclusion of the
Tausch trial.[33]

Holstein clearly realized in what direction Eulenburg was
heading. It would obviously mean the predominance of Wilhelm in
Germany, but without Marschall the government would lack the necessary counterbalance and stability. He reviewed for Eulenburg in a
letter of January 13 the events of 1896 from this point of view, and
he ended with the rhetorical question whether Wilhelm was a man
whom one could follow in confidence.[34]

Even Bülow, to whom Holstein had written, was frightened by
Holstein's considerations. Bülow had received news (independently
from Holstein) that Marschall's position—even in the eyes of some
of his enemies[35]—was such that his immediate dismissal would be
disastrous. Moreover, Eulenburg felt it necessary to note down a
justification of his conduct. These notations show Eulenburg's
strengths, but also—and much more clearly—his severe limitations
and his notorious "byzantinism" in dealing with the Kaiser.[36]

Eulenburg made it clear that Marschall had to go, and defended
his action to Bülow. As to Holstein's reflections, which Eulenburg
summed up in his own words for Bülow, he added that his letter to
Holstein had been a deliberate act to make him realize the contradictions "in which he himself is caught and which seem to be strong
enough so as to gradually think about a change." However, he was
doubtful of the result of this cautious indication, and felt it
necessary to be even more clear.[37] To Bülow he added in a post-
script that if Holstein were aware of the extent of their friendship, he would immediately capitulate: "He writes us, because he
is aware of our power. If it would become clear to him that under
no circumstances can we be separated, then he would hate us."
However, they both (Eulenburg and Bülow) should wait and see, "if
the separation from Holstein could be possible, under what conditions this would have to be done."[38]

Eulenburg took Holstein's warning seriously enough (perhaps
because it was substantiated by Bülow) to caution the monarch once
more not to dismiss Marschall before the end of the Tausch trial,[39]
and he received a reassuring answer from August Eulenburg to the
effect that although the "familiar conditions here are as sick and
unpleasant as ever, before spring there will be no change (before
the end of the Reichstag session)."[40]

In late January the Kaiser awarded Lucanus the "Order of the
Black Eagle." Eulenburg, suspicious of Lucanus's designs but clever
enough to know that it would be better "not to make a move against
Lucanus,"[41] took this opportunity to renew his contact with him for
the projected and inevitable ministerial changes coming in the near
future. After congratulating Lucanus upon his Imperial recognition,
Eulenburg added:

> Recently I received a letter from His Majesty which
> showed me clearly the domestic situation. In this con-
> nection I want to state that I always will stick to the
> content of our conversation we had in Hubertusstock and
> under no circumstances will depart from it....A natural
> development of things seems very important to me, con-
> sidering the situation. As you, I should like to avoid
> His Majesty's being exposed to a greater crisis than is
> absolutely necessary.[42]

This strongly suggests that Eulenburg had told Lucanus about the
necessary dismissal of Marschall, but that it should come neither
before the end of the Tausch trial nor before the end of the Reichstag session; and that Eulenburg had pointed out the necessity of a
calm, not a violent, change. Lucanus confirmed Eulenburg's views:
"The temperature change, which will in all probability come in the
spring, will I hope be accomplished without any crisis." This would
be the case, Lucanus said, especially since Marschall had begun to
realize his politically meaningless victory and would actually (in
Lucanus' opinion) welcome a change. Until then, Lucanus would try
to prevent anything concerning the projected change from leaking out
into the press, lest it alarm the public. When Eulenburg would next
be in Berlin for a while, Lucanus concluded, he should stop by to
talk over a number of things.[43] In this way Eulenburg slowly but
surely tightened the rope around Marschall's neck so as to be able
to strangle him at his own convenience. It is perhaps an indication
of Marschall's political stature that there was keen competition for
the honor of accomplishing this act.

The disillusioned Marschall[44] was awarded one more triumph in
the Reichstag, however meaningless and in fact detrimental to his
already undermined position. It had originally been the intention
of the members of the Reichstag to discuss the Leckert-Lützow affair
shortly after the end of the trial in December. However, this plan
had come to nothing because of the discussion over the *Justiznovelle*
—and also possibly because of the cooperation of the government
with the Center Party.[45]

The notion of discussing the Leckert-Lützow affair had been
brought into the Prussian Landtag by the Conservative representative
Limburg-Stirum in a debate that ranged over a number of issues, from
trade treaties to the current associations law. The debate was
marked by a spirited attack by the Conservatives upon the government's
policies and personalities and the latter's defense by the National
Liberal and Radical representatives.[46]

The Reichstag took up the question of the trial a few days later
on February 5 and 6. It was here that the liberal and radical
majority of that house became an ardent spokesman for Marschall,
who once again (and for the last time) tried meticulously to explain

the necessity of his actions and to defend the Foreign Office against implied misuse of the press. He successfully defended the government by emphasizing the existing unity within the ministry,[47] and he defended himself against the charges of having violated Prussian tradition. The Conservatives were pushed against the wall in this debate, although they—especially the Bismarckians Limburg-Stirum and Count Mirbach—defended the Conservative Party as one that, although in the majority, nevertheless expressed a "re-echoing of that which is being thought in the most widespread circles of the country."[48]

Marschall's parliamentary triumph, although personally gratifying, did not mean much. The Reichstag session had begun as a fiscal debate, and the Polish representatives had then taken the floor to voice their grievances. The Radical representative Munckel had then introduced the Leckert-Lützow affair into the debate, and this debate was ended a day later by the Poles regaining the floor after the Radicals had withdrawn their bill (which was nominally intended to reform the political police) when they had achieved their purpose— an open discussion.[49] With the retraction of the bill, the Leckert-Lützow episode ended for that parliamentary body. Popular and parliamentary majorities in the German Reich were not indicative of ministerial strength and success. In fact, more often than not they seemed to be indicative of the opposite—that success lay with skillful intrigue and popularity among narrow court circles in Berlin. In addition, whereas in the former arena Marschall had been once again the hero of the hour, in the latter he was singularly unsuccessful.

By the time Marschall had gained the confidence of the overwhelming majority of the Reichstag in early February,[50] another issue had somewhat eclipsed the Leckert-Lützow-Tausch affair: the Navy budget and the resultant Hollmann crisis.

2

Although the Kaiser had never really given up his plans for the expansion of the Navy that had been rejected in early 1896 by Hohenlohe, Hollmann, and the Reichstag,[51] this project received new attention as the result of the lengthy Reichstag debate over the naval budget in November, 1896, from the renewed attempts of the Naval High Command to extend and define[52] its powers as opposed to those of the Imperial Naval Office, and lastly from the flaring up once again in early 1897 of the difficulties with Crete.

From January 29 to February 2 the Kaiser resided in Kiel, where he apparently had come under the strong influence of his brother Prince Heinrich and the latter's adjutant, *Korvettenkapitän* Müller, who shared the same views on the naval issue as did Admiral von Senden.[53] On January 3 Wilhelm had informed Waldersee that "in the near future a great deal must be done for the fleet,"[54] and had shown him colored diagrams that indicated the respective growths of the French and German navies.[55] At the same time he created parliamentary suspicion with his speeches against the Poles, the Social Democrats, and ultramontanism.[56]

On February 3 the Kaiser pointed out to Hohenlohe that Germany "should have at least half of the number of the Russian and French ships taken together. Otherwise we are lost. For this a huge loan is needed, and this must be taken up at the end of the year."[57] For Hohenlohe this meant that the monarch would replace the moderate Hollmann with a more forceful personality, a feeling which was reinforced during a conversation with Wilhelm on February 15.[58]

Eulenburg was immediately informed by Hohenlohe and Holstein[59] about this new and portentous advance of Wilhelm. Holstein especially pointed out to him the extreme danger of such a step for the Kaiser—and for Germany. It almost seemed, wrote Holstein, that the Kaiser was placing the "peace, one may even say the existence of the Reich, in jeopardy" for his "limitless Naval plans." In the same letter Holstein again complained about Wilhelm's exasperating dabbling in foreign policy. Last, Holstein mentioned to Eulenburg that the Kaiser's entourage looked upon Botho as the future Chancellor and warned Phili of nepotism—an Eulenburg camarilla, even if existing only in the mind of the public, would come under the most heavy attacks.

Eulenburg was not shaken by this news from Hohenlohe and Holstein. He admitted to Holstein that he could "neither modify the facts nor your opinions." However, the main content of the letter carried a different note: he tried to point out that the most recent idea of the Kaiser in foreign policy—a united action of Germany and France against England—had been discussed by the monarch (and with him, Eulenburg) only from the aspect of *Zukunftsmusik*. In matters of the fleet, Eulenburg pointed out that the monarch could at times demand a great deal in order to achieve something else. Thus on each of the issues Eulenburg went to great lengths in defending Wilhelm, belittling the danger and justifying his actions; he even tried to explain some of the Kaiser's nervousness as a sign of the growing animosity of the monarch against Marschall.[60] As to Holstein's warning about Botho, Eulenburg threw in some flowery phraseology about Holstein's friendship, which he "perhaps deserved a little" and for which he was very thankful. Then he added, "How I think about certain eventualities, you know. I have lost my objectivity as little as at any previous time."[61]

This letter was clearly written with the idea of silencing Holstein.[62] With Bülow, Eulenburg was more truthful. Certainly, he maintained, it would be nice to have a little more stability, but so far no harm had been done. Besides, at present Germany was stronger than ever before, politically speaking, having an "enormous preponderance in all questions." As to Holstein's letter in general, Eulenburg commented: "Everything is just ill-will and hate."[63] This comment throws a clear light upon Eulenburg's "objectivity," as well as on his emphatic assurance of friendship for Holstein.

Eulenburg also began to undermine the position of the Foreign Office. Since at the time the question of Crete had assumed renewed prominence, Eulenburg as the ambassador to the Dual Monarch received more than usual attention. However, knowing the antagonism of Holstein for the Austrian Foreign Minister, Goluchowski, Eulenburg criticized the Foreign Office and informed Goluchowski that Holstein would not stay in office much longer. He took a similar step with the Austrian ambassador to Berlin, Szögyenyi, advising him to bypass the Foreign Office and consult directly with either the Kaiser or

himself in any matter of importance.[64]   At the same time he strongly
complained to Hohenlohe that Holstein wanted to get rid of him
(Eulenburg).[65]   Finally, Eulenburg took the drastic step of complaining outright to Wilhelm about the difficulties he had encountered with the Foreign Office.[66]   It may reasonably be assumed that
this added to the already overwhelming tension between the monarch
and the Foreign Office.

   Just at this time Marschall made some comments about the situation in Crete to the Reichstag, and the Kaiser took strong issue
with him, since the Secretary of State had spoken on the subject
without the express authority of the monarch.   Wilhelm wanted to
summon the Reichstag to the Neue Palais and there proclaim the
position of the government on the Cretan question.[67]   This intention of the Kaiser induced Eulenburg to tell him that the nervousness
of the Foreign Office was partly due to the personal action of the
Kaiser in politics, that the Foreign Office had purposely tried to
offend Goluchowski, that the policy of the Foreign Office was
jeopardizing the alliance with the Dual Monarchy, and that the
Foreign Office *must* be "Your Majesty's machinery . . . that functions with absolute precision."   Moreoever, although Eulenburg
cautiously mentioned to Wilhelm that his interference disturbed
the efficient functioning of that machinery, the point seemed to
be that Wilhelm had the obligation to make the Foreign Office
conform to Imperial intentions and thus bring it under his control.
This meant, in so many words, that Wilhelm was to get rid of
Marschall.[68]

   It would not be going too far to state that Eulenburg consciously
counteracted the Foreign Office in order to eliminate it as a
political factor in the question of Crete so long as it did not
conform completely to the monarch's will and his own.   At this time
the personal interference of the monarch in the field of foreign
affairs had reached its climax.   The acts of the Kaiser and those
of the Foreign Office did not coincide any more at all.   The
Foreign Office was unable to keep up with the rapidly shifting
attitudes and acts of Wilhelm, who did nothing to keep his ministry
adequately informed about his latest personal political feats.   Nor
was the Foreign Office able to counteract Eulenburg's conspiracy
against it.   The result was confusion, distrust, mounting tension
(as reflected in Holstein's letter), and the Kaiser's animosity
toward the Wilhelmstrasse in general and Marschall in particular—a
situation severely intensified by Eulenburg's support of the
monarch instead of the Foreign Office.

   It was during this already rather confused state of affairs
that the question of the Navy once again became acute.   The naval
issue was composed of two main elements: the Navy bill itself, and
the demarcation of authority between the Naval High Command and
the Imperial Naval Office.   The Imperial Naval Office was represented
by State Secretary Hollmann and Chancellor Hohenlohe; the Naval High
Command by Admiral von Senden, Prince Heinrich, Admiral von Tirpitz,
Knorr, and others.

   The feud between the Naval High Command and the Imperial Naval
Office was of long standing.   In 1889 the Admiralty had been dis-
solved and replaced by a Naval High Command and an Imperial Naval
Office; the place of the chief of the Admiralty was taken by a

chief of the newly constituted Naval Cabinet, a Secretary of State of the Imperial Naval Office,[69] and the chief of the Naval High Command.

There were too many chiefs and, perhaps worse, no clear demarcation of responsibility and power among these three offices. Thus, the chief of the Naval High Command had the same rank and privileges as a commanding general in the Army, and he had the right to appeal directly to the Kaiser. The Secretary of State of the Imperial Naval Office, usually an admiral, as a naval officer was directly subordinate to the Kaiser, who also had extensive powers over military (and therefore naval) personnel; but on the other hand, as Imperial Secretary of State, he was at the same time responsible to the Chancellor.[70] Finally, there existed the Naval Cabinet.

The Naval High Command was to be the main agency for military planning and strategy; the Imperial Naval Office was to deal with the Reichstag and prepare the budget and thus to have jurisdiction over the building program.[71] However, instead of the necessary cooperation between these departments and the chiefs, there was a more or less constant struggle for power, especially between the Secretary of State of the Imperial Naval Office, Admiral Hollmann, and the Chief of the Naval Cabinet, Admiral Senden (in conjunction with Alfred Tirpitz, who was appointed chief of staff to the Naval High Command by early 1892). As a result, the "Imperial as well as Hollmann's randomness and confusion" reigned supreme. It was this fact rather than an inherent animosity to the Navy as such that made for such reluctance in the Reichstag on naval matters, as on most other political issues.[72]

By the end of 1895 Senden, Tirpitz, and Knorr were working toward the dismissal of Hollmann,[73] and probably soon also Marschall,[74] with these latter stubbornly fighting back. This state of affairs lasted essentially up to June, 1897, when Senden and Tirpitz were successful in ousting Hollmann and replacing Tirpitz in his post and thereby gaining the necessary cooperation between the naval departments, as well as bringing clarity into the future plans for the Navy.[75]

By early March both departments had once again handed in their respective drafts for the future administrative division between them. It is clear that the Naval High Command took advantage of the parliamentary difficulties of Hollmann as well as the strongly anti-Hollmann attitude of the Kaiser. While their plan would have been a clear demarcation of authority, at the same time it subordinated the Naval Office.[76] Instead of accepting one of them, or proposing changes, the Kaiser wanted these two drafts to be referred to an *Immediatkommission*. At the same time, while the two naval departments were struggling for power and when a showdown was soon to be expected, the Reichstag Budget Commission, to which most of the budget had been referred after the first reading in the Reichstag in November, 1896,[77] took up the debate on the Navy budget on March 1.

It was through Senden that Wilhelm made his intention known about the *Immediatkommission* to Hollmann and Hohenlohe.[78] Apparently under the influence of Hollmann, Hohenlohe (who at first seemed not to have objected to the *Immediatkommission*) changed his mind and held that, according to the Constitution, such a commission did not have power to interfere in any way with a document drawn up by the Imperial Naval Office under the auspices of the Reich Chancellor.[79]

Furthermore, Hollmann went to the Kaiser, who was at Wilhelmshaven to accept the oath of new Navy recruits on March 4 (from where he was to go to Bremen the next day to visit Prince Heinrich), and informed the monarch that he would hand in his resignation if the proposed *Immediatkommission* were convened. Hohenlohe on his part threatened with the cabinet question.[80] The Kaiser did not want a crisis over this issue, so he took a step that had previously been successful—he asked to see Hohenlohe in person. This conference came about on March 7.[81] In response to Hohenlohe's constitutional objections, Wilhelm told him bluntly that "the Emperor has no rights at all," or, as he had mentioned to Hollmann in Wilhelmshaven, "he does not know any constitution, but only that which he wants."[82] Besides, the Kaiser thought that the constitutional aspect was irrelevant, since he possessed 18 Army corps and would know how to deal with the south Germans. Hohenlohe, meekly supported by Boetticher, yielded to the Kaiser on the question of the *Immediatkommission* (in which the Kaiser was supported by Lucanus).[83]

Holstein had kept Eulenburg well informed about the growing Hollmann crisis, but Eulenburg had not taken any action. To Hohenlohe he simply expressed his hope that the crisis which Holstein had signaled would subside, and noted that the loss of Hollmann would be unfortunate.[84] To the Kaiser he wrote a long letter. Significantly, he excused himself for troubling his monarch at a time when "Your Majesty had annoyances and difficulties in Naval-personnel questions," and then he complained about the Foreign Office—a lament which he repeated a few days later.[85]

On March 8 Hollmann went to the Kaiser to report on the session of the *Immediatkommission*, and Wilhelm took this opportunity to demand that Hollmann ask for a vote of confidence. This, in effect, meant that Hollmann would have to hand in his resignation if the Budget Commission—still ardently debating the Navy budget—did not pass the entire budget as originally proposed to the Reichstag.[86] Despite Hohenlohe's protest that Hollmann was only a Secretary of State (and thus responsible to the Chancellor) and that only the Chancellor himself could request him to resign, and despite Hohenlohe's own threat of resignation, the Kaiser did not retreat from his position. On March 13 the Budget Commission approved the Navy appropriation, but with significant cuts, and gave it back to the Reichstag. As a consequence, Hollmann handed in his resignation. Hohenlohe presented it to the Kaiser with the remark that since Hollmann had no authority to take the step that Wilhelm had demanded of him, he as Chancellor could not accept the resignation.

Two days later Wilhelm replied that he had not come to a decision with regard to Hollmann. The act of the Budget Commission did not constitute the acceptance of the budget by the Reichstag. Furthermore, Wilhelm advised Hohenlohe and the entire ministry to mount a vigorous defense of the budget and the original Navy bill. Upon the further plea of the Chancellor to reject Hollmann's resignation in order to strengthen his position in the Reichstag, Wilhelm refused—but again encouraged Hohenlohe: "Not with a lame horse will your Serene Highness appear on the race track, but with a jockey for a tournament with life and death. . . ."[87] He assured

Hohenlohe that he wanted neither Hollmann nor his resignation, and that he did not have a coup d'état in mind over the Navy bill.[88] With Hollmann's pending resignation—a fact well known—the Kaiser, probably accepting the reasoning of Senden, hoped to strengthen his cause in the Reichstag by pressuring it to save Hollmann by accepting the original Navy bill and not the modified proposal of the Budget Commission.[89] However, it was to no avail. On March 28 the Reichstag accepted the cuts proposed by the commission.[90]

From the beginning the Navy bill had faced considerable difficulties. The left-wing slogan of "limitless Naval plans" had never completely died since its conception by the Radical representative Eugen Richten in 1888,[91] and it had been very effectively renewed in November, 1896. Also, a fact probably decisive, there was lack of unity within the Naval Department and between the Kaiser and the government and, moroeover, no clearly defined program.

The budget increase was due mainly to the increased operating expenses of the Navy, and the budget was not so unreasonable that the phrase "unlimited fleet program" might justly have been applied.[92] Nevertheless, the increase was enough to arouse suspicion and antipathy. These were strengthened by an indiscretion which had revealed the eventual total expenditure necessary for a naval program proposed in February, 1890, and by the attempt to justify this in the Reichstag. The way in which Hollmann handled the situation further complicated matters. Very likely under considerable pressure, he had made highly unrealistic promises to the Kaiser with regard to the Navy budget; he had presented a large and somewhat confused appropriation ranging over a number of years. His presentation had to be practically denied and changed so as to discuss only the immediate needs in the parliamentary commission.[93] However, a large share of the responsibility for the Reichstag's negative attitude must also be attributed to the Kaiser himself. In January he had mentioned "several" hundred million marks which were to be used for the Navy.[94] In mid-February he had asked—in the presence of members of the Center Party—for a revival of the *Kartell* policy (an alliance of the Liberals, Conservatives, and Reichspartei) so as not to be so dependent upon the Center (the most important party supporting the government at that time), and he had even hinted at the possibility of dissolving the Reichstag on account of the negative response to the Navy bill.[95] In the latter part of February he had delivered his shocking speech at the Brandenburg provincial Diet referring to Moltke and Bismarck as "pygmies" (*Handlanger*). He said, among other things, that "the party that dares to attack the foundation of the State, that rises against religion, and that does not even call a halt before that person of the Supreme Sovereign, that party must be destroyed."[96] With these words he aroused a great deal of suspicion, fear, and resentment in the majority of the nation and in the Reichstag. He freely spoke about a coup d'état in the near future.[97] Finally, Wilhelm made the Conservative representative Stumm believe that the Kaiser had given him orders to tell the Reichstag that if the original Navy bill did not pass, there would follow dissolution of the Reichstag, a change of voting law, and other similar measures. This "order" Stumm faithfully carried out at the most inopportune time possible, when the Reichstag debated the Navy bill in March. The National Liberal Hammacher was used

to carry a similar message to the Budget Commission.[98]   The result
was that even the moderate supporters now took a stand against the
bill.[99]   One of the leaders of the Center Party, Lieber, even told
Hohenlohe that the cuts had been accepted by the Reichstag not because it had been fundamentally opposed to the bill but "because
one did not want to grant anything to the Kaiser."[100]

3

The crisis, however, was far from over.   In fact, the atmosphere
became even more tense.   The indications for a general crisis—the
possible dismissal of the Chancellor, of the entire ministry, and
even of the Reichstag—took on alarming proportions (an impression
that Wilhelm strengthened to the best of his ability in his conversation with Hohenlohe on March 30).   By this time Eulenburg had
fallen out with Holstein to such a degree that he sent him an angry
letter, for which soon after he felt it necessary to apologize.[101]
Holstein, having suddenly gained knowledge about Eulenburg of such
a nature that he thought Eulenburg would have to leave the service
in the very near future (he did not state the nature of his information), begged Eulenburg for the last time to use all his influence
to calm the situation and counteract all the wild coup-d'état
ideas.[102]   Hohenlohe likewise turned to Eulenburg again for help.
Marschall had already done his part.   By way of Saxon Ambassador
Hohenthal, Marschall urged the Saxon king to persuade Wilhelm to
moderation.   Finally, Marschall made similar requests to the Grand
Duke of Baden.   The Grand Duke, although warmly supporting Wilhelm's
naval plans (at least Wilhelm must have gotten that impression from
his letter), at the same time complied with Marschall.   According
to Marschall, the Grand Duke thoroughly understood the situation in
Berlin, as did the Saxon king, who asked Marschall to "hold out."[103]
However, this time Phili used his influence on a rather modest
scale.   Quite early in the year he had told Holstein that in all
likelihood Senden would be victorious over Hollmann, and Phili
probably knew that by early February the Kaiser had become so disgusted with Hollmann that the latter was indeed a lost cause.[104]
Accordingly, Eulenburg seems not to have taken any serious action
on his behalf.   Besides, he did not take the "limitless fleet plans"
and their implications in personnel and policy too seriously, since
they did not appear to be likely for the immediate future.[105]   On
the other hand, in regard to ministerial changes he had become aware
that "everything pushes toward a solution," and he had asked Bülow
to save a few free days in early April in case it should become
necessary to meet with him.[106]   Consequently, Eulenburg had shrewdly
not stuck his head into the noose of defending either Hollmann or the
Foreign Office. Marschall also seemed beyond recall.[107]   His impression that "postponed" usually meant "cancelled"[108] was not applicable
in this case.   He took the same cautious position when advising
Hohenlohe.   In effect, he told Hohenlohe to dissociate himself from
his ministers and stand "above" any possible crisis (as in the case
of Bronsart the previous autumn), lest he become caught in its
maelstrom.[109]   It is quite obvious that Hohenlohe recognized
Eulenburg's advice for what it was: either go along with the Kaiser,
or accept the fact of dismissal in the near future, as Alexander

in essence pointed out in his reply.[110]

Eulenburg did not answer right away. Instead he wrote to the Kaiser. The Kaiser had calmed down considerably, even if he had not changed his basic position, and was busily preparing new charts for the naval program. However, when the Reichstag refused "his" ships in final reading on March 28, he flared up again. Hollmann was given leave of absence but was not immediately replaced by Tirpitz, only because of the latter's shrewd request to wait three months with the appointment. Wilhelm promised to use the Navy budget as cause for internal conflict by closing the Reichstag, etc.[111] Finally on April 8 Eulenburg reported with satisfaction that the monarch's comment to the Austrian ambassador about his inability to work with Marschall any longer had been correctly understood in Vienna. Then he turned to Hohenlohe and the latter's recent impression that the Kaiser—by inaugurating a "policy of force"— wanted to get rid of him. Eulenburg assumed that Wilhelm was not really considering dismissing Hohenlohe. Moreover, as to the conversation with the Chancellor, he commented, ". . . by thinking that Your Majesty has blown a very loud trombone, in order to awaken a tired old man, I reduce this trombone (in my own mind) to a French horn." Notwithstanding, Eulenburg came back to the question of "policy of force":

> . . . not only a so-called "policy of force" (in terms of which Your Majesty is not thinking anyway), but even already a more *drastic* policy is most likely only possible after the death of the old man in Friedrichsruh; he ties up those elements that are needed for revision, that is the right wing and the parties of the middle, and will only place them at your disposal if Your Majesty capitulates in front of him. . . . This is one part of his policy of revanche. But since capitulation does not exist for Your Majesty, one very likely has to wait until the gigantic angel has ascended to heaven. A government, a ministry, which wants to be *supported* by the parties of the middle or the right, can only be Bismarckian. . . . At the moment I also . . . do not advise cutting the gordian-German federal knot with a Prussian sword. If this would ever become necessary, it is better to do it after the death of that bad man, because he would mobilize the Imperial idea against the King of Prussia, while after his death most likely the Imperial idea would be *for* the King of Prussia.[112]

Such was the motive behind Eulenburg's "doing his utmost"[113] in mediating. It was a far cry from what Holstein and Hohenlohe desired. There was, for instance, no reference to Marschall—and Marschall was, after all, the key figure in the Hohenlohe ministry, next to Holstein. True, Eulenburg had warned against a "policy of force," but he had done it in such a cautious way and had so taken into account the personality of the Kaiser that the seriousness of the situation tended to be obscured. The prime consideration in Eulenburg's mind was to retain his hold over Wilhelm. It was thus necessary to proceed with extreme caution, not to be identified with any one interest group, and not to arouse the suspicion or ill will

of the monarch, particularly in matters concerning the Foreign
Office. No doubt Eulenburg was as sincere a "patriot" as was
Holstein. However, Eulenburg, as unofficial advisor and friend of
Wilhelm, preferred to "believe in the Kaiser." Regarding the
present Hohenlohe ministry as moribund, Eulenburg continued to work
toward the future government, which would consist of "*royalists
sans phrase*" and be dominated by Bülow, the Kaiser, and himself.

No doubt Eulenburg was also sincere in his efforts at mediation.
However, these efforts stemmed from quite different considerations
than those of Holstein. Eulenburg had given up the Hohenlohe
Ministry as a lost cause. The danger to his position and his
political future came not from Marschall's downfall but from a
possible major political upheaval in which one of the extreme factions (Bismarck or advocates of a truly constitutional monarchy),
not Eulenburg, would gain the upper hand. This was an aspect of
the situation that Eulenburg deemed necessary to point out to
Wilhelm.

As Holstein had expected, Eulenburg's mediations did little,
if anything, to support Holstein's own position. Nevertheless,
Holstein sent off another letter to Eulenburg, written in a more
desperate tone than any of his previous communications,[114] again
to no avail. Eulenburg tried to calm him: "In politics I am in
complete agreement with you. Please be quite calm in this regard,
dear friend. You will be satisfied with me."[115] The actual
situation was accurately revealed once again by Wilhelm's uncoded
telegram to Eulenburg on April 20 in which he expressed his indignation over the "negligence of the Foreign Office," which he held
responsible for delaying one of Eulenburg's letters to him.

When Wilhelm met Eulenburg again in Vienna in the latter part
of April, the monarch ardently defended himself against having had
any serious ideas about a coup d'état, and described all such rumors
as outright lies. Eulenburg—perhaps against his better judgment—
agreed with his Imperial friend.[116] Whatever the mediations that
he had promised Hohenlohe and Holstein might have achieved, by now
they had just the opposite effect in regard to the composition of
Hohenlohe's ministry. The Kaiser saw "conspiracy" against him in
Berlin—headed by the Foreign Office—and Eulenburg strengthened
his belief.[117] As before, Eulenburg was determined not to get
involved with the difficulties between the Foreign Office and the
Kaiser.[118]

In Vienna it was agreed between Wilhelm and Eulenburg that
Marschall would receive the embassy in Constantinople, Bülow come
to Berlin, Boetticher be dismissed, and Posadowsky take Boetticher's
place. Every effort was to be made to retain Hohenlohe. In his
case it was recognized that only the military penal code issue and
the associations law could become serious obstacles to the efforts
to maintain his position.[119] These various plans forecast the
actions carried out within the next two months.

In briefly reviewing the two turbulent months of February and
March, 1897, it strongly appears that the cabinets had won a great
victory over the government by using the question of the Navy.
Germany seemed well on its retroactive road to royal absolutism.
As yet the Kaiser's coup d'état was missing, but it was already
brazenly proclaimed by Wilhelm and his entourage. Yet the Kaiser's

entourage and the cabinets did not have control over Wilhelm.
Hohenlohe's several offers of resignation were not accepted; the
threats of an early closing of the Reichstag and a coup d'état
had turned out to be, as Marschall and the majority of the Reichstag
correctly perceived, intimidation tactics lacking serious intention
to implement them, unless the other German princes as well as the
conservative parties would give their support. Wilhelm retained
Hohenlohe in part because of the esteem which he still held in
parliamentary circles. Political influence over the Kaiser, to a
considerable extent, still rested in the hands of Bülow, Eulenburg,
the Grand Duke of Baden, and indirectly Bismarck. Finally, Wilhelm
lacked the necessary courage and firmness to inaugurate energetic
actions. Despite his boastful and sensational behavior, the Kaiser
was and remained an impressionable follower, even susceptible to
intimidation. He was not a leader. It seems quite noteworthy that
the Grand Duke of Baden, who may hardly be accused of promoting royal
absolutism, seemed to support Wilhelm's naval plans. It was, after
all, not so much the content but, rather, the form against which the
Reichstag had objected, and the Navy could still be used as a means
to, gain parliamentary support for the government. The recognition
of the necessity of Reichstag support, combined with the lack of
courage to take actions which might precipitate civil war, prevented
the defeat of the government by the cabinets and entourage. It
implied that a personal regime of a Wilhelm II controlled by cabinets
and entourage was impossible. Possible, on the other hand, was a
constitutional monarchy controlled by the bureaucracy.

NOTES

1. See Marschall Diary, 9.XII.96, mentioning a flood of congratulatory telegrams and messages.

2. As Count Mirbach put it in one of his speeches in the Reichstag at the time of the Leckert-Lützow discussion. See *Stenographische Berichte*, IX Legislatur periode, IV Session, 1895-97,
Reichstag, p. 4479. He was by no means, of course, the originator
of that phrase.

3. See Lerchenfeld to Crailsheim, 10.I.97, G.S.A. München, Ges.
Berlin, 1068.

4. Haller, *Eulenburg*, p. 207.

5. Eulenburg to Holstein, 13.I.97, B.A. Eul. 45.

6. *Hohenlohe*, III, 286-287.

7. Fricke, "Die Affaire Leckert-Lützow-Tausch," p. 1590.

8. *Hohenlohe*, III, 286.

9. Haller, *Eulenburg*, p. 207.

10. See Marschall Diary, 8.XII.96; Hohenlohe to Wilhelm, and
Wilhelm to Hohenlohe, 8.XII.96, Archiv Schillingsfürst, Rep. 100
XXII A-9; *Hohenlohe*, III, 288.

11. Haller, *Eulenburg*, p. 208.

12. *Ibid.*

13. *Ibid.*, p. 209. Lucanus had, of course, been long suspect to Holstein, somewhat later to Marschall and Boetticher as well, who thought him a bad influence on the Kaiser. See Brauer, *Dienste*, pp. 373-374.

14. See Haller, *Eulenburg*, p. 209. In this connection the renewed attacks of the press against Eulenburg seem significant; see *ibid.*, p. 209. Also see Bülow to Eulenburg, 19.XII.96, B.A. Eul. 45.

15. Haller, *Eulenburg*, p. 209.

16. Holstein to Eulenburg, 8.XII.96, B.A. Eul. 44.

17. Eulenburg comment on Holstein to Eulenburg, 8.XII.96, B.A. Eul. 44.

18. Bülow to Eulenburg, 19.XII.96, B.A. Eul. 44.

19. See Haller, *Eulenburg*, p. 208; Franz Fischer to Eulenburg, 16.XII.96, B.A. Eul. 44.

20. See above, p. 229.

21. Haller, *Eulenburg*, p. 207; Marschall Diary, 8.XII.96.

22. *Holsteins Papiere*, III, 594.

23. Marschall to Eulenburg, 15.I.97, B.A. Eul. 45. See also Lerchenfeld to Crailsheim, 11.XII.96, G.S.A. München, MA III 2674; Marschall Diary, 10.XII.96, 12.XII.96.

24. See *Hohenlohe*, III, 305; Brauer, *Dienste*, p. 374.

25. Haller, *Eulenburg*, p. 207; Bülow to Eulenburg, 19.XII.96, B.A. Eul. 44. See also Rich, *Holstein*, II, 523, 524.

26. See Haller, *Eulenburg*, p. 210; Eulenburg to Wilhelm, 5.I.97, Eulenburg to Bülow, 17.I.97 (copy of Eulenburg letter to Wilhelm), B.A. Eul. 45.

27. Eulenburg to Wilhelm, 7.I.97, B.A. Eul. 45.

28. Holstein to Eulenburg, [].I.97; Holstein to Eulenburg, 12.I.97; Marschall to Eulenburg, 15.I.97, all in B.A. Eul. 45; Lerchenfeld to Crailsheim, 10.I.97, G.S.A. München, Ges. Berlin, 1068; Haller, *Eulenburg*, p. 210. Raschdau called Lucanus the main opponent of Marschall. See Raschdau to Schiemann, 14.II.97, Schiemann Papers, No. 107, G.S.A. Berlin, Rep. 97.

29. August Eulenburg to Phili Eulenburg, 9.I.97, B.A. Eul. 45.

30. Holstein to Eulenburg, 7.I.97, B.A. Eul. 45; *Hohenlohe*, III, 290, 291.

31. Holstein to Eulenburg, 12.I.97, 7.I.97, B.A. Eul. 45; Haller, *Eulenburg*, pp. 210-211.

32. Holstein to Eulenburg, 12.I.97, B.A. Eul. 45.

33. Haller, *Eulenburg*, pp. 210-211.

34. *Ibid.*

35. Eulenburg to Bülow, 16.I.97 (parts of the letter are in Haller, *Eulenburg*, p. 212), and Bülow to Eulenburg, 16.I.97, B.A. Eul. 45.

36. Haller, *Eulenburg*, p. 212.

37. Eulenburg to Bülow, 16.I.97, B.A. Eul. 45.

38. *Ibid.*

39. Eulenburg to Wilhelm, 18.I.97, B.A. Eul. 45.

40. August Eulenburg to Phili Eulenburg, 25.I.97, B.A. Eul. 45.

41. Eulenburg to Holstein, 1.II.97, B.A. Eul. 45. See also Bosse Diary, 28.I.97, B.A. Bosse, No. 9; Marschall Diary, 27.I.97; Raschdau to Schiemann, 14.II.97, Schiemann Papers, No. 107, G.S.A. Berlin, Rep. 92.

42. Eulenburg to Lucanus, 3.II.97, B.A. Eul. 45.

43. Lucanus to Eulenburg, 20.II.97, B.A. Eul. 45.

44. In a conversation with Hohenthal, Marschall said that he had for some time been thinking of resigning, but that he was not yet sure, since he did not want to desert Hohenlohe or leave before the Tausch trial. One should not get the impression, he had said, that he capitulates to his political enemies (he could well stand their attacks, etc.); but what in the long run he could not bear was the struggle against the crown. The confidence he had felt in the Kaiser just after the Leckert trial had, owing to the influences that his enemies brought to bear on the Kaiser, turned out to be just the opposite. See Saxon embassy report, 2.II.97, Sächs. H.S.A., Ges. Berlin, No. 252.

45. See Herbert Bismarck to Rantzau, 16.XII.96, Bismarck Papers, Friedrichsruh.

46. Prussian Landtag, *Stenographische Berichte, Haus der Abgeordneten*, 18–20.I.97, pp. 520–599; *Wippermann*, 1897 (I), pp. 147ff.

47. This was, of course, as Marschall knew from his previous experience, not the case. See especially the Leckert–Lützow trial. Herzfeld, *Miquel*, II, 511. It seems that here Marschall was consciously trying to defend the government.

48. *Stenographische Berichte*, Reichstag, 4.II.97, p. 4489.

49. See comments of the representative Eugen Richter, *ibid.*, 5.II.97, p. 4516. See also Marschall Diary, 5.II.97.

50. *Stenographische Berichte*, Reichstag, 4.II.97, 5.II.97, pp. 4477–4516. See also *Wippermann*, 1897 (I), pp. 72ff.

51. Jonathan Steinberg, *Yesterday's Deterrent: Tirpitz and the Birth of the German Fleet* (New York, 1965), p. 97.

52. Rich, *Holstein*, II, 527; Hallmann, *Schlachtflottenbau*, p. 216; Marschall Diary, 30.I.97.

53. Hallmann, *Schlachtflottenbau*, p. 217.

54. *Ibid.*, p. 218.

55. Waldersee, *Denkwürdigkeiten*, II, 390.

56. See Marschall Diary, 1.I.97; Bosse Diary, 28.I.97, B.A. Bosse.

57. *Hohenlohe*, III, 295.

58. *Ibid.*, pp. 295, 298; Röhl, *Germany without Bismarck*, pp. 210-211, esp. p. 211, note 1.

59. *Hohenlohe*, III, 297-298; *Holsteins Papiere*, IV, 8-11.

60. Haller, *Eulenburg*, pp. 216-217.

61. Eulenburg to Holstein, 7.II.97, B.A. Eul. 45. See also Rich, *Holstein*, II, 527.

62. Eulenburg to Hohenlohe, 8.II.97, B.A. Eul. 45.

63. Eulenburg to Bülow, 8.II.97, B.A. Eul. 45. See also Röhl, *Germany without Bismarck*, pp. 204-205.

64. Eulenburg to Goluchowski, 25.I.97, and Eulenburg to Szögyenyi, 13.II.97, B.A. Eul. 45. Szögyenyi accepted this advice; see Szögyenyi to Eulenburg, 27.II.97, B.A. Eul. 45.

65. Haller, *Eulenburg*, pp. 216, 219-220; *Hohenlohe*, III, 308.

66. Eulenburg to Wilhelm, 22.II.97, B.A. Eul. 45.

67. *Hohenlohe*, III, 305; Röhl, *Germany without Bismarck*, p. 211. See also Hohenlohe to his wife, 24.II.97, where he writes that he has talked to Lucanus and that the latter promised to take steps to calm the Kaiser, in Archiv Schillingsfürst, Rep. 101 II H 15; Marschall Diary, 23, 24, 25, and 27.II.97. It is perhaps noteworthy that the Kaiser had apparently been quite satisfied with Marschall throughout February, an attitude which changed radically as soon as the Kaiser had gone to Hubertusstock in the latter part of the month. It was the time also of Wilhelm's incredible provincial Diet speech. When Marschall spoke to Wilhelm on March 1, the latter agreed completely with Marschall and was most amiable. See Marschall Diary, 1.III.97.

68. Eulenburg to Wilhelm, 6.III.97, B.A. Eul. 46.

69. Hallmann, *Schlachtflottenbau*, pp. 67f.; Steinberg, *Yesterday's Deterrent*, pp. 63-64.

70. *Ibid.*, pp. 51, 63-64; Kehr, *Schlachtflottenbau*, pp. 2, 8. See also Walther Hubatsch, *Der Admiralstab und die obersten Marinebehörden in Deutschland 1848-1945* (Frankfurt am Main, 1958), pp. 51ff., 71ff.

71. Steinberg, *Yesterday's Deterrent*, p. 67.

72. Kehr, *Schlachtflottenbau*, pp. 25ff.

73. *Ibid.*, p. 56.

74. See also Eulenburg to Hohenlohe, 29.III.97, Archiv Schillingsfürst, Rep. 100 XXII A, Bd. 10.

75. See Steinberg, *Yesterday's Deterrent*, pp. 70-124; Kehr, *Schlachtflottenbau*, pp. 25-71; Hallmann, *Schlachtflottenbau*, pp. 67ff., 154ff., 171ff.

76. See Röhl, *Germany without Bismarck*, pp. 210, 212.

77. *Wippermann*, 1896 (II), pp. 155-160.

78. Holstein to Eulenburg, 3.III.97, B.A. Eul. 46; *Hohenlohe*, III, 310.

79. *Hohenlohe*, III, 310-311. See also Hallmann, *Schlachtflottenbau*, p. 226; Holstein to Eulenburg, 3.III.97, B.A. Eul. 46; Hohenlohe Journal, 31.II.97, Archiv Schillingsfürst, Rep. 100 XXII A, Bd. 10.

80. *Wippermann*, 1897 (I), p. 6; Holstein to Eulenburg, 3.III.97, B.A. Eul. 46; Marschall Diary, 3.III.97.

81. See Hohenlohe to his wife, 7.III.97, Archiv Schillingsfürst, Rep. 101 II H 15. See also Wilmowski to Boetticher, reporting that the conference had gone off well, that Hohenlohe had the definite impression that Wilhelm absolutely wanted to avoid a conflict. 7.III.97, B.A. Boetticher, No. 96.

82. Holstein to Eulenburg, 5.III.97, B.A. Eul. 46.

83. *Hohenlohe*, III, 310-312. See also Röhl, *Germany without Bismarck*, pp. 212-214.

84. Eulenburg to Hohenlohe, 6.III.97, B.A. Eul. 46.

85. Eulenburg to Wilhelm, 6.III.97, B.A. Eul. 46. See also Eulenburg memo, 20.IV.97, and Eulenburg to Wilhelm, 12.III.97, B.A. Eul. 46.

86. *Hohenlohe*, III, 312; Marschall Diary, 7.III.97.

87. *Hohenlohe*, III, 312-313, 317-319.

88. Rich, *Holstein*, II, 529. Hohenthal reported that although the Kaiser gave a strong appearance of "demanding a person who would go with him through thick and thin," and that in Berlin there existed a political situation of a most confused and unpleasant nature, it would probably end all right, but one ought at the same time be prepared for "unpleasant surprises." See Saxon embassy report, 18.III.97, Sächs. H.S.A., Ges. Berlin, No. 252.

89. *Hohenlohe*, III, 319.

90. On the Hollmann crisis, see Kehr, *Schlachtflottenbau*, pp. 61-71; Steinberg, *Yesterday's Deterrent*, pp. 92-120; Hallmann, *Schlachtflottenbau*, pp. 202-236; Röhl, *Germany without Bismarck*, pp. 214-217; Saxon embassy reports, 10, 15, 16, and 18.III.97, 5.IV.97, Sächs. H.S.A., Ges. Berlin, No. 252; Varnbühler report, 5.IV.97, Wurtt. H.S.A., Ges. Berlin, E 73, Fasz. 61. See also Marschall Diary, 15, 16, and 18.III.97; Bosse Diary, 14.III.97, 15.III.97, B.A. Bosse, No. 9. See also Hohenlohe Journal, 8.III.97; Hohenlohe to Wilhelm, 9.III.97; Hohenlohe to Eulenburg, 10.III.97; Hollmann to Hohenlohe, 13.III.97; Lucanus to Hohenlohe, 14.III.97, all in Archiv Schillingsfürst, Rep. 100 XXII A, Bd. 10.

91. Kehr, *Schlachtflottenbau*, p. 27.

92. Hallmann, *Schlachtflottenbau*, pp. 213-214; Kehr, *Schlachtflottenbau*, pp. 27ff.

93. See Röhl, *Germany without Bismarck*, p. 210; Marschall Diary, 6.III.97, 7.III.97.

94. Hallmann, *Schlachtflottenbau*, p. 217; Rich, *Holstein*, II, 527.

95. *Holsteins Papiere*, IV, 16; Röhl, *Germany without Bismarck*, pp. 210-211.

96. Rich, *Holstein*, II, 528; *Schulthess*, 1897, pp. 56-58; Marschall Diary, 26.II.97; Bosse Diary, 14.III.97, B.A. Bosse, No. 9; Röhl, *Germany without Bismarck*, p. 212.

97. Röhl, *Germany without Bismarck*, pp. 219-220.

98. *Ibid.*, p. 215; Marschall Diary, 9.III.97. Upon hearing Hammacher's words, Lieber went to Marschall and asked his opinion, whereupon Marschall replied not to submit to such pressure tactics ("*Bange machen gilt nicht*").

99. *Hohenlohe*, III, 321-323; Rich, *Holstein*, II, 530.

100. *Hohenlohe*, III, 323; Marschall Diary, 18.III.97. On this whole aspect, see also Röhl, *Germany without Bismarck*, pp. 210-212; *Die Nation*, 13.III.97, 27.III.97.

101. Haller, *Eulenburg*, pp. 219-220.

102. Holstein to Eulenburg, 29.III.97, 30.III.97, B.A. Eul. 46 (parts in Rich, *Holstein*, II, 530-532); Haller, *Eulenburg*, pp. 323-324.

103. Marschall Diary, 20.III.97, 21.III.97; Grand Duke to Wilhelm, 18.III.97, Gr. Fam. Archiv, N 279. See also Röhl, *Germany without Bismarck*, pp. 219f.

104. Holstein to Eulenburg, 3.III.97, B.A. Eul. 46; Rich, *Holstein*, II, 527; Hallmann, *Schlachtflottenbau*, pp. 217-218; Röhl, *Germany without Bismarck*, p. 210.

105. *Hohenlohe*, III, 298.

106. Eulenburg to Bülow, 8.III.97, B.A. Eul. 46.

107. See Eulenburg to Wilhelm, 8.IV.97, B.A. Eul. 46: "I know quite well why Your Majesty has spoken so openly [Wilhelm had said that a change in personnel in the Foreign Office was imminent.] It has also been correctly understood by Goluchowski [!]. The eventual change will be accepted without regret [*ohne Bedauern*]. The communication that Your Majesty will *retain* the chancellor I have also understood as the *real* intention."

108. Quoted from Rich, *Holstein*, II, 525.

109. *Hohenlohe*, III, 326; Archiv Schillingsfürst, Rep. 100 XXII A, Bd. 10. See also Röhl, *Germany without Bismarck*, p. 217, note 5.

110. Alexander Hohenlohe to Eulenburg, 30.III.97, B.A. Eul. 46.

111. Marschall Diary, 25.III.97, 30.III.97, 6.IV.97. To the latter Marschall commented: "I am not scared. The Reichstag must remain and finish its business." See Röhl, *Germany without Bismarck*,

p. 217. The immediate closing of the Reichstag was, of course (and without much objection from Wilhelm), rejected. See Hohenlohe to Boetticher, 1.IV.97, B.A. Boetticher, No. 68.

112. Eulenburg to Wilhelm, 8.IV.97, B.A. Eul. 46.

113. *Holsteins Papiere*, IV, 18.

114. Holstein to Eulenburg, 18.IV.97, B.A. Eul. 46.

115. *Holsteins Papiere*, IV, 25.

116. See Eulenburg to Bülow, 24.IV.97, B.A. Eul. 46. On the coup d'état plans in general, see also Röhl, *Germany without Bismarck*, pp. 217ff.

117. Eulenburg to Bülow, 24.IV.97, and Eulenburg, "Notiz," 20. IV.97, B.A. Eul. 46; Rich, *Holstein*, II, 531.

118. Eulenburg to Bülow, 24.IV.97, B.A. Eul. 46.

119. *Ibid.*

CHAPTER 13

The Collapse
of the Hohenlohe Ministry

Who in Germany can still be surprised with political
surprises? Today they are characteristic of the
policy with which we are blessed.

Die Nation, March 3, 1897

Revolution means that existing conditions end and
completely new ones take their place; . . . and in
this sense we in Germany also find ourselves in the
midst of a political revolution. The old political
center of gravity is lost and we search for a new
political center of gravity.

Die Nation, April 19, 1897

Miquel is to become Vice President of the Ministry of
State and General Deputy of the Reich Chancellor. I
knew about the former, but that a total "Miquel era"
is to be instituted is new. . . . He is for "*Sammlung*."
For the time being the agrarians will smash in the
windows of the government.

Marschall Diary, June 18
and June 25, 1897

1

Although various plans had been considered and partially accepted,
and although some groundwork had been done for another transformation
of the government, Eulenburg was still confronted with considerable
obstacles. It required great skill and maneuvering to carry off a
complete victory.

To describe the crisis that transformed the government in May
and June, 1897, as being the implementation of a plan of the Kaiser,
Eulenburg, and Bülow is somewhat misleading. To be sure, both
Eulenburg and Bülow knew what they wanted; but, recognizing certain
prerequisite conditions for the achievement of their aims, they had
to accept tactical limitations to their activities.

At the end of the crisis, the substance of the Eulenburg-Bülow
plans had been accomplished, but, as will be seen, Eulenburg's
success rested at least in part on circumstances beyond his control.

The question of the military penal code reform came up again in
mid-April, 1897, when discussion of the associations law also reached
a critical stage. The combination precipitated the crisis. Hohenlohe

gained the impression that both questions constituted the "two
levers" to be used against him—probably a hint by Eulenburg. Then
he added, "And this time it will probably become serious."[1] By the
middle of April the state of both the military penal code reform and
the associations law could indeed cause Hohenlohe's despair. He
realized that he could not honor the promises given to the Reichstag
and at the same time satisfy the Kaiser, despite the desertion on
the part of the National Liberals from a substantial associations
law. The Ministry of State early in April had decided to introduce
the bill in the Landtag (therewith inviting another governmental
defeat), only to change their stand by the middle of April and move
for a simple revocation of the anti-association clauses.[2]

It was obvious, however, that this step was by no means the
solution, since Wilhelm would not agree to such a proposal. Despite
Hohenlohe's considered arguments (especially during his interview on
May 5), the Kaiser remained firm; rather, it was the Chancellor and
the Ministry of State which once more changed their latest decision
and basically adopted the position of the Kaiser. This "compromise"
plan was, not surprisingly, accepted by Wilhelm almost immediately.[3]
On May 11 Hohenlohe announced in the Landtag that the government
had consented to drop the existing restrictions on coalitions of
associations, but that simultaneously the general associations law
would be subject to further reforms. This bill was introduced in
the Landtag two days later and came up for debate on May 17.
Hohenlohe's statement introducing the bill did not conceal the obvious
fact that his compromise had been a very one-sided one and that he
had in effect backed down. Nor had Hohenlohe the desire to repeat
his weak justification in front of the Reichstag but, rather,
entrusted the thorny task of defending the government to Boetticher,
who then had to face the famous attack of Richter on May 18 (giving
convenient justification for Boetticher's dismissal for not having
defended the Kaiser and the government).[4] It is only fair to point
out that eventually an acceptable associations law was enacted under
Hohenlohe (in 1899), and in this sense he did fulfill his promise—
but that was the result not so much of Hohenlohe's actions as of the
parliamentary rejection of the bill in 1897 and the pressure
to get a modified law passed before 1900.[5] As far as
the situation in April, May, and June, 1897, was concerned, the
coalition question only helped to accentuate the perpetual government crisis that had started with the Köller affair, as Saxon
Ambassador Hohenthal reported to Dresden.[6] Alexander Hohenlohe
commented very critically upon his father's action, and the latter
in fact could find no other defense for his actions except that at
least he had kept his word,[7] but then he lamented the fact that he
had not been firm enough.[8]

On the question of the military penal code reform, the Kaiser
had notified the Chancellor on April 17 that he had just received
word from Munich that the Bavarian government had rejected the idea
of a central military court. Now the reform question should come
to an end, since the central military court had been a *conditio
sine qua non* in the agreement between the Kaiser and the Chancellor
at the Wilhelmshöhe conference in early August, 1896. Hohenlohe
resigned himself to another postponement.[9] It was not that the
reform question had died down—quite the contrary. Ever since the

replacement of Bronsart, much time, energy, and words had been
applied toward this subject. Symptomatically, the emphasis had
changed. One might say that ever since Bronsart had been dismissed and Hohenlohe had chosen to remain in office, a Chancellor
crisis would not result on the basis of the public-procedure clause
in the reform proposal. However, late in the year a different
problem had begun to develop: the problem of federalism in the
form of a proposed central military court. Bavaria ostentatiously
rejected this proposal and countered with the suggestion of creating a separate Bavarian military court. Was Bavaria to be forced
into submission? Hohenlohe himself pointed out at various times
that he personally would be willing to concede the question to
Bavaria, to honor Bavaria's stand on its special rights (*Reservat-
rechte*), and likewise would his advisors; but he actually could
not do so. Neither Hohenlohe nor most of his ministers took any
actions that risked coming into conflict with the Kaiser and the
Military Cabinet.[10] On the other hand, Gossler sharply and not
without purpose let it be known that he condemned Bavaria's
position, not so much from a military but from a political standpoint. The Kaiser and Gossler went along with the reform only in
order to retain Hohenlohe as Chancellor—and that only because they
thought that Hohenlohe had influence with the south German states,
thus assuring the unity of the Reich. However, Gossler continued,
this attitude toward Hohenlohe might change.[11]

By the end of January an impasse had again been reached; neither
side was willing to end discussions and be accused by their opponents
of having brought about the failure of the reform.[12] Then, from
early February onward, the respective positions of Prussia and
Bavaria began slowly to become more flexible on the surface so that
a compromise solution seemed possible. However, owing to the prolonged discussions and intentional obstructions, the reform proposal
could no longer be introduced into the Reichstag. This fact in
itself had been an important consideration to Eulenburg and to the
Kaiser. By late May, with the threat of the Reichstag as good as
over, the reform question was as far from a solution as it had been
at the beginning of the year.[13] There was no question of its ever
becoming important enough to warrant a Chancellor crisis, not even
in Hohenlohe's own mind. Besides, during this time other and more
immediate issues had eclipsed the old ones.[14]

2

Almost immediately after the issues of the military penal code
and the associations law had again receded into the background, the
final crisis over Marschall and Boetticher arose. It was the time
of the Tausch trial (in the last days of May, 1897), and the
Kaiser's animosity against Marschall had reached its peak.[15] Four
weeks before, Wilhelm (having been told by the Minister of Justice
that Tausch would probably be freed because a conviction on the
basis of perjury was almost impossible)[16] had only talked about the
method of presently dismissing Marschall, and Eulenburg could only
make the best of it and comply. On May 10 Eulenburg wrote to
Holstein, "Finally, I want to mention that Lucanus stepped visibly
into the foreground. He will play a considerable role in the events

that may come to a decision in the near future. But my experience
tells me that the more or less open struggle (in the press, etc.)
against those men that possess the confidence of the Kaiser will be
decided against those that do not have it. It is better to leave
those alone who hold the confidence of the Kaiser."[17] Eulenburg
was afraid of Lucanus, especially if he cooperated with Botho.[18]
However, Eulenburg recognized Lucanus to be a necessary, if not
invaluable, tool (or power that Eulenburg needed to bring into his
camp) if any serious trouble arose. Thus he alerted Holstein about
Lucanus, at the same time warning Holstein not to antagonize or
fight with him.[19]

The actual Boetticher crisis came about quite suddenly on May 30,
1897. The Kaiser had gone on one of his many hunting excursions to
Prökelwitz on May 25. Then on May 28 he had visited Danzig and
Marienburg, and from there returned to Berlin early on the 29th
to review a parade.[20] Eulenburg had met Wilhelm in Prökelwitz to
discuss the Marschall question. The expected crisis seems to have
begun on May 27. Eulenburg sent a telegram to Bülow[21] and then
followed it up with a letter on the same day. There was no mention
of Boetticher in particular, merely of Marschall's "vacation" and
Holstein's vehement opposition to such a move. At this time came
the decision of the Reichstag to extend its session beyond May 28.
It was this latter fact that precipitated matters beyond the
Marschall-Tausch case. Eulenburg wrote:

> Yesterday I sent you a wire of no agreeable import.
> These lines are going to be still less agreeable. I have
> no time to go into particulars. I can only tell you that
> the fight we know of to keep going at all costs the present
> system (and especially Marschall) is being carried on in
> the clumsiest way through the press and so forth. Holstein's
> tactics are—shrewd as he is—he is not far wrong in this—
> to prevent Marschall's going on leave—. . . . Holstein feels
> that his going on leave might lead to a tolerably natural
> solution; and so the poor man, who is as lean as a greyhound
> and getting leaner every day, has to await permission from
> the little, rabid, ruthless terrier. And now comes a sudden
> ring-down of the curtain in the shape of an incomprehensibly
> lengthy prolongation of the Reichstag. Simultaneously, rumors
> about the reason.

Then he added:

> Of course, the Emperor sees through it, and has just
> said very gravely, very much annoyed: "Well, I think you're
> shrewd enough to know as well as I do what all this buffoonery
> means. As it is no use sending the old Chancellor to plead
> Marschall's cause with me, I am to be terrorized in every
> sort of way by the Reichstag. You must see that I can't
> submit to that. There are limits to all things."
> I was in a tight place, my dear Bernhard. I said we
> should certainly have to investigate thoroughly, but one
> thing I did implore of His Majesty—not to make a breach
> immediately after Prökelwitz, for that would do neither
> him nor me any good. "My dear Philipp," he answered,

"whether the decision takes place in three or twelve or any
number of days after Prökelwitz, it will be the same thing—
Prökelwitz will bear the blame! But I will not suffer this
any longer. The situation is unbearable, and Prussia is
being injured by it."[22]

On May 30 came the apparent sudden determination of the Kaiser
(transmitted to Hohenlohe by way of Lucanus) to dismiss Boetticher
immediately on the grounds that he had acted against the crown by
not defending it against Richter's attacks in the Reichstag on May
18.[23]   Thereupon, Boetticher handed in his resignation on May 31.

While at his estate in Liebenburg, Eulenburg was informed by
Lucanus on May 30 that Boetticher would have to go immediately, and
Marschall soon.[24]   The suddenness with which the Boetticher question
had been reopened must have come as something of a surprise to
Eulenburg. When he had left the Kaiser on May 29, there had been
no apparent signs of violent opposition to Boetticher. Moreover,
on that same day he had received the assurance of Lucanus that an
immediate dismissal of Boetticher and Marschall was undesirable.[25]
The main issue during the whole time had always been Marschall, and
Eulenburg—in order to save the moribund Marschall as long as
possible—had come to an agreement with Wilhelm in Vienna and in
Prökelwitz to grant Marschall a lengthy leave of absence. This
later would be transformed into a formal dismissal, so that outwardly Marschall would still retain his secretarial seat for a
while. It was this plan that Eulenburg wanted to work out with
Marschall when he asked Holstein to arrange a meeting with the
Secretary of State,[26] and it was this issue that Eulenburg settled
with Marschall on May 31, after his testimony in the Tausch trial.
Eulenburg reported his meeting to Bülow:

> He [Marschall] is physically and morally *done in*.
> The picture of misery and woe. He told me that he could
> stand no more of it; wants to go on leave on Thursday
> and let it gradually come out that he is unable to ful-
> fill his duties any longer. He is to be let go about
> September—any sooner would be injurious to H.M. As I
> saw that it was a physical impossibility for him to stay,
> I arranged as follows with him: He is not to say anything
> of his intentions to Hohenlohe and Holstein. He is
> positively terrified of them both—and in his wretched
> state of health! I was to suggest to the Emperor that
> H.M. should dispose of Marschall's portfolio in the
> autumn—but keep absolute silence till then, so that
> Hohenlohe may not give us the go-by.[27]

It was at this point that Marschall realized his position
completely. On May 30 he still seemed to have been fairly certain
of continuing—on however precarious a basis (as he had realized
soon after the Leckert-Lützow trial in December, 1896)—as Secretary
of State. With the experience of the Leckert-Lützow case behind
him, with Eulenburg hinting at an embassy post, with the realization
that the chief prosecutor and even Bronsart were siding with Tausch,
Marschall certainly no longer had illusions that the trial would
have any positive effect on his political position.[28]   On the other

hand, until May 31 it seemed that he had not yet comprehended the magnitude of his defeat. During the morning of that day at the latest, however, Marschall decided that he no longer could remain a minister. His diary reports his thoughts:

> In the morning at 8:45 Ph. Eulenburg comes to me for a moment before he goes . . . [to testify in the Tausch trial]. He tells me that H.M. is all right generally, only mad [*erregt*] at Boetticher because he had not responded to the most recent speech of Richter in the Reichstag [on the associations law]. Later Boetticher comes to me and wants to know what is going on. . . . [Hohenlohe] had called him today at 9:30, but then had not received him, because Holstein was with him. At 10:00 . . . Hohenlohe had gone to . . . H.M. At 11 o'clock Ph. Eulenburg comes to me . . . I speak with him in a very frank way about myself, that I consider my position as untenable [*erschüttert*]. The head of the Foreign Office must maintain a neutral position vis a vis the parties. That is not the case with me. As a result of my action in the trade treaty policy I antagonized the conservative parties, upon which the government supports itself in Prussia. Thereby I had become involved, as a result of this enmity, in numerous press intrigues [*Pressetreibereien*] in which I, as the Tausch case shows, have a completely clear record; but the fact of the embittered enmity exists, and I have to take it into account. H.M. has so many difficulties that I could not advise him to burden himself still more with the enmity which a minister had gained for himself. I asked Ph. Eulenburg to speak to H.M. about this and to ask him, if he wants to hear my personal report on this matter. E. thinks that this would be the best way to solve the question; he honors my reasons, even if—as I personally think—sincerely is sorry about my decision.[29]

At the time of this interview neither Marschall nor Eulenburg was fully aware of the Boetticher situation. Marschall made it clear to Eulenburg that he would not continue as Foreign Secretary, as he had done during the many previous crises. Furthermore (again with consistency), Marschall conveyed the impression that he did not wish his resignation to cause a general crisis. It might well be that Eulenburg at this time again mentioned an embassy and that Marschall promised to keep his first intention to resign a secret from Hohenlohe for the time being, lest Hohenlohe and others make an issue of it.

At the time of Marschall's conference with Eulenburg, however, the Boetticher affair was reaching its critical stage with Hohenlohe's intention to resign. Hohenlohe's interview with the Kaiser was at eleven o'clock.[30] Soon after his interview with Marschall, Eulenburg received word from Alexander Hohenlohe that the Kaiser had demanded the dismissal of Boetticher and that, after consulting Holstein, Hohenlohe had decided to resign in the event Boetticher was dismissed.[31]

Initially, Hohenlohe had not objected to the dismissal of

Boetticher. However, when he had "thought matters over," he reversed his position.[32] After having failed to persuade the Kaiser to accept a calmer attitude, Hohenlohe handed in his resignation.[33] He had not made this decision by himself, as he implies in his diary.[34] Alexander Hohenlohe had informed Eulenburg on May 31 that Holstein had influenced the Chancellor to change his position in regard to Boetticher's dismissal, and who very likely caused him to resign.[35] In addition, Eulenburg in a dispatch to Bülow included Alexander with those who were the cause of Hohenlohe's action. It is probable that Marschall also contributed to that end, perhaps more than any other.[36] Holstein wrote,

> At the time of Boetticher's dismissal M[arschall]
> dictated the request for dismissal to Hohenlohe in my
> presence. Two days later, after the reception, he went
> to the Chancellor and urgently advised him not to stick
> to his request for dismissal. Then he went to Boetticher
> and told him, "I do not hold the same viewpoint as . . .
> Holstein [namely] that Prince Hohenlohe should use your
> dismissal for a vote of confidence." So there I was
> suddenly the black sheep, while M[arschall] had dictated
> the resignation. It is understandable that after this
> [incident] I deem Marschall capable of a number of other
> things.[37]

As did Eulenburg, Marschall had come to know about the Boetticher situation soon after his Eulenburg interview of eleven o'clock on May 31. We continue to quote his diary for that date:

> In the meantime I find out what has happened. Yesterday
> evening Lucanus came to . . . [Hohenlohe] and demanded
> the immediate dismissal of Boetticher as a result of
> his conduct toward the Richter speech. Posadowsky is to
> replace him. . . . [Hohenlohe] went to the Neues Palais
> to ask the cabinet question there. At 1:20 . . .
> [Hohenlohe] comes back. The conversation was without
> results, H.M. and . . . [Hohenlohe] maintained their
> standpoints. We advise . . . [Hohenlohe] to hand in his
> resignation, which he does immediately. I speak with
> Ph. Eulenburg, who drives to the Neue Palais in the after-
> noon, and tell him that the immediate dismissal of Boetticher
> is impossible, that it would be a political eclot of the
> worst kind and with the worst effects, since on the 22nd
> of the month the Reichstag convenes about the important
> 3rd reading. But I promised E. that I would work toward
> a compromise, namely that B[oetticher] would be dismissed
> or receive a vacation after the close of the Reichstag.
> In this way the action would be at least politically
> possible, although nevertheless undesirable.[38]

Thus it appears that early in the morning Marschall saw Eulenburg for a moment; then he spoke to Boetticher, who wanted to know what was going on.[39] At eleven o'clock Marschall had his interview with Eulenburg; at about 1:20 in the afternoon he and others conferred with Hohenlohe, who had returned from the Kaiser, and advised him to resign. After this conference Marschall saw

Eulenburg again and at this time discussed with him the Boetticher
question in the manner quoted above.[40]

This course of events caught Eulenburg unaware. It is true
that he had come to recognize the fate of Marschall, and had
skillfully adapted himself to this state of affairs by coming up
with, and carrying out, the plan of veiling the brutal reality of
Marschall's dismissal with a few weeks of vacation and an embassy.
To assure his success, Eulenburg had wrung from Lucanus some measure
of consent not to take any rash action. Up to his conversation
with Marschall on May 31, everything had gone quite well, despite
the disquieting but not alarming news about Wilhelm's indignation.
Then suddenly something had gone wrong: Wilhelm's demand to dismiss Boetticher immediately, Boetticher's handing in his resignation, and, worst of all, Hohenlohe's own intention to resign.

What were Eulenburg's chances to turn the situation to his
advantage? He knew that he had to face the determined opposition
of Holstein, Alexander Hohenlohe, and Kiderlen-Wächter. More than
that, he could not depend on the vague promises given by Lucanus
and Botho Eulenburg; nor could he be sure of August Eulenburg and
Miquel, not to mention the entourage of the Kaiser, which seems to
have been primarily responsible for the action against Boetticher.
Last, there was the Kaiser himself. If Eulenburg did not actually
recall the words of Holstein, he certainly must have harbored the
same general thought: that apparently there were people able to
tune the Kaiser as one does a musical instrument.

Eulenburg immediately went to Potsdam to find out from Lucanus
what really had happened. He found that Lucanus had been sent to
Hohenlohe on May 30 to discuss the dismissal of the "already very
overdue" Boetticher, and the Chancellor had agreed to dismiss him.
However, early on May 31 Hohenlohe had changed his position; since
the Kaiser had not changed his mind, he had handed in his resignation.[41] Lucanus agreed that it was necessary to retain Hohenlohe
and (as Eulenburg had in the case of Marschall) provide a lengthy
leave of absence for Boetticher, which would then culminate in a
dismissal.[42] Eulenburg did not accept this proposal, since he
feared the opposition of Alexander Hohenlohe (and quite likely
also Holstein and others) to such a move.[43] However, whereas in
the case of Marschall the matter was still secret, in the case of
Boetticher it was not.

After having spoken to Lucanus, Eulenburg returned, it seems,
to Marschall and discussed the Boetticher question. Then he
hurried to the monarch, but all he was able to achieve was the
willingness of the Kaiser for "vacation and postponement of the
dismissal of Boetticher for several weeks."[44] Eulenburg thus had
to adopt the plan that Lucanus had proposed to him earlier on the
same day. In the evening Eulenburg saw August Eulenburg, then
Holstein, Alexander, and Kiderlen, from whom he received a very
disquieting impression.[45]

May 31 had certainly been a very busy day for Eulenburg,
including the uncomfortable task of testifying again in the Tausch
trial: the victory apparently in his hands at the end of his
Marschall interview, the sudden turn of events and the facing of
defeat, and finally again gathering the main threads into his own
hands and thereby regaining the initiative.

Eulenburg's coup was delivered on June 1. He saw Marschall
again, and then wrote to Bülow,

> I told him that H.M. would see him to-day before he
> went on leave, and in case of his retirement in the autumn
> had in fact been considering an ambassadorship for him.
> I added that this intention would be frustrated if a
> general crisis came now, for that would sweep everything
> else away. But the general crisis was being prepared for
> (I then related the episode of the night before). He,
> Marschall, could do His Majesty *an immense service* if by
> his intervention he held up this general crisis.[46]

Eulenburg furthermore wrote that Marschall had asked him "to take a
stand against the three fiery men"—Holstein, Alexander, and
Kiderlen—and vividly narrated with all his skill the scene of the
last night where these three had heavily attacked the Kaiser.[47]
Marschall broke down completely. Eulenburg continued to Bülow,
"Marschall quickly caught on. He said that the Monarchy was to
him a principle, and *that he had the last word with Hohenlohe* [!!].
He begged me to write H.M. a few lines and recommend him for the
appointment."[48]   Moreoever, Marschall had also told Eulenburg,

> I have made big mistakes. Never should I have, as
> Secretary of State, identified myself so much with the
> trade policy since I aroused political parties against
> myself—especially the conservatives, without whom
> Prussia cannot be governed in the long run. The
> Secretary of State is to conduct and represent only
> foreign policy.
>   Through Holstein, Caprivi, and finally through the
> parliamentarily powerless Hohenlohe I have been led to
> follow a line that has brought me personal harm and by
> which the ship of state cannot continue for any length
> of time.
>   I will, if you deem it correct, point out these
> viewpoints to His Majesty.
>   The Monarchy is a principle for me—and therefore
> I will never look for a dismissal that might harm the
> Kaiser.[49]

In the presence of Marschall, Eulenburg then wrote to Wilhelm
(who was, characteristically enough, reviewing a parade) that the
situation in regard to Hohenlohe had taken a turn for the worse,
that there were "forces at work . . . who incite him toward resistance," and that the key to solving the crisis lay with Marschall.
He then went on to say that Marschall, "deeply touched by Your
Majesty's kindness, to grant him a long leave of absence and to
hold out a prospect for an Embassy, has bound himself to iron out
the crisis." Furthermore, Eulenburg wrote, "I beg Your Majesty to
grant him an audience as soon as possible this morning and openly
to mention the crisis. He has the last word with the Chancellor—
as he himself admitted. He will use it to the advantage of Your
Majesty."[50]
    The subsequent interview between the Kaiser and Marschall bore
the expected fruits of Eulenburg's planning and gave him the victory.

Shortly after the interview Wilhelm wrote to Hohenlohe and refused to accept his resignation. Boetticher, the Kaiser wrote, must be dismissed; however, in order to show a conciliatory attitude toward Hohenlohe and to induce the Chancellor to remain in office, he allowed Boetticher to get the rest of the proposed government legislative program passed in the Reichstag, "in which case I assume that under no circumstances may the Reichstag be in session, not even one hour longer than three days."[51]

Hohenlohe had not really been in sympathy with a collision course against the Kaiser. It was therefore not too difficult to get him to agree to change his mind about his resignation. Under the impression that the Kaiser had adopted a conciliatory attitude, and under the impact of Marschall's advice not to precipitate a crisis over Boetticher[52] (when Marschall talked to Hohenlohe on June 1), the Chancellor did not push his request for resignation any further and thereby in effect completely gave in to the Kaiser's demands.

In reviewing the Boetticher affair, it is certain that Eulenburg had not pushed for a dismissal of Boetticher at that time. If the Kaiser himself took the action, it seems reasonable to assume that he had been influenced to take such a drastic step after his return from his hunting excursion. Lucanus may have elaborated the issue of the Richter attack of May 18 and taken the opportunity at a time convenient to him to get rid of the "eternal" minister Boetticher—knowing full well that Marschall would not last much longer. The Tausch trial was nearing its end. In this context it is noteworthy that Eulenburg did not mention the Kaiser's violent opposition to Boetticher, as Hohenlohe's version of the Lucanus interview indicated.[53] Had this been the case, Eulenburg (it seems very reasonable to say) would have included this in his letter to Bülow. Until further evidence is found, it is not possible to arrive at a definite answer. Most likely it was a combination of both possibilities. One thing, however, seems quite clear: the Richter attack in the Reichstag on May 18 was only a thin excuse and very likely designed to bring the Kaiser into action, the best that could be found at the time.[54]

3

Eulenburg had successfully overcome the most serious crisis he had yet faced, with the possible exception of the military penal code reform in May, 1896. Marschall confirmed his own defeat and Eulenburg's victory when he wrote to him that "the matter has been settled in the form that we discussed this morning. . . . The men of tonight, Holstein, Alexander, Kiderlen, are furious with me." These had reason enough—completely outmaneuvered as they had been for the moment.[55] In addition, Eulenburg triumphantly proclaimed to Bülow, "The crisis has been overcome—*vivet sequens*—this time I had little hope." However, he added significantly, "But what now?"[56]

As a matter of fact, there still was a lot to be done. The initial victory had to be consolidated and placed on a firmer foundation, lest it should be lost again. Thus far he had temporarily restrained Hohenlohe from resignation—a significant but often previously performed achievement—and he had won over Marschall to his side—an invaluable gain and (everything considered) a brilliant

performance. Marschall had for the present[57] done what was expected
of him, his request for a leave of absence was granted, and he went
off to take his vacation. Holstein, at least to some extent, must
have been aware of what the real significance of this vacation was
(even though he could not be sure), especially when Eulenburg had
indicated to him some days earlier the possibility of Marschall's dismissal; Holstein had begun to try to prevent a leave of absence for
Marschall.[58]   Eulenburg's busy presence and Marschall's radical
reversal in his advice to Hohenlohe in the Boetticher affair must
have increased Holstein's ever-present suspicion to an even higher
degree. Eulenburg thus still had to face the formidable and determined opposition of Holstein, Alexander, and Kiderlen. True, he
seemed to have won over the Kaiser, but who could predict the
Kaiser's future acts, especially when the persuasive presence of
Eulenburg was replaced by that of the Imperial entourage, with its
hatred of the present regime—ministers as well as Chancellors?
Moreover, how could Eulenburg be sure that the other Eulenburgs
and Lucanus would not side against him whenever they so desired?

     Eulenburg wrote (in French) to Bülow, "My efforts with the
Emperor are favorable. He authorizes the postponement of Boetticher's resignation. Holstein, Alexander Hohenlohe, and Kiderlen
push the Chancellor to extreme measures in order to demoralize the
Emperor. I have won over Marschall away from this infamy. Danger
always imminent."[59]   As a result of Eulenburg's maneuvers, the Kaiser
had calmed down to such a degree that "the danger of a sudden decision is overcome." However, under no circumstances were Hohenlohe
and Holstein to know about the true content of Marschall's audience
with the Kaiser,[60] since the crisis had ended (that is, to the extent
that it had) against the wishes of Holstein and Alexander Hohenlohe.[61]

     In Marschall's audience with the Kaiser on June 1 the Boetticher
question had been settled,[62] and the Marschall issue was relatively
safe for the time being. It was rather the question of Boetticher's
successor that perpetuated the tense atmosphere of the succeeding
days. Hohenlohe had soothed his conscience over letting Boetticher
go by making himself believe that he would propose his own candidate
to Boetticher's post and, if the monarch did not accept his choice,
reaffirm his request for dismissal. Doubtless with the backing of
Holstein and despite Marschall's opposition,[63] Hohenlohe's nominee
was von Puttkamer. The Kaiser would have nothing to do with this,
but suggested Miquel—a choice unacceptable to the Chancellor.
Hohenlohe noted in his journal, "There was nothing that could be
done and we parted without coming to an agreement; I, reserving
for myself further decisions. There is still time, since Boetticher does not leave for vacation before July."[64]   By June 7, when
Hohenlohe returned to Berlin, he was still undecided. However, by
that time the situation had fundamentally changed.

     By June 6 Holstein had become a bitter enemy of Marschall. By
then Holstein had been given reason to believe that Marschall, when
he had spoken to the Kaiser on June 1, pleaded for a bestowal of the
position of a Councillor First Class on a former Foreign Office
official, Bothmer (who had been dismissed expressly on the Kaiser's
orders).[65]   However, Bothmer (as Holstein correctly suspected)[66]
had been one of the key figures behind the extremely nasty attacks
on the Foreign Office (and on Holstein and Kiderlen in particular)

in 1894, which had appeared in the satirical Berlin weekly *Kladdera-datsch*.[67] As a result, reinforced by Marschall's changed attitude after June 1, Holstein had come to believe that Marschall had secretly been on the side of his opponents. The result was that Holstein turned bitterly against Marschall and temporarily supported Eulenburg.

It would be interesting to know how Holstein had received his information, which turned out to be false,[68] at this critical time. It seems very probable that this had been a deliberate act to insert a wedge between Holstein and Marschall with the purpose of forcing the former to accept the resignation of the latter without creating a crisis. Although no evidence probably exists, the possibility remains that Eulenburg may have had something to do with this affair. It was he who knew Holstein, as well as the *Kladderadatsch* affair, more intimately than most. Furthermore, he was the only one—besides Marschall and the Kaiser—who at that time knew about the actual content of the June 1 interview. Certainly Marschall would have no interest in discussing the interview with other persons, and espe- cially not in handing out incorrect information about the relation- ship between himself and Bothmer. Nor is it likely that the Kaiser would have invented this matter when talking about the interview (as he did)[69] to others. The whole Marschall-Bothmer affair seems thus to have been a deliberate step with the direct intention of influencing the actions of Holstein in a way that only Eulenburg (and Bülow) would profit from.

On the other hand, it is also likely that Holstein's suspicions had become even greater because of the visit of one of Bothmer's closest friends, Raschdau (a close associate of the Bismarck Fronde), in late May and early June. Raschdau saw a number of high officials in Berlin and complained bitterly about Holstein. After observing Raschdau's activities and the sudden change in Marschall's position, and very likely influenced by cleverly placed rumors such as the supposed incident during Marschall's audience with the Kaiser on June 1 (in this case Lucanus is suspect),[70] Holstein then radically changed his whole attitude toward the Foreign Secretary, holding him responsible for all sorts of intrigues and double dealings.[71]

At any rate, on June 6 Holstein suddenly informed Eulenburg that he placed "special importance" on a meeting with him concerning the Boetticher question.[72] Their meeting took place on June 8. Eulen- burg reported to Bülow:

> Yesterday I met Holstein and dined with him alone at
> Borchardt's. Of course I had expected that he would
> challenge me about my manipulation of Marschall, which
> from its effect on Hohenlohe must have been evident to
> him (though of course he has no idea that Marschall has
> placed his portfolio at H.M.'s disposal)—but I was
> surprised at Holstein's paying me an enthusiastic com-
> pliment on that *coup*, which was to some extent directed
> against him![73]

In fact, Holstein had turned completely against Marschall and at the same time accepted Bülow as the future Secretary of State! Besides that, he made it clear to Eulenburg that he would request his dis- missal if Hohenlohe were forced to resign. Eulenburg could not ask for more: Holstein would give him no trouble about Marschall's resignation; nor, a more important factor, would he oppose the appointment of Bülow. He also would support Eulenburg in keeping Hohenlohe in office, which meant that he would not advise the Chancellor to take for the moment the course that might result in a crisis.

Holstein's "radical change" soon began to be felt. On June 11, after a discussion with Holstein, the Chancellor agreed to drop his nominee, von Puttkamer, and accept Miquel—although both agreed that Miquel should also receive the position of Secretary of Interior so as to force him to defend his plans himself and in front of the Reichstag. At the same time he made it clear (and this was significant) that he supported the Chancellor on the issue of the military penal code reform.[74] Holstein had, therefore, not adopted Eulenburg's standpoint, "no matter what Eulenburg may have assumed."[75] Miquel agreed to accept the position of Secretary of Interior, and so did the Kaiser.[76]

Eulenburg, relieved of one of the most dangerous threats to his plan—the factor of Holstein—was now able to concentrate all his efforts on bringing Hohenlohe under control. While talking to Holstein on June 8, he had carefully revealed that one could not count any more on Marschall. Furthermore, Holstein had accurately carried this information to the Chancellor a few days later. Under these new circumstances the Chancellor could hardly create a crisis over the significant fact that he had suddenly lost his two most important ministers.

To forestall any danger of Hohenlohe's retiring from office, Eulenburg further emphasized his solidarity with Holstein and asked the latter to continue to use his influence on Hohenlohe to remain.[77] At the same time he pointed out to Wilhelm that "the prestige that the old Prince still has in the Empire and in Europe is too valuable for him to lose it without any good reason," and asked the monarch to let his Imperial sun shine on the old Chancellor. With this step Eulenburg hoped to break down any possible resistance by Hohenlohe to the new developments, and at the same time to receive some assurance that Wilhelm would not be influenced into letting himself be carried away, not only with Boetticher and Marschall but with Hohenlohe as well.[78] Wilhelm gave a reassuring reply.[79]

Eulenburg felt assured of Holstein's "radical change" after his conversation on June 8. In this assumption he was further strengthened by Holstein's preoccupation with a renewed threat resulting from recent intrigues of Raschdau against the Foreign Office and particularly against Holstein himself. In fact, this matter went to such lengths that Eulenburg, having had desperately to fight off Holstein a few days before, now had to protect the latter's position against Raschdau by writing the Kaiser,

> At the moment the old Man [Hohenlohe] is beside himself—and with good reason—over Raschdau, who had systematically agitated and has now instigated the old Grand Duke [of Weimar] (since how else could he suddenly have come up with this strange idea?) to ask for more *political reports* of the ambassadors of Your Majesty. . . . I deem it completely justified if the Chancellor (behind

whom stood Holstein), *in order to preserve* his authority, wants to make a "change" due to such continuing "subter-fuges."[80]

On June 17 Eulenburg could summarize his goals and achievements to Bülow thus: after he had realized the impossibility of Marschall's position (at the time of Wilhelm's visit to Vienna), he had to do everything in his power to hold off the change as long as possible, retain Hohenlohe in office, and curb Holstein. "Alas," he wrote, "in all three I seem to have succeeded."[81] The question of Marschall had been decided with the agreement of May 31 and June 1. About Holstein, Eulenburg was confident for the immediate future: "Holstein will not give rise to difficulties any more. For how long is questionable. According to the present situation, I will do everything in order to keep you and Hohenlohe. Therein lies his future—and your advantage. You will therefore not run into opposition with him. Thus you will be in a position to act quite independently, without having to fear a breach."[82]

The weakest point was still Hohenlohe. At the moment Eulenburg repeated his often-voiced consideration: Bülow's immediate succession to the chancellorship would be "a grave matter," and the only other solution—a secretaryship under Chancellor Botho Eulenburg—would not further Bülow's future. Only under the umbrella of the internationally respected aristocratic name of Hohenlohe would he have a favorable entree into the political world of Berlin and Europe.[83] Eulenburg knew that the appointment of Bülow to succeed Marschall would come in the near future, certainly by the autumn of that year. Consequently, he advised Bülow to take a vacation, and he asked the Kaiser to increase the salaries of the Chancellor and the Secretary of State.[84]

The danger of Hohenlohe's resignation seemed to have been pushed into the safe future by the conciliatory attitude of Hohenlohe toward Miquel's proposed appointment to Boetticher's position and by Miquel's apparent acceptance of those positions. The necessity to postpone any definite appointment to Marschall's post until the autumn, and specifically at least until October 1, may be partially explained by the fact that Holstein had made it quite clear to Hohenlohe on June 17 that in the case of a definite appointment of a deputy to take the place of the Foreign Secretary during the summer, Holstein would hand in his resignation: "Never for that purpose (provisional head of the Foreign Office while Secretary of State is on vacation) during the last 10 years has somebody been appointed to this position. If this happens now, immediately after the *Zukunft* has accused me of collaboration with Schumann, the public who are unaware of the details (even if they are objective and not against me), must see in this order an act of Imperial lack of confidence towards me."[85]

Besides, as it turned out, the Miquel issue was far from settled. Miquel, after having thought the matter over, reconsidered his step and, in a long letter to Hohenlohe, declined to take the post of an Imperial Secretary, responsible and vulnerable (at least to some extent) to the Reichstag.[86] Hohenlohe correctly surmised that "Miquel in the background and without responsibility to the Reichstag" would be quite dangerous and, all in all, "impossible." As a

result, the Chancellor once again decided to hand in his resignation if Miquel were to remain in the Prussian Ministry but were
not forced to defend the Reich government in front of the Reichstag,[87] which meant that he should also receive Boetticher's other
position, the State Secretaryship of Interior.

It was at this point, probably not known to Eulenburg, that
Holstein again urged Hohenlohe to resist the Kaiser.[88] In other
words, he reverted back to his previous position and tried to
strengthen the Chancellor against the monarch.[89] However, as
usual, Hohenlohe did not live up to Holstein's expectations.

On June 20 came the expected telegram from the Kaiser to Bülow
appointing him as Marschall's deputy and asking for an interview.
Bülow consented to meet the Kaiser in Kiel on the 26th.[90] At the
same time, he asked Eulenburg to do his utmost to prevent any
rash action on the part of the Kaiser in regard to his appointment,
pointing out that any definite decision must certainly not come
before autumn.[91] The expected event had happened, but it had come
about just a little too early. Eulenburg had not yet fully prepared and safeguarded Bülow's position in Berlin. The question
of Hohenlohe was still somewhat up in the air because of the Miquel
situation and because of Hohenlohe's reintroduction of the question
of the military penal code, over which he and the Kaiser still did
not agree. Although not sorry about the change, Eulenburg could
quite sincerely write to Bülow that he was "inconsolable over this
quick change,"[92] and urgently asked him to a conference on June 23
in Frankfurt before Bülow went to Kiel.[93] There the two friends
discussed the immediate steps and conduct of Bülow that would best
lead to success.[94]

Meanwhile, in Berlin, the Chancellor had again decided to continue his half-hearted defense of his position on the military penal
code reform. Weak himself, with apparent support only from Holstein
(even Marschall wrote a flattering letter, pointing out that he
would not remain in office, and urged Hohenlohe to do so),[95] Hohenlohe succumbed to the consistent pressure to which he had been
subjected.

On June 20 Bülow had been appointed Deputy Foreign Secretary
by the Kaiser. As a consequence, Holstein handed in his resignation on June 24.[96] The changes of the next few days came about
apparently without any objections and interference on Holstein's
part.[97] Again it seems as if Eulenburg, at least to some extent,
had failed, since he had always recognized the importance of
Holstein for Bülow's government and had tried to save Holstein
for Bülow.

Meanwhile, the meeting at Kiel took its due course. The first
communication from Bülow to Eulenburg did not sound reassuring at
all. "My position," Bülow informed Eulenburg in French from Kiel,
"as ever against Hohenlohe and Holstein infinitely more difficult
than you thought."[98] However, everything finally went as well as
could be expected. Hohenlohe gave in all along the line:

> In the final days of June he agreed to another post-
> ponement of the military penal code law in order to give
> the Kaiser time to examine his latest proposals. He
> agreed to the appointment of Miquel as Vice-President of

the Prussian Ministry of State and to allow him to remain as Prussian Minister without accepting the State Secretaryship. . . of the Interior. He agreed to the appointment of Count Arthur von Posadowsky-Wehner, the nominee of Miquel and the Kaiser as State Secretary of the Reich Ministry of the Interior, Deputy Chancellor and member of the Prussian Ministry of State. He agreed to the dismissal of Admiral Hollmann as Chief of the Reich Naval Office and his replacement by another appointee of the Kaiser, Conter-Admiral Alfred Tirpitz. He agreed to the appointment of Lieutenant-General von Podbielski, yet another nominee of the Kaiser, as Secretary of the Reich Post Office. And he agreed to the appointment of Bernhard von Bülow as Deputy State Secretary of the Foreign Ministry.[99]

Nevertheless, Hohenlohe remained in office! Even Holstein retracted his resignation, and his renewed attempts to get Hohenlohe to resign in the face of the momentous changes (in which case he would do the same) came too late and were hardly made with the force of real conviction.[100]

On June 18 Hollmann had already been replaced by Tirpitz. On the 28th Bülow became, in effect, Marschall's deputy; on July 1 Boetticher was dismissed, and Posadowsky-Wehner received the Reich Office of the Interior and Miquel the vice-presidency of the Prussian Ministry of State. The essential issues had been settled, and no crisis had as yet taken place. However, Eulenburg recognized that Bülow's and especially Hohenlohe's positions were far from secure. Thus, from this time on, all the necessary changes having been made, Eulenburg ardently used all his efforts to maintain the status quo, that is, to safeguard the position of Bülow as temporary Secretary of State and to retain Hohenlohe—this eternal problem—for the former's benefit.

Although the main crisis was over by July 1, Eulenburg's objective was still a formidable one—not on account of the independent actions of the old Chancellor but on account of the influence he (as well as the Kaiser) might be subjected to. On the other hand, Bülow was now in Berlin, Marschall was out, and that alone would go far to assure him success. For Wilhelm, at least, the whole crisis had ended. On July 5 he left for his annual cruise into Scandinavian waters, to return only on July 30.

Despite continuing friction and anxiety in regard to Hohenlohe, the latter did what was expected of him. Alexander had written to his father, "You are to hold the nest warm for him (Bülow) until he is ready,"[101] and Hohenlohe did just that. Bülow was formally appointed deputy for Marschall on August 6, and officially became his successor as Foreign Secretary on October 20.

In October, 1900, Hohenlohe was finally replaced as Chancellor by Bülow. On that occasion Hohenlohe noted,

It becomes ever clearer to me that my position had been threatened after the dismissal of Marschall and Boetticher. Each one of them had his faults; but none wanted to become more than what he was, in this

connection both shared with me the same interest, and
thereby they were loyal to me. When Bülow took the place
of Marschall, I had a rival at my side. . . . The work
of Bülow progressed slowly and cautiously, but steadily
toward the goal of replacing me [at the side] of the
Kaiser. Nothing could be done about it. I could not
heave him out of the saddle [in his relationship] with
the Kaiser, who preferred Bülow. In this way destiny
had to take its course until it came to the catastrophe.[102]

Against formidable odds, the combination of Eulenburg and Bülow had
come off with victory. To be sure, their victory was only a pre-
condition upon which to base future action. What had not been
accomplished during the New Course and indeed could hardly have
been possible with the New Course government—namely the cooperation
of industry and agriculture—now became possible with Bülow, as the
future was to show.

NOTES

1. Hohenlohe to Alexander, 22.IV.97, *Hohenlohe*, III, 330. See
also Hohenlohe Journal, *ibid.*, p. 328.

2. See Ministry of State meetings for 2, 9, and 14.IV.97,
D.Z.A. Merseburg, vol. 129; Marschall Diary, 2, 8, and 14.IV.97;
Hohenlohe Journal, 7.IV.97, *Hohenlohe*, III, 328-329; Röhl, *Germany
without Bismarck*, pp. 225-226.

3. See Marschall Diary, 20.IV.97, 26.IV.97, 5.V.97, 6.V.97; Bosse
Diary, 5.V.97, B.A. Bosse, No. 9; Marschall and v. d. Recke to
Hohenlohe, 2.IV.97, Hohenlohe to Alexander, 29.IV.97; Hohenlohe
Journal and memo, 5.V.97; Hohenlohe to Wilhelm, 9.V.97; Hohenlohe to
Kiderlen, 9.V.97, Kiderlen to Hohenlohe, 10.V.97, all in Archiv
Schillingsfürst, Rep. 100 XXII A, Bd. 11; Ministry of State meetings,
28.IV.97, 6.V.97, D.Z.A. Merseburg, vol. 129; *Hohenlohe*, III, 330-
338; Hohenlohe to his wife Marie, 3, 5, and 7.V.97, Archiv Schillings-
fürst, Rep. 101 II H 15; Röhl, *Germany without Bismarck*, pp. 226-227.

4. See *Hohenlohe*, III, 338-341; Röhl, *Germany without Bismarck*,
pp. 227-228; Hohenlohe to Boetticher, 17.V.97, B.A. Boetticher,
No. 68; Marschall Diary, 15.V.97, 17.V.97.

5. See Bachem, *Zentrumspartei*, V, p. 452.

6. See Saxon embassy reports, 6.V.97, Sächs. H.S.A., *Aussen-
ministerium*, No. 1097; Saxon embassy reports of 6.V.97, 24.V.97,
3.VI.97, Sächs. H.S.A., Ges. Berlin, No. 252. The same general
impression of complete lack of governmental unity, extreme uncertainty, and a major crisis to be expected at any moment is also
well conveyed in Varnbühler's report to Mittnacht, 8.VI.97, Württ.
H.S.A., E 46-48, No. 1274.

7. *Hohenlohe*, III, 338-339.

8. *Ibid.*, p. 342.

9. *Ibid.*, pp. 346-350.

10. See Lerchenfeld to Crailsheim, 9.I.97, 14.I.97, G.S.A. München, MA 77753; in the latter report Lerchenfeld wrote that Hohenlohe was not the man to side with Bavaria against the Ministry of State, the Federal Council, and the Reichstag. Bismarck, Lerchenfeld added, could have done so had he wanted to. See also Hohenlohe to Crailsheim, 24.I.97, G.S.A. München, MA 77753.

11. Lerchenfeld to Crailsheim, 9.I.97, G.S.A. München, MA 77753.

12. Lerchenfeld to Crailsheim, 23.I.97, G.S.A. München, MA 77753.

13. For this question, see especially the reports of Lerchenfeld to Crailsheim, 29.I.97, 1, 2, 7, and 12.II.97, G.S.A. München, MA 77753; 27.II.97, 2, 25, and 29.III.97, 5, 7, 11, 12 (twice), 13, 22, 25, 28, and 31.V.97, G.S.A. München, MA 77754; 9.VI.97, 17.VI.97, 3.VII.97, 4.VII.97, G.S.A. München, MA 77755.

14. On this, see also Röhl, *Germany without Bismarck*, pp. 224-225; Marschall diary, 12-15, 19, and 20.V.97; Hohenlohe Journal, 20.V.97, Archiv Schillingsfürst, Rep 100 XXII-A, Bd. 11.

15. Haller, *Eulenburg*, p. 231.

16. Eulenburg to Bülow, 24.IV.97, B.A. Eul. 46.

17. Haller, *Eulenburg*, p. 229.

18. *Ibid.*, pp. 233, 232.

19. See also Rich, *Holstein*, II, 533.

20. *Hohenlohe*, III, 343, note 2; *Wippermann*, XIII (I), p. 9; Haller, *Eulenburg*, p. 230.

21. Haller, *Eulenburg*, p. 230.

22. *Ibid.*, translation taken from Mayne, *Eulenburg*, II, 20-21.

23. *Hohenlohe*, III, 345-346, 348. Another charge was that he had neglected to give a Kaiser-toast in Hamburg. See *Geschichte der Frankfurter Zeitung*, p. 748; Marschall Diary, 31.V.97.

24. Eulenburg to Bülow, 31.V.97, B.A. Eul. 46; Haller, *Eulenburg*, p. 232.

25. Haller, *Eulenburg*, p. 232.

26. Rich, *Holstein*, II, 535, note 1. See also Marschall Diary, 22.V.97.

27. Haller, *Eulenburg*, p. 231; translation from Mayne, *Eulenburg*, II, 201; Marschall Diary, 31.V.97.

28. See Marschall Diary, 25, 26, and 29.V.97.

29. *Ibid.*, 31.V.97.

30. Wilhelm to Hohenlohe, telegram, 31.V.97, Archiv Schillingsfürst, Rep. 100 XXII A, Bd. 11.

31. Haller, *Eulenburg*, p. 232.

32. *Ibid.*, p. 233; Rich, *Holstein*, II, 537; *Hohenlohe*, III, 345.

33. *Hohenlohe*, III, 346; Rich, *Holstein*, II, 537.

34. *Hohenlohe*, III, 349.

35. Haller, *Eulenburg*, p. 232.

36. Holstein to Eulenburg, 31.VIII.97, B.A. Eul. 48.

37. *Ibid.* This is confirmed by Holstein's letter to Eulenburg
dated as "Wahrscheinlich 31.V.97" (B.A. Eul. 46) but more likely
written after June 6: "I do not have a complete picture of what
damage Marschall has caused during the last 14 days. But his goal
seems to have been, to make clear to the world that the Old Man
[Hohenlohe] was helpless without him. . . .
"Precisely at the moment at which the Old Man [Hohenlohe] would
retire into private life, M[arschall] was to get a position outside
[Germany, i.e., an embassy]." The date of the letter should be kept
in mind, since at this time Holstein had turned strongly against
Marschall.

38. Marschall Diary, 31.V.97.

39. Boetticher had not been in Berlin, but was summoned categorically by the Kaiser. See Hohenlohe to Wilhelm, 30.V.97, Röhl,
Germany without Bismarck, p. 230; telegram of Wilhelm to Hohenlohe,
31.V.97, Archiv Schillingsfürst, Rep. 100 XXII A, Bd. 11.

40. On this, see also Röhl, *Germany without Bismarck*, pp. 230-
232.

41. Haller, *Eulenburg*, pp. 232-233.

42. Eulenburg to Bülow, 31.V.97, B.A. Eul. 46.

43. *Ibid.*

44. Haller, *Eulenburg*, p. 233.

45. *Ibid.*, p. 234; translation, slightly modified, taken from
Mayne, *Eulenburg*, II, 24.

46. *Ibid.*

47. Eulenburg to Bülow, 31.V.97, 2.VI.97, B.A. Eul. 46.

48. Haller,*Eulenburg*, p. 234; translation from Mayne, *Eulenburg*,
II, 24.

49. Eulenburg to Bülow, 31.V.97, B.A. Eul. 46. Marschall's own
view of these events is as follows in diary, 1.VI.97: "This night
Ph. Eulenburg sent me a [? probably telegram], everything went quite
well, H.M. wants to speak with me. At nine o'clock he comes to me,
he thinks that H.M., although insisting upon Boetticher's dismissal,
is inclined toward a compromise; in my interview today I am to bring
up the question. . . . I have audience with . . . [Hohenlohe] and
advise to compromise,—that Boetticher will be given a vacation
after the closing of the Reichstag. B., who is present, agrees with
me.
"At 12:30 o'clock *Immediatvortrag.* H.M. receives me graciously
and I explain my personal affair with the same arguments as I did
yesterday to Eulenburg. . . . [The Kaiser suggests an embassy for
Marschall; the latter suggests a place with "favorable climate and
not too far"—a suggestion he had already made to Eulenburg on

May 31.] H.M. gives me a vacation.
"Then H.M. talks to me about the crisis. H.M. was annoyed against Hohenlohe and Boetticher . . . after his conduct Boetticher must absolutely go. He had sent Lucanus to . . . [Hohenlohe] with the proposal [*Anerbieten*] that Boetticher be dismissed after the end of the Reichstag but that he would take a vacation *immediately*. I told H.M. that this way would be impossible. . . . [Marschall succeeds in persuading the Kaiser to give Boetticher a vacation after the end of Reichstag session.] I am glad over my success. . . . Hohenlohe regards the affair as closed. Holstein and cons. [consorts] are mad [*missmutig*]. . . ."

50. Haller, *Eulenburg*, pp. 234-235.

51. *Hohenlohe*, III, 348; Archiv Schillingsfürst, Rep. 100 XXII A, Bd. 11.

52. However, Marschall was not against a crisis. He held essentially the same position as Holstein, urging Hohenlohe to resign in August. See *Hohenlohe*, III, 347-348, 350.

53. It seems that on previous occasions Lucanus had accentuated the formulation of the wishes and expressions of the Kaiser. See Meisner, "Hohenlohe," pp. 138f.

54. See August Stein, *Es war alles ganz anders; Aus der Werkstatt eines politischen Journalisten 1891-1914* (Frankfurt am Main, 1922), pp. 41-43; Fricke, "Die Affaire Leckert-Lützow-Tausch," p. 1600; Harden, *Köpfe*, I, 241. But see also *Hohenlohe*, III, 345-346; *Geschichte der Frankfurter Zeitung*, p. 748; Rich, *Holstein*, II, 537. On the crisis during May 31 and June 1, see also Röhl, *Germany without Bismarck*, pp. 230ff.

55. Eulenburg to Bülow, 31.V.97 (Anlage, 2.VI.97), B.A. Eul. 46. See also Marschall Diary, 2.V.97.

56. Eulenburg to Bülow, 31.V.97, B.A. Eul. 46.

57. But Marschall (as did Holstein) advised Hohenlohe to resign in August, 1897. See *Hohenlohe*, III, 300.

58. Rich, *Holstein*, II, 535.

59. Eulenburg to Bülow, 31.V.97 (Anlage, 2.VI.97), B.A. Eul. 46.

60. *Ibid*.

61. Eulenburg to Bülow, 2.VI.97, B.A. Eul. 46.

62. Eulenburg to Wilhelm, 11.VI.97, B.A. Eul. 47.

63. See *Hohenlohe*, III, 350.

64. *Ibid*.

65. Eulenburg to Bülow, 9.VI.97, B.A. Eul. 47.

66. Haller, *Eulenburg*, p. 235.

67. See Rogge, "Die Kladderadatsch Affaire," pp. 90-130. See also above, p. 108, note 21.

68. Haller, *Eulenburg*, p. 237.

69. See Kiderlen-Wächter to Holstein, 3.VII.97, B.A. Bülow 92. See also *Holsteins Papiere*, IV, 40, note 1.

70. See Kiderlen-Wächter to Holstein, 3.VII.97, B.A. Bülow 92; *Holsteins Papiere*, IV, 39-40.

71. See especially Holstein to Eulenburg, probably 31.V.97 but according to content more probably written in early June, probably June 7. See Rich, *Holstein*, II, 537, note 1; Eulenburg to Bülow, 9.VI.97, B.A. Eul. 47; above, p. 280, note 37. See also Röhl, *Germany without Bismarck*, p. 234.

72. Haller, *Eulenburg*, p. 235.

73. *Ibid.*, p. 236.

74. *Hohenlohe*, III, 352.

75. Rich, *Holstein*, II, 541; *Hohenlohe*, III, 352-353.

76. *Hohenlohe*, III, 354-355.

77. Eulenburg to Holstein, 11.VI.97, B.A. Eul. 47.

78. Eulenburg to Wilhelm, 11.VI.97, B.A. Eul. 47.

79. Wilhelm to Eulenburg, 15.VI.97, B.A. Eul. 47.

80. Eulenburg to Wilhelm, 20.VI.97, B.A. Eul. 47.

81. Eulenburg to Bülow, 17.VI.97, B.A. Eul. 47.

82. *Ibid.*

83. Eulenburg to Bülow, 9.VI.97, B.A. Eul. 47.

84. *Ibid.*; Eulenburg to Wilhelm, 20.VI.97, B.A. Eul. 47.

85. *Hohenlohe*, III, 355.

86. *Ibid.*, pp. 356-358. On Miquel during this time, see also Herzfeld, *Miquel*, II, 514ff.; Röhl, *Germany without Bismarck*, pp. 233, 236f. See also the various embassy reports. Since the Miquel affair is rather the beginning of the second phase than the termination of the one investigated in this study, the necessary details on Miquel during this period have not been presented here.

87. *Hohenlohe*, III, 359.

88. *Ibid.*

89. *Ibid.*

90. Bülow to Eulenburg, 20.VI.97, B.A. Eul. 47.

91. *Ibid.*

92. Eulenburg to Bülow, 20.VI.97, B.A. Eul. 47.

93. *Ibid.*

94. Bülow, *Denkwürdigkeiten*, I, 4-5.

95. *Hohenlohe*, III, 362.

96. *Holsteins Papiere*, IV, 38.

97. See Rich, *Holstein*, II, 542.

98. Bülow to Eulenburg, 27.VI.97, B.A. Eul. 47.

99. Rich, *Holstein*, II, 542.

100. See *ibid.*, pp. 543f.   See also Röhl, *Germany without Bismarck*, pp. 236ff.

101. *Hohenlohe*, III, 371.

102. *Ibid.*, p. 592.

Conclusion

1

By July, 1897, the New Course in all its phases had come to an end. The last step in this development—the change in ministerial personnel—had begun with the dismissal of Berlepsch in June, 1896. This was followed by Bronsart's resignation in August, and the end came with the dismissal of Hollmann, Marschall, and Boetticher by July 1, 1897. Miquel took Boetticher's place as vice-president of the Prussian Ministry of State, Posadowsky assumed Boetticher's former position as Secretary of Interior, Tirpitz replaced Hollmann as Navy Secretary, and Bülow filled Marschall's post as Foreign Secretary.

True to Eulenburg's original intention, the government had, since 1894, taken another turn to the right—not "right about face," but "half right about." To be sure, this meant that neither the conservative Prussian agrarian forces nor the military extremists had come to power. On the other hand, this second turn in mid-1897 had brought affairs back approximately to where they had been before 1890. In this sense, therefore, the New Course had come full circle. Viewed in this light, the position of the government in mid-1897 does constitute a form of capitulation to Bismarck after all; or, from a somewhat different perspective, it may be considered a documentation of political bankruptcy.

After seven years of progressive political anarchy, German politics found a basis upon which it was possible to regain a semblance of stability. In 1890 Kaiser Wilhelm had remarked that almost all revolutions had their origin in the fact that necessary reforms had been neglected. It appeared for a moment that even Wilhelm had "realized" the antiquated nature of Bismarck's policies. However, he was unwilling to translate this insight into a concrete and sustained political effort. In domestic affairs Bismarck's policies had only postponed major problems of adjustment and modernization, and while for some Bismarck had become a red revolutionary, for others he was a "radical" reactionary. In foreign affairs the feeling was expressed with increasing frequency that Bismarck's policies did not adequately provide for Germany's aspirations as a world power.

Bismarck had said that he regarded the Social Democrats, just as he did the Poles, Welfs, Frenchmen, and Danes, as alien people; and that he would treat them as enemies.[1] Wilhelm's professed goal was to provide the New Course with the appearance of a legitimate *raison d'être*, since he sensed the impossibility of maintaining adequate political support merely on the programmatic slogan of opposition to Bismarck. As later interpreted, the New Course was invested with a rationale quite different from what Wilhelm had originally envisioned:

In the field of domestic policy the New Course
represented a broadly conceived attempt at a reform
of the Empire and the Prussian state. The attempt
led to an expansion, if only a very limited one, of
local administration in the eastern parts of Prussia,
a decrease of the tariff on cereals which had been
especially heavy on the poor class of the population;
it led to an introduction of the progressive income tax
in Prussia. . . . It further led to the endeavor to find
a new, positive relationship to the opposition parties
which had been condemned as enemies of Empire and state.
That was the Social Democratic Party. . . . And that was
the Catholic Center Party.[2]

However, the attempt of the New Course (almost from the beginning of
its existence no longer identical with the position of Wilhelm) to
reform and modernize eventually failed. It has been maintained that
"the good intentions of the young Kaiser were alone not enough—his
attitude constantly swayed, he was dependent upon momentary influences and did not give his Chancellor the necessary backing in
relation to affected interests. To this must be added the immaturity
of the German public."[3] It is important to note, however, that the
basis of Wilhelm's "good intentions" was largely negative in nature.
Wilhelm's New Course was not so much meant to solve or even successfully cope with pressing social problems, but was a means to stand
up to Bismarck. The fatal flaw was that Wilhelm found himself in
agreement with Bismarck's publicly revealed domestic views. Without
possessing a Bismarckian sense of proportion, Wilhelm had keen appreciation for visibly displayed Bismarckian power. Yet, while he had
been strong enough to resist and terminate Bismarck's official
position in 1890, he had been faced with the subsequent task of
proving that he could also replace Bismarck—and had been incapable
of doing so. The historian Friedrich Meinecke remarked in 1890
that the Kaiser was drawing an extremely high draft against the
future.[4] Wilhelm proved not to be the man capable of paying.
However strong the institution of monarchy, it was found to lack
personal substance. This created a power vacuum, which in turn
provided constant temptation to grab for power, and thus functioned
as a prime source of political instability. It must not be forgotten
that it was Bismarck who had been instrumental in shaping the
foundation of the precarious political situation that Germany faced
in 1890. It was Bismarck who had endowed the Prussian monarchy with
a greater amount of power than it had ever held previously. On the
surface the system of government with which Bismarck hoped to retard
a dangerously accelerated process of change seemed to substantiate
his reactionary image. In Bismarck's system the only effective
check on the top-heavy power structure of the monarchy could come
from the office of the Chancellor—from Bismarck himself. However,
even Bismarck experienced the collapse of his own work after 1890.
He had not adequately separated the chancellorship from his person.
Consequently, this highest office in the Reich was ineffective in
exercising sufficient restraint upon the monarchy.

2

As a result of the strong, authoritarian, Hohenzollern tradition, and reinforced by Bismarckian dictatorship, the aristocracy (as well as the political parties) had been educated into political incompetence—to give up political responsibility and accept leadership provided "from above."[5] It is characteristic of the Germany of the 1890s that the various political parties and even the monarchy were looking for their own Bismarck who would impose their interests upon everyone else. They all wanted to be successful, but they found no one in their own ranks to exercise sufficient leadership, and they themselves refused to accept political responsibility and discipline. We may note that Hohenlohe, for instance, looked upon the chancellorship in purely negative, passive terms[6] and was, of course, chosen precisely for this reason. Just as noteworthy is Wilhelm's exclamation that Bülow was to become "his" Bismarck. In a political structure which had been trained to accept responsible leadership either from the monarch or the Chancellor, such a clear abrogation of their duty was extremely critical.

The parties on their part lacked discipline as well as leadership and thus were unlikely candidates to take up the burden—to say nothing of the formal, constitutional problem of doing so. The parties of the left during the 1890s were too weak by themselves and were unable to cooperate with each other. The National Liberals, never having recovered from the stroke dealt to them by Bismarck in 1879, were disunited, their various components opposing each other. The Center Party tried hard to become a government party— a difficult task, since the government itself lacked unity and a political program. The Conservatives submitted to Miquel, as later to Bülow, Bethmann-Hollweg, and Ludendorff.

The situation among the various cliques and personnel combinations (all of them powerful enough to obstruct but not enough to construct) was not much better than that of the political parties. The first of the major groups, the Bismarckians (including Miquel as its most astute and able member within the government), wanted to take the negative step of imposing limitations upon the Kaiser and, rejecting the Caprivi era, to reinstate the political basis of 1887. As long as Bismarck was alive, their hope was based on an antiquated political system and a defeated (if still very active and devastating) old man. It was a "personal regime" based on the attempt to control the highest ranking bureaucrat in the Reich— the Chancellor. With conservative support the Chancellor could control the monarch, while at the same time the "personal regime" of the Chancellor was checked by both the necessity of creating and maintaining adequate political consent and by the constitutional position of the monarch. Obviously such a system required not only high bureaucratic mechanical efficiency but also extreme political skill.[7]

The second group, the exponents of the New Course (particularly Holstein and Marschall) also wanted to impose limitations upon the Kaiser, but on the basis of a monarchical system in which the bureaucracy was the controlling element. With the help of Holstein, Kiderlen, and Marschall, and with the technical competency of Boetticher, Caprivi had tried to impose limitations on the Kaiser.

He failed because he lacked an independent power base achieved by
the creation of political consent, and because of internal bureaucratic (ministerial) disunity. Holstein in particular hoped to
rectify the weakness by enforcing bureaucratic unity as had Bismarck
and by formalizing and systematizing bureaucratic control. Holstein
failed because the carrying out of this reform itself necessitated
an independent power base which Holstein did not possess and which
Eulenburg was unwilling to help bring about.

Last, there was the group consisting of the Grand Duke of
Baden, Eulenburg, and Bülow. Confident of finding a new Bismarck in
Bülow and re-establishing authority on the basis of a "personal
regime" analogous to Bismarck and Wilhelm I, this group launched
Bülow in Berlin. Eulenburg fought for and then protected the independence of the Kaiser from the bureaucracy and the Bismarck Fronde.
He was successful because he could use Holstein against the Fronde
and the latter against Holstein. Eulenburg's defense of Wilhelm's
independence, however, was at the same time a move toward isolating
the monarch. The isolated monarch could then be dominated by
Bülow and Eulenburg. Here, too, we may speak of an intention to
impose limitations upon the Kaiser, and here, too, we must record
failure. Eulenburg underestimated his success at defending the
independence of the Kaiser and overestimated his ability to manipulate the monarch and Bülow. As it turned out, Bülow immediately
accommodated himself to the Fronde and the conservatives, which
gave the latter the victory. This was Bülow's price for staying
in office.

Bismarck had lost in 1890 and, despite powerful and sustained
efforts, could not turn the tide during his years of "exile" in
Friedrichsruh. Yet Wilhelm likewise had lost—neither the New
Course (a course dictated to him as a consequence of his struggle
with Bismarck) nor the *Sammlungspolitik* after 1897 (and eventually
even the military dictatorship under Ludendorff) met with success.
Wilhelm, in fact, never was independent enough to carry out a
"personal regime."

After seven years of groping for a new approach to its domestic
and foreign political problems, with an Emperor in a "perpetual
position of constraint" (resulting in that ostentatious but cramped
facade identified as the "personal" regime of Wilhelm), with "a few
politicians of indisputable good will, but no understanding . . . ,"[8]
and with a general political deadlock, no solution had been approached
and the government reverted back to a system that had been
visibly outdated by 1890. Bismarck had been victorious over Wilhelm
after all—but what a victory and at what a cost!

3

The position of the monarchy was of particular importance in
the struggle for stabilization. For a short time Wilhelm had been
on the side of the exponents of the New Course, but had then wavered
and finally turned his back on them and joined the opposition forces.
The period from 1892 until 1897 was essentially a struggle over
control of the Emperor. The result of this struggle was not a
foregone conclusion. The Emperor was quite impressionable and could
be rather easily influenced. In this context, then, the persons

holding the confidence of the Kaiser became the main actors in the
drama. His closest and most influential friend and advisor was none
other than Philipp Eulenburg. As a consequence of the influence that
Eulenburg (and his protégé, Bülow) exerted upon the Kaiser, it was
he who played the decisive role in the struggle for the monarch.
The historian Fritz Hartung wrote:

> The strongest and most lasting influence lay after 1890
> in the very controversial personality of the Count, later
> Prince Philipp Eulenburg. . . . He preferred to remain
> behind the scenes in semi-darkness and from here exerted
> his influence, which the personal friendship of Wilhelm II
> granted him, unseen and uncontrolled. He commanded the
> ear of the Kaiser on the Scandinavian cruises, on the many
> hunting excursions, in all critical hours, at which time
> he put in an appearance, called or uncalled. And in the
> meantime between his visits, he kept up his connection
> with the Kaiser by letters. By this direct relationship
> with the Kaiser he had a great advantage over all ministers,
> even the Reich Chancellors during the years 1890 to 1900.[9]

The position that Eulenburg himself consciously assumed during
the critical period from 1894 to 1897 was that of friend and defender
of the Kaiser. In this role he coquetted with the various opposing
forces at the same time, and played them against each other. Thus
he retained his own advantageous position and simultaneously protected the monarch from any attacks upon his power. Hartung continued:

> Certainly he was not only a flattering courtier, but
> also often a warning and admonishing friend of the Kaiser.
> But when his admonitions remained unsuccessful, it was
> not only as the result of the character of the Kaiser,
> but also lay in the fact that the perfumed, sweet nature
> of Eulenburg, the artificiality and theatrical pose of
> his attitude, but especially his inclination toward
> mysticism and spiritualism underline especially the
> weaker sides of Wilhelm's character. This cancelled
> out the possible effect of the admonitions.[10]

Eulenburg, who had at times stood fairly close to the men of
the New Course, had abandoned them and had even actively undermined
their position. He had done this with the help of the conservatives
and the military. Eulenburg did not intend helping either the
conservatives or their opponents to power. He looked upon himself
as a *"royalist sans phrase"* and promoted royal power in the hope
that the Kaiser, with Bülow and himself,[11] would successfully
replace Bismarck and uphold the Bismarck system as he, Eulenburg,
understood it.

Eulenburg lacked political foresight and political astuteness
precisely because he did not want to realize that even the concen-
tration of royal power that he intended was at the end of the
nineteenth century an impossibility, especially with a person like
Wilhelm II occupying the throne. In his own way Eulenburg, as did
the Kaiser himself in 1890, took a tremendous gamble on the future—
on Wilhelm II and on Bülow, and he was disappointed by both. In
the last analysis Eulenburg "was only a dilettante in everything;

that finally became his doom."[12]

As has been seen, the Kaiser backed down when he encountered determined opposition. The Köller crisis and the fleet proposals of 1895 and 1896 are examples. If Eulenburg had constantly and honestly accepted and promoted (with his customary skill and tact) the viewpoints of the men of the New Course—Holstein, Marschall, Boetticher, and Berlepsch—it might have well been possible to "push the Kaiser" slowly but surely into the position of a constitutional monarch. However, whatever chance of success this development might have had, Eulenburg became the key figure in assuring its failure. It is in this sense that Eulenburg has been described as the evil genius of the Kaiser,[13] and it is for this reason that the figure of Eulenburg assumes special importance.

Eulenburg had been successful in outmaneuvering both the court conservatives (the aides de camp to the Kaiser, the military attachés, Waldersee, and the *casse-cou* politicians and the Bismarckians) as well as their opponents (the Holstein-Marschall group) by bringing Bülow, the "royalist sans phrase," to Berlin. With Bülow, Eulenburg had been successful in carrying out his plan and reintroducing a political system that from his point of view would bring some measure of political stability. Yet this system was really living on borrowed time, since domestically, in this case, "stability" amounted to stagnation. The Bülow regime did not attempt to solve the pressing issues of the time. It made no attempt to reform a political system in which a small minority could irresponsibly dominate a large, alienated majority. Instead, Bülow sidestepped all critical issues by launching a course of "world policy." But this is another story.

With Bülow, Eulenburg had introduced a bastard version of the old Bismarckian system. The era of Wilhelm II continued its course, showing at times frightening similarity to the "era of Louis XVI." The price, moreover, for gambling on the future (by Wilhelm, Eulenburg, Bülow, and last but not least by Bismarck) had to be dearly paid.

4

When reviewing the seven years of the New Course, one of the natural questions to arise is whether it was possible, despite the Bismarckian legacy, despite the character of Wilhelm, despite the faction-ridden bureaucracy, and unofficial entourage, and despite the party political deadlock, to reform the German political structure, bringing it into conformity with a more modern situation and reintroducing a basis for political stability. Was it actually possible to modernize and stabilize Germany politically after 1890?

Samuel P. Huntington, in his stimulating essay on the political modernization of traditional monarchies, posed the problem as follows:

> To cope successfully with modernization, a political system must be able, first, to innovate policy, that is, promote social and economic reform by state action. Reform in this context usually means the changing of traditional

values and behavior patterns, the expansion of communications and education, the broadening of loyalties from
family, village, and tribe to nation, the secularization
of public life, the rationalization of authority structures, the promotion of functionally specific organiza-
tions, the substitution of achievement criteria for
ascriptive ones, and the furthering of a more equitable
distribution of material and symbolic resources. A second
requirement for a political system is the ability to assimilate successfully into the system the social forces
which are produced by modernization and achieve a new
social consciousness through modernization. In due
course, these social groups demand participation in the
political system, and the system either provides for
their participation in ways harmonious with the continued
existence of the system, or it alienates them and produces
overt or covert civil strife and secession.

Huntington goes on to say:

The overthrow of entrenched traditional interests
often requires the mobilization of new social forces into
politics, and the second key capability required of a
modernizing system is the capacity to assimilate into the
system the social forces which result from modernization. . . .
At least equally important is the capacity of the system to
incorporate traditional social groupings which acquire
political consciousness during the process of modernization. . . . The test of a system is, in some measure,
its capacity to respond to these demands. Successful
assimilation depends upon both the receptivity of the
system and the adaptability of the entering group, that
is, the willingness of the group to relinquish some of
its values and claims in order to gain admittance to the
system.[14]

In the policy of modernization on the part of the monarch,
leading to a "crucial struggle . . . between the monarch and his
bureaucratic servants on the one hand and the autonomous centers
of traditional power on the other,"[15] the monarch needs to secure
support. This support he may receive from the state bureaucracy,
the middle class (in Western Europe), the masses of the population,
and possibly some body outside the political system.[16] The history
of Germany during the seven years of the New Course may well be
examined from the standpoint of the conceptual framework that
Huntington has provided. The government in Germany could have had
the large majority of the population on its side. This could have
realistically been the direction of the bureaucracy under Caprivi
and even to a degree under Hohenlohe. The main opponents consisted
of the conservative element and the military. It is questionable
if these elements could have been forced into full modernization,
which would have meant a loss of their traditional social and
political power and status. To a limited extent, this had been
accomplished by Bismarck and even (if still less so) by the leaders
of the New Course and Wilhelm II during the Caprivi era. However,

in 1892, when no new Bismarck was to be had, the monarchy, rather than formulating a clearly outlined program and providing leadership, abdicated its responsibility and became a plaything of the struggling factions surrounding it. The result was that the forces represented by the men of the New Course, lacking a definite program, leadership, unity, and legitimacy in the form of support from the monarch, succumbed to the opposition of both the conservatives and the monarchy. As crucial, however, was the fact that no segment of the variety of forces, including the men of the New Course, was really working toward sustained "modernization," i.e., basic sociopolitical reform, but rather for the streamlining of an autonomous position for the bureaucracy.

Klaus Epstein in his brilliant biography of Mathias Erzberger states that the "imperative need confronting Germany was to transform the bureaucratic monarchy into a parliamentary democracy."[17] Then he sketches a number of factors which "practically forbade" a successful parliamentary-democratic reform. Among other factors, he lists "the strength of the monarchist-bureaucratic tradition in Prussia"; the prestige of the Prussianized Empire; "the socio-economic strength of the classes which had much to fear from an advance to democratic parliamentary government"; the lack of confidence and limited power of the Reichstag; the lack of inter-party cohesion to form a consistent coalition for reform; the acceptance of the constitutional status quo by the Center Party; postponement of potential disruptive internal reforms in light of increasing external dangers; and, finally, the "deep-seated complacency of the German population." In sum, "with complacency in the ruling class and political immaturity in all classes, the problems of the future were rarely properly diagnosed, and remedies were completely ignored."[18]

My investigation, as far as it touches the points above, to a degree corroborates Epstein's comments. Thorough and immediate reforms of the total body politic were not the goal of the bureaucracy. Holstein, Marschall, and Bronsart no less than Bülow and Eulenburg wanted to shield the bureaucratic oligarchy from external interferences of whatever origin. It may even be argued that while differences over particulars did exist, there was consensus as to the basic sociopolitical status quo, which extended no less to the leaders of most political parties. But this approach would obscure the crucial difference of tendency and degree of responsiveness toward the trend of the times between the Holstein-Berlepsch-Bronsart-Boetticher-Marschall element on the one hand and that of Eulenburg-Bülow on the other.

The politics of 1894-97 did not make inevitable the disastrous course of events thereafter, but they significantly contributed toward such a course. The direction of Holstein-Bronsart-Berlepsch-Marschall would in time have made an appreciable difference in the form of a better preparation for, and an easier acceptance of, eventual parliamentary democracy. But it was Eulenburg-Bülow who were victorious. Thus, the specific result of the period 1894-97, as I see it, was the victory of a bureaucratic oligarchy which replaced a tendency toward responsible and innovative statesmanship with short-range, opportunistic, sociopolitical manipulations.

The study has described many typical aspects of the politics of
a bureaucratic oligarchy: lack of a stable and clearly identifiable
repository of power with the consequent contending cliques and a
frequently changing power elite; political scandals implicating
(and uniting in a sense) highest governmental officials, bureaucrats
on the lowest level of hierarchy, journalists, double agents, and
blackmailers; a usually well functioning, elaborate bureaucratic
machinery racing in neutral gear. In the long run this course
contributed substantially to the creation of the crisis of 1914, as
well as to the inability to deal effectively with it. And finally,
it thereby set the stage for the rise of Hitler, the most cata-
strophic of opportunistic manipulators in European history. Perhaps
the road from 1848 to 1948 could have been traveled without the
inclusion of an era of tyrannies and global war.

NOTES

1. Otto von Bismarck, *Die Gesammelten Werke*, XIII (Berlin, 1930),
464.

2. Kotowski, Pöls, and Ritter, eds., *Das Wilhelminische Deutschland*, p. 35.

3. *Ibid.*

4. Friedrich Meinecke, *Erlebtes 1862-1919* (Stuttgart, 1964),
p. 114. I may point out here that Meinecke's discussion of the
constitutional problems of Germany/Prussia in his books, esp.
Radowitz (Berlin, 1913) and *Weltbürgertum und Nationalstaat* (now
in *Gesammelten Werke*, vol. 5, Munich, 1962) are still of great value.

5. This does not, of course, mean that they were not accountable
for their actions, for the formulation and pursuits of their interests. It seems that the great majority willingly and even enthusiastically pursued Imperial policies. But in order to do so,
both the political parties and the government needed to make certain
adjustments. Kehr points out that "the New Course, which had stood
under the sign of the struggle between industry and agriculture for
the power over the legislature (*Gesetzgebungsmaschine*), was (in mid
1897) replaced by the cooperation (*Sammlung*) of industry and agriculture against the proletariat. . . ." He goes on to say that
the Kaiser was successful in carrying through a naval building program not because he as a person and as the monarch called for such
but because the nation's middle classes, who up to 1897 had "looked
upon the Kaiser's naval enthusiasm, partly in resigned helplessness,
partly with annoyance, suddenly saw in world policy and in the naval
building program of the Kaiser a social weapon against the proletariat which promised good successes." See Eckart Kehr, "Soziale
und finanzielle Grundlagen der Tirpitzschen Flottenpropaganda," in
Hans-Ulrich Wehler, ed., *Moderne deutsche Sozialgeschichte* (Neue
Wissenschaftliche Bibliothek, Bd. 10) (Köln, Berlin, 1966), p. 393.
The whole problem of sociopolitical transformation before 1897 as well
as during the years 1897 to 1902 needs renewed detailed investigation.
My study only concerns itself with one aspect of the governmental
side up to June, 1897.

6. See, for example, the witty and sarcastic remarks entitled "Onkel Chlodwig," in Harden's *Die Zukunft*, 33 (1900), 178–182.

7. Cf. also Eberhard v. Vietsch, *Bethmann-Hollweg: Staatsmann zwischen Macht und Ethos* (Boppard am Rhein, 1969), pp. 62ff.; Arthur Rosenberg, *Die Entstehung der Weimarer Republik* (Sammlung "*res publica*," Bd. 8) (Frankfurt am Main, 1961), Chs. 1 and 2.

8. A. J. P. Taylor, *The Course of German History* (New York, 1962), p. 141.

9. Hartung, "Verantwortliche Regierung . . .," p. 319.

10. *Ibid.*, pp. 319–320.

11. See also Harden's article "Praeludium" in *Die Zukunft*, vol. 57, especially pp. 264ff.

12. Hartung, "Verantwortliche Regierung . . .," p. 319.

13. *Ibid.*

14. Samuel P. Huntington, "The Political Modernization of Traditional Monarchies," *Daedalus*, 95 (1966), 766–767, 768–769.

15. *Ibid.*, p. 774.

16. *Ibid.*, pp. 776–778.

17. Epstein, *Erzberger*, pp. 30–31.

18. *Ibid.*, pp. 31–37.

Bibliography

I.   UNPUBLISHED PRIMARY MATERIAL

Bundesarchiv, Koblenz
  Eulenburg Papers
  Bosse Papers
  Harden Papers
  Bülow Papers
  Boetticher Papers

Politisches Archiv des Auswärtigen Amtes, Bonn
  Deutschland 122, No. 3 a/b/c   (Normann-Schumann; Leckert-
    Lützow; Tausch)
  Deutschland 122, No. 2 /d (Marschall)
  Deutschland 122, No. 11 (Hohenlohe)
  Deutschland 125, No. 2 (Thronreden)
  H. Miquel Papers
  Holstein Papers

Deutsches Zentralarchiv, Abt. Potsdam
  Pr. Br. Rep. 30 Berlin C
    Tit. 93, Lit. R and T (Richthofen, Tausch)
    Tit. 94, Lit. V (Leckert-Lützow-Tausch)

Deutsches Zentralarchiv, Abt. Merseburg
  Rep. 90a, Abt. B Tit. III 2 B No. 6
  Prussian Ministry of State protocols, 1895-97

Geheimes Staatsarchiv, München
  Bavarian embassy reports, Berlin (Lerchenfeld), 1894-97

Sächsisches Hof und Staatsarchiv, Dresden
  Saxon embassy reports, Berlin (Hohenthal), 1894-97

Badisches Generallandesarchiv, Karlsruhe
  Baden embassy reports, Berlin (Brauer, Jagemann), 1894-97

Hauptstaatsarchiv, Stuttgart
  Württemberg embassy reports, Berlin (Varnbühler), 1894-97

Staatsarchiv, Hamburg
  Hanseatic embassy reports, Berlin (Krüger, Klügmann),
    1894-97

Fürst zu Hohenlohe-Schillingsfürst, Schillingsfürst
  Hohenlohe Papers (since moved to Bundesarchiv, Koblenz)

Grossherzogliches Familienarchiv, Karlsruhe
  Friedrich I von Baden Papers

Freifrau von Seyfried, Oberkirch
  Marschall Diary

Geheimes Staatsarchiv (Preussischer Kulturbesitz), Berlin-
Dahlem
Schiemann Papers

Pfälzische Landesbibliothek, Speyer
Lieber Papers

International Institute for Social History, Amsterdam
Motteler Papers

Friedrichsruh Archiv
H. Bismarck Papers (courtesy Professor J. A. Nichols)

II. PUBLISHED PRIMARY MATERIAL

Bamberger, Ludwig. *Bismarcks Grosses Spiel, Die Geheimen
Tagebücher Ludwig Bambergers.* Ed. Ernst Feder.
Frankfurt am Main, 1932.

Berlepsch, H. H. *Sozialpolitische Erfahrungen und Erinnerungen.* München-Gladbach, 1925.

Bernhardi, Friedrich von. *Denkwürdigkeiten aus meinem Leben.*
Berlin, 1927.

Bismarck, Otto Fürst von. *Die Gesammelten Werke.* 15 vols.
Berlin, 1923-35.

Brauer, A. *Im Dienste Bismarcks, Persönliche Erinnerungen.*
Berlin, 1936.

Bülow, Bernhard Fürst von. *Denkwürdigkeiten.* Ed. Franz
von Stockhammern. 4 vols. Berlin, 1930-31.

Delbrück, Hans. "Politische Correspondenz: Der Kanzlerwechsel," *Preussische Jahrbücher,* 65 (April, 1890),
461-466.

Deutsches Wochenblatt. Ed. Otto Arendt.

Eppstein, Georg Freiherr von, ed. *Fürst Bismarcks Entlas-
sung. Nach den hinterlassenen, bisher unveröffentlichten
Aufzeichnungen des Staatssekretärs des Innern,
Staatsministers Dr. Karl Heinrich von Boetticher und
des Chefs der Reichskanzlei unter dem Fürsten Bismarck
Dr. Franz Johannes von Rottenburg.* Berlin, n.d.

Gradenwitz, Otto. "Akten über Bismarcks grossdeutsche
Rundfahrt vom Jahre 1892." *Sitzungsberichte der
Heidelberger Akademie der Wissenschaften,* vol. 12 (1921).

Die Grosse Politik der Europäischen Kabinette, 1870-1914.
Ed. J. Lepsius, A. Mendelssohn-Bartholdy, and F. Thimme.
40 vols. Berlin, 1922-27.

Haller, Johannes. *Aus dem Leben des Fürsten Philipp zu
Eulenburg-Hertefeld.* Berlin, 1924.

—————. *Philipp Eulenburg: The Kaiser's Friend.*
Translation by Ethel Colburn Mayne of *Aus dem Leben....*
2 vols. New York, 1930.

Hammann, Otto. *Der Missverstandene Bismarck, Zwanzig Jahre Deutscher Weltpolitik.* Berlin, 1921.

————. *Der Neue Kurs.* Erinnerungen. Berlin, 1918.

Harden, Maximilian. *Köpfe.* 4 vols. 35th ed. Berlin, 1911–13.

Hofmann, Hermann. *Fürst Bismarck, 1890-1898.* 3 vols. 8th ed. Stuttgart, 1914.

Hohenlohe-Schillingsfürst, Alexander von. *Aus meinen Leben.* Frankfurt am Main, 1925.

Hohenlohe-Schillingsfürst, Chlodwig Fürst zu. *Denkwürdigkeiten des Fürsten Chlodwig zu Hohenlohe-Schillingsfürst.* Ed. Friedrich Curtius. 2 vols. Stuttgart, 1907.

————. *Denkwürdigkeiten der Reichskanzlerzeit.* Ed. Karl Alexander von Müller. Stuttgart, 1931.

Holstein, Friedrich von. *The Holstein Papers.* Ed. Norman Rich and M. H. Fisher. 4 vols. Cambridge, 1955-63.

————. *Die Geheimen Papiere Friedrich von Holsteins.* 4 vols. Göttingen, 1955-63. German edition by Werner Frauendienst of *The Holstein Papers.*

Hutten-Czapski, Bogdan Graf von. *Sechzig Jahre Politik und Gesellschaft.* 2 vols. Berlin, 1936.

Kardorff, S. v. *Wilhelm von Kardorff—Ein nationaler Parlamentarier im Zeitalter Bismarcks und Wilhelms II, 1828-1907.* Berlin, 1936.

Keim, August. *Erlebtes und Erstrebtes. Lebenserinnerungen von Generalleutnant Keim.* Hanover, 1925.

Kiderlen-Wächter, Alfred von. *Kiderlen-Wächter: Der Staatsmann und Mensch.* Ed. Ernst Jack. 2 vols. Stuttgart, 1925.

Meinecke, Friedrich. *Erlebtes 1862-1919.* Stuttgart, 1964.

Die Nation. Ed. Th. Barth.

Naumann, Friedrich. *Demokratie und Kaisertum. Ein Handbuch für innere Politik.* Berlin-Schöneberg, 1900.

Penzler, J., ed. *Fürst Bismarck nach seiner Entlassung. Leben und Politik des Fürsten seit seinem Scheiden aus dem Amte auf Grund aller Authentischen Kundgebungen.* 7 vols. Leipzig, 1896-98.

Die Politische Polizei in Preussen. Berichte über die Verhandlungen im Prozess Leckert-Lützow-Tausch am 2., 3., 4., und 7. Dezember 1897 vor dem Landgericht 1 zu Berlin. Berlin, 1896.

Preussische Jahrbücher. Ed. H. Delbrück.

Radziwill, Marie. *Une grande Dame d'avent guerre. Lettres de la Princesse Radziwill au General de Robilant, 1889-1914.* 4 vols. Bologna, 1933-34.

Raschdau, Ludwig. *In Weimar als Preussischer Gesandter. Ein Buch der Erinnerungen an Deutsche Fürstenhöfe 1894-1897.* Berlin, 1939.

──────. *Unter Bismarck und Caprivi; Erinnerungen eines deutschen Diplomaten 1885-1894.* Berlin, 1939.

Reichsbote.

Richter, Eugen, ed. *Politisches ABC Buch.* Eds. of 1896, 1898.

Rogge, Helmuth. *Friedrich von Holstein. Lebensbekenntnis in Briefen an eine Frau.* Berlin, 1932.

Schulthess Europaischer Geschichtskalendar, vols. 37-38. Ed. Gustav Roloff. München, 1897-98.

Snyder, Louis L., ed. *Documents of German History.* New Brunswick, N. J., 1958.

Spitzemberg, Hildegard Baronin. *Das Tagebuch der Baronin Spitzemberg.* Geb. Freiin v. Varnbühler. Ed. Rudolf Vierhaus. Göttingen, 1960.

Stenographische Berichte über die Verhandlungen des Deutschen Reichstags. IX Legislaturperiode, IV Session, 1895-97. Berlin, 1897.

Stenographische Berichte über die Verhandlungen des Preussischen Landtages. Haus der Abgeordneten, 18-20. I. 1897. Berlin, 1897.

Stein, August. *Es war alles ganz anders. Aus der Werkstätte eines politischen Journalisten 1891-1914.* Frankfurt am Mein, 1922.

Tresckow, Hans von. *Von Fürsten und anderen Sterblichen.* Berlin, 1922.

Waldersee, Alfred Graf von. *Denkwürdigkeiten des Generalfeldmarschalls Alfred Grafen von Waldersee.* Ed. Heinrich Otto Meisner. 3 vols. Stuttgart, 1922-23.

Wermuth, Adolf. *Ein Beamtenleben.* Berlin, 1922.

Das Wilhelminische Deutschland: Stimmen der Zeitgenossen. Ed. G. Kotowski, W. Pöls, and Gerhard Ritter. Frankfurt am Main, 1965.

Wippermann, Karl. *Deutscher Geschichtskalendar, 1894-1897.* Leipzig, 1895-98.

──────. *Fürst Bismarcks 80ster Geburtstag.* München, 1895.

Die Zukunft. Ed. Maximilian Harden.

III. SECONDARY MATERIAL

Bachem, K. *Vorgeschichte, Geschichte und Politik der Deutschen Zentrumspartei.* 9 vols. Köln, 1927-32.

Balfour, M. *The Kaiser and His Times.* London, 1964.

Blieffert, Günther. "Die Innenpolitik des Reichskanzlers Fürsten Hohenlohe-Schillingsfürst 1894-1900." Dissertation, Kiel, 1950.

Böhme, H. *Deutschlands Weg zur Grossmacht, 1848-1881.* Köln 1966.

Born, K. E. *Staat und Sozialpolitik seit Bismarcks Sturz. Ein Beitrag zur Geschichte der innerpolitischen Entwicklung des Deutschen Reiches, 1890-1914. Historische Forschungen,* Bd. 1. Wiesbaden, 1957.

Carroll, E. M. *Germany and the Great Powers, 1866-1914.* 1938; reprinted, Archon Books, 1966.

Clapham, J. H. *Economic Development of France and Germany 1815-1914.* 4th ed. Cambridge, 1936.

Engelberg, E. *Deutschland 1871-1897. Lehrbuch der deutschen Geschichte (Beiträge),* Bd. 8. Berlin, 1965.

Eyck, Erich. *Das persönliche Regiment Wilhelms II, Politische Geschichte des Deutschen Kaiserreiches von 1890 bis 1914.* Erlenbach-Zürich, 1948.

Fischer, Fritz. *Krieg der Illusionen. Die deutsche Politik von 1911 bis 1914.* Düsseldorf, 1969.

Fornaschon, Wolfgang. *Die politischen Anschauungen des Grafen Alfred von Waldersee und seine Stellungnahme zur deutschen Politik. Historische Studien,* vol. 273. Berlin, 1935.

Frauendienst, W. "Die Demokratisierung des deutschen Konstitutionalismus in der Zeit Wilhelms II." *Zeitschrift für die gesamte Staatswissenschaft,* vol. 113 (1957).

Fricke, Dieter. "Die Affaire Leckert-Lützow-Tausch und die Regierungskrise von 1897 in Deutschland." *Zeitschrift für Geschichtswissenschaft,* 7 (1960), 1579-1603.

Fricke, G. *Bismarcks Prätorianer. Die Berliner Politische Polizei im Kampf gegen die deutsche Arbeiterbewegung (1871-1898).* Berlin, 1962.

Geis, Robert. *Der Sturz des Reichskanzlers Caprivi. Historische Studien,* vol. 192. Berlin, 1930.

Geschichte der Frankfurter Zeitung. Ed. Verlag der Frankfurter Zeitung. Frankfurt am Main, 1911.

Goetz, W. "Kaiser Wilhelm II. und die Geschichtsschreibung." *Historische Zeitschrift,* vol. 179 (1955).

Goldschmidt, Hans. *Das Reich und Preussen im Kampf um die Führung von Bismarck bis 1918.* Berlin, 1931.

Groth, Otto. *Die Zeitung.* 4 vols. Mannheim, 1928-30.

Hale, O. J. *Publicity and Diplomacy, with Special Reference to England and Germany, 1890-1914.* New York, 1940; reprinted, 1968.

Hallmann, Hans. *Krügerdepesche und Flottenfrage.* Stuttgart, 1927.

————. *Der Weg zum deutschen Schlachtflottenbau.* Stuttgart, 1933.

Hartung, Fritz. "Graf von Hutten-Czapski." *Historische Zeitschrift*, vol. 1953, pp. 548-559.

————. "Verantwortliche Regierung, Kabinette und Neben-regierungen im konstitutionellen Preussen 1848-1918." *Forschungen zur Brandenburgischen und Preussischen Geschichte*, 44 (1932), 302-373.

————. *Staatsbildende Krafte der Neuzeit.* Berlin, 1961.

Heffter, Heinrich. *Die Deutsche Selbstverwaltung im 19ten Jahrhundert.* Stuttgart, 1950.

Helfritz, Hans. *Wilhelm II. als König und Kaiser.* Scientia, A. G., 1954.

Herzfeld, Hans. *Johannes von Miquel. Sein Anteil am Ausbau des deutschen Reiches bis zur Jahrhundertwende.* 2 vols. Detmold, 1938.

Holborn, Hajo. *A History of Modern Germany 1840-1945.* New York, 1969.

Hubatsch, Walther. *Der Admiralstab und die obersten Marinebehörden in Deutschland, 1848-1945.* Frankfurt am Main, 1958.

Huber, Ernst Rudolf. *Deutsche Verfassungsgeschichte seit 1789.* 6 vols. Stuttgart, 1957— .

Huntington, Samuel P. "The Political Modernization of Traditional Monarchies." *Daedalus*, 95 (1966), 763-788.

Jerussalimski, A. S. *Die Aussenpolitik und die Diplomatie des deutschen Imperialismus Ende des 19.Jahrhunderts.* Tr. from the Russian by Leon Nebenzahl. 2nd ed. Berlin, 1954.

Kardorff, Siegfried von. *Bismarck im Kampf um sein Werk.* Berlin, 1943.

Kehr, Eckhart. *Schlachtflottenbau und Parteipolitik 1894-1901. Historische Studien*, vol. 197. Berlin, 1930.

King, David Burnett. "Marschall von Bieberstein and the New Course, 1890-1897." Ph.D. dissertation, Cornell University, 1962.

Krausnick, Helmut. *Holsteins Geheimpolitik in der Ära Bismarck, 1886-1890.* Hamburg, 1942.

Kröber, S. "Der Kampf um die Reform des Militärstrafprozesses (1893-1898)." Dissertation, Gottingen, 1938.

Langer, William L. *The Diplomacy of Imperialism 1890-1902.* 2nd ed. New York, 1965.

Liman, Paul. *Bismarck nach seiner Entlassung.* Berlin, 1904.

—————. *Der Kaiser, Ein Charakterbild Wilhelms II.*
2nd ed. Leipzig, 1913.

Martin, R. *Deutsche Machthaber.* Berlin, 1910.

Meinecke, F. *Geschichte des deutsch-englischen Bündnisproblems 1890-1901.* Berlin, 1927.

Meisner, Hans Otto. "Der Kanzler Hohenlohe und die Mächte
seiner Zeit." *Preussische Jahrbücher,* vol. 229 (1932).

—————. "Der Reichskanzler Caprivi. Eine biographische
Skizze." *Zeitschrift für die gesamte Staatswissenschaft,*
vol. 111 (1955).

Meyer, Klaus. *Theodor Schiemann als politischer Publizist.*
Nord und ost europäische Geschichtstudien (University of
Hamburg), Bd. 1. Frankfurt am Main, Hamburg, 1956.

Müller, Karl Alexander von. "Der Dritte Deutsche Reichskanzler,
Bemerkungen zu den 'Denkwürdigkeiten aus der Reichskanzlerzeit' des Fürsten Chlodwig zu Hohenlohe-Schillingsfürst."
*Sitzungsberichte der Baierischen Akademie der Wissen-
schaften* (Philosophisch-Historische Abtheilung), vol. 3
(1932).

Muschler, Reinhold Conrad. *Philipp zu Eulenburg: Sein Leben
und seine Zeit.* Leipzig, 1930.

Neue Deutsche Biographie. Berlin, 1953.

Nichols, J. Alden. *Germany after Bismarck: The Caprivi Era
1890-1894.* Cambridge, Mass., 1958.

—————. Review of Norman Rich, *Friedrich von Holstein,* in
Journal of Modern History, 38 (1966), 311-312.

Oertzen, D. von. *Adolf Stoecker—Lebensbild und Zeitgeschichte.*
2 vols. Berlin, 1910. Vol. II.

Pinson, Koppel S. *Modern Germany, Its History and Civiliza-
tion.* 2nd ed. New York, 1966.

Pöls, Werner. *Sozialistenfrage und Revolutionsfurcht in ihrem
Zusammenhang mit den angeblichen Staatsstreichplänen
Bismarcks. Historische Studien,* vol. 377. Lübeck, 1960.

Rich, Norman. *Friedrich von Holstein. Politics and Diplomacy
in the Era of Bismarck and Wilhelm II.* 2 vols. Cambridge,
1965.

Richter, Günter. *Friedrich von Holstein, Ein Mitarbeiter
Bismarcks. Historische Studien,* vol. 397. Lübeck, 1966.

Riggs, Fred W. In Joseph La Palombara, ed., *Bureaucracy and
Political Development. Studies in Political Development,*
vol. II. Princeton, N. J., 1967.

Rogge, Helmuth. *Holstein und Harden. Politisch-publizistisches
Zusammenspiel zweier Aussenseiter des Wilhelmischen Reichs.*
München, 1959.

————. *Holstein und Hohenlohe. Neue Beiträge zu Friedrich von Holsteins Tätigkeit als Mitarbeiter Bismarcks und als Ratgeber Hohenlohes.* Stuttgart, 1957.

————. "Die Kladderadatsch Affaire: Ein Beitrag zur inneren Geschichte des Wilhelminischen Reichs." *Historische Zeitschrift*, vol. 195 (1962).

————. "Affären im Kaiserreich." *Die Politische Meinung*, vol. 8 (1963).

Rohl, J.C.G. *Germany without Bismarck: The Crisis of Government in the Second Reich 1890-1900.* London, 1967.

————. "Staatsstreichplan oder Staatsstreichbereitschaft? Bismarcks Politik in der Entlassungskrise." *Historische Zeitschrift*, vol. 203 (1966).

Rosenberg, A. *Die Entstehung der Weimarer Republik. Sammburg "res publica,"* vol. 8. Frankfurt am Main, 1961.

Schmidt-Bückeburg, Rudolf. *Das Militärkabinett der Preussischen Könige und deutscher Kaiser. Seine geschichtliche Entwicklung und staatsrechtliche Stellung 1787-1918.* Berlin, 1933.

Schüssler, Wilhelm. *Bismarcks Sturz.* Leipzig, 1921.

Schütte, Ernst. *Freiherr Marschall von Bieberstein, Ein Beitrag zur Characterisierung seiner Politik.* Berlin, 1936.

Seeber, Gustav. *Zwischen Bebel und Bismarck. Zur Geschichte des Linksliberalismus in Deutschland 1871-1893.* Deutsche Akademie der Wissenschaften zu Berlin, Schriften des Instituts für Geschichte, Reihe I: Allgemeine und Deutsche Geschichte, Bd. 30. Berlin, 1965.

Stadelmann, Rudolf. "Der Neue Kurs in Deutschland." *Geschichte in Wissenschaft und Unterricht*, vol. 4 (1953).

Stegmann, Dirk. *Die Erben Bismarcks. Parteien und Verbände in der Spätphase des Wilhelminischen Deutschlands. Sammlungspolitik 1897-1918.* Köln, 1970.

Steinberg, Jonathan. *Yesterday's Deterrent: Tirpitz and the Birth of the German Battle Fleet.* New York, 1965.

Taylor, A. J. P. *The Course of German History.* New York, 1962.

Thimme, Annelise. *Hans Delbrück als Kritiker der Wilhelminischen Epoche.* Düsseldorf, 1955.

Traude, F. B. "Untersuchungen zur Entstehung und Entwicklung des Verständigungsgedankens der Kontinentalmächte 1897 im Lichte der Presse." Ph.D. dissertation, Köln, 1933.

Vietsch, Eberhard v. *Bethmann-Hollweg: Staatsmann zwischen Macht und Ethos. Schriften des Bundesarchivs*, vol. 18. Boppard am Rhein, 1969.

Wahl, Adalbert. *Deutsche Geschichte 1871-1914.* 4 vols. Stuttgart, 1929-36.

Wehler, Hans-Ulrich, ed. *Moderne deutsche Sozialgeschichte.*
   Neue Wissenschaftliche Bibliothek, Bd. 10. Köln, Berlin,
   1966.

—————. *Bismarck und der Imperiliasmus.* Köln, 1969.

Wertheimer, Eduard von. "Neues zur Geschichte der letzten
   Jahre Bismarcks (1890-1898)." *Historische Zeitschrift*,
   133 (1926), 220-257.

Young, Harry F. *Maximilian Harden. Censor Germaniae. The
   Critic in Opposition from Bismarck to the Rise of Nazism.*
   The Hague, 1959.

Zechlin, Egmont. *Staatsstreichpläne Bismarcks und Wilhelms
   II, 1890-1894.* Stuttgart, 1929.

Zeuner, Hans Joachim. "Hohenlohe und Holstein, Die politischen
   Beziehungen des Fürsten Chlodwig zu Hohenlohe-Schillingsfürst zum Geheimen Rat Fritz von Holstein. Dargestellt
   vornehmlich auf Grund bisher unveröffentlichter Briefe."
   Ph.D. dissertation, Würzburg, 1955.

Ziekursch, Johannes. *Politische Geschichte des neuen
   Deutschen Kaiserreiches.* 3 vols. Frankfurt am Main,
   1925-30.

Index